The Life and Death of the Press Barons

Books by Piers Brendon

The Life and Death of the Press Barons

PIERS BRENDON

ATHENEUM

New York

1983

Library of Congress Cataloging in Publication Data

Brendon, Piers.
   The life and death of the press barons.

   Bibliography: p.
   Includes index.
   1. English newspapers—History. 2. American
newspapers—History. 3. Newspaper publishing—
Great Britain—History. 4. Newspaper publishing—
United States—History. I. Title.
PN5117.B73   1983   072   82-73017
ISBN 0-689-11341-2

To Mae Berger
and to the memory of Mike

CONTENTS

ACKNOWLEDGEMENTS

I WOULD LIKE to express warmest gratitude to all who have helped with this book. I have received assistance from a large number of librarians and archivists on both sides of the Atlantic. In particular I must mention Kenneth A. Lohf, Librarian for Rare Books and Manuscripts at Columbia University, Estelle Rebec, Head of the Manuscripts Division at the Bancroft Library in Berkeley, Diana Haskell, Curator of Modern Manuscripts at the Newberry Library in Chicago, and Archie Motley of the Chicago Historical Society, all of whom went out of their way to make my task easier. I am grateful also to these institutions for permission to quote copyright material. In Britain I owe thanks to A. G. Parker of the Cambridge University Library, to H. S. Cobb of the House of Lords Records Office, to Gordon Phillips, Archivist of the *Times*, and to the staff at the British Library both in Bloomsbury and in Colindale, where so much of my work was done.

Many other people have contributed to the book, none of whom, needless to say, is responsible for its faults. Stephen Koss and Fred Hunter referred me to useful sources of information. James Cornford of the Nuffield Foundation sent me some valuable materials. Rex Bloomstein and Peter Pagnamenta read part of the text and made helpful comments. So did David Farrer, who, together with George Malcolm Thomson, shared lively memories of Lord Beaverbrook with me. Others who perused the book in manuscript are Tom Rosenthal, Peter Grose (a mine of information about the Australian press) and Barley Alison, each of whom improved it in important ways. So did Andrew Best and Nick Furbank: I am immensely indebted to them for the time and labour they invested and for their unerringly perceptive comments.

I have also benefited greatly from the advice and help of a number of professional journalists. Cecil King answered countless questions with patience and candour. Lord Hartwell submitted himself to a similar inquisition with remarkable good humour. Sir John Junor and Sir Larry Lamb generously fitted me into their crowded schedules.

Charles Wintour treated me with exceptional kindness. Murray Hedgcock allowed me access to a treasure trove of newspapers and cuttings. Robert Kaiser gave me a Washington *Post*'s eye-view of journalism in America. And Mae, widow of Mike Berger, one of the New York *Times*'s outstanding journalists, has been a constant source of inspiration. I dedicate this book to her, and to his memory.

Finally I must acknowledge the aid and comfort of my wife and children. Over the last few years they have not only lived with me but with some extremely difficult strangers—a score or more of press barons.

My publisher and I wish to thank William Randolph Hearst Junior for permission to quote copyright material.

LIST OF ILLUSTRATIONS

Illustration Acknowledgements

Page 1 right and 7 bottom: BBC Hulton Picture Library. Page 6: Columbia University Library. Page 10: *Evening Standard*. Page 9: Keystone Press Agency. Pages 14 and 15: *Los Angeles Times*. Page 2 top right and bottom right: Mansell Collection. Page 5 right: National Portrait Gallery, London. Page 12 top right and page 13: *New York Daily News*. Page 2 bottom left: *The New York Times*. Page 12 top left: Press Association. Page 11: Edward W. Scripps Trust. Page 12 bottom: Syndication International Ltd. Page 2 top left and 3, 4, 7 top, 16 bottom: *The Times*. Page 16 top: United Press International.

Illustrations were also taken from the following publications: Page 8: *The American Magazine*, Volume 63, November 1906. Page 1 left: Don C. Seitz: *The James Gordon Bennetts: Father and Son*. Page 5 left: Estelle W. Stead: *My Father*, 1914.

The Life and Death of the Press Barons

INTRODUCTION

IN THE LAST two or three decades a remarkable species has become virtually extinct. The press barons, who first emerged in the 1830s, dominated British and American journalism for over a hundred years. During that time they transformed newspapers from servile little propaganda sheets into great independent organs of information and opinion—the fourth estate. In their prime, around the turn of the century, it seemed as though the press barons aspired not merely to mould men's minds but to direct their lives. One or two might have been elected President of the United States; another could perhaps have become a king; several helped to make or break governments. But on the whole their pretensions outran their power. That democracy should frustrate the dictatorial ambitions of citizens like Kane was hardly surprising. Less predictable was the speed with which such successful, larger-than-life figures disappeared. After a sharp change in the economic climate they were superseded by the vast, anonymous 'communications corporations' and 'media conglomerates' of today. Still, from the historian's point of view their sudden demise is an advantage. It enables him to see the newspaper magnates, for the first time, from a detached position and to trace the steep parabola of their existence to its end. As its title states, this book attempts to chronicle the life and death of the press barons.

Of course, the moment the aim is stated its absurdity becomes apparent. The history of the press barons will never be written; to paraphrase Lytton Strachey, there is too much to be known about them. Their careers are recorded in countless books. Archives bulge with their private correspondence. Whole libraries cannot contain their printed publications, even when reduced to microfilm—for example, the New York *Daily News*, for long America's largest-selling newspaper, is not to be found in the British Library at Colindale. Furthermore, there were simply too many of them. A comprehensive survey, even were it essayed, could be little more than a dry catalogue. This book is therefore highly selective, sometimes arbitrarily so. Thus connoisseurs of the bizarre may be disappointed by the exclusion of

I

Wilbur F. Storey, who wrote the Chicago *Times* with 'the roar of heavenly chariots' in his ears, or of John Norton, the Australian proprietor of *Truth*, who expired surrounded by hundreds of portraits, masks, medals, statues and relics of Napoleon. However typical their behaviour, no mention is made of newspaper magnates from alien traditions of press development, of Axel Springer, for example, whose middle name is Caesar, or of Maurice Bunau-Varilla, who was so afflicted by 'hypertrophie du moi' that he tried to prevent Frenchmen drinking absinthe. The field has been narrowed and the choice of whom to include has been governed by two main criteria.

First, the book restricts itself to the press barons of Britain and America. They are biographically treated in alternate chapters so as to chart the ebb and flow of journalistic influence between the two countries. These currents were naturally strong because of the common ancestry, heritage and language. The detailed historical comparison, never before attempted, proves to be revealing. What emerges in particular is that the press barons of the New World, stimulated by a tradition of freedom and protected by constitutional guarantees, were wilder beasts even than their Old World counterparts. In Britain the national habit of reticence was (and is) backed up by fierce libel laws, stiff punishments for contempt of court and an Official Secrets Act which literally bans the publication of such vital data as how many cups of tea civil servants drink each day. All this helped to tame, though by no means to domesticate, the British press barons.

Importance has been the second factor in determining which press barons were suitable cases for treatment. The score or so whose characters and achievements are discussed here made a significant contribution to newspaper history. All were powerful figures who revelled in conflict. All stamped the mark of rich personalities on their times. Thus Lord Northcliffe is included at the expense of C. P. Scott; William Randolph Hearst is preferred to Adolph Ochs. And if some of the successful candidates seem all too familiar, they may appear less so when juxtaposed in sketches which rely on their unpublished as well as their printed papers. In any case, not all the *dramatis personae* are so famous. Indeed, for a British audience James Gordon Bennett, Horace Greeley, even Joseph Pulitzer, will be little more than names; and the same will apply to W. T. Stead, Cecil King, even Lord Beaverbrook, where Americans are concerned. Other less well-known figures play their part in a study which attempts, as it were, to bridge the Atlantic. So for the convenience of readers on both sides of the ocean a list of leading characters precedes the text, together with the titles of the principal newspapers for which each was responsible.

This cast-list should be especially helpful because, as in a novel by

Dostoevsky, so many different characters possess strikingly similar traits. This may seem rather odd. For a press baron is defined in the following pages by his extravagant display of journalistic independence. What distinguished a press baron from a mere conductor of newspapers, it is suggested, was his will to freedom. He was determined to run his life and his journals with as little interference as possible from outside—from politicians, commercial interests, advertisers, from his own kind, sometimes even from his readers, from popular opinion itself. It is the book's purpose to trace the rise and decline of this ideal of autonomy. Of course, it could seldom, if ever, be realised. Instead independence often expressed itself in the form of eccentricity. The press barons might have sprung fully armed from the head of John Stuart Mill, who valued eccentrics as rebels against conventional opinion which, so he reckoned, had become the new tyrant in a democratic age. Paradoxically, in their extraordinary quirkiness the press barons conformed to type.

That type—vicious, unstable, despotic—became notorious. It was easy enough for politicians to represent the press barons as megalomaniacs, who corrupted the public mind and had evil designs on the body politic. Frequently there was more than a grain of truth in their charges. Often, however, prime ministers and presidents were simply hitting out at a force they could not control, one which disclosed embarrassing information, voiced pertinent criticism and increased the accountability of governments to the people they professed to represent. Perhaps this was a by-product of the press barons' ruthless quest for wealth, power and independence. But whatever their motives, their refusal to endure restraints on journalistic freedom was a real boon. Equally real (and what made their independence possible) was the press barons' commercial success. This was elusive in a business where the competition was as fierce as the wares were ephemeral. The arduous feat of creating and sustaining a prosperous publication was almost always achieved by a lone pioneer of outstanding journalistic ability, a man of mercury who invested his entire personality in his newspaper. It is true that the energy which the press barons unleashed to turn their newspapers into a profitable private business could seldom be harnessed to make them also a disinterested public service. But safety lay in diversity. Between them they created the amazingly rich variety of newspapers which was such a distinctive feature of British and American life before the coming of today's monopolistic companies. The variety, and the ideal of journalistic liberty which it represented, are now under threat from the media giants, with their mass of impersonal publications, consensus-orientated, computer-programmed, boardroom-dominated. What they lacked in integrity

3

the press barons made up for in idiosyncrasy. They may have been villains, but they were heroic villains. The history of modern journalism is the sum of their biographies.

CHIEF CHARACTERS, IN ORDER OF APPEARANCE, AND THEIR PRINCIPAL NEWSPAPERS

James Gordon Bennett I (1795–1872), New York *Herald*
James Gordon Bennett II (1841–1918), New York *Herald, Evening Telegram*, Paris *Herald*
Thomas Barnes (1785–1841), London *Times*
John Delane (1817–1879), London *Times*
Horace Greeley (1811–1872), New York *Tribune*
Henry Raymond (1820–1869), New York *Times*
Charles Dana (1819–1897), New York *Sun*
Lord Burnham (Edward Levy-Lawson) (1833–1916), London *Daily Telegraph*
W. T. Stead (1849–1912), *Pall Mall Gazette*
T. P. O'Connor (1848–1929), London *Evening Star*
Joseph Pulitzer (1847–1911), St Louis *Post-Dispatch*, New York *World*
Lord Northcliffe (Alfred Harmsworth) (1865–1922), London *Evening News, Daily Mail, Times, Mirror, Observer*
Lord Rothermere (Harold Harmsworth) (1868–1940), London *Daily Sketch, Mirror, Mail*
William Randolph Hearst (1863–1952), San Francisco *Examiner*, New York *Journal, American, Mirror*, Chicago *Examiner*, Los Angeles *Examiner*
Lord Beaverbrook (William Maxwell Aitken) (1879–1964), London *Daily Express, Sunday Express, Evening Standard*
E. W. Scripps (1854–1926), Cleveland *Penny Press*, Cincinnati *Post*
Robert R. McCormick (1880–1955), Chicago *Tribune*
Joseph M. Patterson (1879–1946), New York *Daily News*
Eleanor M. Patterson (1881–1948), Washington *Times-Herald*
Cecil King (1901–   ), London *Daily Mirror, Daily Herald, Sunday Pictorial, Sunday People*
Harrison Gray Otis (1837–1917), Los Angeles *Times*
Harry Chandler (1864–1944), Los Angeles *Times*

5

Norman Chandler (1899–1977), Los Angeles *Times, Mirror*
Otis Chandler (1928–   ), Los Angeles *Times*, Dallas *Times-Herald*
   Long Island *Newsday*, Denver *Post*
Rupert Murdoch (1931–   ), London *Sun, News of the World, Times,*
   Sunday Times, New York *Evening Post*, San Antonio *Express, News,*
   Sydney *Mirror, Telegraph, Australian*

CHAPTER ONE

The Birth of
the Barons

DESPITE HIS CROOKED gaze few men have seen straighter than James Gordon Bennett Snr. The pioneer of 'yellow journalism' in America and the first authentic press baron, Bennett made light of his fierce squint. It had been acquired, he said, by his 'earnest endeavours to watch the winding ways of Martin Van Buren',[1] the future President. And in one of those impudent confessional asides with which the New York *Herald* scandalised the age, Bennett wrote:

> I am comforted with the idea that ladies—the sweet and beautiful ladies—who have examined it minutely, do say it is a delicious squint, unlike any one they ever looked into. 'Dear Bennett,' they say, turning up their pretty soft liquid eyes, 'it will make your fortune.'[2]

In a sense, Bennett's vision did make his fortune. He saw clearly that the time was ripe in the 1830s for the creation of a cheap, sensational newspaper. And in conducting the *Herald* he showed an unwavering insight into the mind of the masses. 'The Napoleon of the press in two hemispheres',[3] he called himself. Needless to say, such provocative self-glorification was part of Bennett's stock in trade. But others took him at his own estimation. The *Herald*'s staff referred to him as the 'Emperor'.

Yet only a few years earlier Bennett had been, like his fellows, an out-at-elbows drudge at the beck and call of his political masters. In 1831, for instance, as his unpublished diary reveals, he was still a party hack, a lackey at the court of 'King Caucus'.[4] He trumpeted the virtues of Van Buren in public while privately despising him: 'nothing grand or imposing, has no appreciation of wit, or satire, or learning, or fancy, or imagination'. Bennett was galled by the poverty and restraint he had

7

to endure: 'How my heart burns for distinction'. But newspapers could not attract enough readers or enough advertisements. Unable to attain financial independence, they settled instead for political subservience. Bennett's superb journalistic capacities were frustrated.

> I have endeavoured to procure a higher position in parties, and to settle myself in life. I have done so once, twice, thrice, four times. I have always failed. Why so? It is this restless heart—this eternal craving after some novelty or other—this alternate indolence and action—this never-drying-up ambition.[5]

Bennett was desperate enough to consider returning to Britain in order to prosecute the cause of reform in which, despite the cynicism of his temperament, he then believed. But though he possessed a 'French intellect and Scotch habits',[6] Bennett's aspirations were American. He could anyway have achieved little in his native land, where parliament was doing its best to stifle popular journalism at birth. In the New World he was free to embark on an enterprise which at once transformed the position of the press and revolutionised the status of its controllers.

Single-handed, 'an ink-stained Ishmael'[7] with capital of $500, an underground room for an office and a plank set across two flour barrels as a desk, Bennett liberated the American press from the embrace of its political patrons. By 1839, only four years after its launching, the New York *Herald* had outstripped all local rivals and its circulation of 30,000 matched that of the London *Times*. Bennett had created, in effect, the first yellow journal. He aimed not to inform or to educate but to entertain and to startle. He mixed all the old ingredients of sensationalism into a sulphurous new brew flavoured with his own pungent wit. The *Herald* became a hotch-potch of piquant tit-bits, police reports, commercial news, moral reflections, salacious tittle-tattle, political vendetta, theatrical vignettes, fashion notes, personal raillery, jokes, squibs, puffs and *jeux d'esprit*, all written with wayward effrontery and unbuttoned zest by its 'owner, editor, proprietor, prophet, head man, head saint, head savant, or head devil, just as you please, J. G. Bennett'.[8] The 'head devil' (for most people scented a whiff of brimstone about the cross-eyed, cross-grained iconoclast) rejoiced in his new-found wealth which freed him from 'the hollow-heartedness and humbuggery of these political associations and political men'.[9]

The triumphant *Herald* conferred on its proprietor more than just riches and independence. It raised him from footstool to throne, translated him from servitor into crusader. He was initiating:

> a new movement in the progress of civilisation and human intellect. I know and feel I shall succeed. Nothing can prevent ...

success but God Almighty, and he happens to be entirely on my side. Get out of my way, ye drivelling editors and drivelling politicians.[10]

Soon the *Herald* was so powerful that Bennett himself seemed awed. His newspaper was the steam-engine of the moral world, the living jury of the nation, the permanent committee of the people, the great organ of social improvement, the prime saviour of souls. And because the *Herald* was also the daily expression of its owner's personality, Bennett in folio form, his own pretensions were quite as overweening. Transfigured by power and vanity, he emerged as the first of a new breed of men: the press barons.

Bennett was thus a portent of the future. But with his reckless manner and slashing style he also belonged to an earlier journalistic tradition, that of Wilkes, Junius and Cobbett. To measure his achievement and to examine the milieu in which the press barons were born, it is therefore necessary to turn back a few years—to a singularly unheroic past.

Despite the courage of a Zenger, who resisted censorship in the American colonies, despite the audacity of a Wilkes, who established the right to report parliamentary debates in Britain, the eighteenth-century press on both sides of the Atlantic was venal, corrupt and impotent. Journalism and journalists were held in the lowest possible esteem. It is recorded of Dr Johnson's acquaintance, the Rev William Dodd, who was hanged for forgery, that he once 'descended as low as to become the editor of a newspaper'.[11] Johnson himself defined a reporter as 'a man without virtue who writes lies at home for his own profit'.[12] Benjamin Franklin thought liberty of the press ought to go hand in hand with 'liberty of the cudgel'.[13] And Thomas Jefferson, although in theory a champion of newspapers, found them in practice a 'polluted vehicle'.[14] The fact was that reports of rapes, seductions, murders, accidents, robberies, prodigies, prize-fights, local gossip and national scandal, however copious and enticing, were not enough to keep pre-capitalist newspapers solvent.

Authors, printers and publishers raised additional revenue from straightforward blackmail: they set up scurrilous paragraphs in type and wrested 'suppression fees' from victims too timid to declare, with the Duke of Wellington, 'Publish and be damned!' Or they levied payment for the contradiction of stories already printed. Advertisements also helped, many of them for patently quack remedies, like the pill 'warranted to have been habitually taken during his whole life by Methuselah'.[15] But essentially, before 1830, newspapers relied on political subsidies. And, beholden to parties for information as well as

9

lucre, journalists wrote to order, slavishly about their mentors, abusively about their opponents, viciously about each other. The press was the verbal equivalent of the pillory, the riper the billingsgate the richer the entertainment. Readers bought newspapers in order to find out who was to be vilified next. Respectable journals indulged in the grossest forms of defamation and, with obscene gusto, dog ate dog.

The *Times* described the *Morning Chronicle* as 'that squirt of filthy water'.[16] The *Chronicle* called the *Morning Post* 'that slop-pail of corruption'.[17] In 1823 William Cobbett, who sardonically opposed the spread of education on the grounds that the first thing read by the newly literate would be newspapers, summed up his opinion of the press with characteristic pugnacity.

> Have you ever seen ... a parcel of *toads*, assembled very thickly, on the surface of a muddy, stagnant and stinking pool; communing with one another and reciprocating their filthy breathings and spawning. You have also seen a large stone, or a brick-bat, flung, suddenly, souse into the midst of such collective wisdom. You have seen how the loathsome devils, some diving, others attempting to leap away, others turned on their backs and showing their nasty white bellies, and all croaking out their alarm, and emitting their poisonous matter ... imagine the scene now before your eyes, and you have a true picture of the state of the reptiles of the London press.[18]

This noisome vision of the true nature of the 'kept press' was based on Cobbett's observations in America as well as Britain.

Before the advent of Bennett even the most prosperous owners and the most prominent editors were willing to debauch their organs for political or commercial gain. In England, for example the Rev William Jackson, known as 'Dr Viper' because of 'the acrimony of his pen ... the extreme and unexampled virulence of his invectives ... barbed and poisoned with the ... rankest venom',[19] exploited the *Morning Post* (established in 1772) as an instrument of extortion. Until Leigh Hunt's protest there was blatant collusion between newspapers and the theatres: 'what the public took for criticism of a play was a draft upon the box-office or reminiscences of last Thursday's salmon and lobster sauce',[20] or even an appreciation of the more private performances of actresses. Edward Topham's principal purpose in starting *The World* (in 1787) was to advance the stage career of his mistress, Mary Wells— the jest went that 'Love first created the world'.[21]

His sometime partner in that enterprise, the printer–publisher John Bell, was typical in being at the mercy of his patron, as Leigh Hunt recalled. The rubicund Bell, his 'nose exaggerated by intemperance', had:

> no acquirements, perhaps not even grammar; but his taste in putting forth a publication, and getting the best artists to adorn it, was new in those times ... Unfortunately for Mr Bell, he had as great a taste for neat wines and ankles as for pretty books; and, to crown his misfortunes, the Prince of Wales, to whom he was a bookseller, once did him the honour to partake of entertainment ... at his house. He afterwards became bankrupt.[22]

When, occasionally, news-sheets did display the spirit to resist political threats and financial blandishments it was often just a trimming of sails to meet a change in the ministerial weather. Cobbett employed a racier image to explain the *True Briton*'s volte-face in 1803—its owner had ratted on Addington 'from the same motives that sagacious vermin desert a house which has long been their favourite haunt'.[23]

James Perry himself, the volatile and lubricious proprietor of the *Morning Chronicle* who, it has been claimed, 'created the profession of journalism',[24] was capable of grovelling obsequiousness towards his betters. In 1814 Brougham described the *Chronicle* as 'more prostitute' than its competitors: they remained dumb about the groans and hisses which everywhere greeted the Prince Regent while 'it had the audacity to speak of the *applauses* he met with'.[25] With his blackthorn and bulldog, Perry made a stout show of independence. But having spent three months in Newgate Prison for calling the House of Lords (after Chesterfield) a 'hospital for incurables'[26] and suggesting that its bishops paid less attention to national legislation than to the brevity of opera dancers' petticoats,[27] he had discovered that *lèse-majesté* was a dangerous game. Not only was it a libel 'to possess the people with an ill opinion' of the British government[28] (something difficult to avoid when reporting the proceedings of Lord Liverpool's administration) but attacks on foreign rulers were also judged to be seditious. In 1799 the *Courier*'s controllers were fined and gaoled for uttering the truism that the Tsar of Russia was a tyrant. It was even possible to libel the dead, as the editors of *John Bull* discovered when they were fined for insulting the memory of Lady Caroline Wrottesley.[29]

Thus long before his death in 1821 Perry learnt the value of extreme journalistic unction. He was so inclined to flatter the leaders of his own party that he earned the nickname 'Perrywhig'. Moreover, despite the fortune of £130,000 which the *Chronicle* brought him and Fox's (failed) attempt to have his services rewarded with a baronetcy, Perry was kept Heepishly humble by the social apartheid of the British caste system. It was said that he 'never quite lost his retail manner acquired in the draper's shop at Aberdeen', where he had been born.[30] No wonder that Lord Lowther remarked in 1827, 'newspapers are ... dirty and dangerous things to meddle with, and all *editors* that I have seen are presuming, extravagant and necessitous men'. Or that the Duke of Wellington should speak contemptuously of 'blackguard editors of newspapers'.[31] And this was not merely an aristocratic view: the radical John Stuart Mill, for example, regarded journalism as 'the vilest & most degrading of all trades, because more affectation & hypocrisy, & more subservience to the baser feelings of others, are necessary for carrying it on, than for any other trade, from that of brothel-keeper upwards'.[32]

The American press was in a similarly servile state. By 1830, it is true, a New York editor might be (in James Gordon Bennett's words) 'a distinct and substantial politician—[he] has influence over the mayor and makes the leading men go with him'.[33] But prior to this, as Bennett's biographer, Isaac Pray, wrote, 'journalists were little more than secretaries dependent upon cliques of politicians, merchants, brokers and office-seekers for their position and bread'. And the press was a 'mere engine of trick and trade ... a tool in the hands of those who ruled the offices of public trust'.[34] Jefferson compared editors to clergymen because they lived 'by the zeal they can kindle and the schisms they can create'.[35] But journalistic dissensions were by no means confined to 'epithetical rascality',[36] to the 'coarse insults', 'petty slanders' and 'impudent calumnies' with which Alexis de Tocqueville found American newspapers filled.[37] Often progressing to duels, brawls or riots, they made *odium theologicum* seem almost benign. For example, that brilliant, vicious partisan, Benjamin F. Bache (grandson of Benjamin Franklin) was caned in the street by the Federalist editor John Fenno and skewered thus in *Porcupine's Gazette*:

> This atrocious wretch (worthy descendant of old Ben) knows that all men of understanding put him down as an abandoned liar, as a tool and a hireling ... He is an ill-looking devil. His eyes never get above your knees. He is of sallow complexion, hollow-cheeked, dead-eyed and has a *toute ensemble* just like that of a fellow who has been about a week or ten days on a gibbet.[38]

The belligerent Colonel James Watson Webb, publisher of the *Courier & Enquirer*, involved himself in endless affairs and affrays, honourable and dishonourable. He enjoyed insulting rival editors before assaulting them—'You poor contemptible cowardly puppy' he called Duff Green of the *Telegraph*, announcing that he would 'only pull your nose and box your ears'.[39] And his favourite pastime was applying a horsewhip to the pallid hide of James Gordon Bennett, whom he regarded as an unprincipled adventurer and a moral leper. The Scotsman was unperturbed. On the principle that it was more blessed, and also more profitable, to receive a drubbing than to give one, he made journalistic capital out of the attacks, reporting them in lively detail. The truth was that he could afford to despise Webb, 'a man up to the eyes in whiskers and infamy'.[40] For Bennett had resigned from his position on the *Courier & Enquirer* in 1832 when that journal, 'accommodated' by the United States Bank to the tune of $53,000, renounced Andrew Jackson. With brutal magnanimity Bennett later characterised Webb as 'a frank manly blackguard, a fine-looking, burly, honest kind of savage'.[41]

Before that time, less inhibited than their British counterparts, American newspapermen had earned their patrons' approval by cultivating new refinements in the gargoyle art of vituperation. Its most accomplished practitioner was Francis P. Blair, editor of the *Globe*, the pages of which were said to reek with the blood of his scalped and tomahawked victims. Blair was a tall, skeletal figure with a hatchet face which accorded well with his 'meat-ax disposition when writing about his enemies', yet he had the gall to describe Senator George Poindexter as 'the devil's darning needle'.[42] By 1813 Jefferson was writing 'I deplore ... the putrid state into which our newspapers have passed, and the malignity, the vulgarity and mendacious spirit of those who write for them ... These ordures are rapidly depraving the public taste'. However, he added, it was 'an evil for which there is no remedy; our liberty depends on the freedom of the press, and that cannot be limited without being lost'.[43]

This was a momentous rider and it indicated that in the sphere of journalism America was more than an ocean apart from Britain. The imposition of a stamp duty on newspapers in the thirteen colonies had been a major cause of the Revolution. And the first amendment to the American constitution, in 1791, had guaranteed liberty of the press. An attempt to limit it was made seven years later, in order to contain the Jacobin contagion—'Shall our sons become the disciples of Voltaire and the dragoons of Marat', exclaimed Timothy Dwight of Yale, 'or our daughters the concubines of the Illuminati?'[44] But this repressive measure was largely responsible for the destruction of the Federalist Party in 1800. Jefferson, who then became President, had earlier made his classic declaration: 'were it left to me to decide whether we should have a government without newspapers, or newspapers without a government, I should not hesitate a moment to prefer the latter'.[45]

By contrast, the equally celebrated pronouncement of Charles II's press licenser, Sir Roger L'Estrange, summed up the attitude of the British ruling class:

Supposing the press in order, the people in their right wits, and news or no news to be the question, a public *Mercury* should never have my vote, because I think it makes the multitude too familiar with the actions and counsels of their superiors, too pragmatical and censorious, and gives them not only an itch, but a kind of colourable right and license to the meddling with the government.[46]

By the eighteenth century press freedom had become, in Blackstone's words, 'the birthright of Britons'.[47] But this only meant that editors were not liable to have their ears cut off and that newspapers were not gagged by prior censorship. They remained bound by severe libel laws interpreted by a hostile judiciary, at whose head for many years was Lord Chancellor Eldon, a relentless bigot who wore his wig in bed even though it gave him a headache to do so. Moreover newspapers' circulation was impaired by heavy taxes. Even so Lord Liverpool, Prime Minister during the insurrectionary year of 1819, considered that the 'root of the evil' afflicting the country lay in 'the outrageous licentiousness of the press'. He proposed 'to get rid of the very mischievous cheap publications by extending the principle of the Stamp Duty'.[48]

Terrified by the prospect of 'statesmen at the loom and politicians at the spinning jenny', the authorities raised stamp duties and advertisement levies. They enacted coercive laws and resurrected the archaic penalty of banishment. They harassed newsvendors and had hawkers flogged. They fined and gaoled publishers of the 'pauper press'.[49] A handful of rebels remained defiant. Richard Carlile, for example, invited imprisonment by printing such sacrilegious parodies as this Member of Parliament's prayer:

> Our Lord who art in Treasury, whatsoever be thy name, thy power be prolonged, thy will be done throughout the empire as it is in each session. Give us our usual sops, and forgive us our occasional absences on divisions; as we promise not to forgive those that divide against thee. Turn us not out of our places; but keep us in the House of Commons, the land of Pensions and Plenty; and deliver us from the people. Amen.[50]

However, Carlile was buoyed up by a visionary faith that the printing-press had become 'UNIVERSAL MONARCH, and the republic of letters will go on to abolish all minor monarchies, and give freedom to the whole human race'.[51] Less apocalyptic publishers were cowed by the official persecution. Even that perpetual sergeant-major, William Cobbett, whose unstamped twopenny *Political Register* had achieved sales of forty

14

or fifty thousand copies (despite his avowed intention to fill it with 'dry political matter' and exclude 'everything calculated to amuse the frivolous or to entertain the indolent'),[52] fled to America rather than face arbitrary imprisonment.

In the early 1830s a new eruption of unstamped newspapers occurred as part of the general convulsion of political reform. The government attempted vainly to check it. Then it countered by means of loyalist journals (which the middle classes read and marked) and improving tracts (which the working classes used as fire-lighters and lavatory paper). This propaganda, sneered the *Poor Man's Guardian*, was 'namby-pamby stuff published expressly to stultify the minds of working people and make them the spiritless and unresisting victims of a system of plunder and oppression'.[53] It was a futile attempt to create a proletariat in the image of the bourgeoisie. After a prolonged and indecisive struggle the government hit on a more ingenious manoeuvre. It relaxed controls and in 1836 decreased the stamp duty from fourpence to one penny. This had the appearance of being a liberal gesture but its effect was to smash the illegal press—it was comparable to eliminating smugglers by reducing customs duties. Respectable journals now became cheaper (though at fourpence or fivepence they were still beyond the reach of the masses) and increased their circulation correspondingly, while the profits from publishing an unstamped newspaper were no longer worth the risks of prosecution. The main beneficiary of this change was (in Cobbett's words) 'that cunning old trout', 'that brazen old slut', 'the bloody old *Times*'.[54]

Thus did successive governments stunt the growth and warp the development of the British press. They did not go so far as the French, who in 1825 secretly bought up all the main opposition papers and placed them under ministerial control,[55] much as both Tories and Whigs would have liked to achieve that state of political Nirvana which is the absence of all press criticism. As late as 1840 the *Observer* was receiving grants of Secret Service money. But that entire fund would not have been enough to buy a single substantial journal—London newspapers being so much wealthier than their Parisian equivalents, those cheap 'intellectual brothels' so garishly depicted in Balzac's *Les Illusions Perdues*. Still, a comparison with America best demonstrates the success of the press manipulation in Britain: according to an estimate made in 1833, the United Kingdom (population 24 million) had 320 newspapers, including 20 dailies, with a gross annual circulation of 30 million; whereas the United States (population 15 million) had 850 newspapers, including 58 dailies, with a gross annual circulation of 65 million.[56] Jeremy Bentham understandably saluted America as a place where the press was 'in possession of all that liberty which is conducive to the greatest happiness to the greatest number'.[57]

In Britain the greatest number, the 'fourteen-fifteenths', that 'vast mass of active, stirring life' about which, as Thackeray acknowledged with amazement, the upper and middle classes knew as much as they did of the aborigines of Lapland,[58] were not entirely starved of cheap reading matter. Their craving had traditionally been satisfied by ballads, chap-books, almanacs, broadsheets and pamphlets. These contained everything from bawdiness to superstition, from murders to monstrous births, from riddles to rapes, from executions to elopements, from werewolves to pirates, from jokes to prophecies, from ancient sagas of romance to modern tales of pig-faced ladies seeking husbands.[59] During the Napoleonic period this type of street literature was supplemented by such enterprising journals as the *Terrific Register*, which avoided paying stamp duty by publishing serial stories already issued in book form. Dickens bought it as a boy 'making myself unspeakably miserable, and frightening my very wits out of my head, for the small charge of a penny weekly; which, considering that there was an illustration to every number in which there was always a pool of blood, and at least one body, was cheap'.[60] Gore was of the essence. Witness Edward Lloyd's complaint about the illustration of a Gothic horror he was publishing entitled *The Heads of the Headless*: 'the eyes must be larger and there must be more blood, much more blood'.[61]

It was not enough. The dramatic and mysterious life of the cities of industrial Britain at once fed and whetted the appetites of their increasingly literate inhabitants for news as well as sensation. A regular diet was supplied by the Sunday newspapers, stamped, radical scandal-sheets which by 1829 were selling (often to institutions—coffee houses, barbers—or to syndicates of readers) a total of 110,000 copies (compared to the figure of 28,000 for the seven metropolitan dailies). Typical of these was *Bell's Life in London* which advertised itself as 'a rich Repository of Fashion, Wit and Humour, and the interesting incidents of real life' and provided a vivid miscellany of crime, comedy, sex, politics and sport.[62] Nothing better epitomised the Sunday press, ancestor of today's *News of the World* (itself founded in 1843), than the favoured early headline: 'Shocking Rape and Murder'.

The market expanded in the 1830s and the radical publisher Henry Hetherington gauged its tastes to perfection with the promise that his *Dispatch* would be:

a repository of all the gems and treasures, and fun and frolic, and 'news and occurrences of the week'. It shall abound in Police Intelligence, in Murders, Rapes, Suicides, Burnings, Maimings, Theatricals, Races, Pugilism and all manner of 'accident by flood and field'. In short, it will be stuffed with every sort of devilment that will make it sell.[63]

However, as Hetherington added, his object was not to get rich but to beat the government. He did neither. He never learnt the press barons' vital secret, that their private corridor to political power was carpeted with a thick pile of newspaper money.

Yet by the third decade of the nineteenth century there were fortunes to be made from journalism. The French Revolution and the Industrial Revolution were transforming Britain and America and, like so much else in modern history, the origins of the popular press lay in these two momentous upheavals. The dramatic events in France changed the political climate everywhere. Across the Channel and across the Atlantic there arose (after an inevitable period of reaction) a vibrant enthusiasm for democracy. The reforms of the 1830s, which benefited the middle classes rather than the masses, were the first fruit of that enthusiasm. But the commercial bourgeoisie, who owed their wealth to industrial expansion and the new market economy, did not simply buy newspapers, they bought the wares advertised in them. By the 1830s a proliferation of manufactured goods, displayed in the shop window of the press, had enormously increased its advertising revenue. This was the crucial factor in transforming newspapers into a capitalist industry, founding the fourth estate and spawning the press barons. By concentrating the growing population into cities the Industrial Revolution also created a vast theatre of news, complete with actors and spectators hungry for the kind of personal involvement they had enjoyed in rural communities. Paradoxically, newspapers re-forged these human ties by means of mass production. The technology—the Fourdrinier paper-making machine, the Cowper and Applegarth cylinder press, not to mention the kerosene lamp—was quite as important to the newspaper owners as the techniques, catalogued disparagingly by the historian Lecky, by which journalistic ascendancies were built:

> a knack of clever writing, great enterprise in bringing together the kind of information which amuses or interests the public, tact in catching and following the first symptoms of change of opinions, a skilful pandering to popular prejudice, malevolent gossip, sensational falsehood, coarse descriptions, vindictive attacks on individuals, nations or classes.[64]

Thus newspapers helped to manufacture a community of interest in the place of an organic neighbourhood. In their pages local gossip was writ large and the anonymous citizen became a living, breathing participant. Newspapers forced the growth of social integration, encouraged literacy, even taught immigrants to America the language, as well as keeping the Melting Pot on the boil.

However, in Britain old corruption prevailed against new journalism. State interference arrested the development of the popular press. It also delayed the emergence of the press barons. Only in the United States, wedded to the ideal of journalistic freedom, were conditions right for the evolution of these armour-plated, sabre-toothed behemoths—though many were inclined to explain their birth in other than scientific terms. Carlyle's suggested title for a history of newspapers was *Satan's Invisible World Displayed.*[65] Henry J. Raymond, founder of the New York *Times*, reckoned it worth a million dollars if the devil would appear to him every night, as he did to the evil-eyed Bennett, with instructions about what to write in the next day's paper.[66]

CHAPTER TWO

Satan and Son

T HE JAMES GORDON BENNETTS went from clogs to spats in two
generations. The father established his newspaper empire in the
teeth of fierce competition. The son gorged himself on the imperial
flesh-pots. The father started with nothing but a brutal will. A multi-
millionaire almost from birth, the son was chiefly characterised by a
perverse wilfulness. The father wrote:

> It is my passion, my delight, my thought by day, and my dream by
> night to conduct the *Herald,* and to show the world and posterity
> that a newspaper can be made the greatest, most fascinating, most
> powerful organ of civilization that genius ever dreamed of.[1]

The son declared that he had been trying to kill the *Herald* for thirty
years but was unable to succeed.[2] What the two press barons did share
was the common badge of their order—independence. Like Lucifer,
their besetting sin was pride. The Bennetts stood in awe of no
convention, bowed the knee to no interest, prostrated themselves
before no authority. But whereas the father's resolution was forged in
conflict, the son's capriciousness was fostered by dissipation. The elder
Bennett justly proclaimed, 'I have been a wayward, self-dependent,
resolute, self-thinking being from my earliest days . . . holding with a
death-grasp on the original elements of my soul'. The freakish vagaries
of the younger Bennett were a travesty of the paternal ideal of 'perfect
mental liberty'. They were exercises in arbitrariness, such as dismissing
all the staff whom the *Herald's* editor considered indispensable, or
urinating into his fiancée's grand piano during the betrothal party.

The elder Bennett first asserted his autonomy by sloughing off the
restrictive family faith. Born (in 1795) of Roman Catholic parents at

19

Keith, in Banffshire, Scotland, he was educated for the ministry 'till I became graceless enough to set up for myself, and slap the Pope ... right and left'.[3] Never was an apostate more unbridled. Fascinated by the romantic glamour of Napoleon, Byron and Scott, yet instructed in the stern maxims of the Scottish political economists, the youthful Bennett dramatised himself as leader of the current march of mind, ranged against a Church whose foundations lay in 'the darkness, folly, and superstition of the tenth century'.[4] That Bennett later mounted scoffing assaults on Roman Catholic dogma was a mark of the astonishing licence which he permitted himself—even his madcap son was profoundly relieved when his own drunken editorial, entitled 'To Hell with the Pope', was suppressed by the *Herald*. Yet Bennett senior, tapping a vein of nihilistic humour which makes him seem almost a figure of the twentieth century, poured forth a spate of blasphemous mockery calculated to incense readers of the nineteenth.

Professing to remain 'a liberal Catholic',[5] he described transub-stantiation as 'the delicious luxury of creating and eating our Divinity', a grotesque form of 'religious cookery'. The doctrine of the resurrection of the dead moved him to further profaneness.

> The squabbling will be curious and the movement most astonishing. Bones will get so mixed up as to destroy all title to property both here and here after. A young girl will get hold of the leg of one sweetheart, and the arm of another: and one skeleton may be thus compounded of the bones of a dozen persons, so that he won't know what name to answer to when he hears the roll called over by the recording angel.[6]

Roman Catholics were not Bennett's only butt: 'Great trouble among the Presbyterians', he once reported. 'The question in dispute is, whether or not a man can do anything toward saving his own soul.'[7]

As if this were not enough, Bennett assumed an air of privileged intimacy with the deity, a piece of cosmic impertinence which enraged the devout. Thus he announced his marriage in 1840 with the pious observation, 'I must fulfil that awful destiny which the Almighty Father has written against my name, in the broad letters of life against the wall of Heaven'.[8] And he attributed the *Herald*'s comprehensive society coverage, particularly its exposure of the sexual peccadilloes of the eminent, to a heavenly host of Paul Prys in his employment:

> We receive every night a regular report from these 'spirits of the blue ether' of the doings in every fashionable circle in New York—every saloon in town—every boudoir in Broadway. All movements, good, bad, and indifferent, masculine, feminine, and neuter, are detailed to us.[9]

His enemies, of course, acknowledged the existence of Bennett's familiars but claimed that they were demons. The *Evening Signal* dubbed him 'the Prince of Darkness'. In the first illustration it ever carried the New York *Times* pictured horns beneath his tam o'shanter. The Bishop of New York, provoked by Bennett's condemnation of his failure to break with Rome and free American Catholics from the obligation to 'hug the chain and kiss the toe of every debauchee whom the College of Cardinals may elevate to the triple crown',[10] excommunicated this 'serpent in Paradise'.[11]

Bennett soon shed family as well as faith. In 1819, moved by a sudden impulse to see the country whose 'holy struggle for Independence' he admired,[12] Bennett sailed to North America. A long, rangy man with a high, intellectual forehead, light, sandy hair, hooked nose and wolfish teeth, Bennett would have been an imposing figure but for that wandering eye which imparted a diabolical dimension to his appearance. His sinister countenance actually caused his expulsion from a brothel in Nova Scotia, where he first landed, an adventure which he was to recount with saturnine glee in the *Herald*. 'You are too ugly a rascal to come among us', barracked the girls, 'Keep company only with the virtuous; you can talk; we doesn't [do] them things; mere talk's nothing; we be Demoston's scholars, *all action*'.[13] If, as they claimed, the sight of Bennett gave harlots the ague, it may well have sickened employers. For he slid from one precarious occupation to another before, in the mid-1820s, finding a niche in that nest of stinging vipers, New York newspaperdom.

Writing with fanged nib, he quickly made his mark as a political correspondent and a propagandist in the Jacksonian interest. He served various proprietors, including the eccentric Mordecai M. Noah, who once summoned the lost tribes of Israel, many of them apparently Red Indians, to Grand Island in the Niagara River where he laid the corner-stone of a new Jewish capital, christening the place Ararat in honour of his illustrious ancestor. By 1830 Bennett had become associate editor of James Watson Webb's *Courier & Enquirer*. But though Bennett boasted of the 'fearless independence' of this progressive 'blanket sheet', he was horribly aware that it was yet another journalistic jade to be hired and ridden at will. And when it turned about in response to a massive bribe from the United States Bank, which in Bennett's view threatened to replace political democracy by commercial aristocracy, he resigned in disgust. For years, in any case, his imagination had been (as he wrote in his diary) 'continually chasing some chimera', the creation of his own newspaper.[14]

Almost at once, however, Bennett was ignominiously betrayed by his political allies and reduced to a state of anguish and despair. Far from impressing Van Buren's party by his loyalty, Bennett's show of independence had earned him their 'deadly hostility'.[15] Fearing that, despite his protestations, Bennett was too slippery a customer ever to conduct a safe Democratic sheet, they refused him an essential loan. His purse empty, his pride wounded, his soul embittered, the aspiring press baron made several lonely false starts before founding the *Herald* on 6 May 1835. The first issue to emerge from his cellar reflected Bennett's determination to glory in the role of political pariah. It denounced party principles as 'steel-traps' and vowed to 'be the organ of no faction or COTERIE, and care nothing for any election or any candidate from president down to a constable'. Congressmen of all sorts were social pests and financial parasites. City legislators were 'an unprincipled, illiterate, scheming set of cormorants, foisted on the community' by gerrymandering, ballot-box stuffing and other forms of knavishness.[16] Political morality was 'the grave of honor and the charnel-house of integrity'.[17]

As he began to prosper Bennett reserved his foulest abuse for Van Buren and his associates: 'we have seen them, with these very eyes, enter the house of assignation under the sun's bright rays—and we have seen them even turn the sacred capitol itself into a common brothel'.[18] Such denunciations, Bennett stressed, were not provoked by partisan spleen. Their honesty was guaranteed by his own new-found financial independence.

> I can afford now to tell the truth. My old associates in humbug, Mr Noah and Mr Webb, are yet wallowing in the mire, but Heaven has been more merciful to me. I am beyond the reach of the monster of the United States Bank as well as the 'monster Party'.[19]

At his most extreme Bennett seemed to suggest that now, in what he dubbed 'the editorial age',[20] politicians were altogether a redundant species. Their place would be taken by a kind of mystical union between press and people, over which, like some fiendish pander, Bennett himself would preside. Newspapers were, in a sense, the most immediate form of democracy, for only those echoing public opinion survived. Bennett ensured that the *Herald* was never more than a day in advance of its readers. He insisted, 'An editor must always be with the people, think with them, feel with them, and he need fear nothing. He will always be right, always strong, always popular, always free.'[21] Sometimes, however, the people were unaccountably omitted from Bennett's equation. He was quite capable of maintaining that a penny paper such as his, selling not to subscribers but to the mass market, was 'subservient to none of its readers—known to none of its readers—and entirely ignorant who are its readers and who are not'.[22] Bennett was not content merely to convert the press into the fourth estate. It was his heady ambition to make it the crux of every estate, 'the great organ and pivot of government, society, commerce, finance, religion, and all human civilization'.[23]

Doubtless he exaggerated for effect. One of his subtlest journalistic arts was massively to inflate, in semi-serious, semi-satirical vein, his own and his newspaper's importance. He thus simultaneously guyed and trumped the self-puffery of his rivals. No braggadocio was too outrageous for the *Herald*. Bennett compared himself to Zoroaster, Moses, Socrates, Seneca and Luther. He boasted of having inaugurated a new epoch in world history by infusing into a moribund press 'life, glowing eloquence, philosophy, taste, sentiment, wit, and humour'.[24] He announced that 'Shakespeare is the great genius of the drama, Scott of the novel, Milton and Byron of the poem—and I mean to be the genius of the newspaper press'. He exulted, 'A newspaper can send more souls to Heaven, and save more from Hell, than all the churches and chapels in New York—besides making money'.[25] Bathos and bombast were calculated to amuse Bennett's readers while yet giving them an earnest of his sober purpose. This he explained to a friend:

> I am hard at work—mean to make a commercial newspaper for the million and not for Wall Street—am always serious in my aims, but full of frolic in my means. I must be what Providence intended I should become. What is that? Heaven only knows, but I feel I must be the sum-total of journalism—or a cipher.[26]

The hyperbole was aggressive as well as defensive, but in 1835 the *Herald*'s sole reporter, editor, manager and proprietor might have been forgiven for anticipating only defeat.

The *Herald*'s victory was chiefly gained by its owner's disregard for the accepted canons of propriety. As Charles A. Dana said, Bennett looked on every man and every institution with satirical disrespect and ran 'amuck against the established ideas and usages of society'.[27] In a sharper sketch James Parton (Greeley's biographer) wrote that Bennett could not be called a liar for he lacked any sense of truth. Nor was he a traitor for his heart knew no country, certainly not that of the Scots—'a damned scaly set from top to bottom', hissed the editor, 'and when I pass them in the street, I always take the windward side, and avoid shaking hands as I would the itch'.[28] Nor was Bennett an infidel, for all high and serious concerns were to him a joke. Where honour, patriotism and conviction had their sphere in other men, there was in

23

Bennett 'a mere vacancy'.[29] The truth was that Bennett believed artificial refinement was fatal to a newspaper, sleep to its readers, death to its editors.

He set a ruthless standard of candour in publishing his own affairs. When Webb attacked him in 1836 he reported the brawl in bantering detail. Bennett received a cut on the head and he twitted Webb derisively: 'The fellow, no doubt, wanted to let out the never-failing supply of good humour and wit, which has created such a reputation for the Herald, and appropriate the contents to supply the emptiness of his own thick skull'.[30] Bennett announced his marriage with a series of headlines which diverted the vulgar and affronted the polite: 'Declaration of Love—Caught at Last—Going to be Married— New Movement in Civilization'. It was particularly maddening that Bennett not only flouted the conventions but simultaneously set himself up as an arbiter of taste, informing benighted New Yorkers that it was not *comme il faut* to blow their noses with their fingers, especially in the street, and upbraiding them for dancing to the strains of that immoral Hungarian import, the polka. Of course, Bennett really did loathe the prevailing prudery and he crusaded against such simpering euphemisms as 'limbs' for legs and 'inexpressibles' for trousers. He referred to dancers' 'branches' and wrote, 'Petticoats—petticoats—petticoats—petticoats—there—you fastidious fools, vent your mawkishness on that'.[31]

Not that Bennett was entirely permissive. As he later explained to an employee, 'I don't mind lasciviousness, be as lascivious as ever you like, Altree, but damn it, don't be vulgar!' This specious distinction allowed him a convenient degree of latitude. Thus Bennett censored a passage from Deuteronomy, alluded to by Mrs Gore in her lectures on the anatomy of ladies, observing ironically that 'it is unfit for our columns'. But he printed a lip-smacking report, punctuated with titillating asterisks, of the lectures themselves.

> Mrs Gore proceeded to unfold and develop the beauty and mystery of the internal structure of the female form; in glowing terms she painted the springs of life, action, pleasure, and pain— how each spring was worked—how much tension each would bear—what oil (to speak mechanically) should be used to facilitate the movements of the machinery, and how the strained springs might be braced and renovated—how far we might go and no further. Oh, had you seen the brightening of the eyes and the bending forward of the beautiful necks to catch every syllable of the speaker, you would have given the lovely listeners credit for enthusiasm, if for nothing else.

Men were not admitted to Mrs Gore's lectures so this account is evidently a complete fabrication. But for gratuitous suggestiveness and bland indelicacy it would, even today, be difficult to match.

Bennett was more frankly salacious when describing the rapes and murders which were the *Herald*'s cardinal preoccupation. What really sealed the paper's success was its prurient and shocking treatment of the murder of Ellen Jewett, a beautiful prostitute who, in 1836, was strangled and beaten to death by one of her patrons in a New York brothel. Bennett was quick to appreciate the melodramatic appeal of the story and mounted one of the earliest press spectaculars. He quizzed the police and played the detective himself. He visited the scene of the crime, acting, as one rival put it, like 'a vampire returning to a newly found graveyard—like a carrion bird to the rotten carcase—like any vile thing to its congenial element'. He inspected the corpse: it was 'as white, as full, as polished as the purest Parian marble. The perfect figure, the exquisite limbs, the fine face, the full arms, the beautiful bust, all surpassed in every respect the Venus de Medici.'

Bennett conceived a vivid new journalistic technique, the printed interview, to record his cross-questioning of the brothel-keeper, Rosina Townsend. She was deceitful, which prompted this immodest revenge:

> Rosina's parts for all mankind
> Were open, rare, and unconfined,
> Like some free port of trade;
> Merchants unloaded here their freight,
> And agents from each foreign state
> Here their first entry made.[32]

The *Herald*'s clamorous coverage of both this unexceptional killing and the subsequent trial (which resulted, thanks in part to facts unearthed during Bennett's private investigations, in the acquittal of the accused man) magnified the case into a national *cause célèbre*. And it established Bennett as the star journalist of his age. His sins were scarlet but (to paraphrase Belloc) his newspaper was read.

Of course Bennett did not invent that perennial feature of life and literature, the human interest story. Nor did he originate the means of sensationalising and selling it, for the lowest possible price, to a mass market. In that momentous enterprise he was anticipated by Benjamin Day, who founded the first successful one-cent daily paper in 1833. Based on the English *Penny Magazine*, the *Sun* devoted two lines to the removal of the Secretary of the Treasury, three to the catching of a big shark, quarter of a column to feeding an anaconda at the American Museum, and the main story to Miss Susan Allen, who bought a cigar on Broadway and was arrested after smoking it while dancing in the street.[33] But although the *Sun* sucked every drop of personal pathos from news of crime and sex, infused every particle of human drama into its serialised legends of Davy Crockett and Daniel Boone, and sparkled with outlandish items (of which the most famous was the 'moon hoax', Richard Locke's 'scientific' revelations of lunar life), it was soon eclipsed.

The *Herald*, as Bennett rightly asserted, was prettier, wittier, spicier, saucier, livelier. Bennett revelled in scandal and sensation, as in this recapitulation of the salient points in the macabre case of John C. Colt, who killed Samuel Adams in 1842.

> Take it altogether, the murder—the boxing up of the body—the alleged salting of it— the trial—firing pistols in court—cutting off the head, and bringing the skull of the dead man into Court—the sentence, and defiance of the judge—the Park meeting—the threat to arrest the Sheriff—the money that seemed to flow like water—the various bribes—the mock piety— the holding a sort of levée in the cell on the day of execution—the horrid marriage—the shocking suicide—and the burning of the jail, all combine to form a history that throws fable and romance for ever into the shade.[34]

Day could never effervesce with such shameless vitality. He would never flaunt his wares with such sprightly abandon. He lacked Bennett's evil genius.

Thus Day allowed himself to be provoked into replying to the attacks of this 'goblin-like apology for manhood',[35] attacks which were transparently intended to gain publicity for his paper. When the *Herald* accused the *Sun*, edited by 'the garbage of society', of 'inundating the town with indecent and filthy police reports of drunkards, blacks and negresses', Day replied that Bennett's 'only chance of dying an upright man will be that of hanging perpendicularly upon a rope'.[36] It was a mild enough jibe compared to the barrage of execration which descended on his head in 1840, when puritans and peers allied to declare moral war upon the *Herald*. Then Noah reviled Bennett as 'turkey buzzard, rascal, rogue, cheat, common bandit . . . and polluter of the press'.[37] Webb damned the 'revolting blasphemy' of that 'vulgar, depraved wretch'. Park Benjamin, editor of the *Evening Signal*, branded Bennett an 'obscene foreign vagabond, a pestilential scoundrel, ass, rogue, habitual liar, loathsome and leprous slanderer and libeller'.[38] Bennett was denounced from the pulpit and during one street mêlée an assailant forced open his jaws and spat down his throat. Bennett's paper was boycotted by advertisers and distributors. An infernal device was sent to him by post (but discovered before it could blow him to pieces) and a gallows was erected for his exclusive use.

Even the British, horrified by such excesses of populist vulgarity, contributed to the bombardment. The London *Times* pontificated about the evil effects of 'farthing ribaldry' on enfranchised and uncivilised readers. It concluded that the combination of an unfettered democracy and an unstamped press doomed 'the once hopeful Eden of liberty to remain a wilderness of weeds'.[39] The *Manchester Guardian* pronounced that Bennett's 'sentiments' should no more be taken seriously than those of 'a Chartist Newspaper'.[40] Another journal, *Temple Bar*, concluded that the secret of the *Herald*'s success lay in its being the mouthpiece of the mob; 'and, as we all know, the mob is king in the United States. From first to last Gordon Bennett has pandered to the vitiated tastes of lazy grumbling Irishmen, and ignorant bigoted rowdies in New York; a pack who find their chief gratification in vomiting their rancid dissatisfaction upon this country'.[41] In *Martin Chuzzlewit* Dickens clearly based the *Rowdy Journal* (more blackguardly even than its New York competitors, the *Sewer*, *Stabber*, *Peeper*, *Family Spy*, *Keyhole Reporter* and *Plunderer*) on the *Herald*. And its owner, Colonel Diver, a sallow gentleman with sunken cheeks and a twitching right eye, whose expression was neither a frown nor a leer though it might have been mistaken for either, evidently owed much to Bennett. Dickens waxed somewhat hysterical about the American press in general—he described its conductors as 'the human lice of God's creation'.[42] But both he and his friend and biographer, W. E. Forster, condemned the *Herald* as its most atrocious exemplar. It was a 'broadsheet of lies and filth', a 'foul mass of positive obscenity', 'the *Snake* of Newspapers'.[43]

Bennett sometimes crowed that abuse would make him the greatest editor in the country. Sometimes he growled: 'We are a live lion, and it is dangerous for any long-eared animal to protrude his posteriors towards us in a hostile manner'.[44] Sometimes he ululated:

I bear a charmed existence. Neither fire, nor sword, nor steel, nor competition, nor hate, nor abuse, nor falsehood, nor slander, nor indictments, nor persecutions, of a thousand forms, can quench my spirit, impede my movements, or throw obstacles in my way. I do sincerely believe some superior power watches over me.[45]

Sometimes Bennett savaged his detractors:

Now what is my public and private character as compared with that of my rivals who pass for gentlemen and good citizens? Have I ever broken into a married lady's apartment at night? No. Do I owe $50,000 in debts of honor in Wall Street? No. Have I ever been seen reeling drunk round corners? No. Have I ever been convicted of breaking open sealed packages? No. Have I ever been charged with escaping the State Prison of Massachusetts? No. Have I ever seduced youth and innocence and had its fruits hung up at my door in a basket? No. Have I ever abandoned a wife and followed practices too terrible to name? No—no—no. Yet by the consuming jealousy of the newspaper editors and *employés* of New York, I have been represented as a rogue—a monster—a villain of the deepest die [*sic*]. It is no egotism in me to say I surpass them all in industry, in genius, in talent, in popularity and in success. Hence the real cause. Oh! ye hypocrites, how I will lash you! Beware. Yet even Webb himself, if he would repent, I would forgive. If he does not, I'll have him punished in court.

But there is no doubt that the moral war hurt the *Herald*. Bennett had to employ all his ferocious energy to maintain its ascendancy. He did so by supplying the latest news earliest. He concentrated especially on providing commercial and financial intelligence. Woodcuts, maps, cartoons, sports reports, church news and lampooning paragraphs on smart society all added to the *Herald*'s attractiveness. So did miscellaneous snippets like these:

> Those who can get up in the morning are now gazing their eyes out for the comet.
>
> Lay in your stocks of coal for the winter.
>
> Reader if you desire a bad character, become a candidate for public office—if a good one, die.
>
> The Sun squeaks a little on Saturday. Put your foot on a rat's tail and it ever squeaks so.
>
> No riots now-a-days? What's the matter?
>
> No foundlings were picked up last week.—Quite moral for once.
>
> Brown and Co. corner of Chatham and Mott is the cheap hat store.[46]

Bennett printed increasingly bizarre items about mesmerism, phrenology (a science fit only for 'blockheads', he said) and animal magnetism, likening himself ironically to Alcibiades who docked his dog's tail so that the world might talk about its master. He demonstrated the *Herald*'s effectiveness at selling such necessaries as Dr Goldman's American Anti-Gonorrheal Pills and Hopper's Very

Superior Leeches, extracting—a crucial innovation—payment in advance for each advertisement. Even so he was forced to acknowledge the restraints imposed on him by popular priggery. The *Herald* kept its reptilian style but restricted its risqué content. Bennett promised to exclude further articles of 'a slimy character'.[47]

So, conceived in scandal and reared in scurrility, the *Herald* matured into a *news*paper. As such, it achieved by 1860 a circulation of 77,000, the highest in the world—though even then purchasers might conceal this noxious rag in polite company. Bennett had been first to take advantage of the startling advances in communication achieved by the steamboat, the railway and the electric telegraph. Through ruthless enterprise and lavish investment he revolutionised the news-getting process. During the Civil War he spent over half a million dollars to keep an army of correspondents at the front. But he refused to pay one of them $25 for a horse killed under him in battle because the animal had not been first with the news. Despite such mishaps, Bennett was often better informed about the conflict than Lincoln, who said that he valued the *Herald*'s support more than a victory in the field. In fact Bennett really sympathised with the South, loathing what he was pleased to call the fashionable cant of woolly-minded, woolly-haired, thick-lipped Abolitionists.

But by this time his youthful ideals had withered away. If he possessed a principle it was to provoke news as well as to report it, to stir up the animals in the political menagerie when they showed signs of growing sluggish. He refused to be bound even by the shackles of consistency, remarking cynically, 'I print my paper every day'.[48] Thus Bennett's attachment to the Confederacy was severed not by the President's offer to appoint him ambassador to France (to the press baron a mere bauble) but by the mob's threat to tear down the *Herald* building. Bennett hastily sent a copy-boy to purchase the national banner, which was loyally flown from the paper's flagpole. This gesture, which appeased the rioters, was a symbolic acknowledgement that in the sphere of newspaper patronage the public had superseded the politicians. For although Bennett afterwards purchased an arsenal of rifles and ammunition, they were stored behind the walnut panelling in his office and never used. Shedding its readers' blood would have been bad for the *Herald*'s circulation.

In his later years Bennett received a number of handsome gifts and fulsome testimonials. He sent them to himself. They bore pathetic witness to the fact that, though courted by ambitious politicians and flattered by sycophantic journalists, Bennett had become a lonely, unloved old man. He had few friends, and those were his intellectual inferiors. He had no recreations save to sit in solitary magnificence on

Washington Heights exchanging ribaldry with his pet birds (each of whom was named after a politician, preacher or newspaperman) and perusing the gazettes of his rivals: 'and yet', as he remarked in surly Scottish accents, 'they are mostly domd [*sic*] fools'.[49] His wife had long since fled to Europe in order to escape from the atmosphere of calumny which seemed to be the breath of life to her husband. Yet even for him the polemics, commenced in a vein of jocularity, had turned sour. Bennett, who surely earned his title of the 'best abused man in the world',[50] had become 'implacable in his enmities, and recognizes no principle of honour, or of justice, and no law, human or divine, which would interfere to prevent the exercise of his malignity'.[51] 'Up and down the long editorial room he would stalk distributing in turn their tasks to his editors, who sat in stalls. To one he would say "Pitch into Greeley", to another "Give Raymond hell", and so on.'[52]

The infernal struggles had cankered Bennett's soul. Now an embittered misanthropist, he dismissed all forms of idealism as arrant humbug. The *Herald*, which he had started (at least in part) as a means to improve society, had become a commercial end in itself. Far from controlling the monster he had created, Bennett was its slave. All his powers were subordinated to fostering its growth. To those who worked on the paper, said Henry Villard, Bennett revealed his 'hard, cold, utterly selfish nature and incapacity to appreciate high and noble aims'.[53] Perhaps, shortly before the end, the press baron mellowed; for in 1872 he made his confession to Archbishop McCloskey and he died in the faith of his forefathers. Or was this a senile charade? Maybe even a piece of impious mummery? It is difficult to believe that Bennett readily abandoned his independence, that cherished quality which had made him the most brilliant and original journalist of his age. Perhaps after all it was in the old Voltairean spirit that Bennett secured his everlasting insurance policy from what he called 'the Holy Roman Catholic Church' (adding in sardonic parentheses, 'all of us Catholics are devilish holy').[54]

What Bennett could not ensure was the security of his earthly inheritance, the *Herald*, which he handed over to his only male heir and namesake in 1868. For while the elder Bennett had pioneered the rise of the press barons the younger presaged their fall. What in the father had been lawless self-determination became in the son a refusal to endure any restraint, even that imposed by reason and common sense. Bennett junior indulged his every humour, flouted his every inhibition. He became the prototype of the mad, bad press baron, 'as changeable as a chameleon, domineering, hypersensitive, full of whims'.[55] He was subject to paranoid suspicions, employing office spies, 'white mice' he called them, to sniff out disloyal members of his staff. He was the victim of megalomaniac impulses, dismissing subordinates for fantastic reasons—blue eyes, loose ties, large size, hairiness, drunkenness, sobriety. He was prey to outrageous freaks of fancy, throwing a roll of banknotes onto the fire, attempting to ram a battleship with his yacht, marooning an employee on a Mediterranean island, abducting an entire theatrical company, tattooing owls on his mistress's knees. Bennett treated his minions like rats on an obstacle course, doubling or halving salaries at a moment's notice, appointing two journalists to a single task for the fun of watching their struggle for supremacy. Subjected to his dictatorial crotchets, the *Herald* was beaten to the ground by the time its second proprietor died in 1918. The wonder was that for many years this product of one man's caprice not only survived, it flourished.

The younger Bennett was born to strife. His nativity in 1841 was greeted by the *Sun* as proof of his mother's adultery. For how could the proprietor of the *Herald*, that 'human parody', 'diseased', 'impotent', 'unnatural', have been the father? Bennett senior denounced this 'diabolical' conspiracy to blast his wife's good name, sued the offenders and won.[56] But the soft, musical Irishwoman he had married, Henrietta, née Crean, preferred exile to ostracism and she brought up her children (another boy, who died young, and two girls) in Paris. There bevies of nurses, governesses and tutors saw to it that Jim grew up quite the spoilt darling of fortune, contemptuous of everyone whose father was poorer than his own, which meant that in America he respected only Vanderbilts and Astors. On his return from Europe in late adolescence, the gilded youth of the Gilded Age were happy to welcome such a dashing recruit to their ranks.

Bennett's wild exploits quickly made him their leader. He drank champagne from actresses' slippers, smashed up restaurants, hired entire bordellos for his own and his cronies' amusement. He invented a sport called 'Bennetting', which involved running through schoolgirls' 'crocodiles' causing chaos to pedestrians and traffic. He made extravagant wagers, one of which resulted in his winning the first transatlantic yacht race in 1866. He went on week-long, coach-borne rampages, drunkenly whipping his horses through the New England countryside while sitting naked on the box. Bennett had no head for alcohol. As a *Herald* correspondent declared, 'When sober he displayed the worst qualities of the Scotch and when drunk the worst qualities of the Irish'.[57] And it was liquor which prompted his incontinent behaviour at his fiancée's house on New Year's Day 1877.

Whether Bennett relieved himself into the grand piano or (as some said) the fire-place is unclear. But ladies fainted. Bennett was ejected. Caroline May broke off her engagement. Her brother Fred whipped the miscreant on the steps of his club and then fought a duel with him (both fired wide). Finally Bennett, wearing a bulky coat of mail under his perfectly-cut clothes to ward off further attacks, returned to France, a permanent expatriate. There he expressed his disgust with the United States by parading through the capital on a coach containing one passenger, a jackass, which bore round its neck a sign reading, 'This donkey is the most sensible American in Paris'.[58]

No mere ocean could cause the Commodore (as Bennett liked to be called, in honour of his sailing prowess) to slacken his martinet grip of the *Herald*. At the New York office a fire was kept burning in his grate in case, like the demon king, he should suddenly appear. And twenty sharpened pencils were daily placed on his desk—the chief copy boy's perquisite was to sell them each evening on Park Row. The black lexicon of forbidden expressions and the black list of banned persons (it eventually included Theodore Roosevelt, who had to be referred to as 'the third-term candidate') were constantly revised according to Bennett's specifications. The Commodore spent so much money on transatlantic cables that he finally invested in a cable company of his own. Frequently, too, he summoned editors to pay court to him in person. Arriving at his luxurious Champs-Élysées mansion, they were subject to ritual humiliations, gross or petty.

Some were dismissed outright: his waxed moustache bristling like the tusks of a boar, his blue eyes cold and hard as gems, Bennett enjoyed making men squirm with fear and beg for reinstatement. Others were kept waiting for weeks and then ordered home without having clapped eyes on the Commodore. Still others were harangued:

> De Witt, I have been receiving some anonymous letters about you. They say you are getting fat and lazy. Napoleon and his marshalls won their victories when they were lean. If you become fat you are of no use to me.[59]

All had to undergo the ordeal of being sniffed by the Commodore's pack of Poms, Pekes and Cocker Spaniels, for he was inclined to judge the worth of his employees by the regard in which they were held by these animals. One canny journalist gained the dogs' esteem, and their master's, by sprinkling his handkerchief with anise and placing a piece of raw liver in his top hat. But there was no sure path to Bennett's favour. He was cynical about everyone's motives, including his own. Meeting a young American journalist in Paris, Bennett remarked:

> Working in a newspaper office, eh!!! Bawdy-house, eh!!! I'm a prostitute, you're a prostitute, we newspapermen are all prostitutes.[60]

Bennett was chronically distrustful. He bestowed his confidence, as one foreign correspondent put it, 'somewhat after the fashion of a senile monarch throwing his jewels to the jester who had made him smile'.[61]

Yet although deceit, suspicion and intrigue were the conditions of their employment on the *Herald*, men fought for the privilege of serving the Commodore. For he invested the *Herald* with something of his own animal magnetism. There was a compelling fascination about the way in which this huge organisation was imbued with vigour by a single volatile personality. His sheer fickleness added to the excitement of working in the mercurial medium of journalism. Bennett gloried in his own quicksilver quality, telling the staff of the Paris edition (whom he once visited, dressed in flaming red pyjamas, for the purpose of discharging everyone on the right-hand side of the room):

> I want you fellows to remember that I am the reader of this paper. I am the only one to be pleased. If I want it turned upside down, it must be turned upside down. . . . I want one feature article a day. If I say the feature is to be Black Beetles, Black Beetles it's going to be.[62]

When, after long and heroic exertions, R. D. Blumenfeld finally induced the English *Sunday Herald* to make money instead of losing it, Bennett sent him a telegram from Paris: 'Congratulate you on having made a profit at last. Stop the paper at once. Close the office. Dismiss everybody.'[63] Bennett's best-known display of contumaciousness was his insistence on printing every day, year in year out, an enquiry from an 'Old Philadelphia Lady' about the difference between Centigrade and Fahrenheit. This meant ignoring new readers who answered her question and infuriating old ones who demanded her execution. But it was not just a fad. Its very pointlessness made it a talking-point, and so an advertisement for his newspaper. It was also an indication of the truth about Bennett which his roaring eccentricity tended to obscure— that he was an able and innovating newspaperman whose professional expertise won the grudging admiration of his employees.

Bennett lacked his father's originality, wit and style. But he possessed flair, enterprise and decision. He spared no effort or expense to make the *Herald*, and its sleazy, pink-papered sister, the *Evening Telegram*, founded at his behest in 1867, 'fresh, lively and readable'. He instructed his editors, 'The instant you see a sensation is dead drop it and start on something new'.[64] He insisted on 'scoops' or 'beats', and the *Herald* was first with the news of many notable events, from the battle of Little Big Horn to the sinking of the *Titanic*. More celebrated still was its exclusive story on 9 November 1874, which described the escape of all the Zoo's wild animals and the resulting shambles in New

33

York. Those who read to the end discovered that it was a hoax, a blood-curdling account of what *might* happen should the cages be opened. But for many hours terror really did stalk the city streets, in company with a number of aspirant big-game hunters.

Bennett attended to more commonplace matters, improving the *Herald*'s appearance, condensing the text and expanding the head-lines. He provided excellent foreign and commercial coverage and in-spired weather reports—the temperature being an obsession of his; he festooned his gardens with thermometers and spent much time checking one against another. Above all, Bennett was the first press baron who systematically created news. He sponsored races for yachts, automobiles, aeroplanes, balloons. He promoted 'stunts' like *Herald* soup kitchens for the poor. He financed expeditions, Stanley's successful quest for Livingstone, Long's abortive journey to the North Pole. He had no objection to Stanley's starting small wars in Africa in order to report them. Bennett improved on his father's dictum that newspapers should not educate but startle. He became the earliest exponent of 'the journalism that acts', long before the slogan was adopted by William Randolph Hearst's yellow *Journal* in the 1890s.

Like many newspapers born in sensationalism, the *Herald* was to expire of respectability. Its gradual, inexorable decline in Bennett's final years was caused by the rise of the vigorous 'yellow' press barons, Hearst and Pulitzer. The Commodore despised them and their papers, which he denounced as drivel for kitchen-maids. Joseph Pulitzer he reviled as 'an upstart Jew whose nose was in every putrescent dunghill, rutting out filth for the consumption of the dregs of society'.[65] Yet with this abhorrent creature he managed to preserve a façade of amiability. Pulitzer reported quizzically to his wife from Cap Martin in 1897,

> Bennett called for a few minutes the other day pretending to be friendly. He behaved in rather an eccentric way, rushing out of the room in the middle of a sentence so to speak. Still, he tried to be polite—for whatever reason.[66]

Bennett also tried to meet Pulitzer's challenge, symbolised by the *World*'s gold-domed skyscraper, with a new *Herald* building on 34th Street, dismissing protests that the site was only leasehold and too far up-town: 'Never mind all that, Blumenfeld. Thirty years from now the *Herald* will be in Harlem and I'll be in hell.'[67]

On the other hand, Bennett prosecuted a remorseless vendetta against Hearst, who had been presumptuous enough to enquire how much it would cost him to buy the fading *Herald*. The cabled answer was a devastating snub: 'Price of Herald three cents daily. Five cents Sunday. Bennett.'[68] Hearst's riposte was a combination of effrontery and hypocrisy: in 1906 he instituted court proceedings against the *Herald* for obscenity. The charge was well founded for the *Herald*'s personal column was so notorious (being filled with items of the 'Lady-with-large-chest-for-sale' variety) that the paper was nicknamed the *Whores' Gazette*. But other journals, including Hearst's, played the same lucrative game, albeit more discreetly, and Bennett was livid at having to pay a fine of $25,000. This was chicken-feed to a man who spent during his life between thirty and forty million dollars on pleasure alone; who, for example, not only fitted his yacht *Lysistrata* (named after a 'beautiful and very fast lady') with three separate suites for himself so that, following the practice of his friend Sultan Abdul the Damned, he could accommodate a concubine in each, but also provided a special air-conditioned cabin for an Alderney cow in order to be supplied with fresh milk afloat. However, the *Herald* lost savour, as well as advertising revenue, and soon it was being supported by its spicier sibling, the *Telegram*—described by one journalist as 'the soul of mendacity'.

Among Bennett's more curious idiosyncrasies was his craze for owls. When asleep on duty as a naval lieutenant during the Civil War, he had apparently been roused by one's hooting, just in time to prevent his ship running aground. Bennett's houses were littered with owls, live and stuffed, carved, cast and baked, owls as ornaments, lamps, playthings, receptacles. Owls adorned his blue stationery, his black coaches, his bronze gate-posts. They peered from the top of the *Herald* building. They scowled from the paper's masthead. Bennett even planned an avian sarcophagus, a granite statue of an owl (which must, he insisted, glower 'quite ferociously') two hundred feet tall, to be erected on Washington Heights.[69] Inside its hollow shell a spiral staircase would lead up to the eyes and Bennett's coffin, hung on steel chains, would roost for eternity in the bird's head. Luckily the architect of this bizarre mausoleum was murdered and, interpreting it as an ill omen, Bennett cancelled the project.

But although his talisman was the owl and his newspaper's motto was '*La nuit porte conseil*' (translated as 'Sleep on it'),[70] Bennett exhibited little of the wisdom traditionally associated with the bird of night. True, in 1914 he changed his ways dramatically, doubtless the result of the war and his marriage to Baroness de Reuter, née Maud Potter of Philadelphia, an attractive and sympathetic widow. He became a fanatical partisan of France—within a few months the *Telegram* had killed off more German soldiers than the Kaiser's army contained and it preached the worst kind of bitterness and hate. The Commodore abandoned debauchery and tried to revive the *Herald*, writing stories like 'Routine of Canine Life in Paris Upset by War',[71] and introducing

35

stringent economies. As a foreign correspondent of the paper declared, 'Bennett is dead. The old, drunken, money-spending Bennett is dead. In his place has come a Scotch miser.'[72]

Actually, as he had long prophesied, Bennett expired on reaching seventy-seven (his father's age at death) in 1918, suffering a fatal stroke on his birthday. Moreover a few years' reformation could not reverse the effects of a life-time's decadence. For too long the *Herald* had been a fief in the hands of a fickle tyrant. The paper was Bennett: each letter it sent out was signed with his name, each reporter (even Stanley) was an upstart to be brought low, each editor a mayor of the palace to be garrotted. Journalists found themselves catering for the Commodore's every quirk, supplying him with rare breeds of Japanese dog, with mocking birds (and, shortly afterwards, with mocking-bird food). Bennett's glittering patrimony was, as Walter Lippmann wrote, 'the first independent press which the world has known'.[73] This freedom the most prodigal of sons squandered; not, of course, by truckling to politicians or advertisers, but by making the *Herald* a slave of his passions.

Even now the power of those passions, the manic fury with which Bennett rode his hobbies, the ungoverned frenzy with which he pursued his obsessions, inspires a kind of awe. Certainly he seemed a demigod to Frank Munsey, who bought the *Herald* in 1920 (the proceeds of the sale had been willed to found a home for indigent journalists, many of whom owed their state to Bennett). Munsey, was, in the *World*'s sardonic phrase, 'one of the ablest retail grocers that ever edited a New York newspaper'.[74] No sooner had he installed himself in the *Herald* building than he began to comb his hair and trim his moustache in the Commodore's characteristic manner.

CHAPTER THREE

Thunders from Olympus

IN A MOMENT of unwonted modesty the elder James Gordon Bennett acknowledged that the New York *Herald* was merely 'the face of the Western half of the earth': its other hemisphere was the magisterial countenance of the London *Times*. There were, in consequence, two Napoleons of the press. Two 'master spirits' had breathed upon the new species of art that was journalism and moulded it into 'perfect form'—himself and John Walter II.[1] Flamboyance apart, Bennett was wrong anyway. The second John Walter, the *Times*'s chief (but not sole) proprietor, certainly helped to make that newspaper what Hazlitt called 'the greatest engine of temporary opinion in the world'. Walter stoutly resisted the browbeatings and blandishments of successive governments—Lord Melbourne was to complain that there was nothing the damned fellow wanted. Walter virtually invented the job of foreign correspondent. In 1814 he introduced a momentous change—emblem of the progress of the press—printing by steam power. Critics like Hazlitt could sneer that the *Times*'s heavy columns 'might be imagined to be composed as well as printed with a steam-engine'.[2] But the *Times* was thus able to manufacture 1,200 newspapers an hour and respond to the needs of those usually literate and often liberal-minded new managers of the world's workshop, the middle class. And, evolving in symbiosis with that affluent, citified class, it was also able to print the large number of advertisements on which its prosperity rested. The *Times* thus achieved that *sine qua non* of press freedom, financial independence.

However, unlike Bennett, Walter was loath to exercise this liberty in person. He was 'the shyest and awkwardest of men'[3] and his natural reserve was compounded by a stern Evangelical self-restraint. He

37

could not bear to hear allusions made to the *Times* in mixed company and he imposed a strict rule of anonymity over all aspects of the newspaper: intimate acquaintances who chanced to meet at its headquarters, Printing House Square, were supposed to pass each other without acknowledgement. As soon as possible Walter withdrew to live as a country gentleman on his estate at Bear Wood. He denied the charge that he was 'constantly guiding the affairs of The Times', rightly comparing his infrequent excursions to Printing House Square with those of 'a traveller visiting a foreign country'. Walter became, like the younger Bennett, an emperor in exile. The difference was that he was not afraid to delegate full authority to editors. He thus created, as it were, press barons by proxy.

It was under the editorship of the greatest of these, Thomas Barnes, that the *Times* earned its famous sobriquet 'The Thunderer'. True, before 1817, when Barnes took command, the paper's tone was Olympian enough. But so was that of every common-or-garden Mercury and the *Times* had little claim to be considered the Jupiter of newspapers. Indeed, at the start, it had been the butt of jests and taunts. For the first John Walter was a mixture of crank and crook. He had founded the paper in 1785 to prove the worth of his Laputan scheme for 'logographic' printing, which used founts consisting of words (fifty thousand of them) instead of the twenty-six letters of the alphabet. Of course, this proved entirely impractical—contemporaries joked that the type-founder received orders for a hundred-weight of the words '*murder, fire, dreadful robbery, atrocious outrage, fearful calamity* and *alarming explosion*'.[4]

Frustrated by this failure, Walter made money by 'the vilest arts', employed the *Times* as an instrument of blackmail and extortion and accepted regular bribes from the government (which did not prevent his being twice imprisoned for offending the royal family). The diarist Crabb Robinson reckoned Walter to be as 'worthless a man as I have ever known, at least among those who preserved great appearances'.[5] Matters improved in 1803 when his virtuous though self-effacing son gained control of the paper. But the second Walter's choice of John Stoddart as Barnes's predecessor was uninspired. Dr Slop, to give Stoddart his contemporary nickname, was 'too honest to be a good Tory, and too crotchety to be anything else',[6] and under his auspices the *Times* did not speak with the voice of authority. It issued shrieks instead of thunderbolts. Nevertheless, even in war-time its shrill cadences were audible across the Channel, where they so exasperated Napoleon Bonaparte that he took the opinion of an English counsel about the possibility of suing the paper for libel.[7]

Thomas Barnes (1785–1841) taught the *Times* not to sting but to gore. Almost single-handed he transformed the paper from political irritant into fourth estate of the realm. And he accomplished this in the face of social disdain as well as official resistance. For, as the elder Bennett observed, in England genius and intellect, unless displayed by military men and 'set off with epaulettes and throat-cutting instruments', were not considered fit to consort on equal terms with rank and power.[8] Barnes was the son of a humble attorney and his friends were other disreputable London scribblers like Leigh Hunt and Charles Lamb. All three had attended Christ's Hospital, wearing the blue coats of charity boys, and they shared the same robust sense of humour. To a woman who asked whether he liked children Barnes replied, 'Yes, ma'am, boiled'. Exactly the same story is told of Lamb.[9]

A graduate of Pembroke College, Cambridge, and an accomplished classical scholar, Barnes was a Bohemian and a voluptuary. In youth he had been a fine athlete but with years he grew corpulent and rheumatic. A foaming Toby-jug of a man, variously nicknamed 'the Barrel-organ' and 'Cockney', he ate tripe in the editor's room, had his hair cut by one of the compositors and lived in sin with a lady who, according to Disraeli, resembled a pantomime dame. He usually wore a 'blue body coat, with brass buttons, and the buff waistcoat, of which Charles Fox had been so fond'. And he carried a large bludgeon which he called his 'Conservative stick'—to be used against Tories who had threatened to knock his brains out.[10]

Daniel O'Connell described Barnes as 'the gin-drinkingest editor in London'.[11] But at Barnes's house in Soho the potations were richer and the fare was calculated to increase his already massive girth. The sumptuous table did not impress Lord Chancellor Brougham's Principal Secretary, Le Marchant, who occasionally dined with the editor in order to curry favour with his newspaper.

> We had turtle and venison, Champagne, Burgundy and Hermitage, but our host was embarrassed by his company. Our Hostess was vulgarity personified. Writing as these men do with spirit and taste, feeling as they do and more than they ought their ascendancy in society, still they cannot associate with gentlemen without shewing signs of conscious inferiority. When Barnes lays down his pen he becomes a child.[12]

With his gross appearance and low manners Barnes seemed to epitomise the Grub-Street gutter hack of an earlier age. It was perhaps with Barnes in mind that Queen Victoria later advised Colonel Fitzgeorge to cease running the *Sunday Times* and 'live cleanly like a gentleman'.[13] Yet Barnes was essentially indifferent to royal condescension or patrician patronage. He was, at least in large matters, incorruptible, once rejecting a proffered *douceur* from Louis Philippe of a million francs. He was as personally self-sufficient as his newspaper was politically influential. Barnes valued himself, well before this obituary tribute, as a 'man of colossal talent, who, by a slight exercise of his pen could make ministers of state tremble and crowned heads feel disquiet'.[14]

He never sought the approval of others. He made no public display. He was content to remain all his life a reserved, private, even anonymous, figure. An invincible egotist filled with a proud awareness that he was (in Tom Moore's words) 'devilish clever',[15] Barnes stood in awe of no person and no institution. Indeed he possessed a strain of cynicism which made him seem the total misanthropist, at war with the entire human race. Actually, although he did detest aristocrats—for their ignorance, 'their selfishness, their stupidity, etc. etc.'[16]—he was prodigal in his charities, especially towards destitute newspapermen. The good nature of his temperament vied with the ill nature of his tongue and he would go to any lengths to help people whom, moments before, he had bitterly disparaged. He once remarked that journalism is to literature what brandy is to beverages, but he never seemed to appreciate the devastating effects of his own paper's vituperation. Its acrid character can be gauged from this celebration of Daniel O'Connell:

> Scum condensed of Irish bog
> Ruffian, coward, demagogue,
> Boundless liar, base detractor,
> Nurse of murders, treason's factor!
> Spout thy filth, diffuse thy slime,
> Slander is in thee no crime.[17]

O'Connell said that Barnes had sold his soul to 'literary assassination'.[18] And there is no doubt that the *Times*'s pre-eminence was won, partly at least, by his willingness to publish murderous tirades against the highest in the land. This battering of Lord Palmerston was typical:

> What an offensive union is that of a dull understanding and an unfeeling heart! Add to this, the self-satisfied airs of a flippant dandy and you have the most nauseous specimen of humanity—a sort of compound which justifies Swift in the disgusting exhibition of the Yahoos.[19]

Not surprisingly, it was Palmerston's morning habit to throw his copy of the *Times* into the fire. Barnes wielded his pen like a cudgel, somewhat in the style of Cobbett, whom he ridiculed, incidentally, for keeping a butcher's shop in Kensington and sporting a paunch—a phantom beside his own. Lord Melbourne reckoned that the editor's flailing assaults on the *Times*'s former friend, Lord Brougham, would drive that peer mad.

Barnes chose his contributors for their virile prose and encouraged them to go on the rampage. He selected as his chief editorial writer Edward Sterling, 'an amazingly impetuous, hasty, explosive man, this "Captain Whirlwind"', as Carlyle called him,[20] who delivered his 365 opinions a year in the accents of Jove. Barnes whetted the edge of Disraeli's malice, suggesting, for example, that he should dilate on 'the mean and vacillating character of Lord Lansdowne and the humbuggery of that nest of mischievous drivellers—Holland House'. He printed Disraeli's deadliest stroke, the comment that the appointment of the spindle-shanked Lord John Russell as leader of the House of Commons enabled him 'to begin to comprehend how the Egyptians worshipped—an insect'. Barnes's enemies had cause to claim that he was consistent in nothing except malignity. But even in this he sometimes wavered. Thus he censored Disraeli's reference to the Prime Minister's Sultana, which, though doubtless metaphorical, 'will be thought to refer to a very substantial Siren whose fleshy attractions are supposed to be as agreeable to Lord M[elbourne] as the last patent-easy-chair'.[21] Barnes was more cautious than the elder Bennett. Innuendoes of that kind might alienate the *Times*'s respectable subscribers. It was to their views alone that Barnes invariably deferred.

Indeed, there was a sound commercial logic in the paper's political contradictions. Barnes was an editorial trimmer, a journalist Vicar of Bray. He changed tack in order to anticipate a shift in public opinion and thus keep his readers always, so to speak, behind the *Times*. Having been vehemently ministerialist during the Napoleonic Wars, the paper opposed both oppressive government and abhorred monarch in 1819 and, by favouring Queen Caroline during her divorce proceedings, gained enormously in circulation. Similarly, after sustaining the Tories once more throughout the 1820s, the *Times* rode the crest of the popular wave in the early 1830s. And by coining such phrases as 'The Bill, the whole Bill, and nothing but the Bill', it helped to create the groundswell for Parliamentary reform. At that time Barnes seemed 'a desperate radical'.[22] But by the end of 1834 he sensed an impending revulsion against Whiggery and performed another abrupt *volte-face*—which so incensed Dr Arnold of Rugby that he tried to have the paper excluded from the precincts of his school.

Politicians were also enraged by Barnes's inconstancy. Yet the best guarantee that the *Times* was independent was the fact that no one could depend on it. The *Times*'s spontaneous thunder-clap of approval was worth more than hurricanes of bought applause from a 'jobber journal'[23] like the *Morning Chronicle*. And when the Reform Act created a new middle-class electorate in 1832, members of parliament became much more vulnerable to hostile publicity. Thus Barnes negotiated with governments almost as an equal. He sent a peremptory message to the Whig leaders in 1831 threatening to withdraw his support unless they gave the *Times* their 'full confidence and the full share of patronage and advertisements, etc.'[24] He imposed stiff terms, embodied in the Tamworth Manifesto, for taking the *Times* into Sir Robert Peel's camp in 1834. Barnes helped to draft this document, which marked the transformation of reactionary old Toryism into reforming new Conservatism. Barnes was consulted about ministerial appointments. He was privy to official secrets. The proudest peer in England, Lord Durham, waited in the editor's outer room to intercede on behalf of a crowned head, King Leopold of the Belgians. Lord Lyndhurst, with pardonable exaggeration, pronounced Barnes 'the most powerful man in the country'.[25]

Actually, like most press barons, Barnes exercised influence rather than power. This he relished, all the more so as it was exerted surreptitiously, the editor preserving his incognito behind a regal 'we'. Barnes's only interest apart from the paper, in which he invested every ounce of his brobdingnagian energy, was the extravagant romance of politics. He laughed up his sleeve when ministers consulted him about Cabinet questions. He exulted over the failure of that 'noble grampus', Lord Althorp, to 'manage' or intimidate the *Times*.[26] He rejoiced at Lord Grey's impotent conclusion that the only way to deal with 'newspaper attacks is, as the Irish say, "to keep never minding"'.[27] In private he even expressed feelings of profound contempt for his own readers, boasting that given time he could govern them as he wished. Really, of course, Barnes knew that his strength as an editor lay in reflecting, not directing, their opinions. The leader columns (which, along with the letters to the editor and the superlative foreign news coverage, were the features of the paper which Barnes particularly developed) aimed at the pithy expression of what had often been thought, especially by the middle class. Sometimes this was exaggerated to the point of caricature—the radicals were cannibals. Often it was vociferated in loud polemic—the Irish were hooligans. Usually it was a sublimely articulate commonplace—the poor were pitiable. The *Times* was no longer the voice of ventriloquist governments; under Barnes it had become, to paraphrase Marx, the open mouth of the closed mind of the British bourgeoisie.

Under Barnes's successor its thunders became less strident but its pretensions more overweening. Shortly after his death, in 1841, the paper's newest reporter, John Thadeus Delane, who was aged twenty-three and lately down from Oxford, burst into his St James's Square rooms and announced to his fellow lodger, 'By Jove, John, what do you think has happened? I am editor of the *Times*.'[28] The appointment was astonishing not just because of Delane's youth and inexperience but because of his lack of literary and academic distinction. Moreover, though he might have had some dynastic claim to the editorial throne, his father being the *Times*'s business manager, Delane was the antithesis of Barnes. He was ambitious, avaricious and prone to nepotism. He enjoyed being lionised and was always hobnobbing in Rotten Row with peers and ministers of state. He was no writer of prose and no admirer of poetry: whereas Barnes had esteemed Shelley, Delane greeted a proposal to review his 'Life and Works' with the words, 'Excrement! Excrement!'[29] Unlike the obese Barnes, Delane was a sportsman throughout his life, so keen on riding and hunting that, as his Magdalen Hall tutor remarked, 'he, like the Centaurs of old, is part and parcel of his horse'.[30] Delane was a dandy, while Barnes had been a bear. Delane was to direct the paper from above, where Barnes had conducted it from within. Yet Delane was a heaven-born editor and he took the *Times* to the highest pinnacle of journalistic prestige.

True, it was still possible to disparage the paper under his control. In 1856, for example, a novel entitled *Perversion* was published in which the villain's moral nadir was reached when he became a leader writer for the *Times*. And if Queen Victoria had been able to persuade Lord Palmerston to implement a ban, the *Times*'s representatives would have been excluded from polite society. But the Queen herself was impelled, on occasion, to appear (anonymously) in that supreme forum of British protest, the *Times*'s letter columns. Her Consort acknowledged the paper to be the 'barometer of public opinion'.[31] Edward, Prince of Wales, paid elaborate homage to the editor, shaking hands with him at the end of one dinner no fewer than four times. In general, then, during Delane's reign at Printing House Square, which lasted until 1877, the paper expanded dramatically in both circulation and reputation.

Trollope's accolade to the *Jupiter* and its pope is, perhaps because it piles one metaphor on top on another, the most graphic:

> Who has not heard of Mount Olympus,—that high abode of all the powers of type, that favoured seat of the great goddess Pica, that wondrous habitation of gods and devils, from whence, with ceaseless hum of steam and never-ending flow of Castalian ink, issue forth fifty thousand nightly edicts for the governance of

a subject nation? ... This little court is the Vatican of England. Here reigns a pope, self-nominated, self-consecrated—ay, and much stranger too self-believing! a pope whom, if you cannot obey him, I would advise you to disobey as silently as possible.[32]

The paper's might, majesty and dominion even won transatlantic tributes: Abraham Lincoln said that nothing in the world was more powerful than the *Times*, 'except perhaps the Mississippi'[33]—flattery which did not prevent the paper from suggesting that the President was a butcher, monster and wholesale assassin.[34] Delane's aspiration to exercise power instead of influence, to turn the *Times* into a moulder rather than a mirror of public sentiment, came perilously close to realisation.

What made this possible, and what chiefly distinguished Delane as a potentate of the press, was prescience. Delane was the personification of news sense. He possessed an uncanny insight into how events would unfold, how people would act. In 1845, for instance, he not only prophesied the disastrous collapse of the railway boom (losing the *Times* advertisements but gaining it prestige), he predicted Peel's intention to repeal the Corn Laws. That his political forecasts were so accurate was only in part due to native intuition. Mainly it was the result of his gravitating towards the leading lights in the political and social firmament. He sedulously cultivated the eminent, never losing a friend and seldom acquiring an enemy. Delane ingratiated himself with Lord Aberdeen. He did small favours for Disraeli. He conducted an extraordinarily intimate correspondence with Lord Palmerston: in 1857, for example, the Prime Minister wrote that he had set fire to the chimney of his library at Broadlands while burning letters of resignation from his Chancellor of the Exchequer. (This was Gladstone, who was himself more discreet: he installed a fireproof cabinet at Hawarden in order to preserve letters marked 'Burn this'.)

Discretion, too, was Delane's passport to Society. He revealed secrets but concealed sources. Although he came hot from what George Meredith called 'the very furnace-hissing of events',[35] Delane emitted few sparks in general conversation. He might throw off an illuminating anecdote or a charged comment in the hope of provoking some response. For even ritual exchanges about the weather could fuel his forge. During a chat with Lord Northbrook's doctor about the effects of warm climates on health, Delane divined that this peer would be the next Viceroy of India, though only the Prime Minister and his appointee had even discussed the matter. Usually Delane maintained a vigilant, inscrutable reserve, though the pent-up dynamism of the editor was self-evident. His eyes shone with zeal. His florid countenance glowed with energy. His genial smile beamed between mutton-chop whiskers. His mind quivered in anticipation of those flashes of intelligence which he alone could condense into thunderbolts.

An inveterate snob, given to insulting parvenu Jews, Delane relished exalted company for its own sake. He was once seen, a beatific horseman, riding down Whitehall with a duke walking on either side. He revelled in house parties at which he was 'the only specimen of the British commoner' present,[36] in receptions where every other guest was an ambassador, a cabinet minister or a bishop. Such intercourse was considered illicit. Lord Brougham went so far as to dub Lord Palmerston's association with Delane as 'devil-worship'[37] and the Prime Minister had to justify it in parliament. Disraeli sneered memorably that the 'once stern guardians of popular rights simper in the enervating atmosphere of gilded saloons'.[38] But Delane had not bartered his independence for fashionable invitations. Nor had the *Times* been domesticated by the aristocracy, let alone by the monarchy—Delane despised divine right as an anachronism and dismissed coronations as wearisome and unintelligible. Like most of his readers, the editor revered rank and title without permitting social deference to become political subservience. Indeed, he transferred his allegiance to Lord Palmerston in 1855, after long hostility, largely because that patrician was the embodiment of popular aspirations during the Crimean War.

Then the *Times* denounced the sacrifice of the British army by its blue-blooded leaders in a series of resounding phrases—'lamentable failure', 'fatal neglects', 'grossest mismanagement', 'total disorganisation', 'aristocratic hauteur', 'tremendous crisis', 'human hecatombs', 'national disaster', 'final catastrophe'. It compared the high-born generals, who were trifling away their men's lives around Sebastopol, to the effete peers in Westminster dawdling over the periodical luxury of forming a government. With scathing irony the *Times* even forecast that Lord Raglan and his staff would eventually:

> return with their horses, their plate, and their china, their German cook, and several tons' weight of official returns, all in excellent order, and the announcement that, the last British soldier being dead, they had left our position in the care of our gallant allies.[39]

Such diatribes did not make Delane a democrat or an egalitarian, of course; the *Times* was conservative and capitalist, and had 'very little opinion of the sagacity of uneducated people'. It was just that by refusing to toady to the élite few the editor flattered the bourgeois many, of whom he was the supreme representative. As the *Manchester Guardian* noted, Delane was 'in many respects a typical John Bull ... not over-nice, or over-refined, or over-elevated but strong, self-sustained and self-reliant ... [possessing] small faith in the loftiest motives, but strong trust in self-interest'.[40]

The *Times* became, in effect, the megaphone of the middle class. Their acclaim augmented its thunder and magnified its authority. They emboldened Delane to pronounce sentence of death (speedily executed) on Lord John Russell's administration in 1851. They fortified him in 1852/3 against Foreign Office pressure to abate the onslaught on Napoleon III—an onslaught so fierce that it made the Emperor dance round the room with rage. They licensed him in 1854 to instigate war against Russia, to shatter Aberdeen's government the following year, and to have a stentorian say in determining Lord Palmerston's ministerial and military appointments. They also made Delane confident enough to issue what was virtually the *Times*'s declaration of omnipotence.

The paper resembled the church of the Middle Ages, he said— 'executor of the public will ... informer of the public understanding ... enlightener of the people's consciences ... check against the abuse of power ... monitor against the vices'. But the papacy had abdicated its 'lofty mission' by becoming embroiled in politics.[41] The *Times* would fill the vacuum and become the moral and intellectual arbiter of the globe.

> We aspire, indeed, to participate in the government of the world, but the power we seek is due to no adventitious circumstances, and is exercised solely and freely by the sway of language and reason over the minds of men.[42]

At the time it did not seem an unduly elevated claim. The proofs of the *Times* were said to be corrected as though they were Holy Writ (which did not prevent Delane wishing to kill a proof-reader every time he opened the paper). Archdeacon Denison lamented from the pulpit of Wells Cathedral that if the Scripture said one thing and the *Times* another, ninety-eight per cent of the population would believe the newspaper. The 'great daily miracle' captivated the contemporary imagination.

However, this autocrat of the breakfast table inspired fears as well as fascination. The *Times* sold twice as many copies as all its rivals put together. It seemed set to turn the 'republic of letters' into 'a despotism'.[43] It could be cruel, tyrannical, capricious and unjust. Despite his affability Delane had no mercy for those crushed beneath his Juggernaut. He never explained, never apologised, never recanted.

His pretensions grew with the years. After the Crimean War he quite seriously described the *Times* as a 'perpetual committee of the legislature'.[44] In 1865 Lord John Russell remarked that 'Mr Delane was very angry that I did not kiss his hand instead of the Queen's when I was appointed to succeed Lord Palmerston'.[45] Delane's power seemed the more monstrous for being shadowy, impersonal and undisclosed. Those reverberations from the mountain-top were amplified by anonymity. John Bright termed Delane 'the Man in the Mask'.[46] Yet though the mask enhanced Delane's menace, it hid his vulnerability. He relied on ministers for exclusive political information, which he printed only in leading articles, thus making them a potent blend of news and views. Of course, Delane cherished his independence too much to swap support for confidences. On the other hand, conveniently often the *Times* found itself in a position to commend rising governments and condemn falling ones, to promote waxing politicians and betray waning ones. Gladstone declared that the paper should be prohibited from changing sides more than a certain number of times a year. But Delane justified its inconsistency as the elder Bennett had done, maintaining that he was the editor of today's *Times*, not yesterday's or tomorrow's. Thus it was that the paper not only mirrored public sentiment but monopolised official information. The advantage became crucial after 1855, when the final stamp duty was repealed and a cheap competitive press began to challenge the *Times*. This was the year in which Delane effected his reconciliation with the statesman whom Barnes had dubbed 'Cupid'. Lord Palmerston, puffed as the man of the hour had, in Disraeli's words, 'humbled his old enemy into being his trumpeter'.[47]

Delane's freedom of action was also circumscribed by John Walter III (1818–1894), who interfered with the *Times* more than his father had done in Barnes's day. The third Walter would sometimes appear at Printing House Square in the middle of the night and cause a fuss. He liked to have a say both in the appointments and in the policy of the paper, and occasionally he even usurped the editorial chair. Delane called him 'the Griff'—short for Griffin, or grim and vigilant guardian. The editor resented the proprietor's intrusions and welcomed his absences. Even so their relationship was surprisingly harmonious. The Griff advised and encouraged Delane whereas he instructed and criticised his subordinates when the editor himself was away. But Walter was always modest enough to recognise himself as an amateur. In 1859, for example, he apologised for his inept interference in the running of the paper to Delane's deputy, who noted sourly that Walter lacked the 'capacity and courage' of his employees. In general, however, Walter played the cautious constitutional monarch and

47

allowed his forceful prime minister wide scope to exercise his superlative journalistic talents.

Delane ran the *Times* like a great department of state. He wrote little and supervised much. He selected able contributors and controlled them by forbidding fraternisation—he 'kept his beasts in separate cages'.[48] He spent endless time feeding his 'ravens', instructing his leader writers, correspondents and reviewers. He had a sharp eye for a good rape or murder. He kept a sensitive finger on the pulses of the eminent and was as seldom surprised by the dying as by the living: as a result *Times* obituaries were excellent. He was quick to notice when the paper's policy was going awry; for example, the national hysteria about 'No Popery' in 1850 led it into sectarian excess. And aristocratic hostility to the North during the American Civil War badly warped Delane's judgement—the *Times* suggested that another authoritative publication, the Bible, imposed a duty on slaves to refuse the proffered liberty. But Delane's paper was Janus-faced as well as Argus-eyed. In each case the editor extricated himself by means of the art of journalistic 'curvature'. He gradually modified successive editorials in order to accommodate events, he categorically refuted today what he had demonstrated as self-evident last week.

Above all, Delane applied himself to steady, dogged, relentless toil. Apart from his holidays, spent on continental travel or hunting, shooting and fishing for information at the stately homes of England, Delane worked every day from noon (with an evening break for casting further flies among Society) until the paper was 'put to bed' at five o'clock in the morning. He claimed to have seen more sunrises than any man alive. Eventually the incessant strain shattered his health. Perhaps earlier it had contributed to the 'fatal weakness' of his wife, either insanity or addiction to drink or drugs, which had blighted his domestic happiness and made his life a 'long married widowhood'. Delane had evidently consoled himself with ladies of easy virtue but, like Lord Northcliffe after him, he reserved his love for his mother. She was 'the key stone of my whole existence', and her death in 1869 was a blow from which he never really recovered. By 1876, thin, old, bowed and glassy-eyed, Delane was to be heard quavering, 'I am done, I am done.'[49] More than three decades later Northcliffe was moved to hear an ancient printer's recollection of his last sight of the editor, who gave him a parting present: ' "I want you to take this ring and keep it in remembrance of me." I was so shocked to see the broken condition of my idol that I could not speak, neither could he.'[50] Aged only fifty-nine, Delane retired. Two years later he was dead.

The *Times*'s supremacy stemmed from the pre-eminent skill with which it was conducted. Barnes was the original genius who forged the first bolts from Olympus, Delane the brilliant manager who prevented the 'Thunderer' from becoming, what its rivals called it, the 'Blunderer'. Barnes made the *Times*, whereas the *Times* made Delane. Together the two editors charged the paper with 'an invisible efflux of personal power, a magical force'[51] which haunted and daunted the Victorians. Of course the editors' authority was curbed both by general English restraints and by the particular homage they owed to the Walter dynasty. It has recently been said that the Victorian 'Sovereign–Editor was a myth'.[52] Perhaps so, but Barnes and Delane were exceptional. They deserve to be styled the first English press barons because they largely transcended their limitations. They exercised a degree of journalistic independence which had never before been known in Britain. Under their rule the *Times* became, in the words of one contemporary, 'the "greatest FACT" of our times'.[53]

CHAPTER FOUR

Greeley and Graduates

B Y 1850 THE editors of major English newspapers were anonymous and respectable while their American counterparts were prominent and disreputable. English journalists found it as impossible to mention the transatlantic leaders of their profession 'without using strong language, as it would be to empty a dung-yard with a china plate and silver fork'. Yet to their horror the controllers of the American press became candidates for civil honours and were propitiated by the public 'much on the principle which impels some African tribes to worship the Devil'.[1] The reference was not only to the elder Bennett; it was also to the foul-mouthed printer who by the mid-century had established himself, against all the odds, as the Satanic Scotsman's arch-rival—Horace Greeley.

Greeley's rise had been impeded by innumerable obstacles. When he was born—to drunken impoverished parents of Scottish-Irish descent, at Amherst, New Hampshire, in 1811—Horace was 'as black as a chimney'.[2] Many Southerners believed that he never changed colour. In fact, his skin soon became sheet-white and he was known as 'the Ghost'.[3] The spectral impression was emphasised by his watery blue eyes, wispy bleached hair and massive pearly head. Friendly phrenologists were later to establish that his brain was '*very* large' and (what must have been a comfort to its owner) 'in the right place'.[4] But as a sickly, tatterdemalion child, morbidly sensitive to noise, rustic in manners and ungainly in mannerisms, Horace was apt to be taken for an idiot.

His demeanour grew more outlandish with the years. The moon face acquired an aureole of flaxen throat-whiskers. The weak eyes were magnified behind thick spectacles. The piping voice remained a

The James Gordon Bennetts—father and son

Thomas Barnes

Horace Greeley

Henry Raymond

Charles Dana

John Delane

Lord Northcliffe and Lord Burnham

falsetto whine. The marionette gait became a shambling, tumbling, rolling motion—as Greeley ironically remarked, he appeared to walk 'down both sides of the street at once'.[5] The hayseed habits persisted—Greeley ate as though for a wager and turned somersaults at the office on receipt of good news. The coarse language defied refinement—to someone who said that he used the *Tribune* as lavatory paper Greeley retorted, 'Keep it up, and eventually you'll have much more brains in your arse than in your head'.[6] The farmyard garb—white duster, cravat like a hang-man's noose, low-crowned wide-brimmed hat—became legendary, making him the butt of countless lampoons.

Putnam's Magazine observed that 'the precise boundary between his boots and trousers, like some other boundary questions, is in a state of litigation'.[7] Webb's *Courier & Enquirer* ridiculed him thus:

> He lays claim to greatness by wandering through the streets with a hat double the size of his head, a coat after the fashion of Jacob's of old, with one leg of his pantaloons inside and the other outside of his boot, and with boots all bespattered with mud, or, possibly, a shoe on one foot and a boot on the other.[8]

Manton Marble's *World* was more spiteful: 'Stupid uncouthness and elaborate eccentricity are your daily confession that you desire notoriety even at the cost of some contempt'.[9] Greeley rebutted charges of this kind—for a man of ideas to spend his precious time before a looking-glass 'would be robbing the public'.[10] But it was easy to see why the elder Bennett maintained that a galvanised New England pumpkin would make a better editor than Horace Greeley.

Worse still, Greeley's physical peculiarities were compounded by intellectual quirks which grew more pronounced with age. Though books had been as scarce as toys in his childhood, he was a precocious reader. And his memory was prodigious: after only two lessons he could recite the whole of Murray's grammar, including the rules of orthography, etymology, syntax and prosody. But his endeavours to educate himself were interrupted by juvenile chores on the farm and adolescent grind at the printing press, to which he was harnessed at the age of fifteen. As the university-trained editor of the *Evening Post* said, Greeley's brain was 'crammed with half truths and odds and ends of ideas which a man inevitably accumulates who scrapes knowledge together by fits and starts on his way through life'.[11] Thus Greeley became both a crank and a visionary. He hailed with enthusiasm each passing vehicle which might lead to the betterment of humanity, the socialist omnibus, the cooperative stage-coach, the abolitionist bandwagon, the feminist tumbril. True, he often alighted at the first stop, but disembarkation was made more difficult by his wife Mary, who also rode hobby-horses.

She was a Connecticut school teacher whom he met in New York, where he had arrived in 1831, aged twenty, with no friends and ten dollars in his pocket to pursue his trade as a printer, then as a journalist and, after a decade of penurious drudgery, as founder, editor and publisher of the *Tribune*. Horace courted the bright-eyed, slim-waisted Mary, who was said to be crazy for knowledge, in the prim surroundings of their vegetarian boarding house. But after their marriage, in 1836, she grew increasingly querulous, hypochondriac and odd. 'Mother's sanity', Greeley acknowledged mildly, was 'not of the highest order.'[12] Five out of their seven children died and Mary became deeply immersed in the occult—Horace tried to believe but feared that clairvoyant manifestations were 'brainsick phantasies or blasphemous juggles'.[13] His town house became a 'Castle Doleful' and he was reluctant to return to the 'old, desolate rookery', the bare walls, the meatless, saltless diet, the neurotic nagging.

Nor was there much escape from shrewishness, table-tapping and quackery on his ramshackle 'model' farm at Chappaqua, thirty-five miles outside New York. Despite lavish expenditure of time and money, despite endless chopping and clearing and draining, it remained a stump-ridden swamp known to his friends as 'Greeley's Bog'. Yet he continued faithful to his unstable wife and to his erratic ideals. The *Tribune* campaigned ceaselessly for progress and reform. It was 'Anti-Slavery, Anti-War, Anti-Rum, Anti-Tobacco, Anti-Seduction, Anti-Grogshops, Brothels, Gambling Houses'.[14] There was a cavalier flamboyance about Greeley's style but he looked forward to a puritan millennium.

Even so, in practice Greeley's principles were always vitiated by a spirit of compromise, and the *Tribune*'s readers often complained that he was a bundle of contradictions. Greeley's feminism stopped short of giving women the vote, for example, and involved wives in deferring to their husbands. His pacifism expressed itself by a peace-time campaign to abolish that absurd nuisance, the army, and by the war-time battle-cry 'Forward to Richmond'. His agrarianism, with its inspiring slogan, 'Go West, young man!', aimed to benefit the eastern cities by raising the cost of labour. His humanitarianism embraced white workers enthusiastically, black slaves reluctantly and Red Indians not at all. His protectionism was designed to achieve eventual free trade. His trade unionism was intended to prevent strikes. His socialism was restrained because he despised socialists. His conservatism was suspect because he employed Karl Marx as a correspondent. His radicalism was muted because he distrusted the masses. He was 'a despotic assertor of universal liberty',[15] the spokesman of plain people of the North who tried to negotiate a shifty peace with the South, a Whig founder of the Republican party whose presidential candidature was endorsed by the Democrats. He was editor of a paper intended to be read at the family fireside, yet he opened its columns to doctrines which would abolish the family. Greeley was, as Andrew Johnson said, 'a sublime old child',[16] a puerile sage.

But Greeley's inconsistencies were a strength as well as a weakness. The *Tribune* could never have flourished if its quixotic editor had not also been something of a Sancho Panza. Greeley was egotistical as well as altruistic, cunning as well as curmudgeonly. In fact, realism was the greatest of his isms. Thus he promised that the *Tribune* would never adopt attitudes of 'servile partisanship' or 'gagged, mincing neutrality'[17] towards the parties, but it was founded in 1841 to supply the lack of a cheap Whig paper and Greeley wrote political articles for pay. He believed that disinterestedness was the soul of journalism but he sometimes distorted the news to suit his views. The theatre he always condemned as an extension of the grog-shop and the bawdy-house, but the *Tribune* accepted theatrical advertisements. Greeley denounced other newspapers for printing the 'loathsome details'[18] of murders, rapes and lewd publications, but somehow they found their way into his own pages, prefaced by expressions of outrage. He favoured the establishment of a Fourierist New Jerusalem, but its chief apostle, Albert Brisbane, had to pay to proselytise in the *Tribune*. Greeley espoused international copyright but pirated Dickens and Thackeray. He excoriated patent medicines but printed their puffs. He professed scorn for the dirty spoils of office but became wild when his claims, and the *Tribune*'s, were ignored. He abjured violence but hired thugs to beat up the newsboys of his competitors. There was even an element of calculated showmanship about his appearance and behaviour (though he was actually much less uncouth than the caricatures suggested). The swearing oracle with the scarecrow looks became a unique advertisement for the *Tribune*, the personification of personal journalism.

No publicity would have helped the *Tribune*, though, if Greeley had not been master of the most exuberant vernacular prose since Cobbett. As Lincoln said, 'every one of his words seems to weigh about a ton'.[19] Greeley wrote in a rich, pungent, rumbustious style, redolent of earth and printer's ink. He drew his inspiration from the oratory of the rural pulpit and the urban soap-box. He had a fund of Johnsonian common sense: 'You may eulogize the Dignity of Labor till doomsday, without making a bootblack's calling as honorable as that of an engineer'.[20] His aphorisms were surprisingly durable: for example, he damned a freedom 'so extreme that those who have no shoes are perfectly at liberty to go barefoot'.[21] He could sound like an Old Testament prophet rebuking New Yorkers for worshipping the Golden Calf:

> There prances knavish Bankruptcy in its chariot, spattering the threadbare garb of some ruined creditor, who goes on foot; here trips Fashion in lace; there hobbles Beggary in rags, as, with counterfeited limp and loathsome travesty of the human form, it whines out its petition for alms.[22]

His invective was employed deliberately, for he believed that judicious ferocity was a legitimate journalistic weapon. That 'sewer-sheet', the *Herald*, run by the 'low-mouthed, blatant, witless, brutal scoundrel',[23] Bennett, came in for particular vilification. It was 'eager for the sake of private gain to poison the fountains of public intelligence and to fan with destroying flames the hellish passions which now slumber in the bosom of society'.[24] Another rival was accused of wearing 'mourning for his departed veracity, under his finger-nails'.[25] Public figures were subjected to similar vituperation: President Johnson was 'an aching tooth in the national jaw ... there can be no peace nor comfort until he is out'.[26] Of course, such outspokenness offended the respectable; the poetic editor of the *Evening Post*, William Cullen Bryant, who was said to begin every editorial with a stale joke and end it with a fresh lie, refused to be introduced to Greeley, whispering audibly, 'He's a blackguard, he's a blackguard'.[27] And Bryant's successor, E. L. Godkin, described Greeley as a fungus on the moral and intellectual dunghill of the press. The fact remains that neither of them could write like Greeley.

If the manner made the *Tribune* readable, the matter made it read. Thanks to its earnest moral teachings Greeley became, despite his catholic taste in ideas, the nonconformist conscience of the North. Though he professed himself and everyone else bored by formal instruction, Greeley had always been resolutely didactic. As a boy he used to lecture girls on the folly of wearing stays and he went on lecturing, literally and metaphorically, for the rest of his life. As an apprentice without an overcoat to his back, he laid down the law to mature and affluent members of the East Poultney debating society in Vermont. As a journeyman printer struggling with his first metropolitan gazette, the *New Yorker*, begun in 1834, Greeley hectored his readers about the inadequacy of their contributions: 'We assure P.M. that he *cannot* write poetry, and as the fault is Nature's and not his, he need not hope for its amendment'.[28]

As editor of the *Tribune* he disdained those who published only to sell, comparing them to parsons who preached only to fill the pews. He promised, 'We have plenty of requests to blow up all sorts of abuses, which shall be attended to as fast as possible'.[29] Greeley gloried in the role of public tutor and virtually created the modern editorial page to broadcast his message. The paper's aim, he trumpeted, was to elevate 'the masses through the diffusion and inculcation of intellectual freedom, industry, skill and virtue' and consequently to abolish, or limit, 'ignorance, slavery, idleness, pauperism and vice'.[30] Greeley also saw it as his duty to reprove the people's enemies—exploiters, free-traders, dram-drinkers, slave-drivers, idlers and others who ignored his lessons.

There was nothing personal about this, for Greeley was more interested in principles than people. He once refused a request to help save a sinner's soul from hell on the grounds that hell was not half full enough of sinners as it was. Though generous to the point of improvidence, he valued social blueprints above human sympathy. He fought against slavery not because he liked negroes but because he hated injustice. He contended for temperance not out of solicitude for drunkards but from concern about 'public hygiene'.[31] For similar reasons he espoused factory reform, farm colonies, public parks and direct election of senators; he exposed municipal corruption, child labour, slum housing and sweat shops ('Dens of Death'). Greeley's grammar of reform was mechanical but it had an almost magical appeal to a nation being transformed by the new inventions of industry. And because progress marched in step with poverty, Greeley's explication of American society as a system of 'organized rapacity'[32] found an echo in many hearts.

Often devious and sometimes cowardly, Greeley was no humbug, though Karl Marx dismissed him as such, asserting that the *Tribune* simply represented 'the industrial bourgeoisie of America'.[33] In fact, Greeley was frantic to discover and disseminate some cure for his country's acute growing pains. The golden thread of his social concern could clearly be traced through the paper's labyrinthine isms. It was no wonder then that the weekly edition of the *Tribune*, with its reader-ship of a million, became the Bible of the mid-West, doing all the farmers' thinking for them, as Emerson patronisingly remarked, for two dollars a year. Bennett might be first with the news but his views were generally second-hand, flotsam on the popular tide. Greeley often strove to turn the tide. He resisted the despotism of orthodoxy, minting his message afresh each day. At times he gave the greatest offence to the greatest number, but he forged the *Tribune* into a powerful organ of opinion, becoming in the process the best-known American citizen of his day.

Greeley's free-lance crusades were the more remarkable because so much of his early career had been spent as a mercenary of the Whig party. He harked back to that period when the conductors of the press were, in Jesse Hoyt's words, 'as negotiable as a promissory note'.[34] Greeley never quite shook off the notion that newspapermen were somehow subordinate to politicians. But, declaring that 'I, too, am a man ... I must breathe free air or be stifled', he did resist the dictation of his powerful patron, Thurlow Weed. He even resented political advice from his readers, writing irritably:

> My critics evidently assume that I am a mere jumping-jack, who only needs to know what others think to insure my instant conformity—in short that a journalist is no higher than a waiter at a restaurant, expected to furnish whatever is called for.[35]

In 1854 Greeley broke decisively with the Whig leaders, Weed and Seward. His influence grew with independence. The *Tribune* helped to crystallise the Republican party out of a mass of diffuse opinion in the late 1850s. Greeley himself played an important part in securing Lincoln's nomination in 1860 and during the Civil War the President went out of his way to flatter and mollify the editor.

Paradoxically, the very unpopularity of some of Greeley's causes seemed a guarantee of his integrity. Greeley's reputation was augmented by his initial willingness to grant secession to the South, by his desperate search for any expedient to stop the shedding of blood during the conflict, even by his rash provision of bail for the captured Confederate leader, Jefferson Davis. By 1872 Greeley's prestige was such that he accomplished the hazardous metamorphosis from journalist to politician. He was adopted first as the Liberal Republican, then as the Democratic, champion. Admittedly he was so execrated that he professed not to know whether he was standing for the Presidency or the penitentiary. And despite a whirlwind campaign in the modern style, enlivened by torrents of old-fashioned impromptu oratory, he was trounced by Grant. The fact remains that of all the press barons who aspired to wield supreme political power—and most did—the knight of the albino countenance came closest to success.

Beneath his exalted idealisms Greeley's lust for office, distinction and acclaim had raged with surprising violence. By fusing inchoate views into coherent arguments he had exercised more journalistic influence than any other American of his time. But it gave him little satisfaction. Greeley had yearned to exchange the pen for the sceptre, to seize what he called 'the glittering bait of the Presidency'.[36] His defeat was turned from disappointment to tragedy by the simultaneous death of Mary. Shrill-tongued, vehement and demented, the source of deep domestic unhappiness, she was cherished by her husband to the end. When she was in her grave he wrote pathetically, 'I am not dead but I wish I were. My house is desolate, my future dark, my heart a stone.'[37] Greeley had once described his life as being all a feverish march and at moments of extreme anguish he had been prone to nervous delirium and mental collapse—John Bigelow of the *Evening Post* thought he had been crazy for years. Under the twin blows of bereavement and failure, he succumbed once more.

He felt the *Tribune*, which he now promised to make thoroughly independent, slipping out of his grasp. He was beset by traitors and hounded by malignity. He was utterly ruined and beyond hope. The night was closing its jaws on him for ever. After about a fortnight he was placed in a private asylum and nursed by his two surviving children, Ida and Gabrielle. On 28 November 1872, he died. Whitelaw Reid, the *Tribune*'s managing editor, overheard his last words, which he reported to Greeley's daughters: 'I know that my Redeemer liveth'. This was the revised version. Apparently Greeley had really said: 'Well, the devil's got you at last, you damned old bastard'.[38]

Unlike so many press barons Greeley founded no empire and left no dynasty. Indeed, at his death he possessed only six per cent of the *Tribune*'s stock. He had dissipated his original holdings by vesting shares in his employees, by forking out gobs of cash, as he put it, to all sorts of undeserving people and by speculating in unsound schemes, utopian communities, patent looms, perpetual motion machines, desiccated egg companies. The *Tribune* itself might have landed on the financial scrapheap had it not been for the commercial ability of Greeley's partner, Thomas McElrath. But after his departure in 1859 the paper began to decay as a business despite its editorial vigour. By the end of Greeley's life the presses were old and the type was worn. The building remained a Dickensian warren of dingy staircases, sordid passages and overcrowded offices. The reporters had to write their stories in rotation because there were too few chairs and desks, and even those were prone to collapse. Yet it is not wholly correct to regard Greeley as a journalistic anachronism who was, as E. L. Godkin said, 'fast falling behind his age when he died'.[39] Greeley had never claimed to be a businessman and his business methods were not so much out-of-date as downright inept. It was as an editor that Greeley had shown his consummate ability and he made the *Tribune* not only a medium of public education, but a private school of journalism. Of those he trained, Henry J. Raymond and Charles A. Dana became two of the most prominent press barons of the century. Greeley's graduates were his most impressive legacy.

Both Raymond and Dana had been to college and had profited much from it; indeed, when Greeley first introduced them they immediately plunged into a long discussion about German meta-physics. Greeley was contemptuous of such highly qualified 'horned cattle' in a newspaper office, reckoning that the only real education for a journalist was to sleep on newspapers and eat ink. Not being able to subject his assistants to this healthful regimen, Greeley did the next best thing. He paid like a miser, swore like a trooper and scolded like a drab. He criticised Raymond for being one of the most useless animals endowed with ratiocination, for filling the *Tribune* with slovenly English and for understanding nothing of the art of editing. 'He catches up a pair of shears and dives into a pile of exchanges like a rat in a scrapbook, making his selections on about the same principles'. True, Greeley often left Raymond in charge, but only to bombard him with petulant admonitions:

> Don't you think I won't growl at blunders in the paper, for I will. You make some errors because your heart is not in the business. No man can be an A1 editor (or anything else) who does not regard that as the highest thing—to whom it is not only delight and a sceptre but a recourse.[40]

Greeley did not just teach the techniques of newspaper-making, he demonstrated the vocation. More than this, his craft was an obsession. Infuriated by one proof-reader's misdemeanours, he yelped to an aide, 'You have leisure. Oblige me by going upstairs and choking that infernal fool for nine minutes. Now *do* oblige me.'[41]

Dana was subjected to even more hysterical harangues. From Washington, Greeley complained that he had included news that would keep at the expense of more urgent intelligence especially that sent by the editor himself. Dana was too fond of journalistic slaughter, instead of being mild and meek-souled like Greeley. Dana frightened him more than a border ruffian, caused everyone to curse him, prevented him from sleeping, drove him crazy. Dana was crucifying him:

> The infernal picayune spirit in which [the paper] is published has broken my heart ... No Jew ever managed a pawnbroker's shop in a baser, narrower, more short-sighted spirit than the *Tribune* is managed.[42]

But though he behaved like a baited bear, Greeley appreciated the worth of his subordinates very well, especially as Dana matched, and Raymond actually outmatched, him in capacity for work. But neither Raymond nor Dana relished their treatment at Greeley's hands and both eventually quarrelled with him. They were to differ radically from each other, and from Greeley himself, in the styles of newspaper which they finally espoused. But both owed a deep debt to their early mentor. Greeley had shown them how to change their prose from dry-as-dust academic into cut-and-thrust demotic. He had indicated that newspapers were a ladder to political power. Most important of all, he had demonstrated that independence was the hall-mark of the press baron.

Henry Jarvis Raymond (1820–1869) was the only employee whom Greeley had to rebuke for working too hard. As a delicate, blue-eyed boy with a 'face no bigger than a snuff-box',[43] Raymond had early known what it was to labour. A New England farmer's son, he had learnt to read at the age of three. And, knees bent under him and the family cat as often as not perching on his shoulder, he studied thereafter with 'indomitable nervous energy'.[44] Raymond possessed a powerful mind and at the University of Vermont he toyed with the idea of becoming a professional theologian. But journalism had more to offer and in 1840 he applied for a job on the *New Yorker*—Greeley surprised the slight, dark twenty-year-old by offering instead to sell him the journal. Raymond had nothing to invest but his industry and he made himself so useful as a volunteer office-boy that Greeley found it expedient to pay him a tiny wage. Raymond quickly mastered the principles and practices of journalism. He wrote with astonishing speed (and legibility—a striking contrast to Greeley's drunken hen-tracks) and for reporting speeches he even developed his own system of stenography, 'a kind of long-short-hand'.[45] Despite blinding head-aches, Raymond was soon contributing letters to several country newspapers as well as writing columns of the *Tribune*. By 1842 he had, as he put it, crowded himself into a thousand dollars a year. Perpetual toil in the increasingly rich field of journalism was bringing Raymond the harvest he craved. For, as Greeley wrote in his obituary of this 'over-worked, over-anxious, over-eager man', Raymond was 'ambitious, liking position, liking money, liking all the prizes and all the warm, sweet gifts of life'.[46]

The passionate idealist of the *Tribune* was fundamentally out of sympathy with the calculating pragmatist who created the *Times*. Greeley found it almost as much of an embarrassment to have lucre as to lack it, and he regarded the *Tribune* as his mission to erring humanity. Raymond saw the *Times* as a money-making machine and an oyster-opening instrument. It was a profitable business which would enable him to become what he eventually became, the dandy with the gold-topped cane who belonged to the smart set, philandered with women, held public office, received the confidences of presidents. Though fond of the 'glorious, jolly' Greeley as a person, Raymond was from the first contemptuous of his isms. In 1841 he wrote:

Some delectable asses here (among whom I am sorry to say is Greeley) have started a plan for reorganising society—elevating the social condition of the universal dogdom and allowing puppies to hold their proper rank in the scale of being . . . Brisbane is at the head of it—a flippant, brainless jackanapes—ridden by this one idea of 'elevating folks'.[47]

Raymond continued to protest against utopian socialism in the famous printed debate he held with Greeley after his own ambition and his editor's stinginess led them to part in 1843. For an extra five dollars a week Raymond joined Webb's *Courier & Enquirer* which was soon mocking Greeley for wanting 'all the world [to] live upon bran-bread and sawdust'.[48] Against Greeley's rhapsodical notion of small cooperating communities which would eradicate human exploitation and reconcile the interests of capital and labour, Raymond mustered a host of traditional arguments. He proved, 'to the entire satisfaction of everyone who agreed with him',[49] that Greeley was undermining the rights of property, polluting the sanctity of the family and flouting the precepts of revealed religion. As is usually the case in disputes of this sort, the essential difference lay in opposing views of human nature. Greeley maintained that mankind would never learn to swim towards perfectibility if it refused to enter the water of improved social organisation. Raymond replied that since it was weighed down by moral evil, humanity would sink if it quitted the firm ground of existing institutions. This down-to-earth philosophy appealed to a city whose business was business and it was adopted by the great conservative newspaper which Raymond founded in 1851. The New York *Times*, he said, 'shuns all fantastic schemes of reform—the offspring of fanaticism rather than reason—it gives its hearty cooperation to all judicious plans for removing existing evils'.[50]

All newspapers are commercial enterprises and most have been inspired by the profit motive, but the New York *Times* was the first to be deliberately established as a great industry. One day in 1851 Raymond was walking across the ice of the Hudson River when his companion and friend, George Jones, who had once worked in the business office of the *Tribune*, mentioned that it had made sixty thousand dollars in the previous year. There and then the editor and the manager decided to implement a long-cherished plan to start their own newspaper. Trading on Raymond's journalistic reputation (for which he was given a fifth of the stock), they raised a hundred thousand dollars—ten years earlier Greeley had started the *Tribune* with perhaps three thousand, much of it borrowed. Though first housing the *Times* in a barren, unheated garret, illuminated with candles held upright by three nails in blocks of wood, Raymond not only spent the original capital, he needed more in order to make the paper pay. This was because he refused to print advertisements which savoured of fraud or sex. He also shunned Bennett's vulgar sensations and Greeley's romantic crusades, aiming to steer a middle course, as Dana neatly said, between the moral eccentricity of the one and the mental eccentricity of the other. Raymond was determined that the *Times* should be decent, reliable, full and fair—even at the cost of some dullness. Building a newspaper on the bedrock of respectability was an exacting and expensive business.

Nevertheless, Raymond was well equipped to succeed. At his behest the *Times* did not merely print the news, it aspired to print all the news or at any rate, in the words of the later slogan, 'All news that's fit to print'. Raymond was a journalistic Gradgrind who believed that a newspaper's essential function was to publish facts, facts, facts. As he showed with his swift, vivid eye-witness accounts of the battles of Solferino and Bull Run, he was a first-class reporter. Where opinions were concerned Raymond was on more dubious ground. His leading articles were lucid, weighty, persuasive and acerbic. But he confessed to feeling aware, before he reached the end of each sentence, that it was only partially true. Despite Greeley's training Raymond remained, as Bennett said, a 'doughty little blue-stocking'.[51] At heart he was a scholar, given to refining and qualifying. This did not mean that his paper was insipid. For, like its London namesake, the New York *Times* was ever strong upon the stronger side, and sometimes it was savage. Greeley complained bitterly that 'Little Villain' (as he soon dubbed Raymond) gained many readers by pandering to popular prejudices and 'by ultra abuse of Abolitionists, Women's Rights, Spirit Rappers etc., which I cannot do'.[52]

But Raymond never lost his temper. No cause stirred him emotionally and, whatever their subject, his editorials were cool forensic exercises. As he wrote in the first issue of the *Times* (swiping, incidentally, at Greeley):

> We do not mean to write as if we were in a passion unless that shall really be the case; and we shall make it a point to get into a passion as rarely as possible. There are very few things in this world which it is worth while to get angry about; and they are just the things that anger will not improve.

Lacking the fervour of partisanship and the power of passion, lacking Bennett's originality and Greeley's picturesqueness, Raymond was not a great editor. He was so anxious to attain balance that he toppled into banality, pontificating in his introductory 'Word about Ourselves':

'We shall be *Conservative* in all cases where we think Conservatism essential to the public good; and we shall be *Radical* in everything which may seem to us to require radical treatment'.[53] Still, if this was scarcely a trumpet-call from Zion, it was a sentiment from which moderate men of goodwill could not easily dissent. And long before Arthur Brisbane (Albert's son) coined the epigram, Raymond assumed that his readers did not want to know what he thought but what they thought. Thus the *Times* gained circulation not only as a comprehensive record of events but as a cheap testament of orthodoxy. Once established, it paid handsome dividends. Like the London Thunderer on which it was modelled, the New York *Times* soon became an institution. It received the imprimatur of John Walter himself, who found the American press 'as bad as can be'. He told Delane, 'The N.Y. Times is the only respectable paper I have seen'.[54]

Yet not until shortly before his death did Raymond grasp the implications of what he had achieved. Initially he was affected by the traditional notion that newspapers were the adjuncts of political parties and the elavetors of editors. Indeed, General Grant compared him to a 'jumping-jack. He is heads up or tails up just as Seward or Weed move him.'[55] Grant exaggerated, but those political leaders did exercise some influence over the *Times*, despite its standard declarations of independence. Moreover Raymond accepted the Lieutenant Governorship of New York at Weed's hands in 1852 (to Greeley's envious chagrin) and promoted Seward's attempt to become Republican presidential candidate eight years later. Sustaining Abraham Lincoln and Andrew Johnson during the 1860s kept Raymond so busy that he had to conduct the *Times* by remote control: Thurlow Weed said that each morning Raymond was 'as surprised at his editorial columns as the hen with a brood of young ducks'.[56]

Still, this could have worked had not Raymond alienated both his fellow Republicans and many of the *Times*'s readers by a remarkable display of dithering after the Civil War. First he supported placatory policies towards the South but, when they proved unpopular, he deserted their chief advocate, President Johnson. This fiasco taught Raymond a crucial lesson—that there should be no illicit intercourse between governments and newspapers. Too close a relationship between them is bound to corrupt both. For however seductive their words, politicians invariably approach journalists with rape in their hearts. The *Times* must hold aloof from these advances. As Raymond said, when he returned from Washington to take personal command in 1867, unless the paper was 'independent of the ruling political hierarchy' it could not render 'service of the slightest value to the country'.[57]

Thus in the last two years of his sadly abbreviated life Raymond showed that the true press baron was his own man, uninfluenced by, and uninvolved with, Presidents or Governors, business juntas, Tammany Rings or Union Leagues. Even so, he evidently hankered for the dangerous liaisons of the past. The *Times*, with a circulation of about seventy-five thousand, was now worth well over a million dollars. But Raymond yearned for new worlds to conquer, new objects on which to expend his super-abundant energies. He suffered from soul sickness and even talked of selling his share of the paper (a third by 1869). Whether he would have done so, it is impossible to say. And one can only speculate about whether he would have achieved a permanent reconciliation with his beautiful but temperamental wife, Henrietta, whom he had alienated by his addiction to cards, theatres and actresses. For in the company, and perhaps in the arms of one of these last, Rose Eytynge (whose public performances the *Times* had praised extravagantly) Raymond had a fatal stroke. He was brought home at the dead of night by two mysterious strangers and deposited, gasping, on the floor of his hall. He never regained consciousness.

World-weariness was the besetting affliction of the successful press baron. If Charles Anderson Dana (1819–1897) never suffered from it as acutely as Raymond, his career nevertheless affords a startling contrast between initial hope and ultimate despair. For Dana started life as idealistic as Greeley and finished it as cynical as Bennett. Of old Puritan, New England stock, he was educated at Harvard and equipped with a thorough knowledge of the classics, literature and philosophy, as well as many languages dead and living (including Red Indian dialects). Having ruined his eyesight by reading *Oliver Twist* into the small hours, Dana spent five years among George Ripley's Transcendentalists at Brook Farm. This was a cooperative community devoted to spiritual uplift through a combination of manual and mental labour. It was also an escape into simple living from a society blighted by industrial competition and urban squalor. Dana by no means submerged his identity in the association, wearing his hair uncurled and refusing to don the uniform of brown or blue holland tunic, black belt and tasselled, visorless cap. Perhaps he was vain about his appearance: tall, blond and virile, he was said to resemble a Greek god and he soon married a fellow member, Eunice MacDaniel. In other respects, however, Dana conformed to the customs of Brook Farm. He waited at table, milked cows, supervised the tree nursery, taught Greek and German, sang bass in the choir and wrote articles and poems for literary magazines.

In 1847 this 'republic of lovable fools'[58] collapsed—for a variety of reasons: coarse food and poor sanitation, too much regimentation and too little privacy, witty rather than well-dug potato patches, inadequate capital, bloomers, fire, small-pox. But before this happened Dana had met Greeley, who regarded the Brook Farmers as lazy individualists and helped to convert them into a socialist 'Phalanx'. In 1848 Dana went to Europe as the *Tribune*'s correspondent (he was also perhaps the first journalist whose letters were syndicated in other American papers) and he sent back reports brimming with revolutionary ardour. In that heady year he propagated the whole radical gospel, including Proudhon's famous text that 'Property is theft', though he also evinced some scepticism about the purity of the reformers' motives. This was the first faint shadow of his future misanthropy. But it cast no cloud over his relationship with Greeley, who addressed him ironically as 'Fellow Citizen'. Dana returned in 1849 to become the *Tribune*'s managing editor and to study the tortuous ways of his 'great exemplar in journalism'.[59]

Dana admired Greeley for his adhesive memory, for his rich fund of humour and for the smashing power of his prose, but felt he lacked an educated man's critical faculty. Dana therefore set out to provide the *Tribune*'s sense of judgement, to give the paper intellectual coherence. This was fine where he agreed with his editor, as over slavery, a protective tariff, freedom of conscience and of labour, the development of American resources human and material. But where Greeley was inclined to shuffle, especially on the question of permitting the South to secede from the Union, the uncompromising logic of his lieutenant vexed him as much as one of his perennial boils. Dana possessed a bulldog savagery once he had grasped an issue or an enemy, whereas Greeley, like some ill-coordinated mongrel, engaged merely in flurries of fury. As the country drifted towards civil war Dana's sophisticated mind reacted impatiently against Greeley's crackerbarrel platitudes. However eloquently expressed, they were evasions.

Dana grew more peremptory and malicious, and as this exhortation to one *Tribune* correspondent shows, his methods were scarcely those of his chief:

> What a desert of news you keep at Washington! For goodness sake, kick up a row of some sort. Fight a duel, defraud the Treasury, set fire to the fueling-mill, get Black Dan [Webster] drunk, or commit some other excess that will make a stir.[60]

Once the conflict began Greeley's *volte-face* into frenzied aggressiveness suited Dana, who was responsible for reiterating the *Tribune*'s war-cry 'Onward to Richmond'. But when this headlong policy led to the disastrous repulse at Bull Run, Greeley imagined that Northern blood was on his hands and became distracted with grief and remorse. He tried to exculpate himself by publicly blaming Dana for the catchphrase and he fell into a mood of irresolute defeatism. Dana remained staunch for victory and in 1862 Greeley sent a message dismissing him. He gave no reasons, then or afterwards. The ambivalence of Dana's subsequent attitude towards his mentor was well summed up in Beard's cartoon, drawn in 1872: it showed Dana assisting Greeley to scale the White House wall with the point of a pitch-fork.

By that time, after sterling service as Assistant Secretary of War—Lincoln called him 'the eyes of the government at the front'[61]—Dana had embarked on the main business of his life. This was, in the words of its advertisement, to make the *Sun* shine for all. The paper had passed through various hands and vicissitudes since Benjamin Day's time and Dana bought it (with the help of junior partners) for $175,000 in 1868. He at once revolutionised its character. The *Sun* became lighter, brighter, less diffuse and more wayward. Dana created the term 'human interest', which consisted not only of rapes and murders but of anything that tickled the fancy—a new kind of apple, the weight of a presidential candidate, the vagaries of the City Hall clock, the latest fashion in beards, being shaved by a lady barber. The prism of Dana's mind refracted such news into his variegated 'Sunbeams' section:

The mules are all dying in Arkansas.
A printer in Texas has named his first-born Brevier Fullfaced Jones.
Real estate is looking up in New Orleans.
Venison costs six cents a pound in St. Paul.
Queen Victoria says that every third woman in Cork is a beauty.
Goldwin Smith is coming to America.
The Pope denounces short dresses.[62]

Of course, Dana by no means ignored the familiar subjects of sensationalism, crime, scandal and disaster, even anticipating the yellow press with headlines like 'The Skull in the Chimney', 'A Man Hanged by Women' and 'Horrors of a Madhouse'. But he compressed such items into scintillating crystals of intelligence, the like of which had never before appeared in a newspaper. Dana had always scorned England's penchant for heavy editorials and elaborate *belles lettres*; they were 'the mere perfumeries of his profession'.[63] He replaced them by what was, in content, the first 'tabloid' newspaper—Lord Northcliffe was later to tell W. R. Hearst that he had 'modelled his *Daily Mail* largely on the ideas of the old New York Sun'.[64] Dana had proved that the public liked brief, trenchant paragraphs of hard news. (It was his subordinate John B. Bogart who coined the classic formula, 'When a dog bites a man that is not news; but when a man bites a dog, that is news'.)[65] Dana's competitors sneered that the *Sun* was read only by horse-car drivers. But by 1876 he had tripled its circulation: a hundred and thirty-one thousand buyers were daily perusing his luminous and lively photograph of the world's doings.

This photograph was distorted by Dana's Swiftian disgust, increased by the war, for humanity in general and for those who tried to improve its lot in particular. As with Swift, his savage indignation was exacerbated by the practice of journalism itself, which he defined cynically as buying white paper at two cents a pound and selling it at ten cents. In person, admittedly, Dana was an amiable father who loved to work surrounded by his children, a generous connoisseur of Chinese porcelain and rare trees, a benevolent chief who paid well and conducted conversations while simultaneously dictating articles and spitting tobacco juice. In print, however, Dana became an embittered nihilist who derided all forms of altruism as sham or cant and regarded nothing as sacred, nothing as even serious.

The *Sun* ridiculed those who tried to prevent cruelty to animals, scorned civil service reform, disdained the clap-trap of Christian Science, scoffed at negro education, suggested that the city should raise a statue to honour its villainous Boss Tweed and mocked Dr Parkhurst, the campaigner against immorality, for his morbid curiosity about the subject. Dana seemed almost to welcome blatant forms of corruption because they indicated an absence of the cancer of hypocrisy. He reserved his most withering contempt for the puritanical high-mindedness of the *Evening Post*. This was America's equivalent of C. P Scott's *Manchester Guardian* and it denounced the newly risen *Sun* for outdoing even the *Herald* in ribaldry, levity, indecency and dishonesty. Dana detested the *Post* as a mixture of whited sepulchre and white elephant—it was so heavy, he said, that transporting it across the new Brooklyn Bridge would provide a complete guarantee of that structure's soundness. And he despised its priestly editor, E. L. Godkin, who was said to disapprove of everything that had occurred since the resurrection of Christ, as a 'stupendous humbug'.[66] The contrast between their two papers suggested to one contemporary a succinct explanation for the depravity of New York: 'What can you expect of a city in which every morning the *Sun* makes vice attractive, and every night the *Post* makes virtue odious?'[67]

Of course, readers expected editorial rivalry. They enjoyed Dana's proposal than an Alaskan river should be named after the *Times*'s con-troller, George Jones, because it was shallow, muddy and discoloured the sea round its mouth. They relished Dana's mock concern that

Greeley, whom he nicknamed 'the Woodchopper of Chappaqua', was a 'profane swearer' and the associate of 'Free Lovers'.[68] But there was something more than asperity and wit behind Dana's vendettas, a perverse malignancy, a wilful exercise of power somewhat in the manner of the younger Bennett, but more vitriolic. As one of Dana's acquaintances wrote, 'He was extraordinary in his malevolence. He had hatreds, queer hatreds, based on grounds unthinkable to any other human being.'[69] For example, quite without justification Dana publicly blamed Whitelaw Reid, new editor of the *Tribune*, for Greeley's death. He pursued a number of Presidents with a vindictiveness which Rutherford B. Hayes described as lunatic. Grant, for instance, was characterised as a drunken despot, a heathen boor, a blackmailing, anti-semitic jobber with a tendency towards kidnapping and a sympathy for bigamists. Even more remarkable was the assault on Grover Cleveland in 1884. Although the Democratic leader favoured many of the editor's policies, Charles 'Assassin' Dana (to employ the *Times*'s sobriquet) reviled him as a dummy who got his speeches from an encyclopaedia and a debauchee who would turn the White House into a brothel.

In this campaign Dana deliberately affronted popular opinion and lost almost half his circulation in the process. Yet he himself defined press power as 'the power of speaking out the sentiments of the people' and warned that any newspaper which exceeded this authority risked impotence and bankruptcy.[70] That Dana ignored his own maxim was partly due to the overflow of indiscriminate rancour which had poisoned his mind. Partly it was the result of an ungoverned assertion of independence which he rightly saw as the press baron's vital credential. Dana 'despised the scribbling flunkey, the parasite whose life or conduct was governed by the subserviency'.[71] His whole career had been dedicated to escaping from this condition of bondage. Liberty, he concluded, was best maintained by exercising licence. As the *Sun* reached its zenith Dana's confidence in his own star waxed. He approached the occupational condition of so many press barons at their apogee—megalomania. That this never grew into such an exotic bloom as, say, the younger Bennett's, is doubtless due to the fact that during Dana's last years the *Sun* was eclipsed by Joseph Pulitzer's brave new *World*—physically as well as figuratively: on Park Row the gold-domed *World* skyscraper overshadowed the *Sun*'s modest premises.

On 18 October 1897, an austere two-line announcement appeared in his paper: 'Charles Anderson Dana, Editor of the Sun, died yesterday afternoon'. His passing coincided with the transformation of the press into a modern industry, which was caused by a growing city readership, more department store advertising, cheaper paper and the introduction of linotype machines, type-writers and telephones. Throughout America lesser newspaper lords flexed their muscles and stood on their dignity—men like Samuel Bowles of the *Springfield Republican*, E. W. Scripps of the Cleveland *Press*, Murat Halstead of the Cincinnati *Commercial*, Henry Watterson of the Louisville *Courier-Journal*, Joseph Medill of the Chicago *Tribune*, Carl Schurz of the St Louis *Westliche-Post*, Charles de Young of the San Francisco *Chronicle*. Whatever their disputes on other matters, they agreed that during the last third of the nineteenth century the press had reached man's estate. As early as 1864, Medill was saying that wealthy newspapers had outgrown their early political tutelage. Whereas twenty-five years before the press had been 'a little shallop' trading along an almost empty shore, it was now 'a proud steamer, bidding defiance to the tempests, and laden with the mails and commerce of the world'.[72]

This was modest beside the pronouncements of his fellows which, though they sounded like the flippant grandiloquence of the elder Bennett, were meant in solemn earnest. Samuel Bowles was their most eloquent spokesman and he explained that the mission of the mature newspaper was to be:

> the high priest of history, the vitalizer of Society, the world's great informer, the medium of public thought and opinion, and the circulating life-blood of the whole human mind. It is the great enemy of tyrants and the right arm of liberty, and is destined, more than any other agency, to melt and mould the jarring and contending nations of the world into ... one great brotherhood.[73]

Such pretensions were the fruit of an independence which Bennett senior had pioneered, which Greeley and Raymond had eventually, and in different ways, attained, which the younger Bennett and Dana exulted in. This independence became the prerogative of newspaper owners all over the United States at the dawn of what was to be the golden age of the press barons. The idealistic Greeley, the ambitious Raymond and the irresponsible Dana had provided three contrasting but influential illustrations of just how the press barons might exercise their new-found freedom.

CHAPTER FIVE

The New
Journalists

IN 1851 HORACE GREELEY astounded a British parliamentary committee, before whom he was giving evidence, by revealing that
American artisans read the newspaper after breakfast 'just as the
people of the upper classes do in England'.[1] Moreover, Greeley
claimed, the cheap popular press of America was not nearly as bad
(Bennett's *Herald* excepted) as it had been painted. It was both refined
and educational, worth more than all the schools in the country.
Greeley's factual testimony was unimpeachable, but few members of
the committee would have allowed his estimate of the value of the
transatlantic press to alter their traditional view:

> Our common idea of the American newspaper is that of a print
> published by a literary Barnum, whose type, paper, talents,
> morality and taste are all equally wretched and inferior; who is
> certain to give us flippancy for wit, personality for principle,
> bombast for eloquence, malignity without satire and news
> without truth or reliability; whose paper is prolific of all kinds
> of sensational headings; and who is obliged, in the service of
> advertising customers, to become enthusiastic on the subject of
> hams, exuberant in the praises of hardware and highly
> imaginative in the matter of dry-goods.[2]

Although they feared that a cheap English press would imitate this
atrocious model, British governments were under increasing pressure
to repeal newspaper duties by the 1850s. 'Taxes on Knowledge' seemed
indefensible in a country which was at once anchored to *laissez-faire*
and drifting towards democracy. The Crimean War stimulated an
enormous voracity for news in Britain just as the Civil War was to do in

the United States (that rabid precursor of the yellow press barons, Wilbur F. Storey, told a Chicago *Times* correspondent, 'when there is no news, send rumors').[3] Politicians at Westminster and aspiring magnates in Fleet Street saw the chance of creating effective rivals to the *Times*. For these and other reasons the British press was gradually relieved of the 'taxes on knowledge'. The objections of Lord Salisbury, who opposed their repeal on the grounds that newspapers did not contain any knowledge, were ignored. So was what Karl Marx sarcastically described as 'the tragicomic, blustering rhetoric with which the Leviathan of the English press—*The Times*—fights [for hearth and home] i.e., for the newspaper monopoly, now modestly comparing itself with the Delphic oracle, now affirming that England possesses only one single institution worth preserving, namely *The Times*; now claiming absolute rule over world journalism'.[4] In 1853 the levy on advertisements was lifted, the stamp tax was removed two years later, and paper duty was abolished in 1861. Soon a flood of new penny papers was pouring into the streets of London and provincial cities. The historian G. M. Trevelyan was to call it the 'White Peril'.[5]

The first and most successful of these popular journals was the *Daily Telegraph* which was issued at a penny in September 1855. Its Jewish printer-publisher was Joseph Moses Levy. But his son Edward, who changed his name to Levy-Lawson and his religion to Christianity, was effectively editor and proprietor of the paper until 1903. Then, aged seventy, he was raised to the peerage as Lord Burnham. A quick, capable journalist, he realised the worst expectations of the genteel by deliberately copying the techniques of the New York *Herald*, though the *Telegraph*'s sensationalism was diluted to suit English taste. Even so, typical early headlines read: 'Extraordinary Discovery of a Man-Woman in Birmingham', 'Felonious Assault on a Young Female', 'Shocking Occurrence. Five Men Smothered in a Gin Vat', 'Horrible Atrocity. A Child Devoured by Pigs'. Like Bennett, Levy-Lawson emphasised the human note. He gave detailed coverage to crime, divorce, public executions and sport. He conducted crusades against capital and corporal punishment, bishops, hereditary peers and prostitution. He engaged in stunts, entertaining thirty thousand children in Hyde Park, organising relief funds, protesting against the sale of Jumbo the elephant to Phineas T. Barnum.

The *Telegraph* included features on subjects like 'The Velocity of Light', 'What is the Best Religion?', 'Spontaneous Generation' and (an evocative title) 'Steam Intercourse with Australia'. It sponsored expeditions, going halves with Bennett in financing Stanley's search for Livingstone. It reviewed books, music, drama and feminine fashions (from a masculine point of view, as in this early comment on cosmetics:

'What a horrifying discovery it would be to find that one's wife was enamelled').[6] Above all, the *Daily Telegraph* made use of the electric telegraph to report news from all over the world. The American formula worked in Britain. By 1861 the *Telegraph*, with 65,000 readers, was overtaking 'Old Grandfather' *Times*. By 1877 its circulation approached a quarter of a million, the highest in the world. Of course, the *Times* remained aloof. The chief proprietor, John Walter III, refused even to acknowledge the existence of the *Telegraph*, or the press revolution it heralded. After all, though the *Telegraph* aspired to please everyone from aristocrat to artisan, its readership, as one contemporary sneered, consisted chiefly of 'virtuous publicans and intelligent greengrocers'.[7]

Such snobbery was one reason why Edward Levy-Lawson failed to become, despite the *Telegraph*'s pre-eminence, the outstanding press baron of his age. More important, though, he was hampered by lack of personal charisma and social confidence, to such an extent that subordinates sometimes dominated him and the paper. When Thornton Hunt was chief editorial writer, for instance, he overruled the policies of the proprietor. This was not, as the editor of *Truth*, Henry Labouchere, asserted, because Levy-Lawson possessed fewer political ideas than 'a vendor of fried fish in Petticoat Lane'. It was, at least in part, owing to the racial prejudice which inspired that and other barbs. Labouchere, especially, attacked him in vicious anti-semitic terms and called him Judas for betraying Gladstone and the Liberals in 1866—a quarrel that culminated in a fist-fight outside the Beefsteak Club. And the *Telegraph*'s best writer, George Augustus Sals, would sometimes storm drunkenly into Levy-Lawson's office bawling, 'You bladdy Jew, give me some money!'[8]

It was actually Sala's personality more than Levy-Lawson's which pervaded the *Telegraph*. A colourful exhibitionist, he possessed a massive nose which was said to be Fleet Street's most prominent landmark. It was inflamed by alcohol and had been split down the middle during a brawl in a brothel catering for his taste in flagellation—to a guardee who spoke disrespectfully of this organ he remarked: 'You must be the snot that ran down my nose'.[9] But Sala was not just a bohemian exotic. He was an extraordinarily accomplished journalist-of-all-work who could turn out swift, vigorous articles on any subject—he was especially famed for his eloquent leaders on the blessings of temperance written during or after bouts of drunkenness. Sala's versatility can be gauged from this message which Levy-Lawson sent him in 1881: 'Please write a leader on Billingsgate and the price of fish, and start for St Petersburg this evening'.[10] Long after Sala's death, his spirit seemed to haunt the *Telegraph* building in

Peterborough Court, a monstrous rookery in which even Levy-Lawson regularly lost his way.

'The Guv'nor', as he was called, did little to modernise the plant or the paper, and it was ill-equipped to resist the *Daily Mail*'s challenge at the end of the century. This was perhaps the real reason why Lord Northcliffe paid him such generous tributes. In fact, Levy-Lawson's only original contribution to journalism had been the invention of the box number, which gave a great fillip to the *Telegraph*'s small advertisements. Otherwise he was a counterfeiter of American innovations. Having gained the *Telegraph* popularity by imitating Bennett, he won it respectability by copying Raymond. And after 1886 he was an adamantine conservative. He followed a safe, undistinguished and profitable policy, appealing to solid, middle-class readers who saw nothing odd in the *Telegraph*'s printing items like this: 'I was greatly struck by the deferential attitude of the man who was washing the face of Queen Victoria on the Temple Bar monument'.[11] In Labouchere's graphic phrase, the *Telegraph* became full of 'senile adulation for the powers that be'.[12]

Such toadyism was anathema to the fervent republican who overshadowed Levy-Lawson and established himself as the most creative force in English journalism between the demise of Delane and the coming of Northcliffe. This was William Thomas Stead (1849–1912) who, by the vigour of his personality, style and convictions, founded the 'new journalism'. Stead was England's version of Horace Greeley and between 1884 and 1888, in the opinion of the New York *Sun*, he 'came nearer to governing Great Britain than any other man in the kingdom'.[13] Much of Stead's strength as an editor stemmed from his belief that he was a messenger divinely appointed to save humanity from the Abyss. For he was a Puritan of the Puritans: his father was an earnest, needy Congregationalist minister and his mother was said to be 'half a priest herself'. Young William conceived a more passionate love for the patron saint of Puritanism, Oliver Cromwell, than he did for Jesus Christ. He wished that God would give him a big whip so that he could scourge the wicked out of the world. He proselytised among his fellows: 'turn, oh turn, why will ye die, have you any objection to come to Him who is altogether lovely'. He knocked down a boy for ogling a girl as she tied up her garter—moved, significantly, as much by jealous calf-love as by outraged propriety.

Aged fifteen, he was inspired by James Russell Lowell's preface to the 'Pious Editor's Creed':

What a pulpit the editor mounts daily, sometimes with a congregation of fifty thousand ... And from what a Bible he can choose his text . . . the open volume of the world, upon which, with a pen of sunshine or destroying fire, the inspired Present is even now writing the annals of God! Methinks the editor who should understand his calling and be equal thereto, would . . . be the Moses of our nineteenth century . . . the Captain of our Exodus into the Canaan of a truer social order.[14]

Aged twenty-two, never having seen the inside of a newspaper office, Stead was appointed editor of the *Northern Echo*.

This was the first English halfpenny morning paper (founded at Darlington in 1870) and its owner, J. Hyslop Bell, had been so impressed by Stead's free-lance contributions that he gave this meagrely educated merchant's clerk full editorial and managerial control. Stead was delighted to have the opportunity of preaching the gospel of social reform and lambasting those children of the Devil, the Tories. He soon breathed his own vitality into the paper, increased its circulation, gave it more of a national than a regional character and tried to lead, not to follow, his flock. In 1875 he wrote of the *Echo*: 'It is myself. Other papers could not bear my image and superscription so distinctly. I have more power and more influence here than [I could] on almost any other paper.'[15]

Stead became the noisiest journalistic evangelist in the country, determined, as he told Gladstone, 'to secure the final overthrow of the Powers of Darkness in high places'.[16] He campaigned for the creation of a global English-speaking confederation. He conducted a mission against the Contagious Diseases Acts, which licensed compulsory medical inspection of prostitutes in garrison towns, a subject about which he professed himself 'mad'. In 1876 he felt the call of God to agitate over the Turkish atrocities in Bulgaria, a crusade which was so successful that Gladstone himself became its champion. Stead also felt the call of Madame Novikoff, the attractive Russian propagandist for whom he conceived a 'sinful passion' which nearly wrecked his three-year-old marriage. And once more the wrongs which seemed to concern him most were those suffered by women: 'the honour of Bulgarian virgins', he emphasised, 'is in the custody of the English voter'.[17] The fact was that, like Stead's other sensational crusades, this one was the product of a deep religious impulse allied to a powerful sexual drive.

It was the control of that drive, according to Havelock Ellis, who knew Stead well, which supplied much of his dynamism as an editor. True enough, he did eventually exercise a degree of sexual control. Having sired six children, Stead for many years practised *coitus interruptus* twice a week with Emma, his 'responsive and affectionate' wife. This actually gave him more pleasure than complete intercourse, though when he 'worshipped my wife with my body' as many as three or four times a week it induced wax to form in his right ear and made him deaf.[18] But the very fact that he, a pious Victorian, recorded this at all showed an extraordinary lack of restraint. Stead also loved to talk about sex, often in Rabelaisian vein— T. P. O'Connor was later to say that he was monomaniac on the subject, comparing him to Sinclair Lewis's carnal revivalist, Elmer Gantry. Nor did Stead exactly repress his inclinations when pretty young ladies appeared at the office—he pulled them onto his knee and embraced them. He did this, he explained, because he enjoyed it; and he told a colleague that there were 'five-and-twenty women in London who would give their little finger for a kiss from me'.[19] Stead was passionately interested in women (too much so in the opinion of his daughter Estelle), especially in those who had not lost what he believed they should prize above life itself. Far from being a form of sublimation or self-control, his newspaper campaigns were a spontaneous overflow of these powerful feelings. As if to clinch the point, Stead referred to those editors who did not espouse his virile form of journalism as the eunuchs of their craft.

Stead's course in life was governed by a series of premonitions or 'signposts' supplied by his 'Senior Partner', as he called God. In 1879 he suddenly felt that he would be summoned to edit a London newspaper. The following year, accordingly, he accepted the offer of a post as deputy to John Morley on the *Pall Mall Gazette*. This was a small twopenny evening paper, founded in 1865 and partly modelled on Thackeray's fictional journal 'written by gentlemen for gentlemen'. Everyone said that Morley, an aspiring Liberal politician and later Gladstone's biographer, was such a perfect gentleman—everyone, that is, except Lord Rosebery who commented, 'such a perfect lady'.[20] Morley was, indeed, somewhat prim, but he was also a free-thinker. He was notorious for spelling 'god' with a small g (reserving the capital, it was said, for Mr Gladstone). Thus his relationship with his unconventional though devout assistant was fraught with difficulty. Morley was pained to hear that Stead actually ran up and down Pall Mall. He must have been appalled by some of Stead's other habits, his fondness for catching, cooking and eating mice, for example—he had heard that this was done during the siege of Paris, tried it himself at the office and discovered that these rodents were particularly toothsome when served on toast.

Then there was Stead's appearance, the shaggy red beard, the deplorable snuff-coloured suits, the strange pyjama-like under-garment, tied with a tassel at the neck, which served for a shirt, and the ancient sealskin cap which gave him the air of a dog-stealer. Footmen at the great houses, undeterred by the piercing blue eyes with which Stead was to stare down Popes, Tsars, Empresses and Prime Ministers, tried to show him to the tradesmen's entrance. Morley was more concerned about Stead's Greeleyish fads, his insistence that those who wished to communicate with him at a distance should do so telepathically instead of telegraphically, his inclination to fill the paper with fanatical articles about vivisection. Morley disliked his tendency to bawl in print even more than his custom of sprawling all over the office like some character out of the Wild West—Stead preferred to think of himself as a barbarian from the North. Despite all the drawbacks this 'union of classical severity with the rude vigour of a Goth', as the *Times* called it, was an outstanding success. Morley admired Stead's capacity to do the work of six men, his splendid journalistic resource, and his unshakeable good humour. Even so, Stead could not have remained a subordinate for long. Luckily in 1882 he received a premonition that he would shortly become autocrat of the *Pall Mall Gazette*, fulfilled the following year when Morley entered Parliament. On being appointed Chief Secretary to Ireland in 1886, Morley remarked that he felt particularly well qualified to govern that country because he had kept Stead in order for three years.

Once in command Stead initiated the 'new journalism'. The phrase was originally his own, although it is usually attributed to Matthew Arnold, who employed it to disparage the high-minded but *'feather-brained'* sensationalism of the *Pall Mall Gazette*.[21] Actually the 'new journalism' contained much that was as old as journalism itself—the lurid treatment of news, for example. Stead's crusades belonged to a tradition begun by Delane. Stead became notorious for having introduced the interview to England but both William Howard Russell of the *Times* and J. M. LeSage of the *Telegraph* had anticipated him in copying Bennett's invention.[22] And many other innovations were simply pirated from America; eye-catching headlines and cross-heads, signed articles, a gossip column, the frequent use of maps, diagrams and drawings. A colleague who had observed the workings of the New York *Herald* and the *World* was 'struck by the wonderful way in which you have assimilated all the features of American journalism'.[23] The new element which Stead brought to journalism was himself. By sheer force of character he breached the wall of anonymity which surrounded the Victorian press in Britain, a barrier so strong that it even preserved editorial incognitos posthumously: when Nicholas Byrne of the *Morning Post* was stabbed to death in his own office, the paper merely published his name, age and address.

Refusing to 'twaddle about chrysanthemums or the fashions at Goodwood',[24] Stead imprinted his rich personality on the *Pall Mall*

Gazette. Writ large in its pages were his individual idiosyncrasies, moral preoccupations and intellectual vagaries. Like Stead himself, who would pace round the dingy Northumberland Street premises beating himself on the leg with a long-handled clothes brush, the paper 'palpitated with actuality'.[25] It effervesced with his unique blend of rash egotism and restless idealism. The energy of these competing impulses can perhaps best be gauged from Stead's account of his daily physical jerks:

> First, I use my legs—six kicks forward with each foot, and, to put vigour into them, I say with each kick, 'That's for Joe!' [Chamberlain] Having finished with 'Joe', I think of myself and give myself two half-dozen kicks to the rear; kick my own behind and repeat each time, 'William, be humble!'[26]

As for mental exercise, Stead took this in the columns of the *Pall Mall Gazette*, which at once reflected his craving to exert supreme power throughout the country and his desire to be a meek executive of the Senior Partner.

Stead's early campaigns show how quickly he became adept at influencing a small but important segment of the ruling class, at leading the leaders of public opinion. First he joined in the bitter cry against the London slums, which led to the appointment of a Royal Commission on Housing. In 1884 he interviewed General Gordon and agitated to have him sent to deal with the Mahdi's uprising in the Sudan. The proposal had a wide appeal, it was echoed by other newspapers and in due course was implemented. Stead was overjoyed. He proclaimed that he was 'running the Empire for Northumberland Street'.[27] He admired Gordon extravagantly, sharing many of his Biblical preoccupations—about the exact site of the Garden of Eden, for example, which the General had finally located in the Seychelles because of the striking similarity between the ripe fruit of its giant palms and Eve's pudenda, and the no less singular resemblance between the breadfruit and Adam's sexual organ. Unfortunately Stead received no premonition of Gordon's fate at Khartoum.

Strangely enough for someone who was to be a prominent advocate of international arbitration and global peace, Stead's next 'escapade' (his word) was to clamour for a stronger navy. Once again, this was a popular cry and the government was obliged to increase the estimates. Then, in 1885, Stead embarked on the crusade which was to make him famous all over the world. He exposed the traffic in juvenile prostitutes in a series of articles collectively called 'The Maiden Tribute of Modern Babylon'. This dramatic title was a fertile cross between mythical and Biblical allusion. It was also an earnest of Stead's determination to employ the techniques of the 'new journalism' to propagate the cause of old puritanism.

Having invoked the support of the Archbishop of Canterbury, Cardinal Manning, General Booth and others, Stead conducted a personal investigation into the worst haunts of London vice. He concluded it by purchasing a thirteen-year-old girl, Eliza Armstrong, from her mother for the sum of five pounds. Stead took Eliza to a brothel where he posed as a rake, drinking champagne and smoking a cigar to sustain the role. Eliza went to bed and Stead satisfied himself that he could have accomplished her defloration if he had so desired. When she had been medically examined and pronounced *virgo intacta*, Stead placed her in the care of the Salvation Army. He then proceeded to publish his spectacular revelations. He stirred up interest by issuing a preliminary warning that the squeamish and the prudish would be shocked. He announced that 'The report of our Secret Commission will be read to-day with shuddering horror that will thrill throughout the world'.[28] He printed explicit details of the 'veritable slave trade', accompanied by an illustration of a rape victim. He spiced the articles with piquant cross-headings, 'How Girls are Bought and Ruined', 'The Confessions of a London Brothel-keeper', 'The Violation of Virgins'. He introduced a note of class warfare, lambasting the sons of the rich for exploiting the daughters of the poor. He condemned the church, parliament and the press for engaging in a conspiracy of silence about the scandal.

There had never been a sensation like it. Tumultuous crowds packed Northumberland Street and the presses ran day and night without satisfying the demand. Eventually the *Pall Mall Gazette* ran out of paper. Stead was vilified in the House of Commons and in the public prints. He was accused of publishing pornography and lowering the tone of sexual refinement in England. He was christened 'Bed-Stead'. Ironically (in view of the notorious *Life and Loves* in which Stead was denounced as a prig) Frank Harris, then editor of the *Evening News*, was one of his most vehement critics: he likened the *Pall Mall Gazette* to 'a vile insect reared on the putrid garbage of the dunghill'.[29] On the other hand, Stead was saluted by social reformers of all denominations throughout the world. Britain's greatest moralist, John Ruskin, who damned the whole output of Fleet Street as 'so many square leagues of dirtily printed falsehood',[30] said that the *Pall Mall Gazette* was the only newspaper with a conscience (though he was most upset by a vulgar article about being buried alive). Public meetings all over the country endorsed Stead's case, the justice of which was recognised by the government when the Criminal Law Amendment Act raised the age of consent to sixteen years. (Stead did not want it to go any higher or young prostitutes would be deprived of their livelihood—he aimed to prevent crime not vice.) Of course, Stead revelled in all this publicity and pursued his side of the controversy with zest. According to Alfred Milner, who served under him on the *Pall Mall Gazette*, 'Stead talks, writes and thinks of nothing else but his virgins, past or present'.[31]

When Stead was threatened with prosecution for obscenity he expressed delight at the prospect of calling princes of the blood, judges, statesmen and half the legislature, to testify about brothels from their personal experience. But, for whatever reason, he failed to subpoena these witnesses when he was brought to trial, on the charge of abducting Eliza. He was found guilty on a technical point; he had not obtained her father's consent. Despite the jury's plea for clemency, Stead was sentenced to three months' imprisonment. So strong had been his presentiment that the term would be two months that he was tempted to ask the judge whether he had made a mistake. In the event he served just over two months, all but three days of it in the 'first division'. This meant that he could live quite comfortably, conduct the paper's business as usual, play blind man's buff with his children and wear his own clothes—ever afterwards, though, he donned a yellow, arrow-stamped prison suit on the anniversary of his conviction, which raised eyebrows as he travelled up to London on the suburban train from Wimbledon. In Holloway Gaol Stead was deluged with letters and presents, including a toy lion wearing a muzzle which roared when it was squeezed, sent by his staff. The gift was more symbolic than its donors knew. For during his incarceration Stead gave way to extreme delusions of grandeur. Towards the end of it he told John Morley:

> As I was taking my exercise this morning in the prison yard, I asked myself who was the man of most importance now alive. I could only find one answer—*the prisoner in this cell*.[32]

It was now that Stead began to formulate his ideas on 'Government by Journalism' (published in 1886), the most audacious assertion of press power ever made in Britain.

The rule of monarchs and noblemen was past, Stead argued, and the press was taking over the functions of the Commons. The editor was 'the uncrowned king of an educated democracy'. (Stead was later to inform the Prince of Wales that he would on no account exchange places with him.) The editor received a daily (instead of a septennial) mandate from the people. They elected him every time they bought his newspaper, which, unlike parliament, was in perpetual session. He was able through it to inform the public, to utter the views of the dumb masses, to conduct missions, expose abuses, judge grievances and right wrongs. The press was the 'engine of social reform', the 'Chamber of

Initiative', the 'voice of democracy', the 'apostle of fraternity' and the 'phonograph of the world'.[33] All this might be dismissed as windy rhetoric but for two facts. First, Stead did try to practise what he preached. As well as exerting considerable influence over politicians, the *Pall Mall Gazette* became a bureau for dispensing practical benevolence. Newspaper offices always attract, and always strive to repel, cranks, bores and lunatics. Stead welcomed them. He endeavoured to help 'the oddest set of creatures outside Bedlam',[34] everyone from the Yorkshireman obsessed by the sinfulness of soft mattresses to the little girl whose mother sent her to inquire how best to sell a sewing-machine.

Secondly, Stead formulated a remarkable programme by which the press could actually exercise civil power. He proposed that each newspaper should have its own whip in parliament, should be vested with the right to inspect all official institutions and should be assisted by press agents in each government department. Inspired by the administrative scheme of his idol, Oliver Cromwell, Stead further suggested the appointment of journalistic 'major-generals' throughout the country. They were to play the hybrid role of twentieth-century public opinion pollster and seventeenth-century puritan patriarch. As the 'interrogators of democracy' they would keep their editors abreast of popular views. And in their local districts they would be the 'indispensable members of the greatest spiritual and educational and governing agency which England has yet seen'.[35] Stead was no more specific than this, but he seemed to visualise that at the centre of this journalistic network there would be a Victorian edition of God's Englishman in a bushy red beard and a shabby check suit. Certainly, he felt that, as a competent editor, he could make himself the most influential man in the British Empire. And soon, apparently, he was to buttonhole the Prime Minister in these terms:

> Look here Mr Gladstone! If you and I were to put our heads together we could settle this business in half an hour, without troubling any of those fellows—

a reference to the other members of the Cabinet.[36] Someone remarked, in an expression which Stead took to repeating, that he behaved as though he were 'superintending the universe'.[37]

Ironically, however, as Stead's pretensions grew his editorial hold on the *Pall Mall Gazette* weakened. Of course, the paper's circulation benefited enormously from the 'Maiden Tribute'. Northcliffe's associate, Kennedy Jones, saw what sensationalism could achieve and noted that the stagnant waters of Fleet Street cannot be troubled without stirring up some mud.[38] However, the rise in sales was only temporary and many of the *Pall Mall Gazette*'s regular subscribers and advertisers were alienated. Consequently the proprietor, Henry Yates Thompson, insisted that his journal should be as others were. He wanted it to air safe Liberal topics like church reform. Above all, he stipulated that there should be 'no more virgins'.[39]

This was a severe restriction on Stead's hitherto complete freedom of action, but one which he effectively circumvented. Thus in 1886 he vigorously exploited the famous scandal of Sir Charles Dilke, who was cited as co-respondent in the divorce proceedings of his fellow member of parliament, Donald Crawford. What made the case so sensational was the accusation that Dilke had inveigled his nursery maid, Fanny, into bed at the same time as Mrs Crawford. Equally shocking, Dilke was allegedly attracted to Mrs Crawford, whom he taught 'every French vice',[40] because her mother had earlier been his mistress. The verdict at the trial was peculiarly inconclusive: the divorce was granted but Dilke was declared innocent, implying that Mrs Crawford had committed adultery with him but not vice-versa. Stead beat the big bass drum of righteousness and rattled the tambourine of purity in public life. He persecuted Dilke unmercifully declaring that he was no more fit to hold public office than Jack the Ripper. He even took Mrs Crawford onto the staff of the *Pall Mall Gazette* in order to pursue the vendetta. Stead was similarly unrelenting towards Edward Langworthy, a millionaire who deserted his wife, and towards Charles Stewart Parnell. Apparently Stead employed private detectives to shadow Parnell to Kitty O'Shea's house in Eltham and he hounded the Irish leader when the affair became known.

Inevitably Stead's mania for sensations of this kind and his itch for another martyrdom put further strain on relations with Yates Thompson. So did his resistance to any kind of control—when accused by Joseph Chamberlain of inciting Stead to attack him John Morley replied, 'You might as well suspect me of inspiring the north-east wind'.[41] Anyway, Stead's 'signposts' had been pointing to his imminent departure from Northumberland Street for some time. So, in 1890, he resigned. Like Barnes and Delane, Stead was only an editor, though an inspired one. True, his great admirer, Cecil Rhodes, offered to buy him the *Pall Mall Gazette* (or some other paper). But Stead refused. As yet no press baron had appeared in England who combined, in the American manner, editorial flair with proprietorial independence.

Stead's trouble was that he dissipated his huge energies. This is not to say that he lacked concentration: using relays of shorthand writers he was quite capable of transferring an editorial from his head to type in fifteen minutes. With phenomenal rapidity he could assimilate confused masses of detail and reduce them to brief, lucid statements. He once wrote 70,000 words in six days. But, lacking balance, judgement and self-discipline, he could never resist intellectual distractions. He was perversely open-minded, a journalistic Toad of Toad Hall forever puffed up with some new conceit, a quack cure for cancer, a miraculous fertiliser, Esperanto, spirit photography, a process for distilling gold out of sea-water, a circulating library of human beings instead of books (this was G. K. Chesterton's idea of a joke—Stead took it seriously).

His next Fleet Street venture, begun in 1890, faithfully reflected his queer brand of apocalyptic eclecticism. This was the *Review of Reviews*, a hotch-potch of significant snippets digested from other journals all over the globe, quickly named 'Fagin's Miscellany' or the 'Magazine Rifle'. Of course, as Stead's partner Georges Newnes discovered, the editor had no intention of making this a literary version of his own popular rag-bag, *Tit-Bits*. When, after three months, the two men agreed to part company, Newnes delivered an interesting 'sermonette' to Stead on the differences between their respective forms of journalism:

> There is one kind of journalism which directs the affairs of nations; it makes and unmakes Cabinets; it upsets Governments, builds up Navies and does many other great things. It is magnificent. This is your journalism. There is another kind of journalism which has no great ambitions. It is content to plod on, year after year, giving wholesome and harmless entertainment to crowds of hard-working people craving for a little fun and amusement. It is quite humble and unpretentious. That is my journalism.[42]

The summary omits two vital points. Newnes's journalism was exceedingly lucrative; Stead's was increasingly messianic. By 1890 Stead had realised that he was called to found 'a city of God which will be to the age of the printing press and the steam engine what the Catholic Church was to Europe of the 10th century'. The *Review of Reviews*, which soon had American and Australian editions, was to be the first step towards establishing 'a world-wide journalistic civil church'.[43] It would have associates in every town and village; it would democratise the best thought on earth; it would reveal the Senior Partner's will to men; it would be read as the Bible had been. The telegraphic address adopted by the *Review of Reviews* was Vatican. Stead clearly saw himself as a secular pope, if not as the chosen saviour of the English-speaking world.

The capital of this world, in Stead's view, was destined to be Chicago. And his flamboyant descent on that city, described in his book *If Christ came to Chicago* (1894), provides a striking instance of his salvationism at work. Stead raised money and founded organisations to relieve social ills. He agitated against corrupt municipal administration and competing religious denominations. He dressed in ragged garb and worked with a gang of labourers at cleaning the streets (catching a nasty chill in the process). He toured the city's 'sporting houses' and declared that rich and self-indulgent women were more disreputable than 'the worst harlot on Fourth Avenue'.[44] The Chicago *Tribune*, which had outraged local 'Pecksniffs' by printing full details of the Maiden Tribute, said that his present work should be suppressed as obscene literature. Despite such criticism Stead never lost his urge to redeem the world. But his ventures grew more and more paradoxical: the imperialist opposed Britain's war in South Africa and her Raj in India; the pacifist rampaged for an invincible navy; the brilliant journalist began two daily papers which failed disastrously (despite advertising schemes which included showering London with money from a balloon); the puritan was converted into an ardent playgoer after his first visit to the theatre, made at the age of fifty-five.

However, for the last twenty years of his life Stead became obsessed by the world of what he jovially called 'spooks'. He was first drawn towards spiritualism because the subject was ripe for journalistic exploitation. He was able to extend the scope of interviewing dramatically, for example, by quizzing both the quick and the dead. He once obtained a fluent (and quite exclusive) interview with the spirit of Mr Gladstone. But soon Stead discovered that he possessed the occult power of automatic writing. He took dictation from various spooks, including Tennyson and Catherine the Great, but his main spiritual contact was a young American, whom he had met shortly before her death, called Julia Ames. She transmitted messages, with suitably spectral punctuation, like this:

> No you are not a weak miserable wretched creature you are a poor mean worm in yourself But you are the destined instrument of the truth and it will be mighty mightier far than you imagine Oh my dear dear friend how I envy you the opportunities you will have You will deliver mankind from the fear of death and bring them into the living presence of spirit. Yes that paper [the *Review of Reviews*] will be your throne the world will hear and listen and believe. My dear William have you lost hold of the Hand of God? Julia Ames.[45]

Even more stimulating were Julia's accounts of sexual ecstasy behind the veil. Apparently spirits could remain monogamous. But posthumous promiscuity was also permitted. Stead looked forward to an

W. T. Stead in prison uniform

T. P. O'Connor by Spy

Joseph Pulitzer

Lord Northcliffe acknowledging
his welcome to Australia

Lord Rothermere

William Randolph Hearst in politician's garb

eternity of incorporeal copulation, merging himself blissfully with other spooks whenever 'the vibrations of our souls coincide'.[46]

Towards the end of his life beliefs of this sort inevitably harmed Stead's reputation as an editor. But one transatlantic press baron, William Randolph Hearst, knew good copy when he saw it. Stead urged him to put 'soul' into sensational journalism and Hearst took him literally. He not only published the Englishman's articles (such as 'How I Know the Dead Return'), he also appointed him special correspondent for the New York *American* at £1,000 a year, a sum shrewdly fixed by Julia in order to finance a Bureau, named after her, to facilitate communication with other spooks. Among her various prophecies, Julia had always confirmed Stead's premonition about how he would meet his end. After two more imprisonments, he was fated to be kicked to death by an angry mob. Consequently, when he set off for the United States in April 1912, to deliver an address about world peace to the 'Religion Forward Movement' at Carnegie Hall, no 'signposts' pointed against his embarking on the *Titanic*. After it struck the ice-berg Stead behaved with the unearthly courage which had so distinguished his journalism. He helped women and children aboard the boats and refused to wear one of the scarce life-jackets. He was last glimpsed standing alone on the deck in 'a prayerful attitude of profound meditation'.[47] His final request was that the heroic bandsmen, who went on performing as the ship sank, should play 'Nearer my God to Thee'.[48]

Predictably, Stead's followers maintained that he was just as active in spirit as he had been in the flesh. Even after death he retained the showman's knack of stirring up controversy. It was to this faculty that Bernard Shaw referred when writing to T. P. O'Connor (1848–1929), who had extended the scope of Stead's 'new journalism' by founding London's evening *Star* in 1888. In that year Shaw wrote:

> today the journalist-in-chief must be above all things an apostle, a man of convictions, illusions, fanaticisms, everything that made a man impossible in the days when the *Star* was impossible ... nobody hates, curses or fears you, as so many do Stead.[49]

This was true. Nevertheless, O'Connor deserves credit for having elaborated Stead's practices so as to draw a large audience—the radical *Star* quickly gained a circulation of 150,000.

After an impoverished Irish childhood and a hand-to-mouth Fleet Street apprenticeship, O'Connor had worked briefly for both Bennett's *Herald* and for the *Pall Mall Gazette*. As editor of the *Star* he consciously took American papers for his model. In particular he imitated transatlantic typography, importing extended informative headlines into Britain for the first time. O'Connor also favoured entertainment at the expense of information. Like Northcliffe after him, he acted on the principle enshrined in this verse:

> Tickle the public and make them grin
> The more you tickle, the more you'll win.
> Teach the public, you'll never grow rich;
> You'll live like a beggar and die in a ditch.[50]

In its terse, anecdotal way, the *Star* stressed the human side of every issue. The snuff-taking T.P. (as he was called—he hated 'Tay-Pay') announced that people in the public eye 'shall be presented as they are—living, breathing, in blushes or in tears—and not merely by the dead words that they utter'.[51] He was well aware that there was nothing new about personal gossip. But, as he observed in 1889, the kind of intimate allusions to individuals now prevalent in the press would, a decade or so earlier, have been regarded as impertinent, if not indecent.[52]

Thus Stead and, following in his footsteps, O'Connor, did much to revolutionise journalism in Britain. Before their day the respectable press had conceded little to human feeling. It had assumed that men (and, in so far as it thought of them, women) wanted to read political news from home and abroad, law reports, market and shipping intelligence. The *Pall Mall Gazette* and the *Star* throbbed with emotion and touched life in all its parts. Of course, every revolution has its evolutionary aspects and since the 1850s other journals had been adapting themselves to changing conditions. Growing city populations, improved standards of living, compulsory education and the rise of literacy, helped to swell the market for newspapers. New technological methods, increased advertising revenue, speedier forms of communication and the distribution of news through Reuter's agency, helped to supply it, cheaply yet profitably. Moreover, successful newspapers like the *Telegraph* and the *Daily News* appealed to a popular readership by anticipating, piecemeal, some of the practices of the 'new journalism'. At the same time the casual old fashions died hard: as late as 1879 Labouchere could decide that in view of a dearth of news he might as well not bring *Truth* out for a week.[53] Genteel people continued to think of journalists as inhabiting the same moral plane as actors. In 1894, for example, the clergyman conducting the funeral of Edmund Yates, creator of the *World* and in some respects godfather of the 'new journalism', made a Freudian slip at the graveside: 'We commit his body to the flames'.[54]

Politicians, however, recognised the enhanced role of the press in swaying the new voters, though they jeered at one another for truckling to such an unreliable medium. John Bright went so far as to condemn Disraeli's government for being influenced by 'the raving lunacy of the *Pall Mall Gazette*, and, if the House would forgive the alliteration, the delirium tremens of the *Daily Telegraph*'. But by the 1880s peers, who had been accustomed to regard reporters in much the same light as poachers, were happy to dine with them in Willis's Rooms, under the presidency of a royal duke, and to toast the press as an estate of the realm.[55] Even so, as Stephen Koss has shown in the first volume of his monumental survey of the British press,[56] editors and proprietors were slow to emerge from their political tutelage. After the repeal of the 'taxes on knowledge' newspapers did not suddenly abandon their party affiliations or renounce their client status. For even when official controls were lifted the habits of subordination were hard to break. Not until they were broken could the press barons come into their full ascendancy.

By the 1890s Fleet Street, which had earlier been dominated by a few strong voices, was 'a babel of competitive roarings'.[57] The despotism of the Thunderer was over—among other misfortunes the *Times* had been badly damaged by attempting to implicate Parnell in crime through the publication of what Stead, when they were offered to him, guessed to be forged letters. Levy-Lawson was certainly not qualified to succeed Delane. And, despite his superlative gifts as a journalist, Stead lacked the drive to build himself a financial as well as an editorial power base. O'Connor lacked the stamina. Yet the time was ripe for combining the methods of the new journalism and the techniques of mass-production to construct a newspaper for the million. It was left to Alfred Harmsworth, later Lord Northcliffe, to achieve this feat and thus to establish himself as the pre-eminent British press baron.

CHAPTER SIX

The Caged Eagle

I<small>N THE</small> U<small>NITED</small> S<small>TATES</small> the feat had been achieved a few years earlier by the pre-eminent American press baron, Joseph Pulitzer. If ever there was a journalist of genius he was one. Pulitzer possessed a more cultivated intellect than any of his peers, with the possible exception of Dana. At the same time he had an intuitive understanding of how to appeal to the popular mind. This, combined with great commercial acumen and immense funds of nervous energy, enabled him to revolutionise New York journalism. It was his unique distinction to create a sensational newspaper with a serious editorial page. With geometric clarity Pulitzer explained his reason for wanting the *World* to address the nation and not a select committee: 'circulation means advertising, and advertising means money, and money means independence'.[1]

Independence meant that Pulitzer could try to realise some of the ideas which he shared with W. T. Stead about the power of journalism. Admittedly, his pretensions were more Napoleonic than theocratic, though he did regard his later blindness as being part of a divine plan to benefit the *World*:

> Why? Because I don't meet anybody, I am a recluse. Like a blind Goddess of Justice I sit aloof, uninfluenced. I have no friends. The *World* is therefore absolutely impartial and free.

But in their way Pulitzer's ambitions were almost as overweening as Stead's. He considered that the *World* was the most important teacher and moral agent in America. He believed that it should determine who should be elected President and 'should be more powerful than the President'.[2] He was fond of quoting Benjamin Constant's remark that

'The press is mistress of intelligence, and intelligence is mistress of the world'.[3] He even envisaged that the *World* might influence beings on other planets. Quite seriously Pulitzer canvassed a scheme to erect an advertising sign in New Jersey so enormous that it could be read on Mars; the project collapsed when one of his entourage asked, 'What language shall we print it in?'[4]

Finding the right language always presented a problem to Joseph Pulitzer and his use of English affords graphic evidence both of his neurasthenic temperament and of his journalistic capacity. It was not just that he possessed the most caustic tongue on Park Row, roused his subordinates with explosions of sulphurous blasphemy, went so far as to interpolate curses in the middle of the words—'re-goddam-porting', 'inde-goddam-pendent'. Every syllable that Pulitzer uttered was eloquent of his tempestuous personality. The anxious elaborations, the emphatic inversions, the hysterical reiterations, all testified to the manic intensity of the man. A simple complaint about the length of the *World*'s editorials became a protracted lament that they were 'too verbose, too prolix, and not incisive, terse and direct enough'. An appeal to the *World*'s editor for more love and murder stories containing 'concrete, living dramatic movement', was couched in these insistent terms:

> Primarily you are there to carry out *my* wishes, *my* ideas, *my* judgement of what is romantic, thrilling, mysterious, of deepest human interest whether a love story or *anything*. I have not the remotest idea you can print my ideas fully, for if you had a few of my ideas, I have no doubt you would have a paper of your own, but inasmuch as I am most intelligent, try to be most friendly, most kindly to your limitations, yes limitations.[5]

Of course, German was Pulitzer's mother tongue. Product of the union between a prosperous Jewish grain merchant and a beautiful Austrian gentlewoman, he was born in 1847 and well educated in Budapest, where he learnt French as a second language. He had an adventurous nature and sought a military career. But he was handicapped by weak eye-sight and a skeletal frame (at six foot two he had to stoop in order to let his adored mother box his ears). Only the hard-pressed Union army would accept him. Accordingly, in 1864 he took ship for America, swimming ashore at Boston in order to collect his own recruitment bounty. Proud, humourless and irritable, he was victimised by other troopers and he saw little or no action before being demobilised. He spent an indecisive and poverty-stricken period in New York—because his shabby presence annoyed the patrons he was moved away from the front of French's Hotel, which he was later to buy and demolish in order to erect the *World* skyscraper. Then, probably because he knew that there was a substantial German-speaking community in St Louis, he went West, selling his silk handkerchief for twenty-five cents in order to finance the journey. There he did various hand-to-mouth jobs, stevedore, waiter, clerk, debt-collector and ostler ('The man who has not cared for sixteen mules does not know what work and troubles are').[6] Finally, in 1868, he obtained employment as a reporter on the liberal, German-language newspaper owned by Emil Preetorius and Carl Schurz, the *Westliche Poste*. Within four months he had acquired a vital tool of the trade and was speaking his own guttural, colourful, comical brand of English.

'Joey the Jew' at once became the butt of his fellows for he looked, as well as sounded, the part. His appearance was always something about which Pulitzer was self-conscious. He once instructed a barber not to make him look like an orang-outang and later on he refused to bare even a shoulder for the sculptor Rodin, who riposted by sheathing his bust in what seemed to be the beginnings of a frilly nightdress. Pulitzer's face was dominated by a large aquiline nose, then a temptation to pranksters who liked to tweak it with a cry of 'Pull-it-sir', subsequently a gift to caricaturists. He had a broad forehead, blue bulbous eyes, a small chin disguised by a tufty red beard, a prominent, mobile Adam's apple and slender expressive hands. His complexion, too, reflected his moods: normally pink, it became grey when he was harassed and fiery red during his frequent tantrums. He wore rough workman's boots, white nankeen pantaloons inches too short for his spindly legs, a coarse shirt without a collar or tie, a dirty linen 'duster' and a fifteen-cent hat with a band made out of grocer's cord. Pulitzer's industry was as distinctive as his clothes but it did not amuse his rivals. All day and for most of the night he laboured without ceasing. Preetorius was amazed by his 'perfect passion for work', remarking that 'His time for work seemed to be all the time'.[7] Pulitzer kept no regular hours, snatched meals when he could and sometimes forgot them altogether, sacrificed his health, mental and physical, on the altar of that 'inky-nosed, nine-eyed, clay-footed god called News'.[8] Soon rival reporters were having to obtain translations of his voluminous contributions to the *Westliche Post*.

In 1869 Pulitzer became news editor but was still enough of a laughing stock to be nominated as a joke for a seat in the state legislature which the Republicans could not hope to win. He accepted the challenge in all seriousness, canvassed tirelessly and was elected, using his new position to mount a vigorous assault on local corruption. Pulitzer showed that he meant business when a dishonest contractor insulted him: he shot the man in the leg with his four-barrelled pistol (despite which he was shortly afterwards appointed a St Louis police commissioner). Pulitzer was, in his own words, 'absolutely crazy and absorbed in politics'.⁹ He would have been an anarchist or a socialist in despot-ridden Europe but in the free air of America he was an aggressive liberal who campaigned hard for Greeley in 1872. As a naturalised American he could never become President himself and he was determined to excel in the one profession that could transform him into a President-maker. Thus in 1872 he took the opportunity to buy cheaply (with his savings and a small legacy) a controlling interest in the *Westliche Post*, discredited as an organ of Liberal Republicanism by the fiasco of Greeley's candidacy. Pulitzer rebuilt the paper's fortunes with sensational stories about child-murder, rape, suicide, white slavery, seduction, adultery, embezzlement, fire, feud, burglary, romance, mystery, horror and scandal. Within a year he was able to return to Europe in search of a cure for the blinding headaches which plagued him, having sold his share of the *Post* back to its original owners for thirty thousand dollars.

Although Pulitzer was liable to sudden eruptions of energy his genius was essentially the pains-taking variety. For the next five years, until 1878, he appeared to lie dormant. He travelled. He qualified for the bar. Fascinated by languages he studied Plato and Aristotle in Greek, translated a German translation of Shakespeare back into English and compared it with the original. Pulitzer invested his capital shrewdly and spoke ironically of taking a 'favourable chance to make myself contemptible by making money'.¹⁰ He dabbled in politics, becoming a committed Democrat in 1874. He worked intermittently for Dana's *Sun* (which he reckoned the best newspaper in the world), sending back hasty, graceless reports filled with repetitions and alliterations from Washington and London. He conducted a stormy courtship with Kate Davis, an attractive, high-toned, frivolous Southern girl, distantly related to the Confederate leader. In his first love letter Pulitzer confessed that he was too cold and selfish to merit her affection but:

> I have an ideal of home and love and work—the yearning growing greater in proportion to the glimpse of its approaching realiz-ation. I am almost tired of this life—aimless, homeless, loveless, I would have said, but for you.¹¹

It was an improbable match but, having set his heart on it, Pulitzer was not to be denied, though Kate was mortified after the honeymoon when he revealed what he had previously concealed—his Jewish ancestry.

The episode, like this whole latent period of his life, explains much about Pulitzer both as a man and a journalist. Far from acting with speed and resolution, he was slow, devious and apt to vacillate. He knew that, as he later said, 'The big things, the great opportunities must not depend upon chance, as there will be very few of them unless they are reached out for and hunted with patience and perseverance'. Pulitzer pursued his opportunities relentlessly, though there was little room for patience in his seismic temperament. He concentrated the whole force of his intelligence on each project, prepared the ground indefatigably, moved only when he was satisfied that there could be no mistake. Yet he agonised over every detail of every decision. In 1874, for example, he determined to make a simple journey from St Louis to New York only after interminable heart-burning and soul-searching. He wrote, 'The battles of Salamis, Sadowa or Sedan were nothing compared with the struggle that has just closed in my breast'.[12] One of his secretaries was to remark that Pulitzer possessed a will of iron but a nervous system of gossamer. In fact his internal state resembled more a vial of lava perpetually on the boil.

In 1878, after an anguished period of hesitation, Pulitzer bought the bankrupt St Louis *Post* for $2,500. Its only real asset was an Associated Press franchise, something the ailing St Louis *Dispatch* lacked. By merging these two worn-out sheets and by working on the new 'carcass like a slave',[13] Pulitzer was able to create, within five years, the most potent newspaper in the mid-West. Moreover, he did so without innovation. For his genius as a press baron lay not in originality but in first stimulating and then exploiting the talents of his employees. The typography of the St Louis *Post-Dispatch* remained traditional, though Pulitzer inserted more news on the front page. Its policies were those of the liberal middle class and it exuded the standard provincial patriotism. Its stories were still told chronologically—it was not until later that Pulitzer began to insist that the most important news should come first. There was nothing new about his use of fiction, illustrations, women's features or humour. Or about stunts like sending a reporter up in a balloon; or about simultaneously raising funds and publicity, a trick which Pulitzer borrowed from the younger Bennett. Similarly, Greeley had anticipated his crusades against corruption and social evils. In fact, the *Post-Dispatch* contained all the familiar ingredients of sensational journalism, including gossip ('Does Rev Mr Tudor Tipple?'), scandal ('Environed by Vice, The YMCA Block Completely Given Over to Sin') and salacity ('Death's Delilah: The Startling Position a Frail Woman Awoke in this Morning: A Well Known Citizen Stricken Down in the Arms of His Mistress'). There were also many precedents for alliterative headlines though Pulitzer was inordinately fond of them—'Bosom Beautifiers', 'Vagaries of Vice', 'A Dastard's Deed', 'Baptized in Blood', 'Mangled by Mongrels'.[14]

What was new about the *Post-Dispatch* was the energy and enterprise which Pulitzer infused into every page. By now he had become something of a dandy, with immaculate nails and beard and a penchant for soft felt hats and blue chinchilla overcoats tailored in New York. But every day and for much of each night he stripped to his shirt-sleeves in order to drive the paper forward. He was everywhere and concerned about everything, excited about a story of a runaway horse, raging at some hapless compositor over a misprint, goading a reporter to score a 'beat', harrying the advertising department to obtain more 'want ads', scrutinising the account books for errors, inventing an eye-arresting headline, writing, correcting, polishing, condensing and re-writing an editorial, forging 'bullets, sharp, pithy bullseye paragraphs scattered in [the] news columns daily'. Pulitzer's sanctum was a corner of the reporters' room, cut off by a dusty curtain which, every few minutes, he would sweep aside with a bony arm. Out would poke the proprietor's beaky nose, his plume of dark hair, his fierce bulging eyes and long scraggy neck. In shrill tones he would pour forth a stream of ideas, suggestions, commendation, criticism or abuse, often mixed with outbursts of such profanity and filth that even hardened journalists shuddered. Like the other great press barons in their hey-day, Pulitzer controlled an enterprise which, however massively prosperous it became, was small enough to respond to its proprietor's slightest impulse. His inner tensions were so powerful that he generated around himself an atmosphere charged with excitement, anxiety and fear. It was precisely the medium, Pulitzer believed, in which the most brilliant newspapers were created.

Unfortunately the atmosphere surrounding Pulitzer was not only stimulating but corrosive. It ate away at the devotion and loyalty which he inspired in so many of his employees. They were attracted to him by high salaries and great expectations. Before being hired each was subjected to a merciless inquisition. What were his antecedents? How old was he? Was he married? Children? How many mothers-in-law? What had he done? What did he like doing? Why? Had he news instinct, energy, originality? Was he 'suggestive'? (Pulitzer meant full of suggestions.) It was the beginning of a long process of attrition. Whatever efforts his staff made, whatever triumphs they achieved, Pulitzer always wanted more. And he wanted it for less: despite his grand vision of the role of journalism he was quite prepared to haggle over a few cents worth of expenses. He wrote, 'Ding Dong Ding Dong Ding Dong Ding Dong the word economy into [E.O.] Chamberlin until he has nervous prostration'.[15] Pulitzer was to take as the *World*'s motto 'Forever unsatisfied'. In the course of a harangue lasting six hours he admitted to O. K. Bovard, later editor of the *Post-Dispatch*, 'I am a terrible critic and fault-finder ... crazy to improve the paper'. Subsequent memoranda illustrate the compulsive way in which he hectored and bullied his lieutenants. A typical exhortation, to Don C. Seitz of the *World*, ran:

> I expect you to think, think, think!!! To read the papers critically, intellectually, comparatively; to make as many suggestions as you possibly can on the distinct understanding that you are in my place;—that any editor depends on the proprietor; is controlled by the proprietor, must carry out the proprietor's wishes and policy. My being disabled ... involves the necessity of your thinking, as nearly as possible, what you think I think. This was the theory by which Cockerill and Ballard Smith, in fact, every man I trained, were guided.

Ballard Smith, whose first intimation of dismissal from the *World* was its owner's cabled order that he should be given a farewell dinner at Delmonico's, was one of two editors employed by Pulitzer who ended their days in a lunatic asylum.

John A. Cockerill, editor of the *Post-Dispatch* from 1879 to 1882, was more resilient. He was a fierce, versatile journalist who had the additional distinction, in Pulitzer's eyes, of being able to swear fluently for ten minutes at a time without repeating himself. He was also one of the few subordinates who would not be intimidated by Pulitzer. He deplored his chief's incessant nagging: 'Mr Pulitzer was the damndest best man in the world to have in a newspaper office for one hour in the morning. For the remainder of the day he was a damned nuisance.'[16] Pulitzer stood by Cockerill when he was accused of murder in 1882 (he had shot a threatening visitor in the *Post-Dispatch* office), putting him in charge of the *World*. But his relationship with the pistol-packing editor illustrated a paradox which the press baron could never resolve.

Pulitzer insisted on employing only bold, creative spirits, but he mistrusted anyone independent enough to challenge his authority. In fact, he refused to delegate, became increasingly paranoid about those occupying senior positions on his newspapers, provoked rivalries among them, placed two men in the same job, employed office spies and further spies to spy on them, practised a policy of divide and rule. After he left St Louis, in 1882, Pulitzer justified his refusal to appoint a deputy on these specious grounds:

> Authority alone does not furnish ideas, brains, knowledge, experience, judgement, tact—yes, tact,—anxiety for more talent,

anxiety for self-improvement, for new blood and new men. But any man can have,—will have this authority very quickly after he had demonstrated his fitness and ability to manage a very large, able and experienced staff.

It was like saying that he would not trust them behind the wheel of a motor car until they had learnt to drive. Although the *Post-Dispatch* flourished, its journalists suffocated in a miasma of jealousy, suspicion and betrayal. The truth was that Pulitzer wanted employees he could respect but he unconsciously despised anyone who would work for him.

Yet Pulitzer sometimes displayed an elephantine joviality. He would reward successful reporters by pulling their ears, like Napoleon, or giving them silk top hats. He enjoyed romping with his infant children, though he was later to become a capricious domestic tyrant, who subjected his offspring to bullying and emotional blackmail. In so far as Pulitzer was capable of happiness—and as his son Joseph told him, 'You have never come anywhere near learning how to enjoy life'[17]—he was happy during the St Louis years. Even so he chafed at the narrow provincialism of that city. He resented the fact that its 'Bourbons' snubbed his wife despite his wealth and her breeding. He yearned to dominate the national stage. As Theodore Dreiser said, he was 'a disease-demonized soul' who cherished a vaulting ambition to be the greatest journalistic force in America.[18]

So in 1883 he leapt at the chance of buying the New York *World*. This was a well-written but little-read paper which had begun life in 1860 as a religious organ. It had passed through various metamorphoses before being acquired by Jay Gould, the millionaire 'skunk of Wall Street', who used it to puff his nefarious railway ventures.[19] For the opportunity of breaking into the charmed circle of New York newspaperdom, Pulitzer paid Gould $346,000, much more than the loss-making *World* was worth. But despite panic-stricken doubts at the last minute, Pulitzer was making an investment not taking a gamble. He explained his programme simply. First he called the staff together and announced, 'Gentlemen, you realize that a change has taken place in the *World*. Heretofore you have all been living in the parlour and taking baths every day. Now I wish you to understand that, in future, you are all walking down the Bowery.'[20] Then he proclaimed to the citizens of New York:

> There is room in this great and growing city for a journal that is not only cheap but bright, not only bright but large, not only large but truly Democratic—dedicated to the cause of the people rather than that of the purse-potentates—devoted more to the news of the New than the Old World—that will expose all fraud and

sham, fight all public evils and abuses—that will serve and battle for the people.[21]

Within two years the *World*'s circulation had increased tenfold, from 15,000 to 150,000. In an unwonted excess of jubilation Pulitzer got boisterously drunk and fell into the arms of the constabulary. 'Look here othifer', he expostulated, 'I'm a congrethman. You can't arreth me.' The policeman was unimpressed by this dignity (as was Pulitzer himself, who resigned from the legislature after a few months). But as he proceeded to hurry the prisoner away he was informed by Pulitzer's companion in revelry, the cartoonist Walt McDougall, that the congressman was also proprietor of the *World*. 'Holy Chessus! Why didn't you say so?' came the reply, 'I'll get you a carriage and you can take him home without anybody seeing him.'[22] In the eyes of the law, evidently, the press baron was mightier than the politician.

The growth of such journalistic power, vastly magnified by the new mass audience, attracted increasingly hostile attention on both sides of the Atlantic. In Britain Lecky expressed horror that unknown men, merely by virtue of owning newspapers, should assume the language of the accredited representatives of the nation and rebuke, patronise and insult its elected leaders. The Democratic Mayor of New York, Abram Hewitt, accused Pulitzer of being the personification of a new kind of boss,

> the newspaper boss. Sitting in his editorial sanctum like a brooding Buddha, he does not hesitate to claim omniscience and to endow himself with omnipotence. The political boss was responsible to his party; the newspaper boss is responsible only to his own pocket. He is as dangerous as he is despotic.[23]

Pulitzer was stung by the attack and retorted with what by then did not seem unduly inflated justifications of press power. The newspaper was responsible to its readers. Its highest mission was public service. It was the supreme moral and educational force of the day. The *World*'s first duty, he maintained, was 'Teaching, teaching, teaching, not only truth per se but puncturing falsehood, humbug, demagoguery, etc. President-making may be a consequence of this.'[24] Jefferson himself had said that public opinion was lord of the universe: the press was its voice and the *World*'s vernacular was the truest echo of the accents of the common people. More specifically, Pulitzer claimed that by the mid-1880s the extension of plutocracy, the tyranny of the great corporations, the ominous unrest among labour unions and corruption or incapacity in politics, posed problems which could not be solved without the help of the press. The newspaper would thus become 'a power for promoting public good which shall exceed any other influence in the land. It is the *World*'s ambition to lead in this cause.'[25] Ideas ruled the world, as Pulitzer said, and the *World* was master of ideas.

Pulitzer was also denounced for building his editorial platform over a sink of sensationalism. His power stemmed from the fact that he spoke with the voice of Greeley (less the eccentricity) but his hands were those of the elder Bennett (minus the salacity). The charge was well-founded and Pulitzer responded to it with furious ambiguity. He insisted, 'I dislike the term "sensational" and never use it'. He denied that the *World* had 'at any time been in any sense a "sensational paper"'. It had 'never printed Pall Mall Gazette scandals' (though it did report the 'Maiden Tribute', in copious detail and with an unattractive combination of prurience and prissiness) but had always presented 'the cleanest legitimate news of the day'.[26] On the other hand, the paper could not function as the national conscience without reporting vice and crime. It could not expose evils or deter malefactors without writing about them (though the *World*'s fascination with the seamy side of royal and aristocratic life in Europe hardly accorded with this explanation). Moreover, to be effective the *World* had to be read and must therefore contain 'all that is romantic, dramatic, unique, yes,— even thrilling. Whatever represents that much abused, almost ridiculously maltreated word: "human interest".' Despite this emphasis, the *World* acted as a moral agency because it faithfully mirrored current affairs (though even in New York two of the paper's favourite subjects, cannibalism and human sacrifice, were scarcely everyday events).

In less guarded moments during his first years on the *World* (he was later more cautious and conservative) Pulitzer frankly acknowledged his craving for 'a good sensation'.[27] But he was no Stead. He always paid lip service to the canons of Victorian prudery. He instructed the *World* to substitute the term 'criminal operation' for 'abortion'. He protested against the portrayal of women in fashionable low-necked dresses and waxed furious on the rare occasions when the paper was banished from respectable clubs. This did not mean that Pulitzer abjured titillating headlines, the odd 'artistic' nude or pictorial features such as 'The Paroxysmal Epoch. Kisses in every known and unknown Language.'[28] It did mean that the *World* seemed spicier than it was.

However, the paper owed its immediate success to performance rather than promise. Indeed, its frenetic self-promotion would have been ineffective unless 'The only two-cent eight-page paper' really was, as Pulitzer's 'ears' proclaimed, 'Bright, Newsy, Gossipy and Entertaining'. The 'ears' were the little boxes on either side of the paper's title and Pulitzer set great store by them. He weighed them 'with the utmost care as a druggist weighs poison'.[29] They were the 'windows of a newspaper' he said, and 'I judge a business manager largely by his ears'.[30] Pulitzer is often credited with having invented 'ears' though they were to be found adorning the London *Observer* in the early nineteenth century. In fact, apart from the introduction of coloured comics into the *Sunday World*, no particular journalistic innovation can be attributed to Pulitzer. As on the *Post-Dispatch*, so on the *World*, he merely injected new vitality into old techniques.

Thus the headlines were more lurid ('Death Rides the Blast', 'Blood on Mother's Lips'). The serials, cartoons, competitions, features, sport and women's pages were bolder and more varied. The humour was simpler ('Cyrus H. McCormick invented a great reaper, but the Reaper whose name is Death cut him down and now he is no mower').[31] The style was plainer, aimed at readers with little education or sophistication: Pulitzer favoured maps, diagrams and illustrations; he 'begged and implored' his staff to 'condense, condense the dry, the serious, the intricate, the complicated'; he banned 'un-understandable' words. The stunts were bigger and some even possessed a global appeal—raising a fund to erect France's gift, the Statue of Liberty; or sending star reporter Nellie Bly round the world in seventy-two days in order to beat Jules Verne's fictional record. National as well as local muck was raked. Pulitzer campaigned against bad housing, the contaminated milk supply and the sweated labour of immigrants in New York. But he also conducted crusades against transcontinental targets such as the Bell Telephone monopoly, Standard Oil, and the Equitable Insurance Company, recognising that the trusts were 'the tremendous terror-inspiring riddle of the day'. In short, Pulitzer was a novel exponent of old-fashioned ballyhoo. It quickly made him a millionaire.

But if the *World* was a stage on which he presented the news in its most dramatic form, it was also a podium from which he addressed his countrymen. Pulitzer was part impresario, part sage, and the *World* reflected this dichotomy. The front page was an exhibition of Pulitzer's seething emotions, his restless curiosity about the most exciting, spectacular and quirky aspects of human behaviour, his delight in histrionics. The leader columns gave expression to Pulitzer's soaring intellect, to his obsession with politics, to his belief that a realisation of Jeffersonian Democracy would be the American dream come true. Pulitzer lavished all his ardour and ingenuity on making the *World*'s editorial page into a 'million-candle-power torch of liberty and intelligence'.[32] He was always partisan but never subservient; he praised Cleveland (perhaps helping him to win the Presidency in 1884), flayed Hanna, condemned Bryan, attacked Roosevelt (a 'military megalomaniac' with the 'manners of a horse').[33] He was always liberal but, despite protestations to the contrary, never radical; he championed the cause of the underdog, whether labour, immigrant or female (though he occasionally succumbed to racial prejudice and was inclined to assert that women needed babies not votes); he lambasted predatory plutocracy (but measured success in terms of riches); he opposed imperialism, militarism and jingoism (though he capitulated to the national hysteria during the Spanish-American war).

Despite the effort which he expended on editorials, Pulitzer did not, as is often asserted, despise the popular sections of his paper. The *World* was a property as well as a pulpit, he insisted. His distinctive achievement was to invest it with this dual personality. Each part, every minute detail, was vital to the well-being of the whole. Pulitzer devoted no more energy to dictating editorials than to agitating for items about scientific marvels, pet dogs, sex changes, fasting, Monte Cristo millionaires, bigamy, female athletes, poison plots ('I am not opposed to murders, quite the contrary').[34] Needless to say, this frenzied industry took its toll on the human cogs in Pulitzer's machine. Theodore Dreiser noticed that the *World*'s staff had in their eyes an expression of nervous, resentful terror, as have animals which are being tortured. On occasion Pulitzer subjected them not just to tongue-lashings but to actual bodily assault. One journalist, driven beyond endurance, hit back. With malicious glee Bennett's *Herald* reported that 'as the room was small, [the blow] necessarily landed on Mr Pulitzer's smeller'.[35]

The famous nose remained intact but by 1888 Pulitzer's health was in ruins. The *World*, with a circulation of a quarter of a million, had outstripped all its competitors and forced them into an ignominious lowering of their prices. Its twenty-storey building, the highest in New York at the time, was rising from its Park Row foundations. From this eyrie the *World*'s master could literally 'spit on the *Sun*'.[36] But Dana's vicious editorial, instructing 'Judas Pulitzer' to 'move on' from New York and become the Wandering Jew of journalism, was taking on the character of a prophecy. Pulitzer was tormented by asthma, insomnia, headaches and nervous indigestion. His cyclothymic rhythm had quickened, moods of euphoria being succeeded by outbursts of despair, joy giving way to rage at a moment's notice. Worst of all, poring over print had damaged his eyes. Hardly able to see, he ranged over the earth in search of health. The doctors urged him to rest but they might as well have tried to convert a bird of prey to vegetarianism.

Pulitzer kept in constant contact with his editors by cable. He fought the *World*'s battles and chafed over its management from afar. Then, one bright morning in 1890 as he was sailing out of Constantinople, Pulitzer remarked to his secretary, 'How suddenly it has gotten dark'. 'It's not dark', came the reply. 'Well it's dark to me,' said Pulitzer. His retina had become detached and he was almost totally blind. So the dark fragment of Pulitzer's life began, and with it what was perhaps the greatest feat of journalistic virtuosity ever achieved by a press baron. A lesser man would have relinquished control of his newspapers; Pulitzer continued to mould them in his own image. A fainter spirit would have come to terms with his shadowy world; Pulitzer sought to change it, to accommodate the world to himself. Irvin Cobb described Pulitzer, imprisoned in darkness, as 'a caged eagle furiously belaboring the bars'.[37]

Not only did Pulitzer lose his eyesight, he also suffered a severe nervous breakdown. Ever afterwards he referred to himself as a wreck and an invalid, constantly in pain. He had always worried neurotically about his health. But now he had serious grounds for hypochondria. In particular, he was afflicted by a pathological aversion to noise. The slightest sound affected him like a pistol shot. The click of a door, the striking of a match, the harsh inflection of a voice, provoked paroxysms of disquiet. Meal times were specially hazardous. Instead of drinking their soup, visiting journalists were apt to inhale it. When a careless secretary broke an almond in half, Pulitzer felt as though he had been murdered and the nuts were banished from his table. One of his grown-up daughters scraped her knife and fork on a plate and she and her brother fled the house rather than endure their parent's wrath. In fact, although Pulitzer complained that no human being had ever been so 'truly forsaken and deserted and shamefully treated by his family',[38] he was too overwrought to endure the presence of his wife and children for long and he seldom saw them. Instead he surrounded himself by secretaries (appointed after the most gruelling and exhaustive selection procedure) and spent his life in an endless quest for silence.

Wherever he went elaborate precautions, spelt out with 'voluminous verbosity', were taken to exclude noise. At hotels, for example, all the rooms surrounding his suite were kept empty, heavy carpets were laid down, hinges were oiled and thick plate-glass windows were installed. But everywhere he was driven mad by hubbub. In London it was the shrieking of the peacocks in Kensington Palace. In his insulated house at Bar Harbor, Maine, it was a foghorn—he tried to bribe the lighthouse-keeper never to blow it. On board ship it was a determined piano-player—Pulitzer pretended to be a composer finishing an opera in order to mute him. Finally he constructed a completely sound-proof annex to his mansion on New York's 73rd Street. Known as 'The Vault', it was connected to the main house by a passage hung on ball-bearings to prevent vibration. It had padded doors, cork floors, double walls and triple-glazed windows. But, like Carlyle's similar venture in Chelsea, it was haunted by noise. Not until the ventilation chimney had been hung with thousands of silk threads to absorb every resonance, did Pulitzer attain quiet. But he could never be at peace.

Tranquillity was a living death, alien to his nature, unendurable in others. Pulitzer's form of vitality was irritability, especially during his sightless years. His fundamental attitude to life was that he was surrounded by damned fools and whatever was, was wrong. The unease which he radiated is well caught in this ironical report about his rheumatism and dyspepsia which George Hosmer, his friend and doctor, sent to Kate Pulitzer:

> He was frightened a great deal this morning and was nearly frozen, because Dunningham [Pulitzer's valet] put the thermometer out of the window and said that it showed twenty-eight degrees. When it proved that it was really thirty-eight he felt a good deal warmer. He is not easy to feed. He is tired of chicken. He is tired of quail. He says the ducks taste like geese. He never eats veal. The mutton is not good, and Dunningham, his medical adviser, says he must not eat roast beef. Somebody has been fool enough to tell Dunningham that there is such a thing as uric acid and he is on guard. His theory is that Mr Pulitzer must live on vegetables but not the starchy ones and that he must not drink any claret. This reduces him to living on spinach and cold water and yet he cannot be happy if he does not gain three pounds a day.[39]

In short blindness and infirmity provoked rather than prostrated Pulitzer. And as with health, so with the *World*: he fretted over every detail. Although he only entered its new building on three occasions his restless personality still dominated the paper. Its employees could sense the 'feverish and disturbing and distressing . . . tang of his presence . . . as definitely as though he were there in the flesh'. According to Theodore Dreiser, the air inside Pulitzer's gold-domed skyscraper 'fairly sizzled with the ionic rays of this black star'.[40]

Pulitzer enforced his will by means of a bombardment of memoranda. These were extraordinary documents, dictated at white-hot speed and couched in code (Pulitzer designated himself 'Andes'). They covered every aspect of the paper's existence and performance. Pulitzer used them to quiz each department; he demanded reports written 'in the fewest possible words and with the largest possible amount of point, pith and knowledge'.[41] Morbidly suspicious, he

99

checked one set of answers against another and required explanations of every inconsistency. He also determined editorial policy by cable, urging his journalists to employ the *World*'s 'greatest and most unique asset of complete independence and freedom to tell exact truth'. Pulitzer demanded 'incessant, daily, striking, town-talk-making, continuous, accumulative features' and suggested what many of them should be. He badgered reporters to provide concrete details about people in the news, their age, height, weight, colour of hair, shape of head, how many cups of coffee they drank in the morning, whether they wore pyjamas or a night-shirt. He needled about accuracy and condensation. Like a demented gadfly, he whined and flitted and stung: 'Don't echo flapdoodle ... sharpen your memory, stiffen your upper lip, quadruple your backbone ... don't slobber'.[42]

The progress of each important member of staff was monitored. Amid the firings, scourgings and threats to withdraw 'goodwill and generosity' from miscreants, an occasional unexpected compliment would flash over the wires. For example, Charles Chapin, the *Evening World*'s sadistic city editor, was congratulated for his 'ferocity in the news hunt'. (Chapin, who was later sent to Sing-Sing for murdering his wife, exclaimed over a photograph of Mayor Gaynor's being shot, 'What a beautiful thing! Look—blood all over him! And exclusive, too!'[43] Yet even Chapin was shocked by Pulitzer's capacity to swear, remarking that with him it was an art rather than a vice.) Pulitzer also hired men by memorandum, once ordaining the employment of a drunkard in order to infuse more spirit into the paper. The experiment proved a failure when the reporter in question, defending himself from the attentions of a 'blue dog', smashed a glass door and cut his wrist so badly that he nearly died. Pulitzer was by no means consistent. He counselled moderation one minute and the next damned the paper for neutrality. He wanted less government but more state intervention against malefactors of great wealth. He demanded political balance and then decreed that some legislator should be burnt in effigy. And from a distance he could only give belated and general instructions which might easily be overtaken by events. But the paper would not have excelled in its prime function, the dissemination of up-to-the-minute news, unless driven by that electric current of memoranda. The *World* was Pulitzer's pylon and he was its dynamo.

After 1895 the paper required every watt of his energy to withstand the most dangerous challenge it faced during his life-time. In that year William Randolph Hearst descended on New York, breaking in (to employ a famous phrase of the day) 'with all the discreet secrecy of a wooden-legged burglar having a fit on a tin roof'.[44] Hearst bought the *Journal* and secured a mass audience by beating Pulitzer at his own game. His sensationalism was more lurid and his headlines were of a size which, as old journalists would say, should have been reserved for the Second Coming. The *Journal* added injury to insult by stealing both the *World*'s stories and its staff, including the cartoonist R. F. Outcault, whose comic-strip hero, the Yellow Kid, gave his name to the style of journalism which Hearst was pioneering. It is often said that Pulitzer despised Hearst's brashness. In public, it is true, he was contemptuous about the vulgar hullaballoo raised by his rival. In private, however, he was quick to accuse his subordinates of 'self-delusion' and 'semi-lunacy' for attributing Hearst's success purely to his enormous expenditure:

> Money of course is an extraordinarily important factor, but Geranium [i.e. the *Journal*] has brains and genius beyond any question, not only brains for news and features but genius for the self-advertising acts which have no parallel.

Pulitzer directed his own editors to show more 'artistic horn-blowing instinct', which resulted in stunts like the firing of bombs from the *World*'s dome to bring rain during the dry spell. He raised journalists' salaries and lowered the *World*'s price. Its typography became bolder, its contents racier, its hue more saffron. Soon there was little to choose between the two yellow dogs. By 1898 the competition was so fierce that Pulitzer succumbed to the national mood of jingoism.[45] Three years earlier he had won international acclaim for supporting the unpopular policy of arbitration between the United States and Britain over the Venezuelan boundary dispute. Now, quite cynically, he shrieked for war against Spain. It would only be a little one, he hoped, and it would enable him to measure the effect on his circulation figures. So the *World* gave itself over to scare headlines, to fraudulent stories, to fake pictures and to the violation of Pulitzer's principles. The paper's editorial Dr Jekyll became enslaved by its sensation-mongering Mr Hyde.

This state of bondage points up the paradox that the Spanish-American conflict exposed the smallness rather than the greatness of the press barons' power. To all appearances they reached their apogee during what was often called 'the newspapers' war'. Pulitzer and Hearst were accused of spreading war fever, dictating their country's foreign policy, provoking hostilities and usurping the functions of government. For example, instead of sending correspondents to report the war, they dispatched 'special commissioners' to take diplomatic and military initiatives. Certainly newspapers aggravated the bellicose mood of the nation. They inflated the pretensions of their proprietors, whose faith in the puffing words of their own prints affords a touching instance of human gullibility. For instance, like Stead, both Pulitzer and Hearst claimed that their newspapers were the permanent spokesmen of democracy, whereas elected leaders only held office for a fixed term. Credulous politicians genuflected towards these capricious embodiments of press power. But the newspaper magnates loomed larger in public life than was warranted by the actual influence which their journals exerted on the masses. For the truth was that the newspapers, bent on popular appeal, were reflecting rather than directing public opinion.

Pulitzer, the most high-minded and strong-willed of the press barons, capitulated to the overwhelming commercial pressures. Prosperous and independent as the *World* was, the *Journal* posed a serious threat to it. No one knew better than Pulitzer that a newspaper which did not go forward went backward. So the sound and fury over Spain signified not a presumptuous accretion of press power in the political sphere but a bitter struggle for dominance in the market-place. The cost of this paper combat was enormous, for the expense of reporting the war far outweighed the revenue earned by ballooning circulations. Thus, after Spain's defeat, Pulitzer sought a pact with Hearst 'which would substitute combination for competition'. Long negotiations were carried on by intermediaries, in an atmosphere of superficial bonhomie and underlying distrust. They concerned everything from fixing the price of the papers to agreeing on the amount of red ink to be used on their respective front pages. Plans were even made to pool the profits of the *World* and the *Journal* and divide them equally between the two owners. Suddenly Hearst and Pulitzer found the monopolistic manoeuvres of the great trusts less reprehensible. It was the first portent that vast corporations were destined to replace the one-man newspaper fiefs. At their zenith, it augured the decline and fall of the press barons.

Of course, this was not apparent at the time. Moreover, no formal treaty ended what one commentator called 'this contest of madmen for the primacy of the sewer'.[46] There was simply a tacit agreement that the *World* and the *Journal* would find their separate audiences. Pulitzer did not want to lose his 'hold on the masses'. But his willingness to 'aim at a better class of readers' was an acknowledgement that the *World* had betrayed its trust. He never admitted to any feelings of remorse. During the last decade of Pulitzer's life the main theme of his memoranda was that the paper, under its excellent new editor Frank Cobb, should put its faith in reliability and respectability, not in sensationalism. It must never imitate the *Journal* in reckless disregard for good taste. Pulitzer wrote:

a newspaper can never be influential if it seeks no more than to please the unthinking, or echo the cries of ignorance and passion. Indeed to become truly commanding, a newspaper must have convictions, must sometimes fearlessly oppose the will of the very public on which its existence depends.[47]

Mr Hyde still made his presence felt in the pages of the *World*, but Dr Jekyll was once more in the ascendant.

In many ways these were Pulitzer's finest years. He denounced America's 'vampire empire' with its policy of 'leprosy and loot',[48] exposed much hidden corruption in her government and society, advanced the cause of enlightenment and progress. So vigorous were the campaigns he waged that Cobb remarked, 'There will soon be nothing left to reform except the weather'. Pulitzer decreed that, without abating a tittle of its force, the *World* should adopt a position of magisterial impartiality. Even the trusts should be treated fairly. Hearst himself must be given his due, though Pulitzer regarded him as a socialistic demagogue and Cobb yearned to 'scatter his intestines from the Battery to the Bronx'.[49] It was at this time, too, that Pulitzer arranged his most famous legacy, the prizes for distinguished writing. And he endowed a school of journalism at Columbia University. The main subject on its curriculum, he argued, should be ethics.

> Above knowledge, above news, above intelligence, the heart and soul of a paper lie in its moral sense, in its courage, its integrity, its humanity, its sympathy for the oppressed, its independence, its devotion to the public welfare, its anxiety to render public service.[50]

Thus, with the advent of the twentieth century, Pulitzer rose from the depths of yellow journalism and set himself up as the conscience of America.

The contrast between the public pieties he uttered and the private brutalities he practised became correspondingly more pronounced. John Singer Sargent's distinguished portrait of Pulitzer captures the contradictions and complications of his nature, with its mixture of altruistic geniality and Mephistophelean cruelty. One eye is alight with piercing intelligence while the other is dull, sullen and half-closed. Like sailors on the look-out for storms, Pulitzer's entourage learnt to watch the expressions which flitted over that mobile countenance. In an instant his mood could alter from sympathetic interest to impatient boredom, from winning animation to forbidding contempt. One moment he could be rewarding a minion with a cigar, the next belabouring him with a riding crop. His secretary, Alleyne Ireland, gave a vivid report of a characteristic diatribe:

> What I need is rest, repose, quiet, routine, understanding, sympathy, friendship, yes, my God! the friendship of those around me. Mr Ireland, I can do much, I can do everything for a man who will be my friend. I can give him power, I can give him wealth, I can give him reputation, the power, the wealth, the reputation which come to a man who speaks to a million people a day in the columns of a great paper. But how am I to do this? I am blind, I'm an invalid; how am I to know whom I can trust ... I've had scores of people pass through my hands in the last fifteen years ... and my God! what have I found? Arrogance, stupidity, ingratitude, loose thinking, conceit, ignorance, laziness, indifference; absence of tact, discretion, courtesy, manners, consideration, sympathy, devotion; no knowledge, no wisdom, no intelligence, no observation, no memory, no insight, no understanding. My God! I can hardly believe my own experience when I think of it.[51]

Even with its expletives deleted, this is an intensely dramatic speech. At its climax Pulitzer's fists were clenched, his arms were raised in stark gestures, his eyes glinted and the sweat stood out on his forehead.

The press barons wielded unfettered power in their own domains, a state of affairs which fostered weird excesses of behaviour and bizarre distortions of character. But they could be victims of *lèse-majesté* when venturing out in public. Pulitzer, for example, while walking along the front at Menton, was accosted by a stranger. Exhibiting signs of acute nervousness, he cried: 'My God! What's this? What's this? Tell him to go away. I won't tolerate this intrusion. Tell him I'll have him arrested.'[52] So, for the last few years of his life, Pulitzer created a hot-house world where he could cultivate his eccentricities in isolation.

Changeable as the sea himself, Pulitzer found much relief from his crippling ailments afloat. From 1907 onwards he largely confined himself to his splendid new yacht. It had been specially built for him and every detail was designed to suit his unique requirements. For instance, the bridge was placed near the stern in order to prevent any of the seventy-five felt-shod crew members from walking over his head. The promenade deck was unencumbered by nuts, bolts, stanchions or ventilators. Pulitzer's magnificent private quarters, equipped with quilted bulkheads and padded floors, were hermetically sealed off from the rest of the ship. Even his wash-basin was raised so there was no need for him to stoop and risk a rush of blood to the head. Characteristically, Pulitzer christened his yacht the *Liberty*; his secretaries nicknamed it the *Liberty Ha! Ha!* or the *Prison Hulk*. Their own cabins were known as 'The Cells'. Certainly these wretched hirelings found that a voyage with Pulitzer was a sentence of penal servitude with hard labour. They were refined and educated men who had fallen on evil days—Pulitzer preferred Englishmen as being more subservient. As many as six of these secretaries were kept busy all the time. Their duty was to ease the pain of Pulitzer's existence. For he could find no repose save in ceaseless mental activity. However exhausted he was, he needed a constant flow of words to keep his brain racing and his psyche calm. Unless someone was reading or talking to him each waking minute he was liable to fall into moods of black dejection or suicidal self-pity.

So his secretaries not only read Pulitzer the *World* and its rivals every day, transmitting his verbal thunderbolts back to New York, they also combed the light and heavy literature of Europe for items that would interest or entertain him. To keep such a giant intelligence occupied was an exhausting task and one that required almost superhuman delicacy. Nothing must be read or said to excite Pulitzer at breakfast or his whole day would be ruined. He had no sense of humour but he required to be amused—though not too much or the laughter would kill him. He insisted on stimulating talk at dinner, but gratuitous expressions of opinion bored him. He liked facts but his appetite for them could never be satisfied—he once instructed a daughter to send him a full description of every girl in her school. His secretaries gutted encyclopaedias but under Pulitzer's ruthless interrogation they revealed gaping holes in their knowledge. One man, incautious enough to announce at dinner that he had read the complete works of Shakespeare, was made to give a summary of each play, its plot and characters. When he had accomplished this heroic feat, Pulitzer snapped: 'Well, go on, go on, didn't you read the sonnets?'[53]

Secretarial assistance was necessary if Pulitzer was to take his afternoon nap. He would lie down while one of his minions read aloud. Soon Pulitzer would say, 'Softly', and the words became barely audible. After a few more minutes the command would come, 'Quite softly'. Then the reader would reduce volume still further and would cease to articulate the words. This non-verbal murmur might continue for two hours (and woe betide the secretary who coughed, sneezed or varied the pitch of his voice) until Pulitzer awoke and the reading proper could recommence. 'His Majesty' (as the secretaries called Pulitzer) even depended on them for sexual pleasure: he luxuriated in bed while they read him erotic German stories.

Pulitzer struggled against his handicaps to the end. He never ceased to beat against the bars of his prison-house. His final great campaign over the misappropriation of Panama Canal funds caused Theodore

Roosevelt to threaten to have him gaoled in earnest, for uttering a criminal libel on the American government and people. This proved a legal mare's nest. But the worry perhaps hastened Pulitzer's death. It also caused him to shuffle onto his editors the responsibility for what had appeared in the *World*. This was a brief and solitary aberration. Pulitzer so cherished the paper's freedom of action that he encouraged it to rake the muck of commercial concerns in which his own money was invested. The investigation into the Panama scandal demonstrates that at the last he was trying to exercise the independence he had won and to live up to the high standards he espoused. As he wrote:

> Our Republic and its press will rise or fall together. An able, disinterested, public-spirited press, with trained intelligence to know the right and courage to do it, can preserve that public virtue without which popular government is a sham and a mockery. A cynical, mercenary, demagogic press will produce in time a people as base as itself.[54]

Pulitzer's extraordinary career does not quite reveal the squalid depths to which a press baron could fall. But it surely illustrates the exalted heights to which he could rise.

The passing of Joseph Pulitzer, which occurred quickly and quietly in October 1911, also shows the extent to which his vitality had sustained the *World*. Before his death he established a trust to ensure that the paper would go on for ever. But, as he had feared, his heirs proved too feeble (though his son Joseph continued the *Post-Dispatch* in the father's spirit) to bear his burden. Pulitzer's liberalism, though not without its limitations, had been of the militant, crusading variety; theirs was a wishy-washy apology for a creed. Under them the paper lost its cutting edge. For a time its fast-talking, high-living executive editor, Herbert Bayard Swope, seemed capable of saving the *World*. At any rate he hypnotised Pulitzer's son Ralph into thinking so, as he did many other leading figures of the day. Listening to him as he received telephone calls from Franklin Roosevelt, Governor Smith and Bernard Baruch, Swope's psychoanalyst concluded that he was paranoid, having hired impersonators of these important men to ring him up while he was on the couch. Swope's magnetism was only exceeded by his egotism. He took a proprietary attitude towards everything, even the weather, once looking out of the window and commenting on the state of 'my snowstorm'.[55] But Swope only prolonged the *World*'s Indian summer and he resigned in 1928.

Without firm control the paper's always split personality began to disintegrate still further. It had, in the words of James M. Cain, 'an editorial page addressed to intellectuals, a sporting section addressed to the fancy, a Sunday magazine addressed to morons, and twenty other things that don't seem to be addressed to anybody'.[56] The losses began to mount and, as Alexander Woollcott said, having first milked the paper, Pulitzer's heirs then murdered it.[57] Breaking their father's will, they sold the *World* for five million dollars to the Scripps-Howard chain who joined it together in unholy matrimony with the *Telegram*, once the evening organ of James Gordon Bennett. By 1931 the economic climate was growing colder and many other newspapers were seeking security in mergers and consolidations. All but the best protected and most ferocious press barons faced extinction.

CHAPTER SEVEN

Northoleon

O<small>N</small> 1 J<small>ANUARY</small> 1901 the *World* performed a stunt which indicated the shape of things to come in journalism. Pulitzer invited Alfred Harmsworth, the young man who was in the process of revolutionising the press in Britain, to edit his New York paper for the first day of the new century. Pulitzer offered the Englishman freedom to do what he liked with the *World* for a single issue. It was a challenge which Harmsworth, who admired Pulitzer to the point of plagiarism, could not resist. He at once began to make impossible demands, wanting to produce a small wire-stitched booklet instead of a newspaper. Eventually a compromise was reached and the *World* was printed as a twelve-page, four-column 'tabloid', about half its normal size.

While it was going to press the gold-domed skyscraper was illuminated by a dazzling display of electric lights. Everyone on the paper wore evening dress in the Englishman's honour. (There was one exception, the news editor, Pomeroy Burton, who regarded it as an affectation: Harmsworth, always obsessed with finding 'the right man, the man! The Man! THE MAN!!!', admired this show of independence, observed Burton's 'bulging brow which indicated intellect' and later inveigled him onto the *Daily Mail*.)[1] During the evening Harmsworth went round the office urging that no story should be longer than two hundred and fifty words. The *World*'s 'ears' proclaimed 'All the News in Sixty Seconds' and 'The Busy Man's Paper'. Harmsworth's front-page editorial forecast that this type of condensed journalism was appropriate to 'the Twentieth or Time-Saving Century'. At the stroke of midnight he and the *World*'s workforce toasted the new epoch with champagne, while, according to the paper's headline, there rose from the celebrating multitude in City Hall Park a 'Roar Like Niagara Gone Mad'.

The tabloid had already been pioneered by the New York *Daily Graphic* and Frank Munsey's *Daily Continent*. So Harmsworth's experiment was widely disparaged in the press, a typical criticism being that 'Americans do not want to take their roast beef in "essence" nor their drink in capsules'.[2] But as a stunt the tabloid was a breathtaking success. Don Seitz told Pulitzer, 'Nothing for years has attracted so much attention in the newspapers of the country as your Harmsworth edition'. He added that if the circulation department had shown more faith in the venture 200,000 extra copies could have been sold. Overnight Harmsworth found himself famous in the United States and for the rest of his life Americans tended to regard him as 'the British Empire's greatest single human force'.[3] Pulitzer himself picked his brains, sending a lieutenant to find out how Harmsworth chose effective serials for his journals. Seitz called at his hotel before breakfast and held a conversation with the English newspaper magnate which was instructive, if 'a trifle confused with his toilette'.

> He said his method was to study melodramatic stories and then, out of the lot, create something that seemed to combine all the powerful elements. He then cited the use he had made of *East Lynne* [by Mrs Henry Wood—the stage version contained the most famous line in Victorian melodrama: 'Dead! and . . . never called me mother!'] . . . *East Lynne* is a very old favourite and I find that he has . . . floated numerous publications on it . . . He is a hard man to talk to as his mind runs far ahead of the matter in hand and it is difficult to pull him back, especially when in a bathrobe.[4]

This episode was a brief diversion in a headlong career. But it anticipated important developments in the press. For Harmsworth both founded the *Daily Mirror*, Britain's most successful tabloid, and stimulated Joseph Patterson to create its New York equivalent, the *Daily News*. And in 1929 Hearst urged his editors to adopt Northcliffe's style of lively, peptonised journalism and ate his earlier words about the tabloid *World*: 'We all thought it was a clever stunt, but few of us realized the vital importance of the principle'.[5] The press barons reacted on each other and the Atlantic was no bar to the flow of influence. Pulitzer had given Harmsworth some of his first lessons in management (appointing two men to the same job) and in publicity (the *Mail* borrowed the *World*'s 'ears'). He had taught him the art of putting, as Harmsworth called it, 'the big strawberry at the top of the basket'.[6] But Pulitzer was not too proud to seek journalastic tips from his former pupil. In an affectionate obituary Harmsworth (by then Northcliffe) recalled their 'delightful conversations on a thousand and one subjects'.[7]

He was perhaps flattering himself. They certainly talked at length—on one occasion each tried to outdo the other in stressing his passion for newspaper accuracy, until the preposterousness of their claims (newsboys selling the *Mail* used to cry out 'Daily Liar') suddenly struck them and both became wreathed in smiles. But as this early glimpse of Northcliffe suggests, he was incapable of producing a consistent sequence of ideas and relied instead on brilliant flashes of intuition. Beside Pulitzer, Harmsworth was an intellectual pygmy, though an extremely nimble one. Yet in terms of journalistic flair, vaunting ambition and empire-building enterprise he surpassed Pulitzer. Northcliffe was to break with the old free-booting tradition of the press barons. In an age of mass production he produced reading-matter for the masses. Though designed to an ancient formula, his publications were manufactured in a modern way, standardised, assembled and sold cheaply, like the goods in Woolworths. Northcliffe was not satisfied with running one journal, or several, on the old commercial lines. Instead he initiated the momentous transformation by which newspaper magnates turned their private fiefs into public companies. And, by attracting massive investments of capital, he created the greatest press confederacy in the world. His enemies named him Northoleon.

Alfred used to joke that he was born (near Dublin, in 1865) with a swollen head, and early photographs confirm that it really was rather too large for his body. Its size was a source of some concern, especially when 'Baby Alf' began to have 'fits' which the doctors diagnosed as 'congestion of the brain'. But his formidable mother could not devote much attention to the 'Firstborn', as Northcliffe always signed himself in letters to her, the one serious love of his life. For Geraldine Harmsworth was preoccupied with her expanding family—she bore fourteen children in twenty years—and with stiffening the backbone of her feckless husband, Alfred Harmsworth senior. At her insistence this schoolmaster of peasant stock qualified for the English bar. But he found it difficult to secure briefs and consoled himself with drink and the reflection, almost certainly spurious, that he was 'descended from kings'.[8] Alfred junior thus spent his London youth in shabby-genteel circumstances and perhaps his earliest acquaintance with newspapers was being wrapped in them when there were no blankets. He taught himself to read with the aid of a toy printing set and attended various down-at-heel private schools, but he was never more than superficially educated. H. G. Wells, who taught at Henley House, where Alfred had earlier édited the school magazine, said that the institution imparted no mature or coherent outlook to its pupils. It launched them 'as mere irresponsible adventurers into an uncharted scramble for life'.[9] He added that Harmsworth's own adventure bore an absurd resemblance to Bonaparte's.

By the age of sixteen, when Geraldine expelled him from the house for seducing the parlour-maid and he embarked as a free-lance journalist, Alfred had acquired a magnetic presence. His body, hardened by long-distance bicycle rides, had now caught up with that magnificent head. With his fine blond hair and mesmeric blue eyes, with his bold, regular features and proud, upright carriage, Alfred was an extraordinarily arresting figure. People called him the 'Adonis of Hampstead'. However, behind that impressive façade he remained the eternal schoolboy, a state symbolised perhaps by his single physical blemish; Alfred bit his finger-nails until they bled. At heart and in mind he was the Peter Pan of press barons, charming, mischievous, sentimental, superstitious and occasionally violent. 'Dodger' had been his nickname at school and all his life Alfred had a penchant for toy tricks and practical jokes, some of them tinged with cruelty. He was convulsed by humour like this:

> Office Boy: There are two men out there, sir, who want to see you; one of them is a poet, and the other a deaf man.
> Editor: Well go out and tell the poet that the deaf man is the editor.[10]

Alfred loved 'novelties'. Much of his adolescence was spent in mulling over 'get-rich-quick' schemes. He even manufactured mountebank concoctions like 'silk hat revivers' and 'Tonks's Pills', guaranteed to 'Cure All Ills'.[11] One of his first ventures in journalism, serialised several times in his own publications, was entitled 'A Thousand Ways to Earn a Living'. Above all, Alfred never lost his taste for glittering scraps of useless information. He was intrigued by the fact that Mr Gladstone wore red socks, that Queen Victoria was only fifty-eight inches tall, that Napoleon could not bear cats. But although Alfred snapped up trifles he had the courage and vigour of a young lion. J. L. Garvin, editor of the *Observer*, went so far as to say that, 'In his heightened vitality and the vivid, ceaseless play of his temperament, he was more like a legend of the Renaissance than any later man'.[12] In short, Alfred possessed 'the common mind to an uncommon degree'.[13] It was precisely right for Fleet Street.

After a knock-about apprenticeship, during which Harmsworth edited *Youth* and *Bicycling News*, he launched his own weekly in 1888, *Answers to Correspondents*, soon shortened to *Answers*. This followed the formula invented by George Newnes, whose *Tit-Bits* was a collection of jokes, puzzles, curiosities and odd facts, many of which were true. Harmsworth produced a refinement on this jackdaw journalism, a request programme. He invited his readers to ask for their own tit-bits; they thus did much of the work for him. Of course, many of their questions were unanswerable, especially satirical enquiries about why all bus conductors were bald or whether a nice girl should poison her father. Harmsworth had to remind those who sent in impossible sums that the editorial wastepaper basket was capacious. But there was a steady supply of just the kind of intellectual gewgaws which he found fascinating. 'Can Fish Speak?' 'Why Don't Jews Ride Bicycles?' 'Do Dogs Commit Murder?' 'Can a Clergyman Marry Himself?' 'Do Tortoises Mew?'

Harmsworth supplemented his replies to these conundrums with countless scraps of editorial bric-à-brac, much of it gleaned from American journals: 'A Parrot that Went Mad from Fright', 'A Night in a Snake's Throat', 'Facts about Fairies', 'Buried Alive in Salt', 'The Strange Things Found in Tunnels'. He printed cliff-hanging serials, featuring crime and adventure. Royal anecdotes abounded: 'The Queen never travels at more than 35 miles an hour'. The jokes, often music-hall puns, imposed little strain on the intelligence: 'A swallow may not make a summer, but a frog makes a spring'. Harmsworth gave earnest hints on etiquette: 'There is no doubt that "I am extremely sorry!" "Oh, don't mention it", sounds infinitely better than "Beg pardon!" "Granted"'. Obvious preoccupations apart, his readers turned out to be most interested in stamps, banknotes, quack remedies, Dickens and, above all, inconsequential statistics: 'If all the hair that is shaved off the men living in London in a day was collected, it would be equal in bulk to $3\frac{1}{2}$ tons of hay'.

Despite this alluring miscellany and the editorial determination to succeed ('the word "fail" . . . is not in our vocabulary'),[14] *Answers* might have gone the way of its many rivals had it not been for the competitions. Readers were asked to estimate, for example, how many people crossed London Bridge each day. The winners received prizes, a winter outfit of clothes, a post in the *Answers* office, a £100 banknote. Then Harmsworth discovered from one of the tramps whom he liked to engage in conversation that his dream of wealth was 'a pound a week for life'. This was offered to the person who guessed the value of the gold in the Bank of England on a particular day. Nearly three-quarters of a million people entered and the circulation of *Answers* rose to 200,000. Harmsworth's own vision of opulence expanded correspondingly.

He began to evolve his 'Schemo Magnifico'. *Answers* would be the first link in a great chain of publications. Each one would support the next and economies of scale could be introduced. They would advertise each other. They could use and re-use the same material. Thus *Comic Cuts* was born in 1890. It specialised in visual as well as verbal jokes

('Crookedness in money matters frequently results in financial straits'), copied many of the melodramatic features from *Answers* and soon proved even more of a success. Later in the same year came *Illustrated Chips,* quickly followed by *Forget-me-Not, Home Chat, The Marvel, The Wonder, Union Jack, The Sunday Companion* and so on. In 1893 *Answers* Ltd. became a public company and moved to new premises. Harmsworth's office was at the top of some steep stairs: 'Makes it easier for me to kick people down', he remarked. By 1894 the combined circulation of his journals approached two million and Harmsworth had created the largest publishing business in the world.

A magazine magnate sells a commodity to customers whereas a press baron dispenses a charter to citizens. With a single bound Harmsworth made the change. In 1894 he bought the moribund *Evening News* and, by combining *Answers* techniques with the methods of the new journalism, he flogged it back into life. Two years later, after soliciting the advice of W. T. Stead and preparing over eighty 'dummy' issues, he founded the *Daily Mail.* While its first edition went to press Harmsworth was prostrated with anxiety. But on hearing that it had sold nearly four hundred thousand copies he exclaimed, 'We've struck a gold mine'.[15] The *Mail*'s immense and immediate popularity stemmed in part from its liberal resort to the standard *Answers* subjects: 'Do Fish Suffer Pain?', 'Is the Sun Burning itself up?', 'Shooting by Electric Light', 'Bread from Wood'.[16] These perennial items were often given a topical context and presented in the manner of Dana's 'Sunbeams':

> Rome is now lit by electricity.
> About 10,000 Americans visit England yearly.
> The first steel pens cost the manufacturers 5s. apiece.
> The deepest mine in the world is the Lambert coal mine in
> Belgium, 3,490 feet deep.
> The Arabs think infinitely more of the pedigree of their horses
> than of those of their own families.
> The signal 'men' on American railroads are women.
> It is calculated that there is property of the value of £10,000,000
> at the bottom of the Atlantic.[17]

But the *Mail* succeeded for other reasons too. Its news was nearly as condensed and quite as piquant as its *Answers* fare. The features, social gossip, sports reports and 'Chat on 'Change' were bright and entertaining. The jokes were amusing without being vulgar. The crime stories were exciting without being lurid. Instead of leaders there were short, sharp editorial comments. 'Most of the ordinary man's prejudices are my prejudices', Harmsworth observed, 'and are therefore the prejudices of my newspapers'.[18] As for the correctness of these prejudices, it was surely self-evident that the test of truth was general acceptability. When J. A. Spender, editor of the *Westminster Gazette*, complained about the *Mail*'s Boer War-mongering Harmsworth called for the circulation ledger: 'Look, Spender', he said, 'here we began our campaign. See, up, up, up. No Spender, we are right.'[19] The *Mail*'s 'Magazine Section' appealed directly to women. It was full of items like 'Is Love-Making Pleasanter in Town or Country?', 'Hints on Engaging Servants', 'What a Girl Should Know' (how to keep the house clean).[20] Men bought the paper because it was a cheap, slick, dependable article. Moreover typographical sobriety and advertisements on the front page gave the *Mail* a respectable appearance, something Harmsworth set great store by. The young man in a hurry might almost mistake it for the *Times*.

The *Mail* was a Juggernaut which was pulled by readers and pushed by advertisers. The readers, mostly impecunious white-collar city-dwellers, were not so much the newly educated as the recently better-off. As the huge circulation of Sunday papers showed, literacy had been widespread before the 1870 Education Act but standards of living had risen since then. The improvement was marginal: while editing *Answers* Harmsworth had received many letters containing 'sad revelations of the poverty of the lower middle classes'.[21] But he realised that clerks earning £75 a year would be willing to spend a halfpenny where they might baulk at a penny. He was able to cut costs by producing the *Mail* according to the latest techniques.

This was where his brother Harold, later Lord Rothermere, played his vital part. Northcliffe was the impresario while Rothermere was the entrepreneur. Northcliffe was often accused of finding journalism a profession and turning it into a branch of commerce. This is nonsense. What really happened was that together the Harmsworth brothers found it an old-fashioned, ramshackle business and transformed it into a modern, stream-lined industry. They converted Grub Street into Fleet Street. Harold introduced sophisticated accounting procedures, 'knifed' 'rags' that did not pay, bought raw materials at knockdown prices, changed the under-capitalised family firm into a flourishing public company, diversified into lumber and paper mills. He installed the new technology, telephones, type-writers, lino-type machines. The British market, unlike the American, was compact. By using newspaper trains, as Northcliffe told Pulitzer, he could deliver the *Mail* to 'the forty million English people at his door' in time for breakfast.[22] Thus, with his brother's help, Northcliffe created the first truly national newspaper.

He could never have done so without the advertisers, large and small. In a sense the cheap mass press was a by-product of the cheap mass production of consumer goods. These were increasingly sold in new department stores, which paid huge sums to display their wares in the newspaper's shop window. Harmsworth resented his reliance on this revenue and declined to 'perform Byzantine genuflexions' before the big advertisers.[23] He was later to appoint the commissionaire at Carmelite House, the *Mail*'s headquarters, as a censor of the coarse and abominable advertisements being submitted to the paper. But his rage about pictures of ladies' underwear ruining the *Mail*'s appearance merely stimulated the growth of professional advertising agencies. And his behaviour when this source of income was threatened moved Hannen Swaffer to coin his celebrated aphorism, 'Freedom of the press in Britain means freedom to print such of the proprietor's prejudices as the advertisers don't object to'. That bohemian journalist provoked a typhoon by innocently posing a typical *Answers* question, 'Is Oatmeal a Poison?' 'What's all this nonsense about oatmeal?' yelled Northcliffe, 'You've cost us thousands of pounds. All the proprietors of patent foods are damning us. Get this contradicted by three o'clock or you're fired.'[24] Luckily Swaffer was able to procure medical testimony to the effect that oatmeal had saved the human race.

'The important thing is poise', said Harmsworth.[25] But he never possessed it. Indeed, the secret of his success was an inability to stand still. Lloyd George compared him to a flea and a grasshopper. He jumped to conclusions with the alacrity of the intellectually insecure. Where his growing newspaper chain was concerned he hopped from one expedient to another. J. A. Spender averred that 'Nature had made him as sensitive as a seismometer, not only to the earthquakes of the popular mind, but to all the premonitory symptoms'.[26] But though Harmsworth's powers of divination seemed magical—he was apparently able to locate buried silver coins, flicking them out of the ground with his stick—he was by no means infallible. His spring-heeled intuitions let him down completely in 1903 when he founded the *Daily Mirror*. This was announced as a 'newspaper for gentlewomen' staffed by ladies. They proved all too lady-like, prone to tea-drinking, fainting fits, genteel archaisms and innocent *doubles entendres*. The *Mirror* missed its market and was soon losing £3,000 a week. 'It's taught me something anyhow', Harmsworth remarked, 'that women can't write and don't want to read.'[27] Perhaps instead the public would like a paper written by men with 'pictures stuck in anyhow and hardly any words at all'.[28] Pioneering the use of half-tone blocks, Harmsworth turned the *Mirror* into the illustrated tabloid which, by mid-century, was to have the world's largest daily sale.

His journalistic agility and his powerful, if erratic, support for the

Conservative cause were rewarded in 1905 with a peerage. The Tory Prime Minister, Arthur Balfour, claimed that he did not read newspapers (and his uncle, Lord Salisbury, had sneered memorably that the *Mail* was written by office-boys for office-boys). But Harmsworth had stood as a Tory parliamentary candidate and invested large sums in Conservative organs like the *Manchester Courier*. Balfour's secretary was to remark on 'how admirably our Party is served by the Daily Mail. It is the most potent auxiliary. Everyone reads it.'[29] Moreover its owner implicitly acknowledged his allegiance to the Conservatives when Max Aitken solicited his aid for Bonar Law, who succeeded Balfour as their leader in 1911: 'I do not suppose that I shall have any difficulty in giving him my full support, though I am not, as you know, a strict Party man'.[30] So Alfred Harmsworth became Lord Northcliffe. He incorporated the Napoleonic bees in his bonnet into his coat of arms. Humbert Wolfe voiced the general cynicism which such press ennoblements provoked:

> The House of Lords
> are waiting for
> The Newspaper
> Proprietor.
> Soap, attention!
> Listen, Beer!
> 'Glory to the new-made peer!'
> Hark! the Heralds'
> College sing
> As they fake the quartering.[31]

Far from providing him with greater equilibrium Northcliffe's new dignity actually seemed to increase his volatility. He see-sawed from bouts of demonic energy to moods of valetudinarian lassitude. Opportunism and improvisation were his watchwords. He took up causes in his newspapers only to drop them the moment public interest showed signs of waning. His crusades were invariably stunts, for English libel laws prohibited muck-raking in the American style. For example, when Northcliffe attacked the Lever 'Soap Trust', which he did partly in emulation of Pulitzer and partly because he feared the effects of a monopoly on his advertising revenues, his fingers were badly burnt in the courts. So instead he determined to 'force everybody in the country to eat Standard [wholemeal] bread and grow sweet peas'.[32] And later he tried to make them wear the *Daily Mail* hat, a cross between a bowler and a Homburg.

More seriously, he campaigned for mechanical progress. He pioneered the reviewing of films and records, and once complained that the *Mail*'s Gramophone Notes 'remind me of what a French cynic said of women—a good idea badly carried out'.[33] Northcliffe had a sublime understanding of the concrete. He saw the revolutionary potential of automobiles, aeroplanes and wireless when they were still widely pooh-poohed. 'We live in tremendous times', he said, and his excitement was infectious.[34] But even his most heartfelt crusade, preparing the British Empire for the inevitable war with Germany, was not consistently sustained. Northcliffe commissioned a book entitled 'The German Menace' but on returning from a trip to America he demanded that the title (and the tenor) should be changed to 'Our German Cousins'. Northcliffe was a bright new comet in the political firmament. But his influence was generally overrated and always unpredictable, for his enthusiasms were as fleeting as the wares he sold. A. G. Gardiner, editor of the *Daily News*, called him a 'Mad Dervish'.[35]

Northcliffe discharged men as summarily as he discarded measures. It was said in Fleet Street that he sucked journalists' brains and then threw them away. Any excuse would do. He asked one employee if he was happy in his work and, on receiving an affirmative answer, Northcliffe retorted, 'Then you're dismissed—I don't want anyone here to be content on £5 a week'.[36] Sometimes he conducted executions by telephone: 'Who's that?' 'Editor, *Weekly Dispatch*, Chief.' 'You *were* the editor.'[37] One day Northcliffe would invite a journalist to dinner and prophesy fame and fortune for him; the next the chief would fail to recognise his new protégé. Other hirelings were subjected to ritual humiliations: one was commanded to kneel in his presence; another was directed to eat in the kitchen. Like Pulitzer, he surrounded himself with an entourage of lackeys and lickspittles, sparring partners on whom he could punch out his aggressions and caprices without the danger of being hit back. In Northcliffe's 'Yes Man's Land', it was said, 'sickening scenes of subserviency' took place, which both delighted and revolted him.[38] One journalist wrote that 'the regime resembled a petty German court with its heel-clickings, grovellings, slander, espionage and jealousies of those who so desired to bask in the sunshine of patronage.'[39]

But there were sunny days and there were admirers among his staff who were not sycophants. Edgar Wallace regarded Northcliffe as a 'visible tangible genius . . . Why it was like meeting Courage in a top-hat or Faith wearing gloves.'[40] After his death Wallace wrote, 'The Chief remains for me an almost sacred personage'.[41] Northcliffe could be the most exhilarating companion in the world, gay, ebullient, comical, confiding, generous and endlessly curious about the foibles of human beings. A hypochondriac himself, he was excessively open-handed to employees who were ill. For others in favour nothing was too much trouble. He would take them off on schoolboy jaunts in his motor car, here stopping to buy ginger beer, there enquiring about a strange new hat worn by a pedestrian, somewhere else quizzing a tramp about his life, everywhere indulging in fantasy, laughter, romance, the thrill of life on the move. Of course, much of Northcliffe's fizz stemmed from an over-active ego. Everything was interesting because it was happening to him. But if Northcliffe was 'the most egotistical man' Irvin Cobb ever met, he had 'a thousand excellent reasons for being the most egotistical man anybody ever met'.[42]

Such a man longed for a monument to his self-esteem. Northcliffe yearned to possess the most famous and influential paper in the world. The *Times*, as he said, was wallowing in a 'forty-year slough of despond'.[43] Ever since Delane's dotage it had been in decline and the circulation had fallen to 38,000—not much higher than in Barnes's day. Its affairs had been ineptly handled by the business manager, Moberly Bell. According to Kennedy Jones, Bell could only count up to five. The *Times*'s accounts were kept in a penny note-book or on the backs of old envelopes; it is said that when Harold Harmsworth came to inspect them he burst into tears. By the Edwardian age the *Times* was less a newspaper than a court circular, a diplomatic gazette, a university register. It was a clubman's shroud with appropriately lifeless contents, an Establishment chronicle with suitably Victorian typography. The paper's essential heresy, Northcliffe maintained, was 'News, like Wine, improves by keeping'.[44] The editor, G. E. Buckle, was a scholar rather than a journalist. He wrote with a quill pen, scarcely knew how to operate the telephone and, a symbol of the paper's Dickensian fashions, he opened letters with his thumb. What is more he wore a beard, always a suspicious circumstance in the opinion of Northcliffe, himself clean-shaven. 'Find out at once what that fellow has got to hide', he would instruct his secretary on sighting a bewhiskered employee.[45]

With all these disadvantages the *Times* faced bankruptcy. Clearly this ancient damsel had to be rescued from her distress. Northcliffe was no knight in shining armour, of course. He was crass, brash and crude (though never coarse—mistresses notwithstanding he was a 'Pecksniffian Nonconformist' about 'smut'). But the majority of the co-proprietors preferred Northcliffe to his chief rival, Arthur Pearson, whose *Daily Express* actually printed news on its front page. Northcliffe was more respectable; he valued the *Times*'s prestige; he revered its past achievements about which he knew a good deal; he honoured Barnes as the paper's greatest editor; he was fond of repeating Delane's maxims, for example, 'Rather twice late than once wrong'.[46] Was it not possible that Northcliffe could perform a miracle with the *Times*, bring it up to date without changing its character, make it profitable without dictating editorial policy? In uncannily similar circumstances, nearly three-quarters of a century later, the same questions were to be asked of Rupert Murdoch.

As soon as Northcliffe acquired the paper, in 1908, he received an ingratiating letter from J. L. Garvin: 'You are Jove now and the *Times* will take a back seat'. Those were Northcliffe's sentiments entirely but he found it difficult to impose his will on the 'Brethren' or 'Black Friars', as he called the denizens of Printing House Square. After all, he had guaranteed to maintain the *Times*'s independence. And its staff thought of themselves as the trustees of a venerable and esoteric institution rather than the employees of a commercial concern. Moreover, Northcliffe himself had no idea what to do with the *Times*, apart from transforming it into a modern, efficient newspaper. At the very least he was determined to make it 'worth threepence'.

Northcliffe acted with circumspection, employing spies or 'ferrets', giving men long vacations on the principle he had learnt from Pulitzer that holidays were the time to find out who was who in a newspaper office. Gradually Northcliffe's suggestions became criticisms and his criticisms hardened into orders: 'One rigid rule I would make for the future is that on the personal page there should be nothing like "Scottish History Chair at Glasgow", which is of no interest to the distinguished Nuts and Flappers we are trying to pursue'. Soon he was bullying: the 'priggish slackness' at the *Times* must be utterly eradicated.[47] Then there were feral rages, one over the dreadful fate which consigned to him the responsibility for a paper which he did not control. Just as fear stalked the corridors of the *Daily Mail*'s Carmelite House, so Printing House Square was pervaded by 'an atmosphere of intense uneasiness and stifled revolt'.[48]

Yet for some time the Black Friars managed to foil Northcliffe. What is more, in a curious way he connived at their obstructiveness. For though he reorganised the paper as a business, there was little he could do to increase the *Times*'s readership via the familiar techniques of condensation, simplification and topicality. These would destroy the paper's élite status and land him with a threepenny edition of the *Daily Mail*. Thus he was never able to evolve a consistent plan for the *Times*. Northcliffe was not, as one employee wrote, 'a genius without a soul'; he was 'A Genius without a Purpose'.[49] In a memorable image H. G. Wells compared him to 'a big bumble bee puzzled by a pane of glass'.[50] Northcliffe was intensely frustrated by the experience and his buzzing grew more frantic as his failure became more obvious. In 1911 he goaded Buckle to resign and worried Bell to death. Mrs Arthur Walter, wife of the *Times*'s former chief proprietor, observed that 'moral chaos' now reigned at Printing House Square.[51] Polite society, which bored Northcliffe, whispered that he was syphilitic, a madman in the making. Yet he was sane enough to make the *Times* pay—against all the odds. After six years of arduous, incessant, disappointing labour it was still not worth threepence. So, in 1914, he reduced its price to a penny. Circulation at once rose threefold, to 150,000. At a stroke the *Times* ceased to be a noble relic of the past and became once again a great newspaper. It was a magnificent coup, achieved in the teeth of the Black Friars' opposition by a man whose determination matched his vision.

Perhaps the success went to Northcliffe's head. Perhaps there was something in the rumours about his mental health. Perhaps the First World War stimulated his incipient megalomania. At any rate, in the last decade or so of his life Northcliffe increasingly aspired to be Northoleon. Of course, the joke had been current for some time. As early as 1905 he had been lampooned as the producer of an elixir called 'Napolio, guaranteed to expand the imagination, fortify invention, destroy reticence, render domestic privacy impossible, convert an accident into an assassination, and produce Marvels out of Nothing'.[52] Northcliffe even encouraged the comparison, snapped out Napoleonic phrases, signed himself with a single N, surrounded himself with busts of the Emperor (one of which he presented to Winston Churchill). On a famous occasion he even tried on Bonaparte's hat at Fontainebleau, discovering with superstitious delight that 'It fits!' But by 1914 Northcliffe seemed to be quite intoxicated with his own power. In October that year, after a visit to the Admiralty, Northcliffe was found by Geoffrey Dawson, the *Times*'s new editor, to be 'in the wildest state of mind, denouncing Churchill not as a bad First Lord but as "having spoken disrespectfully" of him, N.!'[53] Later on in the war, when storming out of No 10 Downing Street, Northcliffe slammed the door so loudly that nearby policemen thought a bomb had gone off. After such outbursts he would chide himself, 'A man as powerful as I am ought not to let his temper get away with him'.[54]

Part of his anger must have stemmed from a baffled awareness that in reality he was having little impact on events. Of course, he never admitted it, quite the opposite. 'There is no doubt about our power over the public', he told R. D. Blumenfeld, 'we can cause the whole country to think with us overnight whenever we say the word.'[55] This was not only a conscious exaggeration, it was also an inversion of the truth. Only one in every six houses took a Northcliffe newspaper—enough, in all conscience, but scarcely the whole country. Moreover Northcliffe always echoed popular sentiments. During the war, for example, his journals were rabidly xenophobic. And his own reports from the front, with their mixture of atrocity stories and sporting similes ('A good artillery battle reminds one very much of a quick lawn-tennis volley')[56] were just what people at home wanted to read—though they helped to breed among the soldiery an ineradicable scepticism about the press. As Wickham Steed, Dawson's successor as editor of the *Times*, noted, all Northcliffe's 'impressions were received through a medium which might be called the public eye in miniature'. He 'automatically censored' his observations in order that they should reflect the prevailing will to win. They also mirrored every tiny shift in the national mood, which Northcliffe habitually gauged by riding in workmen's buses and trains. Similarly, when Asquith resigned from the premiership in 1916, Northcliffe crowed to his brother Cecil, 'Who Killed Cock Robin?' and received the dutiful answer, 'You did'.[57] In fact Asquith lost his office as a result of a political intrigue, itself the product of widespread dissatisfaction (fomented, indeed, by Northcliffe and other press magnates) about his indecisive leadership. Northcliffe was a beater, not a shooter.

The only occasion on which Northcliffe seriously tried to lead public opinion was in 1915 when he attacked Kitchener for failing to supply the army with sufficient high-explosive shells. In a sense, this display of independence was Northcliffe's finest journalistic hour. Yet, paradoxically, it was also a triumph of the patriot over the journalist: 'Better to lose circulation than to lose the war', said Northcliffe. The attack led to threats on his life, bonfires and bannings of the *Daily Mail*, and it provoked a fierce new devotion for the moustached icon of the people. Soon, responding to the defection of his subscribers, Northcliffe abandoned his campaign against the warlord. He thus confirmed what the perceptive had always known, that his buzz was worse than his sting. Yet this was the hey-day of the press barons. Newspapers had a mass as well as a class readership; there was no rivalry from radio or television; during the war censorship of official information (against which Northcliffe raged) and a docile parliament left a vacuum which the press rushed in to fill. Northcliffe might, as he said, 'believe the independent newspaper to be one of the future forms of government'.[58] After such a display of impotence, he could scarcely claim that it was a present form of government.

Nevertheless ministers were intimidated by Northcliffe's dictatorial behaviour and out of their weakness came his strength. They tried to enlist his support by showering him and his family with honours, titles and offices. Lloyd George, a premier without a party, felt himself particularly vulnerable to pressure from the press. Later he fancied exerting it: after Northcliffe's death and his own defeat, in 1922, he seriously considered buying and editing the *Times* himself. On two occasions Lloyd George snared Northcliffe by creating attractive posts specially for him, leader of the British War Mission to the United States in 1917 and Director of Propaganda in Enemy Countries the following year. Northcliffe accepted them because he craved to traffic, as his papers kept urging the government to do, in deeds not words. The moment his capable, podgy fingers grasped the levers of power Northcliffe realised that he had fallen into the pit which gapes for all press barons. For they cannot be at once performers and critics (though Beaverbrook nearly managed it). If they take an executive post in government they sacrifice their freedom to pass judgement on it. They exchange general influence for particular power. Northcliffe writhed in this trap. 'Do you realise', he exclaimed petulantly, 'that, if I enter political life, I have to abandon all connection with the Press, which is my sole source of power?'[59]

Actually, he was effective at drumming up American support for the war. He also damaged German morale by means of his ideological poison gas, according to Ludendorff and the Kaiser. Doubtless the compliment was a way of excusing their own military failures, but Hitler flattered Northcliffe by imitation. He told Rothermere that 'Much in our Nazi propaganda methods is based on the tactics so successfully employed against us by your brother'.[60] Despite these gratifying achievements Northcliffe felt constrained and frustrated by office. Scarcely a week passed in which he did not submit his resignation. True, when he finally went he hankered to return. Personifying as he did the spirit of revenge against the Huns, Northcliffe particularly resented his exclusion from the British delegation at Versailles, where it was his unequivocal intention to lay the foundations for a just and lasting war. But really he acknowledged that 'politicians and newspaper owners are best apart'.[61] In a letter to Northcliffe, Pulitzer had complained of being the loneliest man in the world because he eschewed any human contact that might threaten his integrity as a newspaper magnate. To this aloof ideal Northcliffe himself fitfully aspired. After the war rumour had it that he was to be offered the Lord Lieutenancy of Ireland: Northcliffe snorted, 'Does any human being imagine that I would compromise my power and independence by a footman's job like that that', adding quickly, 'or any other job?'[62]

He preferred the unofficial titles, dignity without responsibility, such as that bestowed on him by A. G. Gardiner: 'the visible autocrat of English affairs'.[63] But although by 1920 he controlled 110 publications, Northcliffe's despotic character was chiefly manifested in wayward exercises of will-power. He insisted, for example, that all numbers in the *Times* should be spelt out in words—until Stock Exchange Prices were mentioned. He sprang at the *Mail*'s advertising manager, Wareham Smith, 'like a tiger—I thought he was going to knock me down'. He raved for twenty minutes without stopping: 'Who are you, a whipper-snapper clerk, to thwart me? I'll break you, etc. etc.' Smith was made to compose a fawning apology and, in the presence of a third party, to read it out to the Chief who instantly dissolved into smiles and amiability.[64] Northcliffe had always reckoned that he possessed a 'corkscrew' brain which went round and round in circles but eventually achieved its object.[65] Now his mind resembled more a runaway whirligig. His mental condition was symbolised by the futile health-seeking trip round the world on which his doctors sent him in 1921.

This strange, sad odyssey exhausted Northcliffe's body, not least because lacking golf to keep his bulk in check, he dieted compulsively—'I am on the road to skeletonhood'. And it effected no improvement in his mind. Indeed his lively, inconsequential account of the journey made it seem like a global quest for *Answers*: New Zealand contains 'caterpillars with trees growing out of their heads'; 'tea is really a flowering camellia, just as the chrysanthemum is a daisy'; the hook-worm 'enters the foot and goes right up the body into the lungs, then into the mouth and down to the stomach, where it breeds like rabbits'; 'there are about three hundred kinds of fleas, and only one conveys the plague'; Malayan moths are 'as big as swallows'; rats in ships' refrigerators grow 'fur like a bear'; with a Chinese '"cash", worth one-fortieth of a farthing ... you can buy hot water'.[66] Thus the record of his tour reveals the triviality and, in its racialist comments on the 'natives', the callowness of Northcliffe's intellect. Paradoxically, it also displays his sensitivity and prescience. It projects luminous shafts of insight into the future, as in Northcliffe's forecasts about the fate of Palestine and his vision, at its apogee, of the imminent decline of the British Empire. One *Times* journalist said that Northcliffe had 'the gift of innumerable mental angles'.[67] Many were obtuse, many acute.

Northcliffe returned, he thought, fuller than ever of vigour and venom. But the last few months of his life were a pathetic travesty of his earlier career. Whether he was suffering from malignant endocarditis as the official diagnosis asserted, or whether, as many suspected, he was a victim of general paralysis of the insane, cannot now be known. It scarcely matters. His psyche was splintering at the edges. Northcliffe himself had horrifying intimations of madness. He consulted specialists and even told the *Mail*, with a flash of macabre humour, to put its best reporter onto the case. He was afflicted by delusions and persecution mania. He saw two moons, became, Pulitzer-like, morbidly sensitive to noise, worried about being poisoned and carried a pistol to ward off assassins. He successively abused his staff, insulted his estranged wife Molly, uttered blasphemous obscenities (denouncing God as a homosexual), rampaged through a Boulogne hotel stark naked, smashing mirrors, crockery and glasses and threatened his entourage with violence. He was brought back to England, put under restraint, dosed with morphia and finally isolated, for the sake of fresh air, in a hut on the roof of his neighbour, the Duke of Devonshire, in Carlton Gardens. There, in August 1922, he died. His last intelligible utterance was, 'Tell mother she is the only one!'[68] So passed the creator of modern English journalism. Despite his glaring faults, the pettiness of his character and the incoherence of his mind, Northcliffe achieved a kind of greatness. In Britain he was pre-eminent among what he called 'the Sacred Caste of Newspaper Proprietors'.[69] Indeed, Northcliffe's stature was such that his celebrated title was bandied about with scarcely a trace of irony: 'the Napoleon of Fleet Street'.

Northcliffe's journalistic flair had founded his newspaper confederation but it had been sustained and expanded as a business by his unexciting brother, Lord Rothermere (1868–1940). Alfred had rather despised Harold's commercial preoccupations and even excluded his brother from the planning stage of the *Daily Mail* in case his cheeseparing should restrict its growth. But Rothermere received his proper reward in 1922 when he gained control of Northcliffe's popular journals (the *Times* was bought by Major J. J. Astor). Rothermere was responsible for building up the newspaper network which, with its complex offensive and defensive corporate structure, has changed not only the nature but the spirit of modern journalism. To give an inkling of how this system worked: Rothermere possessed more than half of the 700,000 £1 ordinary shares in Daily Mirror Newspapers Ltd., which controlled the *Daily Sketch*, the *Sunday Herald*, the *Sunday Pictorial*, Empire Paper Mills and the Daily Mail Trust. The last owned $53\frac{10}{3}\%$ of the deferred shares of Associated Newspapers Ltd., which in turn owned the *Daily Mail, Evening News, Weekly Dispatch, Overseas Daily Mail* and other journals. In 1926 the combined share and loan capital amounted to nearly £7½ million and the Stock Exchange value was £24 million. In other words, the public invested money, financed growth and took risks, while Rothermere maintained control. He also juggled with the companies and the profits, inflated share prices by increasing advertising at the expense of news and behaved like any other captain of industry, though he was generous as well as greedy.

Rothermere did not resemble such press barons as Lord Southwood or Lord Thomson in being merely an animated cash register. Lucre, indeed, was his measure in most things, even art and sex—in his experience, he once said, old masters were cheaper than old mistresses.

But when he stepped out of the long shadow cast by Northcliffe, Rothermere proved just as anxious to use his papers for political purposes. In his choice of causes, however, Harold was less judicious than Alfred. He flirted with fascism, urging Lloyd George and Oswald Mosley to become dictators at home, and supporting Mussolini and Hitler abroad. And he involved himself, as a vacillating junior partner, in the fiasco of Lord Beaverbrook's Empire Free Trade campaign—of which more later. Rothermere also mounted an inexplicable crusade against the territorial injustice done to Hungary at Versailles. It was a cause which led to the most bizarre proposal ever put to a press baron—some Hungarian monarchists offered him their country's crown. Rothermere professed to be shocked by the idea and refused. But, no doubt remembering the royal blood which was said to run in Harmsworth veins, he was secretly delighted. That such a design should have been mooted at all was not an acknowledgement of his mythical ancestry. It was a tribute to the legendary power which shone like an aureole around the press barons in their golden age.

CHAPTER EIGHT

The
American Dreamer

'THE SUPER-NORTHCLIFFE of America':[1] this was perhaps the least insulting title bestowed by his detractors on William Randolph Hearst. For, despite fierce competition, he surely wins the award for being the most vilified press baron in history. The Northcliffean analogy itself was dismissed, by H. L. Mencken: 'As well compare the Matterhorn to a load of cinders'.[2] The founder of yellow journalism was likened in his megalomania to Caligula and to Hitler. Hearst was said to be the nightmare in the American dream and the punishment inflicted on the United States for her sins. He was reviled as a demagogue, blackmailer, charlatan, victim of intellectual halitosis and moral entropy, poisoner of the wells of knowledge, debaucher of the public taste, pander to the degraded passions of the multitude, cosmic pyromaniac, werewolf. Biographies appeared which were little more than lexicons of invective—Hearst was accused of every crime from trying to buy his way into the White House to sinking the battleship *Maine*. His mind was described as a mass of corruption and his soul as a howling wilderness. He moved Presidents to obscenity and Senators to execration. In Congress Howard Minton denounced Hearst as:

> the greatest menace to the freedom of the press that exists in this country, because instead of using the great chain of newspapers he owns, and the magazines and news agencies . . . to disseminate the truth to the people, he prostitutes them to the propaganda that pursues the policies he dictates . . . He would not know the Goddess of Liberty if she came down off her pedestal in New York harbour and bowed to him. He would probably try to get her telephone number.[3]

Finally, of course, Hearst's character was assassinated by Orson Welles in *Citizen Kane*. This film projected a classic vision of press barons as sinister and rapacious monsters and fixed Hearst in the popular imagination as their prototype.

Welles later claimed that apart from the famous telegram in which Hearst promised to start the war with Spain and his 'crazy art collection (much too good to resist), in *Kane* everything *was* invented'.[4] This is nonsense. As the film critic Pauline Kael has shown, and as the script's real author Herman J. Mankiewicz acknowledged, 'many of the incidents and details came from Hearst's life'. Hearst himself was 'defiantly—almost contemptuously—undisguised',[5] and there was no mistaking the stifling futility of Marion Davies's existence spent amid gin bottles and jig-saw puzzles. Certainly Hearst was angry enough about the portrayal of himself and his mistress to issue 'a definite "MUST" instruction' to his editors. They should not print anything about 'those crooks' at the RKO studio, which was responsible for the film; a reporter on the New York *Journal* should 'come to California incognito' and conduct 'a complete study of the entire cast of bit players' in *Citizen Kane* with a view to writing an exposé of 'Communistic activity in the motion picture industry'; Welles himself (who had earlier impersonated Hearst in Sidney Kingsley's Broadway play *Ten Million Ghosts*) should be branded as a Bolshevik. Hearst sought to discredit Welles because he feared that the cinematic image of Kane would survive when all the cruder caricatures were as dead as the dust on library shelves. Hearst does indeed live on as Kane and it is more difficult to disentangle the man from that potent myth than to disinter him from reams of abuse, hyperbole and misrepresentation.

Yet even that exhumation presents its problems. For Hearst baffled his critics as much as he incensed them. In the words of one contemporary:

> He was inscrutable, Buddha-like in his detachment . . . I could not classify him. He evaded understanding. There seemed something Oriental in his mentality: a kind of unsocial quality that freed him from the influences that were usually important to men.[6]

As *Newsweek* put it, 'Trying to find out what makes Hearst's mental wheels go round has driven many level-headed managing editors to nervous breakdowns, and many rival publishers to cutting out paper dolls'.[7] The contradictions between Hearst's character and his actions, between his pronouncements and his achievements, seemed to defy explanation save in terms of double-dyed hypocrisy. The shy, courteous publisher spawned a brash, unscrupulous journalism not seen in America since the elder Bennett's time. The capitalist with a taste for feudal extravagances professed to be a radical and a progressive. The puritan who shuddered at bar-room stories and privately deplored best-sellers 'full of "By Jesus" and other oaths and of "whores" and "tits" and of merry gentlemen feeling up serving-maids' legs', lived openly with first a prostitute and then an actress. The paradoxes are legion and countless attempts have been made to explain them. In 1906, one journalist in search of the real press baron was:

> assured with equal positiveness that Mr Hearst was the only genuine champion of the Have-Nots against the Haves, that he was a political mountebank and a buffoon, that he was nothing but a notoriety-hunter, that he was a myth, and that his show of power was due to the dexterity of an adroit and supremely capable committee in the background.[8]

The last was for long a fashionable account of what went on behind Hearst's basilisk stare—nothing. There was no real Hearst because there was no Hearst at all. He was simply a personification of plutocracy who purchased his editorial ideas from Arthur Brisbane, his business skills from Solomon Carvalho, his news instinct from Sam Chamberlain and his flair for sensationalism from Morrill Goddard. Cartoons represented Hearst as a figment of Brisbane's imagination— they depicted the press baron as an empty bladder being inflated by the star columnist. But the failure of multi-millionaires like Jay Gould and Andrew Carnegie, who tried to sustain newspapers on cash instead of talent, showed that there was more to Hearst than mere money, and strangely enough, he himself often repeated Pulitzer's admonition that extravagance was no substitute for intelligence.

People persisted in trying to open the locked vault of his character, most with high explosive, some by finding the combination, and others by cutting a single key. Lincoln Steffens was the ablest of these safecrackers. He found everything about Hearst elusive, even his personal appearance: 'his blonde hair is browning; his blue eyes are grayish'. But Steffens concluded that the cool, aloof, soft-voiced, hard-eyed press magnate was possessed by a ruthless egotism, 'the unconscious egotism of absolute self-sufficiency'.[9] Hearst's most thorough and most recent biographer, W. A. Swanberg, tries to resolve the enigma by propounding a cliché: his subject was not one person but two, a split personality, Prospero and Caliban. What all these appraisals have in common is that they view Hearst from the outside. Now, however, a huge assortment of his papers has been made available at the Bancroft Library in Berkeley. For the first time[10] it is possible to anatomise the man from within, a vital step towards assessing what part he played in the history of the press barons.

The Hearst family fortune was made by Willie's father, George, a miner with a Midas touch. He was born of Scottish stock in 1820, but he found life on the slave-worked Missouri plantation too slow and became a prospector. Rough, wild and almost illiterate, he took to California like a native and often said that he would like to have been a Red Indian. He abandoned his early Presbyterianism and became a smoker, drinker, gambler, swearer and 'hard woman-chaser'.[11] He also struck precious metals whenever he dug. What is more he held on to his claims, employing the rugged methods of the West to do so—one contemporary maintained that when George was stung on the testicles by a scorpion it was the insect that died. In 1862 he married the nineteen-year-old Phoebe Apperson (having earlier been in love with her mother). 'Puss', as he called her, was a prim, bird-like school-teacher with aspirations to culture and gentility. George was a trial to her, particularly on account of his reluctance to wash and wear clean linen.

Moreover he indulged their only child, who first saw the light of San Francisco sunshine in 1863. Willie was fed on cake, jelly and ice-cream, and nicknamed 'Billy Buster'. He was entertained with fireworks, theatricals and Punch-and-Judy shows. He was given dogs, horses and gold nuggets. By the age of five Willie had grown abnormally wilful. In order to gratify his desires he bullied, cajoled and bribed. When playing trains with other boys, his mother observed, he insisted on being 'Conductor, Brakesman, Engine and all'. Partly to stop the rot, partly to console herself over George's unfaithfulness, partly to expose Willie to European civilisation, Phoebe took him off on extended tours, suffocating him with her own exclusive affection. When he was only eleven Billy Buster had acquired 'a mania for travel', was 'picture crazy', began collecting stamps, coins and porcelain. He wanted to live in Windsor Castle and asked his mother to buy him the Louvre. In fact she had difficulty in convincing him 'that we could not buy all we saw'. She also found it impossible to control him when he was bent on mischief. He was especially fond of practical jokes, letting off flares in his room and pretending the hotel was on fire, simulating deafness so that strangers had to shout at him. One day in Paris he was returned to his mother by a gendarme who had caught him angling for goldfish in the ponds of the Tuileries Palace.

As an adolescent Willie grew even more determined to have his own way. One tutor made futile efforts to discipline his seventeen-year-old charge, trying to quell his 'idiotic attempts at fun' and threatening violence in order to make him work when he wanted to visit the theatre. Willie was besotted by the romance of the footlights and the glamour of the grease-paint. But he liked not only to watch but to participate in dramas—rows, skylarks and occasionally more symbolic performances. In Rome, for example, he delivered one of Cicero's orations from the spot where it was first spoken. He also tried to find a way of extinguishing the eternal flame. In Aix-la-Chapelle he solemnly sat in Charlemagne's chair. Before Napoleon's tomb he reverently doffed his hat.

At Harvard, where he was 'blue and homesick', Willie completed his education by neglecting his studies. Not being interested in scholarly disputes about the 'as-it-wereness-of-the-sometimes',[12] he spent much time perfecting a negro-minstrel song-and-dance act which was much acclaimed by his fellows. And, supported by an allowance of 250 dollars a month plus almost unlimited credit, he tried to convert Harvard into a gigantic stage where he could play the leading role in a pageant of his own devising. He let loose roosters and exploded fireworks on the campus, entertained his cronies, male and female, to lavish late-night junketings, threw custard pies in Boston theatres, squirted soda-water at his instructors, made his pet alligator drunk and when the animal died, had it stuffed. George apparently encouraged him to have fun. Phoebe complained about his 'utter indifference and extreme selfishness' and pleaded with him to reform: 'It would almost kill me if you should not go through College in a creditable manner'. He replied in mock-heroic vein: 'I assure you that I will not get "full" nor will I in any other way injure my constitution, damage my reputation or stain my immaculate record'.

Willie's protestations were as facetious in content as in style. He was first rusticated and then, after sending his professors chamber pots with their faces painted on the bottoms, expelled. He recounted the final scene to his mother:

> I don't propose to eat any more crow myself nor to secure any to the rest of the family so if you please we will proceed to the next course. Moreover, for fear that you would insist on being helped twice I have just practically upset the pepper in the plate. I assured the gentlemen of the Faculty of Harvard College that I didn't regret so much having lost my degree as having given them an opportunity to refuse it me, and an abject grovel in the characteristic Japanese style would hardly be consistent with the above statement.

When Willie told Phoebe that he would be home for the long vacation

she replied, sourly but accurately, that he had been enjoying one long
vacation all his life.

The comedy of Hearst's university career was played out, but his
time at Harvard had not been entirely wasted. First, the seeds of his
political ambition had been sown. Despite his bashfulness Hearst
craved office, any office. Though he had no real intimates and
alienated rather than attracted contemporaries by his long cigars,
independent ways and ostentatious spending, Willie hoped desperately
to obtain 'the third marshalship of the class'. He also referred to himself
ironically as 'W. R. Hearst, statesman and patriot' and dreamed of
sitting in Congress. He took a lively part in celebrating the election of
Grover Cleveland: 'the band played, rockets shot up into the night and
the glorious flag unfurled'. But when someone on the rostrum
congratulated the Hearsts, father and son, for contributing to the
Democratic victory from opposite ends of the continent, Willie 'was
quite overcome and ran away and hid so that I would not have to make
a speech'.

Secondly, he became permanently addicted to journalism, bearing
on his arm for the rest of his days the emblematic scars. These were six
small burn marks inflicted during the initiation rite prior to his joining
the staff of Harvard's satirical magazine *Lampoon*, of which he became
successful business manager. Hearst studied the methods of Delane as
well as those of Pulitzer and later briefly worked on the *World*. He told
his father, who 'knew no more about newspapers than the man in the
moon' but had bought the ailing San Francisco *Examiner* to promote his
political ambitions, that he wanted to run that paper. Willie drew up a
forthright indictment of the *Examiner*'s shortcomings:

> It is a positive insult to our readers to set before them such pictures
> of repulsive deformity as these and yet such abortions are not
> entirely out of place in an article that comes to a climax with a
> piece of imbecility so detestable that it would render the death of
> the writer justifiable homicide.

By imitating the *World*, by employing 'enterprise, energy and a certain
startling originality', by improving the lay-out and typography, by
printing advertisements and illustrations that would 'attract the eye
and stimulate the imagination',[13] he promised to make the *Examiner* the
best newspaper in the West. If his journalistic talent failed him and 'I
find I am fit for nothing in God's world', Willie told his father, who was
shortly to become Senator for California, 'I shall go into politics'.

Just as important as the prospective quality of the *Examiner* was the
hope that its losses would be turned into profits. It is often said that

Hearst, perhaps the greatest spendthrift in history, despised and disregarded money. Charlie Chaplin, for example, never met anyone who threw wealth around as he did: 'Rockefeller felt the usual burden of money, Pierpont Morgan was imbued with the power of it, but Hearst spent millions nonchalantly, as though it were weekly pocket money'.[14] In fact, Hearst thought about lucre all the time, though he valued it not for its own sake but as power in cold storage. More than this, it was the stuff that dreams are made of. He recognised that newspapers had reached a stage when 'the opportunities for profit are immense'. But at the very time when he was pleading for control of the *Examiner*, he was also badgering his father to buy him some real estate, 'procure some kind of ranch, mine, line of steamships', 'something that will not slip through my fingers and leave me alone in a cold cold world'.

Willie even went to inspect George's Anaconda Mine, which was then producing a fifth of the world's copper, and pronounced it 'the damndest hole I ever struck'. He knew nothing about mining, 'could not tell a drift from a vein' and was happy to leave the 'redish yellow leprous looking hills' in Montana for the spectacular scenery of San Francisco. By 1887 this tall, moustached youth with the diffident manner, the girlish complexion and a voice 'like the fragrance of violets made audible'[15] was ensconced in the *Examiner*'s office. He was delighted to have found 'an occupation that is pleasure as well as business'. To this romantic prankster journalism was, as James Creelman (later Hearst's foreign correspondent) wrote, 'an enchanted playground in which giants and dragons were to be slain simply for the fun of the thing; a Never Never Land with pirates and Indians and fairies; a wonderful, wonderful rainbow, with uncounted gold at the other end of it'.[16]

'Monarch of the Dailies' was the slogan which Hearst coined for the *Examiner* and he now started to promote the paper in princely fashion. 'Wasteful Willie' bought readers as they had never been bought before. In the twelve months after August 1887 he doubled circulation, to 40,000, at a cost of $187,513. Hearst pioneered a new trend among press barons. Previously they had started with little or nothing, had served an apprenticeship in one of the branches of journalism and had risen the hard way. Now the expense of complicated machinery and an increased labour force made this much more difficult. Press barons of the future tended either to inherit their newspapers or to purchase them with capital acquired elsewhere. Hearst did both. And, like other 'magnate-owners'[17] involved in diverse enterprises, he was inclined to let the financial tail wag the journalistic dog—another portent of the future. But although his newspapers were often at the service of his fortune, his fortune was always at the service of his newspapers.

Hearst spent money in a way that amused his father and horrified his mother. He installed modern equipment and hired better journalists. In 1889 he appointed as Managing Editor the elegant, monocled Sam Chamberlain, whose panache can be gauged from the younger Bennett's comment: 'My secretary? No, damn him! He made me *his* private secretary!'[18] Chamberlain had also served Pulitzer and was the living embodiment of Dana's dictum that journalists who quit drink quit work. Between alcoholic sprees, tolerated amiably by Hearst, he helped to make the *Examiner* a more brazen version of the *World*. All the familiar techniques were employed, condensation and illustration, stunts and crusades, sensations and self-promotion, scandals and fakes. When there was no news Chamberlain would shout at the reporters, 'Get excited, damn it!'[19]

Insofar as he was able to unbend, Hearst got excited. He danced jigs in the office, sang cowboy songs, drew sketches for cartoons, sorted through pictures with his prehensile toes, wrote headlines for editors, tore the paper to pieces just before going to press, and sent his newshounds out in packs, hiring special trains to take them to distant scenes of action. Hearst also initiated a number of populist campaigns. For example, he attacked the corrupt Southern Pacific railroad whose trains were so slow, according to Ambrose Bierce, that they exposed passengers to the perils of senility. In what was essentially a frontier town Hearst used the tactics of the frontier. When the Fire Commissioner sued the *Examiner* for accusing him of selling municipal fire engines in Mexico for his own gain, Hearst blandly admitted the man's innocence on this particular charge but claimed that he was so crooked in general that it was impossible to libel him—the paper was fined one dollar. Hearst invented or distorted news to suit his own ends, employed gangsters to distribute his papers (and destroy those of rivals), invoked his father's aid to dismiss local politicians who denied official advertising to the *Examiner*. He worked in spasms of energy and relaxed in orgies of indolence. He flew kites, set off fire-crackers, launched balloons, attended vaudeville performances and indulged in his own brand of buffoonery. A favourite jape was to squeeze the handle of his trick cane thus emitting a piercing whistle which he liked to direct at bearded men in the street. Willie had the ambitions of a crown prince but the instincts of a court jester.

This suggests why there was such a flagrant discrepancy between his virtuous utterances about the press and the vicious practices of his own journals. Life for Hearst was simply a huge spectacular and newspapers were its programme. They not only provided a running commentary on the show but were, in a sense, part of it. No more than the plot of a pantomime did they aspire to truth. As well indict their evil genius as prosecute the demon king. In a revealing unpublished letter Hearst acknowledged that:

> the modern editor of the popular journal does not care for facts. The editor wants novelty. The editor has no objection to facts if they are also novel. But he would prefer a novelty that is not a fact to a fact that is not a novelty.

When he prints a novel fiction 'the public is startled and the paper sells'. Neither the editor nor the public are to blame: the former achieves circulation and the latter a thrill. The judicious may grieve but they are only a minority. 'And after all, too,' Hearst concluded, 'no harm is done.' The public does not believe the newspaper, which it reads for entertainment not information, and welcomes 'as it welcomes Salome dancers, to be shocked'. Hearst was essentially a fantasist. His visions, often genuinely comic, bore only an incidental relationship to reality.

The world was his extravaganza. In Munich he bought so many beer mugs that 'there are only a few left in the town and they are retained by the shopkeepers as souvenirs'. In Portugal he indulged in a reverie about King Manuel running away from revolutionaries with such speed that he lost all his clothes, and was discovered 'with nothing on but a royal flush'. The hoteliers in Belgium were so greedy ('we are leaving with what little money we have left') that had he died there they would have stolen the pennies out of his eyes. On the other hand, as he told his mother in a characteristic conceit, New Orleans was an ideal place in which to expire:

> the part of the town that isn't a cemetery nevertheless looks like one and everything suggests obsequies, from the great live oaks draped in funeral plumes of Spanish moss to the processions of sad-eyed mourners tramping with slow and measured steps from store to store ... The clothing dummies in the windows, wearing the fashions of a dead and gone past, have a sort of late lamented look about them and seem not so much to have been draped by a window dresser as to have been laid out by an undertaker. There is a sort of spectral character to the whole town and when you look up at the melancholy, tomb-like houses it almost seems as if the signs should read 'Here lies Jacob Epstein, Haberdasher' or 'Sacred to the memory of Jones and Jenkins, Ladies' Tailors and Dressmakers'. We rode around the town in a solemn sort of way, one carriage after the other like a cortège, and when we stopped to gaze reverently at the placid face of this ancient city it seemed as if we were taking one last look at the remains before the greatest of

all funeral directors, Father Time, screwed down the lid of oblivion upon the relic of departed things.

Willie was similarly fanciful about his private life, assuring his mother, 'I am not going to be giddy. I am going to be a highly respectable citizen.' In fact, as Phoebe complained to George, he was living openly in Sausalito with 'a *prostitute* [named Tessie Powers] and utterly ignoring his mother. He will surely have his punishment.'

So he did, and it was a severe one. Willie was starved of funds— relatively speaking. By 1890 the *Examiner*, responding to the massive injections of cash and effort, was beginning to thrive. But Hearst was bored by small-town success. He wished that San Francisco 'were bigger or that the *Examiner* were in New York' for he was no longer 'afraid of Pulitzer men'. In 1891 he canvassed ways of challenging the *World* on its own ground, discussed a possible partnership with its editor John Cockerill, 'talked newspapers till we were black in the face' with Ballard Smith, met 'every newspaperman in New York'. Without money, however, his dream of a transcontinental chain of journals was doomed. In his final years George Hearst, surrounded by leeches and parasites, seemed bent on spending it all himself.

Willie even rebuked him in a long cable, the irony of which must have amused them both.

> Please telegraph me whether or not it is true that you have paid forty thousand dollars for a colt. If you have I shall let everything here to thunder and come East and take care of you. In the meantime you had better get a nurse. I mean this. I shall leave immediately . . . If you insist on squandering all your money I will stop working and see what I can do in that line myself but [if] you simply want to become notorious I think I can suggest cheaper methods and some that will reflect less on your intelligence.

On his death in 1891 George managed to leave mines worth a nominal 18 million dollars but the potential of producing wealth enough to realize even Willie's dreams. Every cent was bequeathed to Phoebe. Resenting Willie's immoral and boorish behaviour (she wished he would 'talk *not grunt* and be ugly') she disbursed her money in thimblefuls. But in 1895, after several crises, mother and son were reconciled. Tessie Powers went into exile with a handsome gratuity, and Willie received 7½ million dollars with which to build his journalistic castles.

He at once bought the ailing New York *Journal*. This paper had been founded by Joseph Pulitzer's sybaritic brother, Albert, and was said to purvey sex in words of one syllable. In Dana's acidulous phrase, it was 'edited by fools for fools'.[20] Hearst had no objection to that. Indeed, he was fond of quoting his father's remark that it was lucky for clever Willie that the world was full of fools. They were providentially ordained to purchase the *Journal* and as a sales gimmick Hearst even mailed them pennies with which to do so. He simply bought readers for a paper whose size he increased to sixteen pages and whose price he lowered to one cent. 'The great crowd that only sees but never thinks'[21] was then mesmerised by what Hearst described, in a flash of candour, as 'sensational features of the Goddard type, very vivid fiction', and human interest stories about '"What the Baby said", "My first proposal", "How to Boil an egg", and a lot of that kind of junk'. It was indeed Morrill Goddard, one of Hearst's earliest acquisitions from the *World*, who set the tone for the new *Journal* with a magazine section so lurid that it made the penny dreadful seem like a religious tract.

Goddard had a ghoulish imagination and an eye for the visually arresting—he anticipated Northcliffe in the use of half-tone photographs. He specialised in freaks, monsters, pseudo-scientific marvels and sexual titillation. Under his auspices the *Journal* was filled with tales about two-headed virgins, prehistoric creatures roaming the plains of Wyoming, surgeons cutting the jugular vein of cancer patients, Siamese twin marriages. Goddard could transmute the most prosaic item into a sensational headline: he billed *The Other House* as 'Henry James's New Novel of Immorality and Crime';[22] he even made a 'Shocking Discovery about the Bad Habits of Ants'.[23] In a single issue there were garishly illustrated stories about adventures among head-hunters, the suicide of a French criminal at his wife's suggestion, the career of a Connecticut cocotte (whose downfall began when she answered a personal advertisement in Bennett's *Herald*), the torture of prisoners in Siberia, the murder of a black rapist by his intended white victim in Georgia, an operation to remove Queen Victoria's cataracts (the picture showed a scalpel slicing through her eyes). The *Journal* virtually acknowledged that it dealt in fables scarcely more real than the comic strips before whose polychromatic effulgence, so it claimed, the kaleidoscope paled with envy and the rainbow resembled a lead pipe. One of the paper's advertisements actually promised 'News novelettes from real life; stories gathered from the live wires of the day and written in dramatic form'.[24] This approach attracted Hearst almost as much as it did the new substratum of readers, many of them immigrants, which (like press barons before and since) he discovered and exploited.

Of course, much of the *Journal*'s success was due to Hearst's being a master of pyrotechnics. His stunts were more explosive, his self-puffery was more blatant and his crusades were more enterprising than those of his competitors. His sob-sisters were also more lachrymose, as this (none too broad) parody, concerning a colliery disaster, illustrates.

> I sobbed my way through the line, the stern-faced sentinels standing aside to let me pass with a muttered, 'the lady is from the Journal; let her by'. I was the first to reach the wounded and dying. 'God bless Mr Hearst,' cried a little girl as I stooped to lave her brow; and then she smiled and died. I spread one of our comic supplements over the pale, still face and went on to distribute Mr Hearst's generous bounty.[25]

Absurd as this is, it suggests another important element in Hearst's appeal to the masses—his sympathy for the underdog.

It is easy, particularly in view of Hearst's reactionary old age, to dismiss this as a mixture of opportunism and cynicism. But there is no denying his real, if romantic, devotion both to the Democratic party and to demos. In Portugal, for example, he was genuinely indignant about the poverty and execrated King Manuel for 'wasting on jewelry for a jade the money that ought to be spent for schools and public works'. At home he championed strikers, attacked trusts and supported the progressive side on most social and political issues. He made good his claim that the newspaper was the attorney of the people. In 1918 he even urged immediate recognition of the Bolsheviks, who had created 'the most democratic Government in Europe'.[26] And as late as 1925, in a private letter to Arthur Brisbane, he remarked, 'we are running radical papers in the most conservative country in the world'. In 1929 Winston Churchill found him a strong liberal.

The very fact that Hearst inveigled Brisbane away from Pulitzer is evidence of his youthful idealism. For Brisbane had made his name by writing socialistic articles for the *World*. Its blind proprietor liked these so little that he was prepared to allow their continuance only 'if his regular pay is reduced'.[27] He must have known that this condition would be rejected for, despite his left-wing views, Brisbane's personal avarice was entirely unabashed. Characteristically, he made a fortune from real estate as a direct result of having studied the works of Henry George. He made another fortune by writing for Hearst. Indeed, as the highest paid working journalist in the world (his annual salary rose to $260,000) he was able to buy a string of small newspapers and become a pocket press baron in his own right. At first Brisbane believed that the *Journal* could never beat the *World*. 'Jo Pulitzer has a head as long as that of a horse,' he remarked sagely, 'compare it with Hearst's.'[28] But soon Brisbane's front-page column, full of information divorced from knowledge and pithy commonplaces ('Brisbanalities') about the vicious rich and the virtuous poor, was helping to prove that the *World* was not, as its owner had once maintained, invulnerable.

Even so the Park Row philosopher could not resist the rewards of prostitution. Hearst's business manager Moses Koenigsberg wrote:

> Brisbane everted the human soul to prove why housewives should do their shopping on the days preferred by the biggest advertisers; he recaptured from the planets a formula to demonstrate the superiority of the latest automobile transmission; he dug from the strata of the Silurian age a fossil to illustrate the virtues of a new cleansing liquid ... [The advertisers were so excited that they] submitted proposals for articles expatiating on the connubial bliss to be derived from the use of a trade-marked bunion-eradicator; the winning personality to be developed in business as well as romance by the wearing of a certain patented garter.[29]

Hearst himself, though frequently instructing the columnist to campaign for municipal changes (such as the building of a new bridge over the Hudson or the siting of subway stations) which would increase the value of his New York property, complained mildly that Brisbane's 'personal plugs' were making 'our biggest feature a promotion medium'. Brisbane was aware of other dangers. For example, the more free puffs he gave to the Ziegfeld Theatre, in which he and Hearst owned shares, the less paid advertising the paper would receive, not to mention the fact that other impresarios would be offended. The question of morality did not arise. Brisbane calculated rewards as though journalism were a branch of accountancy, while Hearst gauged effects as if it were a variety of show business.

Appropriately, then, the slogan Hearst chose for his eastern paper was 'While Others Talk, the *Journal* Acts'. Its most extravagant performance featured the conflict with Spain. Hearst saw this as 'a war of adventure. A knight errant war. A war in the ancient manner ... a crusade.'[30] From the outset he seemed to lose himself in the illusion he was creating. However implausible the story, however gimcrack the scenery, he willingly suspended disbelief. He took every stunt and every scare with the utmost seriousness. For example, the release from prison of Evangelina Cisneros ('the Cuban Joan of Arc'), accomplished by the *Journal*'s reporter Karl Decker, was the most blatant piece of hokum. But as the paper's editor-in-chief W. J. Abbott wrote, Hearst gave every sign of believing that he was 'battling a powerful State to save the life and liberty of a sorely persecuted girl martyr ... Hearst felt himself in the role of Sir Galahad rescuing a helpless maiden.'[31]

By the same token the Spanish military commandant, General 'Butcher' Weyler, was solemnly represented as a monster who craved 'to quench his thirst with American gore'.[32] Hearst lacked not so much the knowledge of good and evil as the knowledge of fact and fiction. The *Journal* invented atrocity stories, manufactured interviews, published fake pictures, perverted real incidents. It conducted the most sustained campaign of jingoism in American history. When the battleship *Maine*, on a friendly visit to Havana, was sunk (under circumstances that still remain a mystery) the *Journal* shrieked, 'War Sure! Maine Destroyed by Spanish; this proved absolutely by torpedoed hole.'[33] By the time hostilities commenced, in April 1898, the paper's streamer headlines were $5\frac{1}{2}$ inches high. This was an unprecedented expansion which permanently changed the tone of modern journalism. Headlines no longer told the news, they sold the news. Hearst became so excited that he resolved to participate in, as well as to direct, the unfolding melodrama.

He volunteered to serve in both army and navy and, when the government was slow to accept his offer, he personally led the *Journal*'s large corps of newsmen to the front. Hearst published a Cuban edition of his paper for the troops, reported all aspects of the war himself, and faced shot and shell with unflinching courage. But bravery does not imply veracity. The *Journal* invented battles where they had never been, inflated minor engagements into major victories and, in general, printed 'a series of fabrications almost without parallel in newspaper history'.[34] On a personal level, the two incidents usually cited to reveal Hearst in a heroic light reek of journalistic artifice.

The first occurred during an attack on the fortified village of El Caney. Hearst, a dashing figure in black clothes, a flat-brimmed straw hat with a brilliant scarlet ribbon round it, a starched white collar and a tie to match the hat band, came upon one of his reporters who had been wounded in the shoulder. It was James Creelman, an expert counterfeiter of news, and according to him Hearst behaved just like a *Journal* sob-sister. The press baron knelt by his side, 'put his hand on my fevered head' and, declaring what fun it was to have Mauser bullets whining all round him, jotted down Creelman's story in his note-book. '"I'm sorry you're hurt, but,"—and his face was radiant with enthusiasm—"wasn't it a splendid fight? We must beat every paper in the world."'[35] It is impossible—and perhaps Hearst himself found it impossible—to determine how much of this is embroidery. But some of it must be because there are small inconsistencies in Creelman's two accounts.

The second episode, however, was clearly staged for the benefit of the *Journal*'s readers, though that too had a factual basis. While examining the wreckage of Admiral Cervera's fleet off Santiago, Hearst spotted a group of disconsolate Spanish sailors on the beach. He and his entourage landed and made them prisoners of war. But in his anxiety to dramatise the event he published a photograph of the capture which was taken from the landward side. It must therefore have been posed afterwards. By Hearst's standards the falsification was minimal, legitimate journalistic licence, and he probably never even noticed it.

The characteristic feature of yellow journalism was to act (with the avowed aim of promoting the public interest) in a spectacular fashion. Before the war Hearst had planned that the *Journal* should rescue Dreyfus from Devil's Island. During it he ordered Creelman to prevent a Spanish fleet from sailing eastwards by purchasing a steamer and scuttling her in the Suez Canal. The war itself had been started, he claimed, by the *Journal*—actually many factors had contributed to the mood of national belligerence, including a search for new markets, hostility to European imperialism, humanitarian zeal, not to mention other newspapers. Anyway, after the final victory Hearst became convinced that a press baron with panache could accomplish almost anything. He formulated one of the most magniloquent proclamations of press power ever printed. Newspapers were 'the greatest force in civilization'. Not only did they 'form and express public opinion', 'suggest and control legislation', 'declare wars' and 'punish criminals', they also, as representatives of the people, 'control the nation'.[36]

Hearst actually proposed an alliance between the proprietors of this puissant new force: 'I urge upon the men whose power gives them such great responsibilities the importance of a formal editorial union—not for private profit but FOR THE PUBLIC GOOD'.[37] Perhaps this self-appointed trust-buster hoped to dominate the merger. But, though an interesting anticipation of the 'media trusts' of the future, it was still-born. Instead Hearst began to expand his personal confederation of newspapers. If each was as potent as the *Journal* they would surely enable Hearst to satisfy what Morrill Goddard called his 'positive craze for public office'. It was delightful to rule the state by proxy, to lord it over presidents and parties through the medium of the press. But the exercise of direct power from the Oval Office was, as Hearst confided to his mother, a much more 'alluring proposition'.

As they watched Hearst's journals proliferating across the continent like cancerous cells, Americans became terrified of the malignant effects they might have on the body politic. By 1904 Hearst had invaded Chicago, Boston and Los Angeles. His newspaper chain, though not the first, was the strongest. It was already syndicating material and buying paper in bulk more cheaply than local rivals. Moreover it was a far cry from the unifying, uplifting organisation once envisaged by Whitelaw Reid, with a staff of Stanleys to collect the news and Shakespeares to write it. Hearst's papers were daily election addresses wrapped in tinsel to attract the masses. Never before had a democratic office-seeker possessed such an instrument for manipulating the voters.

Yet Hearst's political career was a resounding failure. After his election to Congress in 1902, he was rejected as the Democrats' presidential nominee in 1904, lost the race to become Mayor of New York in 1905 and Governor of the State in 1906, and was crushingly defeated as an independent candidate for the presidency in 1908. His subsequent attempts to gain office were hopeless. In part all this was due to the entrenched power of machine politicians, with whom Hearst negotiated even as he reviled them; in part to the unpopularity of his policies, many of which were regarded as revolutionary. But mainly it was due to public disapproval of the newspapers themselves. As Creelman said, Hearst 'studies the American people from the standpoint of the vaudeville theatre'.[38] Indeed, he instructed his editors to 'Make your readers enjoy reading your paper just as they would enjoy going to an entertaining play'. But the American people turned out to be less malleable and more discerning than he realised.

They saw stunts like the rushing of relief trains to scenes of disaster for exactly what they were. They recognised that Hearst was actually discrediting the genuine muck-rakers of the progressive era by a sensational travesty of their efforts. They disliked Hearst's casually unscrupulous methods, even when these were employed in a good cause—for example, the use of stolen letters to expose senatorial corruption. Most of all, they resented the apparent assumption, made in an editorial and a verse (by Ambrose Bierce), that it was legitimate to murder politicians opposed to Hearst. This kind of journalistic demagogy made it easy to blame President McKinley's assassination on the press baron and after it he was hanged and burnt in effigy. Hearst destroyed all incoming parcels in case they contained bombs, took to carrying a gun and changed the *Journal*'s name to the *American*. He also coined a number of aphorisms exalting the standard of journalistic ethics, for example, 'Honesty is the best publicity'.

Hearst was concerned with what, in current jargon, would be called image-building and bridging the credibility gap. He was anxious to 'establish a reputation for truth and accuracy'. 'We have got to convince our readers of our fairness and our sincerity,' he told his editors. A definite policy must be followed to inflate 'the prestige of the paper, to impress the public with the importance of the paper; to counteract the statements of competitors that the Hearst papers are sensational and contain no matters of dignity'. All types of promotion, like all types of Southern whisky, were good, though some were better than others. Issuing a paper without publicity was like winking at a girl in the dark. Hearst's language was entirely that of the advertiser. Indeed, he had long considered that the newspaper should take the place of the advertising agency and he paid his advertising managers twice as much as his business managers.

Hearst made spasmodic efforts to ensure that the product bore some relation to the claims being made for it. He demanded more plausibility and more decorum. 'No sensation is a sensation unless the reader believes it is true.' A ukase went forth (never enforced) banning words like 'blood' and 'rape' from the headlines. Again:

> We do not want our human interest stuff to be murders and divorces and scandals and things of that kind. We want to relieve these—you may say, criminal human interest stuff,—with human interest stuff of a more refined and reputable kind.

After exhortations of this kind Hearst's publications might become a little less jaundiced. But he soon grew bored with their modest pallor. Unless his journals reverted into their old state he would complain that they were less interesting than the telephone book. Hearst wanted both sensationalism and respectability, both mass circulations and newspapers that appealed to the 'NICEST KIND OF PEOPLE', the middle class.[39] As a pedlar of illusions, he was convinced that self-advertisement could do the trick, provided that it was both insistent and persistent. 'Repetition is reputation,' said Hearst.

Actually, the evil reputation of Hearst's journals stemmed precisely from the contradiction between rhapsodic publicity and squalid reality. In Chicago, for instance, he employed men and methods which reveal *The Front Page* for what it was, a sentimental romance. The *Examiner*'s Walter Howey, the model for Hecht and MacArthur's city editor Walter Burns, was far from being a rogue with a heart of gold. Behind the dreamy manner, the polka-dot bow-tie and the whiff of eau-de-Cologne, was a journalistic thug who 'could plot like Caesar Borgia and strike like Genghis Khan'.[40] Once, however, a victim struck back: Howey had lost an eye in a bar-room brawl when his own tactic of using a smashed whisky bottle as a rapier was turned against him. Howey's glass eye was said to be the one which expressed human warmth and feeling. His character is epitomised by a macabre visit he engineered to the condemned cell on the night before Carl Wanderer's execution. Howey 'seized the bars, jumped up and down like a caged baboon and kept yelling at the prisoner, "Yah Carl! You're going to hang by the neck! By the neck, Carl, by the neck!"'[41] In addition to inventing the 'rewrite battery', where raw news was processed into condensed mush, Howey practised bribery, extortion and fraud, especially the last. A particularly flagrant case concerned a corpse found in a Chicago sewer, which the *Examiner* triumphantly identified as being that of the missing heiress Jean DeKay. On closer inspection the body proved to be indisputably male, whereupon Howey personally dumped it in the river.

The rest of Hearst's staff used similar tactics, for in choosing them he worked on the principle that 'a crook who is a go-getter is better than a Sunday school superintendent who is not a go-getter'. More elevated principles, he remarked drily, were the impediments of small men. When challenging the Chicago *Tribune* (whose ruthless might he much admired) Hearst provided the kind of regular paid employment for criminals not equalled until the rise of bootlegging during the prohibition era. Hearst's circulation department was filled with hoodlums and eventually headed by Dion O'Bannion, one of the most cold-blooded killers in the country. (Needless to say, the resulting gang warfare, in which some thirty newsdealers were murdered, received little or no publicity. Nor did Hearst's use of gangsters to terrorise his own striking journalists qualify as news.) Hearst was also served by minions such as Roy Benziger who, like Howey, possessed a glass eye. This 'he would pluck out of its socket while pleading with some already hysterical parent for a likeness of her ravished and throttled daughter. The gesture usually gained him five minutes of uninterrupted search while the hostess lay in a faint.'[42]

Such conduct was standard practice. Hearst's Chicago journalists thought nothing of starting a riot to make news during the silly season, as one did when he telephoned all the black funeral directors in the city with instructions to undertake the burial of the same corpse. Blackmail was also a great stand-by. It was used with special effect to solicit advertising from a reluctant store. The paper planted a woman in the early stages of smallpox as a shop assistant, 'discovered' her and set up the exposé in type. The store capitulated and the report was never printed. Hearst regarded this carnival of horrors with detached amusement. After some particularly outrageous misdemeanour he might discharge a man, only to employ him again a few weeks later at an increased salary. The hirings and firings occurred with bewildering rapidity: in one period of thirty-seven months the Chicago *American* had twenty-seven city editors. Hearst sacked just as he paid, by results. But he also operated on the whimsical principle, so beloved by press barons, that dismissals helped to keep things moving. His newspaper offices resembled lunatic asylums and their inmates were, if anything, even more neurotic and competitive than the employees of Pulitzer and Northcliffe. As one exclaimed bitterly to Hearst, 'It takes a lot to break my spirit but you surely are a giant'. But as another remarked, at least Hearst never bored anyone who worked for him.

Neither did Hearst bore his countrymen, though he often managed to infuriate them. They abominated Hearst's attempts to use his lengthening chain of newspapers to fetter the public mind. Hearstian policies, even when they commanded support, were too often expressed in the strident tones of the mob orator to command respect. Thus during the First World War he gave isolationism a bad name. Actually in 1914 Hearst did try to intervene. He sent Northcliffe a frantic cable prophesying 'riot and revolution and red anarchy in the centers of government, and relentless revenge of the masses, resentful of their needless sacrifice'.[43] Hearst asked his English counterpart to use the press to halt the conflict. Never was an appeal more fruitless. Northcliffe, who in 1909 had assured the Black Friars that Hearst was not 'a bad man' but a rich one who 'devotes himself to trying to purify American politics', now denounced his publications for their 'damnable' hostility to Britain and soon told him to his face that he was a poor journalist.[44] In fact Hearst commanded his editors, 'In printing war news, please be absolutely neutral and avoid alarmist or biased matter in any way'. But as popular sympathy veered towards the Allies he tried to counteract it. Quite rightly, for example, he exposed atrocity stories about Huns raping nuns as propaganda. Quite grotesquely he went on to suggest that the sinking of the *Lusitania* was due to the incompetence of her crew.

No matter how lavishly his papers displayed the stars and stripes in order to prove their owner's patriotism, no matter how eagerly he cultivated the society of English duchesses, it was impossible to eradicate the impression that Hearst was really pro-German. By the time the United States entered the war he was perhaps the most hated man in the country. He was said to be so mistrusted that he could not have secured congressional endorsement for the Ten Commandments. Bonfires were made of his newspapers and in response to a tumult of cat-calling in cinemas the Hearst-Pathé News Company dropped his name from its title. The mood of national belligerence was such that Hearst was even vilified for being unduly fond of dachshunds. The charge was true: he liked them 'long and racy, like a pirate craft and with long ears and a long prow—I mean nose'. But Hearst's sinister sentimentality embraced all sorts and conditions of dog—he was later to banish James Thurber's canine caricatures from the pages of the New York *American* with the remark, 'I wouldn't have them peeing on my cheapest rug'.[45]

After the war Hearst was still unable to win public favour, even when his papers echoed popular opinions. For example, his opposition to the League of Nations was unconvincing: the man who had in 1914 advocated aggression against Mexico to protect his vast land-holdings there now posed as a lonely pacifist ranged against a wicked gang of international financiers. Similarly his abhorrence of communism might have reflected the national feeling had it not become an obsession which expressed itself in a series of witch-hunts, most notoriously against radical university teachers. In view of his own relationship with Marion Davies, Hearst's assault on Bertrand Russell was the acme of hypocrisy. Russell argued that sexual relations which did not involve children should be regarded as a purely private affair: Hearst wanted him to be banned from New York's City College for preaching 'moral standards of oriental barbarism'.[46]

Finally, Hearst's supposed fondness for fascism provoked a furious campaign of boycott and obloquy during the depression years. One manifestation was the *Anti-Hearst Examiner*, a short-lived publication whose message was summed up in this rhyme:

> Hearst in war, Hearst in peace,
> Hearst in every news release,
> Spreads his filth and desolation,
> To increase his circulation.[47]

Actually, as always, Hearst put America first. He regarded fascism as another European perversion (like British imperialism) whose only useful function might be to fight communism. On the other hand, though he disliked anti-semitism, he was quite prepared to give the Third Reich 'fair treatment' in his papers after signing an agreement in 1934 to supply its press with American news—this was normal business practice. Moreover, he found it difficult to resist the glamour of that 'marvellous man' Mussolini.[48] Hearst told an awed Marion Davies that the Duce had an office which was nearly as big as Louis B. Mayer's at MGM Studios. As late as December 1940 Hearst was instructing his editors that no 'unnecessarily offensive' cartoons of the two Axis leaders were to appear in his newspapers.

By the mid-1930s Hearst's publishing empire had expanded to its furthest extent. He owned twenty-six daily and seventeen Sunday newspapers which took, respectively, 13.6 per cent and 24.1 per cent of the national circulation. He controlled King Features Syndicate which sold its articles to most of the 2,500 papers in the United States and to many more abroad. He also possessed thirteen magazines, including *Cosmopolitan, Harper's Bazaar* and *Good Housekeeping*, three news services, eight radio stations and two film companies. It was the largest communications business in the world and it produced curious contortions among contemporary politicians.

Franklin D. Roosevelt, for example, made the most fulsome overtures to the press baron. In 1932 Hearst had used his influence with the Californian delegation to clinch Roosevelt's nomination as Democratic candidate—the only time he made a president. Before taking office Roosevelt solicited his continuing support. Employing Hearst's editor E. D. Coblentz as an intermediary, he promised to initiate public works, introduce a sales tax, press for government control (eventually state ownership) of railroads, and appoint a 'radical' cabinet. 'There will be no one in it who knows the way to 23 Wall Street,' the President-elect guaranteed, 'No one who is linked in any way with the power trust or with the international bankers.' He concluded:

> Please tell Mr Hearst that I appreciate more than I can say his interest. We are working to a common end and it won't make any difference to me if he disagrees with me on details so long as we are in agreement on the big methods.

Hearst replied that he was 'in enthusiastic accord' with this progressive programme.

He also made the significant remark that 'reasonable reflation is not radicalism. It is intelligent conservatism'. And, growing more conservative as the Depression continued, Hearst was soon accusing Roosevelt of 'wild-eyed radicalism' and incipient dictatorship. So virulent did his campaign against the New Deal become that he eventually had to instruct his papers to find something about the administration to commend: 'Our criticism is almost too uninterrupted to be effective'. As the 1936 election approached Roosevelt rounded on his tormentor via two bitter speeches made by the Interior Secretary, Harold Ickes ('a bad egg', in Hearst's view), and rode triumphantly back to the White House. Hearst felt as if he had been run over by a steam-roller. He was bemused by a victory which seemed to demonstrate the unimportance of the press. From his ivory tower he wrote to J. F. Neylan, his lawyer:

> Do you know why we got such an *awful* beating? . . . I think we are in a new America . . . It's like the new art. There doesn't seem to be any reason for it *but* people want it. There are fashions in politics as in clothes. Old American ideals seem to be as much out of fashion as the frock coat.

Yet despite the breach between them, Roosevelt was still angling for Hearst's support as late as October 1937, when he had another long meeting with Coblentz. The President tried to reassure the press baron that the government's foreign policy would not lead to war. But he also felt able to volunteer some gratuitous counsel calculated to send Hearst into one of his rare tantrums.

Please tell W. R. I advise him to get rid of his poorest papers, to print more news, not to print too many features, keep just the good ones, and to kill his editorial page. Tell him to use it for the good features and to print only the occasional editorial on Page 1.

The fact was that Hearst's empire now showed clear signs of internal decrepitude. Indeed, it was close to collapse.

Hearst had learnt nothing new about journalism since Pulitzer's day. Consequently by the 1920s most of his publications had a time-worn air, of which he was uneasily conscious. Between the wars he constantly attempted to galvanise them into renewed vigour. In 1925 for example, he told Brisbane that the New York *Journal* was 'hopelessly dull and commonplace', and demanded 'a real sporting editor . . . good writers . . . big bold pictures . . vivid circulation making fiction . . . big type . . . Two pages of comics . . . a smashing news page.' But somehow none of this ever materialised. He ordered crusades against vivisectionists and standing armies, cock-fighters and dope-pedlars, bankers and boxers, hangers and strikers, reds and rats. But his editors regarded them as 'bunk' and so did the public. He made the New York *American* adopt the layout of Lord Beaverbrook's *Daily Express*. But though, as Brisbane remarked, 'the mummy wriggled out of its old-time wrappings', no magic ingredient could be found to restore it to life, let alone to give it eternal youth.

Since Goddard's death, Hearst chided, his papers had resembled 'a cotton apple', good to look at but containing 'froth' instead of 'nutriment'. Brisbane himself could think of no sales gimmick more inspiring than 'big type and pink paper', and he complained to Hearst, 'I am an old gentleman, going out the back door'. Occasionally he did conjure up a 'novel stunt', such as his campaign to persuade readers of Hearst's New York *Mirror* to 'Get Married—Have a Baby—Buy an Automobile'.[49] It was pointed out to him that this slogan reversed the normal sequence of events in modern America. He persevered with the endeavour, but it proved a miserable failure.

Like Hearst, Brisbane had become a reactionary. He praised Hitler for murdering homosexuals and Mussolini for massacring Ethiopians. Nero, he maintained, was the greatest man who ever lived: 'He had the courage of his convictions and used the ignorant rabble to achieve his own ends'.[50] Brisbane also deplored the new fashions in morality. He once addressed this stern memorandum to Emile Gauvreau, the *Mirror*'s Managing Editor: 'It is possible to be successful in journalism without borrowing ideas from swine'. The *Mirror* was Hearst's attempt to keep up with the tabloids. It challenged Joseph Patterson's *Daily News* which critics asserted surpassed even Hearst's journals 'in the art

147

of gathering garbage from the gutters of life'.[51] Also in the field was Bernarr Macfadden's *Graphic* which specialised in 'hot news', typified by headlines like 'Three Women Lashed in Nude Orgy'.[52] It was nicknamed the Pornographic and in its offices time was said to stand still, at sex o'clock. Hearst acknowledged that the *Mirror* was unable to compete with the *Graphic*, first because 'we do not want to run that immoral kind of sheet and second because if we did want to run it we could not run it as well as McFadden'.

As it happened, the less scandalous but more virile *News* was to destroy both the *Mirror* and the *Graphic*. Hearst recognised the familiar process of journalistic evolution:

> Tabloids are merely going through the development that standard papers went through in converting sensationalism into genuine merit ... Consider as a guiding motto the statement that the future of newspapers is as tabloids, and the future of tabloids is as Newspapers.

The law of the journalistic jungle was inexorable. Try as he would Hearst, who was prudish enough to deplore a photograph in the *Journal-American* of young ladies playing leapfrog, seemed powerless to make all of his own newspapers fit to survive. His New York flagship became known as 'the vanishing American'. Writing to Lord Beaverbrook in 1932, Roy Howard pronounced what was almost an obituary on his fellow press baron:

> Mr Hearst will rate as one of America's greatest journalists. But the parade has passed him. Today his force is a negative one. He can do no more to retard progress and befuddle political thinking than any other man in America. As a constructive force (which he once was) he is through. I say this with regret because despite his journalistic code and a technique for which I have no respect, I take my hat off to his many great accomplishments, and America has much to thank him for.[53]

Hearst's legendary extravagances were also to blame for the desperate plight of his organisation. Like other contemporary press barons, he had issued shares, raised loans, juggled with holding companies and diversified his interests (mainly into real estate). Unlike his peers, Hearst ploughed little of the money which he raised back into the business. He used the bulk of it to pay for his gargantuan purchases. Indeed, he borrowed more. He seemed to assume that his credit was infinite, writing to Neylan with bland insouciance, 'Do not be alarmed regarding Mr Fleischhacker. We owe him some money. If we do not want to owe it to him, we could owe it to somebody else.' Hearst even raised $600,000 on his principal residence, San Simeon—unwittingly he mortgaged it to the owner of the rival Los Angeles *Times*, Harry Chandler, whom he despised as an 'old maid . . . except for the fact that the comparison is rough on the old maids'.

Hearst lived in a world of financial fantasy and it is in these terms that his mania for acquisition, so often described, must be explained. Hearst bought to create an illusion. He admitted that he took to art as other men take to the bottle. It was a method of keeping reality at bay. This he effectively did with perhaps fifty million dollars worth of Gothic tapestries, medieval panels, Renaissance pictures, Georgian silver, Egyptian mummies, Greek statuary, Roman sarcophagi, Moorish pottery, Spanish monasteries, German armour, Italian choirstalls, French fireplaces, English furniture, Mexican saddles and so on and so forth. This art was not collected for art's sake so much as for the sake of decoration. It was designed to adorn Hearst's various castles. As A. J. Liebling satirically observed, Hearst might feel 'a sudden need of a Louise XV encoignure to make a guest bedroom seem more cozy, or a set of Irish wine fountains and cisterns for an informal supper'.[54]

Hearst's treasures were magnificent props in sets calculated to make Cecil B. DeMille gasp. There was the mock-Bavarian village at Wyntoon, for example, where Hollywood scene-painters provided fairy-tale murals and the three main dwellings were called Angel House, Bear House and Cinderella House. Most famous of all, needless to say, was San Simeon itself, the alabaster palace on the Enchanted Hill. There Hearst slept in Cardinal Richelieu's bed, dwelt in the Celestial Suite, indulged his passion for charades and fancy dress parties (often appearing as Napoleon), surrounded himself with star-spangled celebrities and exotic animals, created dazzling special effects like having the gardens planted overnight with blooming Easter lilies, built towers and tore them down on a whim. He and his architect, Julia Morgan, were alike, according to one who saw them at work, in being 'long distance dreamers'.[55]

Hearst's castle-building took other forms, all of them exorbitantly expensive. Most notorious was his involvement in the tinsel world of stage and screen. His infatuation with showgirls was scarcely assuaged by Millicent Willson, member of a dancing troupe called 'The Merry Maidens', whom he married in 1902. She bore him five sons and he, as Millie complained, 'undid all my discipline by giving them everything they wanted'. She also tolerated his infidelities with other actresses. But when he established a permanent liaison with Marion Davies, in 1915, Millie responded by purchasing a pearl necklace from Tiffany's and sending her husband the bill, which ran into six figures.

Marion Davies was initially unenthusiastic about the affair but, as one of Hearst's cousins said, she 'simply couldn't bypass all the money that was thrown at her'.[56] 'Hearst come, Hearst served,' became her motto, uttered with a delicious stammer. Marion was, by her own admission, a 'silly, giggly idiot'.[57] She appeared to believe that the Second World War had been fought against the Russians, though perhaps this was not surprising, given Hearst's habit of calling the USSR, long after the German invasion, a 'semi-Axis partner'.[58] But Marion's vacuousness was matched by her vivacity. Her angelic face was set off by an impish manner. She enjoyed ice-cream eating races and said that her idea of bliss was to drown in a tub of gin. There was no meeting of minds between them because Marion had no mind to meet, but Hearst preferred women who were built, as he put it, for pleasure rather than business. Marion made him feel young again and he doffed his sombre politician's garb in favour of a pantaloon's outfit—green suits and hand-painted ties. He showered gifts on her with regal profusion, some of them incongruous enough, in all conscience. Dorothy Parker, who was expelled from San Simeon for drinking too much, noted in the visitor's book:

> Upon my honor,
> I saw a Madonna
> Standing in a niche,
> Above the door
> Of the famous whore
> Of a prominent son of a bitch.[59]

Hearst's most lavish present to Marion was her career as a film star, though, paradoxically, he smothered her talent as an actress. He prevented her from playing the tough-moll and comic parts for which she was best suited. Instead he favoured sentimental ingénue roles and costume dramas so chaste that she almost invariably disguised her comely figure in trousers. Cinematic magic was his aim. In 1921 Hearst had maintained that there was 'no such thing as intelligent censorship', but by 1939 he was calling for just that in order to preserve films from the intrusion of reality, or, as he put it, to make them 'a medium of decent entertainment'. The press baron was more entranced by Hollywood's glamour than any professional film mogul. He described it as 'a wonderland of beauty and genius'. But the cost of sustaining his celluloid afflatus was prohibitive. When asked whether there was any money in the motion picture industry Hearst replied dispassionately, 'There are several millions of my money in it'.[60]

With the owner haemorrhaging dollars from every pore it was hardly surprising that his organisation was bleeding to death. Its business manager, Sol Carvalho, had done everything possible to economise, even stumping round the offices on his wooden leg switching off lights. Hearst raided the tills and safes of his newspapers to provide himself with petty cash. He turned his journalists into buyers at a global bazaar. Alice Head, for example, controller of his British magazines, was forever being distracted by cables telling her to purchase the Doge's bonnet, or to procure the bells of Bruges Cathedral and two giraffes in good condition. At the drop of a hat editorial errand-boys had to provide Pomeranian pigeons, a quantity of Chinese musk, ice-cream moulded in the shapes of Mickey Mouse and Donald Duck, a chastity belt for a dachshund. Journalists even supplied Hearst with jokes: he once demanded a list of 'scrambled proverbs' from 'Bugs' Baer, who obliged with such as 'The rich get richer and the poor get children', 'Marry in haste and repent in Reno', 'A miss is as good as she wants to be'.

Hearst's profligate course could only be checked by a financial crash. In 1937, indebted to the tune of well over a hundred million dollars, he found that he could neither borrow more money nor issue more stock. His credit with the Canadian paper companies had run out—he owed them so much that their industry was almost on its knees. To avert bankruptcy he surrendered financial control of his organisation to his old friend Judge Clarence Shearn, counsel of the Chase Manhattan Bank, and a group of trustees. Acknowledging his journalistic skill and accepting his principle that 'no accountant can run a newspaper anywhere but into the ground', they left him as editorial overlord. But they cut his salary to $100,000 a year, despite his objection that this was less than he had paid to Arthur Brisbane.

'I have no money,' he lamented, 'I am just a cheap skate.' In fact he still had about eleven million dollars worth of art objects which the trustees were doing their best to turn into ready cash. They even held sales at Gimbel's store in New York where bric-à-brac from what Hearst called 'the greatest private art collection in the world' covered three and a half acres of floor space. He protested that this was no way to sell antiques, whose value depended on their rarity, and was rebuked by the bankers for not making 'sincere efforts to dispose of personally owned assets'. Everywhere his trustees liquidated and consolidated. But when their work was over Hearst still possessed the biggest publishing institution on earth. By 1942 he had seventeen daily and twelve Sunday newspapers. They were poised to take advantage of the seller's market provided by a war which Hearst, like Beaverbrook in England, had said would never happen. Hearst rightly warned that the glut of advertisements could only damage the papers if they were printed at the expense of news. His instructions were disregarded, which led eventually to a further contraction of his newspaper chain.

But in the short term increased revenue enabled him to regain complete control of it.

For a brief Indian summer Hearst once more played the press baron. He exhorted his sons not to be gentleman-journalists, telling George that he had never worked and ought to try that form of amusement, suggesting that John should be paid by the day in order to compel his attention. Hearst persecuted his editors, campaigned for General MacArthur, denounced the United Nations as a communist plot. Age conferred respectability and he received ingratiating letters from the famous. The Duke of Windsor, for example, subscribed himself 'an ardent admirer of yours and the policy of your press'. Hearst even took to writing a column of his own, somewhat in the style of Brisbane. With their snappy sentences and short paragraphs Hearst's articles were effective journalism. They were marred only by excursions into faddishness and a kind of occult sentimentality: one weird essay about lemmings was punctuated by the mystical refrain, 'Beware of the sea'.[61] But despite all this activity it seemed as though Hearst was only going through the motions. His dreams had been shattered by the curtailment of his independence in 1937 and he never recovered from that rude awakening. He would not acknowledge that he had been overtaken by history. He never recognised that the trustees' success in saving his newspapers symbolised the rise of corporate management and the decline of proprietorial domination. Without grasping the significance of the spectacle, Hearst had witnessed the passing of the press barons.

But he himself refused to pass. Throughout his life Hearst had shunned all reference to death. He had even deplored Arthur Brisbane's 'talking about old age. It is bad for you. Nothing makes you so old as feeling old ... Cut out that old age stuff. You just give me a pain.' Hearst had used his newspapers to explore a variety of more or less scientific methods of rejuvenation. But by the time he reached the age of eighty-eight, in 1951, even the injections of Dr Myron Prinzmetal, a heart specialist (and ironically a secret vivisectionist), could not keep Hearst alive. A friend of Aldous Huxley's visited the press baron some time before the end and gave a gruesome account of conditions at Marion Davies's Beverly Hills mansion:

> The old man, who is dying, emaciated almost to the vanishing point, but desperately clinging to life; (he won't lie down, for fear of not being able to get up again, but spends all his time sitting bolt upright); Marion Davies permanently drunk, dressed only in a dressing gown which constantly flies open at the front, expressing a genuine adoration for Hearst but meanwhile sleeping with the

young Jewish [...] and announcing to all the world that she does so and saying what a stinker he is both in bed and out; in the next breath confiding triumphantly to fellow-Catholic [—] that she has persuaded the old man to leave two million dollars to the convents of Southern California.[62]

Finally, Hearst instructed Marion to 'Stop the bed'. He did not want to get off, merely to arrest the automatic rocking device and die in peace.[63]

There was no rest for his corpse, however. While Marion slept the sleep of the drunk, Hearst's sons, informed of his death by one of the nurses, snatched his body away from her house. She was deeply mortified:

> Old W. R. was gone, the boys were gone. I was alone. Do you realize what they did? They stole a possession of mine. He belonged to me. I loved him for thirty-two years and now he was gone. I couldn't even say goodbye.[64]

After being embalmed Hearst's body was placed under guard to prevent anyone seeing him without an appointment. The funeral was held at Grace Episcopal Cathedral on Nob Hill in San Francisco, not far from his birthplace. Marion was not invited.

But under the complex provisions of Hearst's will, which preserved most of his assets by leaving them to a charitable trust, it looked as though she might be able to take over control of his newspapers. She even tried to exercise authority, talking inebriated nonsense over the telephone which malicious journalists tape-recorded and played back to the organisation's senior executives. It was into their hands that the power eventually fell when Hearst's sons wrested Marion's voting rights away from her. Privately owned (as it still is), the empire was professionally managed and bore many of the hall-marks of a public communications company. For instance, its revenue from newspapers (an abbreviated chain of thirteen dailies) probably constitutes less than a third of an estimated billion-dollar annual income. In fact Hearst's personal fief was finally transformed into a 'multi-media conglomerate'. So ended an epoch which had begun some two generations earlier, when the youthful press baron had first dreamt of becoming 'God Almighty's ghostwriter'.[65]

CHAPTER NINE

The Crusading Imp

WITH THE ADVENT of the twentieth century the press barons developed a sense of common identity. Competition between them was no less fierce than before. Indeed, most would have shared the view which Rothermere, advocating all-out war against the opposition, put to Beaverbrook in 1931: 'The newspaper market is far too crowded. There are not enough readers, or advertisements, to go round. Some elimination would help.' However, despite the open rivalry and the secret back-biting, dog was now reluctant to eat dog. The lords of the fourth estate used their organs of publicity to confer privacy on one another. As the American journalist George Seldes said:

> Publishers [of newspapers] are hardly human beings. They never get shot, they never shoot, they are never co-respondents, they never commit adultery, they are rarely divorced, they know nothing of the 'love-nests' the press talks about; they never sue anyone, they are never sued. They dwell among the untrodden ways, half-hidden from the eye, the faintest violets by the mossy stones of publicity.[1]

This was scarcely an over-statement. In San Francisco, for example, Hearst issued instructions in 1924 that 'nothing unpleasant about Mr de Young [owner of the *Chronicle*] is to be printed whether it is news or not. I think it would be a good policy to adopt not to print any unpleasant things about any newspaperman.'[2]

In London this kind of voluntary embargo extended to the families and sometimes even to the friends of the press barons. '*I loathe personal attacks*', thundered Rothermere, particularly, he added, when they were directed against himself and his intimates. Fleet Street uttered no word about the imprisonment of the homosexual stepson of Lord

Astor, who owned the *Observer*. And when Beaverbrook's son Peter became involved in a court case Lord Southwood assured his father that it was 'not a matter for publicity'—despite the fact that their papers, the *Express* and the *Herald*, were at daggers drawn. 'The Sacred Caste of Newspaper Proprietors' (the phrase, it will be remembered, was Northcliffe's) was increasingly concerned to uphold its own dignity. No one was more devoted to this cause than Beaverbrook. The House of Lords, he maintained, was 'the real and rightful Newspaper Proprietors' Association' and its members must observe the rule of chivalry, at least where their fellows were concerned. He told Lord Camrose that 'newspaper proprietors should endeavour to work together in unity'. When the Beaverbrook press cartooned Lord Rothermere it obtained his prior approval of the drawings. Beaverbrook's partiality for his own order extended across the globe and beyond the grave. The *Daily Express*'s obituary on William Randolph Hearst stated that his hostility to Britain had been exaggerated and that he was one of the great American figures of his age. In dealing with his press peers the imp of Fleet Street invariably played the cherub.

Of course, those inclined to look for it could find in this baleful camaraderie a conspiracy of international proportions. Leo Maxse, for example, editor of the *National Review*, claimed (quite wrongly) that Hearst's press was financially interlocked with Beaverbrook's. Baldwin, when Prime Minister, described Hearst, Beaverbrook and Rothermere as a power-intoxicated triumvirate intent on dictating, domineering and blackmailing. Upton Sinclair proclaimed that the press was 'a gigantic munition-factory, in which the propertied class manufactures mental bombs and gas-shells for the annihilation of its enemies'.[3] Marxist historians today argue that the press barons were a cartel of capitalists plotting to exercise 'social control' by means of ideological indoctrination.[4] But all this is to ignore the operations of a newspaper magnate like E. W. Scripps, whose revolutionary creed was 'God damn the rich and God help the poor'.[5] It is also to deny the most striking characteristic of the press barons—an individuality so pronounced that it constantly teetered into eccentricity.

True, there were many superficial similarities between Beaverbrook and Hearst, private prurience and public puritanism, for instance. Early in his career as a press baron Beaverbrook even sent the editor of the *Express* to pick Hearst's brains: he found the lord of San Simeon 'a weird and dangerous proposition'. But Beaverbrook sought advice voraciously and took it abstemiously. He can no more be identified with Hearst than with Northcliffe, who provided him with a challenge rather than a model.

Northcliffe was so infinitely the greatest figure in the Fleet Street of 1920 that I never considered anybody else in relation to my own journalistic ambitions. I definitely set out to compete with that overwhelming personality and all the power it stood for.

Thus Beaverbrook saw himself as belonging to a journalistic tradition and a proprietorial freemasonry. Though preferring to be called 'the Lord' rather than 'the Chief', he adopted many familiar policies and practices. For example, in harrying his staff he matched Pulitzer, Northcliffe and Hearst. He was capable of sending his editors 147 directives in a single day and delivering peremptory summonses to his secretaries while they were in the lavatory. One was so exasperated that he bellowed at the butler through the door, 'Tell the Lord I'm having a shit, and I can only deal with one shit at a time'.[6] Far from being offended by this riposte Beaverbrook roared with laughter. He did resemble his peers, especially in being unpredictable, unique, his own man entirely.

Lord Beaverbrook accounted for his nonconformist character in various ways. He liked to suggest that he had become a pioneer in response to the harsh and impoverished circumstances of his Canadian childhood. Pursuing the geographical theme, he would dramatise himself as a cataclysmic natural force:

> On the rockbound coast of New Brunswick, the waves beat incessantly. Every now and then comes a particularly dangerous wave that breaks viciously on the rocks. It is called 'Rage'. That's me.[7]

Elsewhere Beaverbrook attributed his exceptional nature to having been run over by a mowing machine. He explained that the crack which the wheel gave his boyish skull allowed the brain room to expand. Beaverbrook was as prone as most successful men to indulge in fantasies about his childhood. The facts are that he was born, plain William Maxwell Aitken, in 1879 and spent his early years amidst a large, prosperous family at Newcastle, New Brunswick. His mother, whose drive and energy, quicksilver mind and effervescent spirits he shared, was the daughter of an affluent Canadian store-keeper. His Scottish father, from whom he learnt a stern Calvinistic ethic, was the local Presbyterian minister. That ethic Beaverbrook obeyed occasionally, breached often, but honoured always. He did not conform even to Nonconformity.

However, throughout his life Beaverbrook's most profound conviction was that an Inferno of fire and brimstone awaited the souls of the damned. So it should be, Randolph Churchill remarked, 'seeing that they've been getting the place ready for him specially all these years'.[8] His deep-rooted and sincere belief in hell-fire was no joke, even if Beaverbrook himself sometimes treated it as such—one of the many paradoxes into which he was led by his religious beliefs. He might flippantly declare, 'My Christianity is quite simple ... God is Moderator of the Church of Scotland'.[9] He might intone Presbyterian hymns when drunk, climbing up the book-case like a monkey at any reference to being heavenward bound. But this verse, which Beaverbrook was fond of reciting, indicates that he felt himself predestined to eternal torment.

> I know that God is wroth with me
> For I was born in sin.
> My heart is so exceeding vile
> Damnation dwells therein.
> Awake I sin, asleep I sin,
> I sin with every breath.
> When Adam fell he went to hell
> And damned us all to death.[10]

There are many exits from Calvin's labyrinth. Beaverbrook's peculiarity was that he tried them all, sometimes simultaneously.

Thus he attempted to convince himself that he was saved, issuing divine propaganda from a Presbyterian press and erecting a large illuminated cross in the grounds of his country house 'to remind myself that I am a Christian'.[11] Then he acquiesced in damnation, letting himself (in the words of one editor of the *Express*) be 'possessed of a devil like some figure in the Old Testament',[12] eschewing post-coital remorse in the arms of his mistresses in favour of a great laugh at the point of orgasm. More frequently, like the adroit go-between he was, Beaverbrook endeavoured to reconcile the powers of light and darkness, wanting to be Prime Minister and Leader of the Opposition at the same time, planning a compromise peace with Hitler in March 1940.[13] H. G. Wells wrote, 'If Max gets to Heaven he won't last long. He will be chucked out for trying to pull off a merger between Heaven and Hell . . . after having secured a controlling interest in key subsidiary companies in both places, of course.'[14] Earthly entrepreneurship was Beaverbrook's final refuge from the wrath to come. Like many Protestants, he believed that accumulating capital here below, through industry and thrift, was a means of laying up treasure in heaven.

Actually Beaverbrook became a 'Maxi-millionaire' (his term) before he was thirty by shunning these traditional virtues. He was energetic rather than industrious, an 'imp of mischief' at school who was bored by formal instruction and kept 'switching from one idea to another'.[15] The records, some of which he destroyed, do not show whether Beaverbrook was dishonest in his Canadian dealings, though one of his private secretaries believes that his fortune was founded on a swindle. Certainly Beaverbrook was devious and deceitful and he never lost the reputation of being a 'shady financier'.[16] As for thrift, he alternated between neurotic penny-pinching, calculated generosity and extravagant gambles. Even as a boy he loved the drama of speculation and knew the exchange value of every marble in town. But appropriately he made his first money from selling and then writing for newspapers. At the age of thirteen he even founded, printed and published a news-sheet of his own, entitled *The Leader*. It closed down abruptly when his father discovered that Max was working on it during the Sabbath.

Anyway there was no quick cash to be made in running a one-man press. On leaving school Max dabbled in law but found that too slow. Then he worked as a 'sky-blue drummer', a pedlar of hope in the insubstantial form of life-insurance. Finally, after what he later compared to an Evangelical conversion on his twenty-first birthday, which shrivelled up his idle, poker-playing ways like a devouring flame, he became a seller of bonds, a promoter of companies, a fixer of deals. His take-overs and consolidations flourished during Canada's boom years after the turn of the century. The young Aitken completed each transaction, took his profit and moved on. In 1910, having pulled off a huge, rewarding and much-criticised cement merger, he made a pilgrimage to the land of his father. In Britain an ardent patriot with a fortune at his disposal might effect a true merger between the increasingly separatist elements of the Empire. Failing that, he could at least enjoy the thrill of being at the hub of events, which was situated somewhere between Fleet Street and Downing Street. Beaverbrook evidently decided that the spot was marked by Stornoway House, which he later bought. It was decorated with flying cherubims and flanking its majestic portals sat two wooden lions which were said to wink whenever a virgin entered the premises.

In Canada Aitken had cultivated the press and once he nearly bought a newspaper (the Montreal *Gazette*) in order to advance his commercial ventures. So it was natural that he should seek an instrument of propaganda to realise his political schemes in England. These developed apace. In 1910 Aitken lavished cash, push and an urchin charm which seemed to transform complete strangers into boyhood chums overnight, on the constituency of Ashton-under-Lyne. Despite his incomprehensible accent and his habit of referring to dollars and cents instead of pounds and pence, he was elected as

Conservative member of parliament. In 1911 he helped to promote his friend Andrew Bonar Law as the compromise candidate who succeeded Balfour as leader of the Tory party. Aitken was widely regarded as being Law's evil genius (long before he became Churchill's) for they seemed to have nothing in common except a Scottish-Canadian ancestry and a manse upbringing. In fact the bright Aitken gave the dour Law devil-may-care entertainment, receiving in exchange 22-carat respectability. He assisted Law in business as well as politics and, to the scandal of their countrymen, the 'arch-mergerer' and 'wholesale stock waterer'[17] took his reward in the shape of a knighthood.

In the same year Sir Max established his connection with the *Daily Express*, which had been founded in 1900 as Arthur Pearson's answer to Northcliffe's *Daily Mail*. Pearson had gone blind and (unlike Pulitzer) relinquished control of his newspaper, which was slowly sinking into a morass of debt. Its popular American-born editor, R. D. Blumenfeld, an apprentice of James Gordon Bennett's, appealed to Aitken who bailed out the *Express* with his own and Conservative party funds. According to Rothermere, Aitken effectively controlled the paper from 1912 onwards. But he did not formally become its owner until December 1916, a fact he concealed from the public because it coincided with his involvement in the 'honest intrigue' by which Lloyd George replaced Asquith as Prime Minister. Insiders were not deceived, of course. 'The newspaper world of London is like a great telephone exchange,' Rothermere observed. 'All interested know who is behind each paper.' And in a bitter missive to Beaverbrook Margot Asquith described the removal of her husband as a triumph of 'light principles, heavy purses and a large "controlled press"'. Beaverbrook was to boast that the coup was the greatest thing he ever did.

In fact his achievement was limited to effecting a shaky alliance between the two men who could topple Asquith, Bonar Law and Lloyd George. For this he was ennobled. He later claimed that by going to the upper house, that 'mausoleum of weary titans',[18] he had committed political suicide. But at the time he 'very much wanted to be a peer'.[19] Taking his cue from Northcliffe (who received a telegram from him signed 'Titken' and expressed the amiable hope that this was not to be his new title), Baron Beaverbrook was soon investigating and interfering with the government's business. Unpropitiated the press barons could, Lloyd George believed, tear his coalition apart like the Whig dukes of old. So he contrived to give them office without power. In 1918 the Ministry of Information was created, as H. G. Wells wrote, 'to prevent Lord Beaverbrook from becoming too well-informed'.[20]

It was naturally gratifying to be what Blumenfeld called 'de facto a monumental nabob not behind but in front of the curtain'. But, like Northcliffe, Beaverbrook learnt the painful lesson that in government he was bound by party ties and gagged by red tape. He discovered that his main enemy was not the Germans but the British—the aristocratic Foreign Office deprived this parvenu of the intelligence he needed to do his job. Beaverbrook was thus intensely frustrated during the rest of the war and delighted to demobilise his ministry, in two days, when hostilities ceased. He vowed never to join another government save in time of national emergency. Nothing, he was determined, would henceforth compromise his independence. His resolve was soon put to the test.

In peace-time Beaverbrook began to devote more of his energies to the press. The occupation was a marvellous stimulant: if sex was his 'social champagne',[21] journalism was his political whisky. 'There is surprise after surprise for the man who is connected with a newspaper,' he said. 'Every day a newspaper grows more exciting.'[22] It became quite intoxicating when mixed with mischief and served without restraint. The Conservatives, who held a substantial minority share in the *Express*, complained that the paper was not acting in the traditional way of subsidised organs—making a show of independence while really disseminating party propaganda. Beaverbrook refused to toe the Tory line. Instead he resolutely pursued 'my only quest ... the Holy Grail of Empire',[23] which in 1921 took the somewhat unheroic form of campaigning against an embargo on imported Canadian cattle. The Conservatives' chairman, Sir George Younger, actually blamed the maverick *Express* for the breakdown in Bonar Law's health. Beaverbrook was unmoved by this specious charge and declared that the prerogative of the press barons was 'complete independence'.[24]

Over the next few years Beaverbrook established himself as the champion of Greater Britain and the hammer of governments which were weak in the imperial faith. In the process he justified and asserted his own power as a press baron. Formerly, he said, journalists had fawned on politicians in return for scraps of information. A few press potentates like Delane had been strong enough to resist the system but they had operated within a small circle and among a privileged electorate. Northcliffe had created the popular press and inaugurated a period in which newspaper proprietors treated with statesmen on equal terms. Now conflict between Fleet Street and Downing Street was inevitable; it was also desirable, for each force acted as a check on the other. So far this was a standard account. But in 1926, spurred on by his hostility to the new Tory Prime Minister, Stanley Baldwin, Beaverbrook began to conjure up the press barons' familiar fantasies about using newspapers to coerce governments.

In a remarkable speech, revised by Rothermere, who himself talked blithely about making and breaking ministries, Beaverbrook set out to demonstrate:

> the efficacy of the weapon of the Press. When skilfully employed at the psychological moment no politician of any party can resist it. It is a flaming sword which will cut through any political armour ... That is not to say that any great newspaper or group of newspapers can enforce policies or make or unmake Governments at will, just because it is a great newspaper. Many such newspapers are harmless because they do not know how to strike or when to strike. They are in themselves unloaded guns. But teach the man behind them how to load and what to shoot at, and they become deadly. It is only genius which can so load and point. The risks of its control are therefore limited seeing that genius is rare. And this is well for if it ever fell into the hands of a thoroughly unscrupulous man of genius, there is no limit to the harm it might do. It might become a power which would have to be curbed at all costs.

Beaverbrook went on to envisage the havoc that might be wreaked in Britain by a brilliant and ruthless press magnate using the 'personal' methods of American journalism—he mentioned no names but obviously had Hearst in mind. Beaverbrook concluded by saying that if he really had been prosecuting a vendetta against Baldwin, as Conservatives alleged, he would have adopted the transatlantic techniques. Instead, just as Clive was astonished at his own moderation, Beaverbrook marvelled at 'my own strict adherence to journalistic scruple'. Baldwin had been warned, and so had England. The crusader of the *Express* was on the march and his sword would not sleep in his hand until he had built an imperial New Jerusalem.

Beaverbrook's confidence stemmed from the fact that in the decade after the war he taught himself to be a press baron. As Beverley Baxter, Blumenfeld's successor on the *Express*, wrote to Beaverbrook, 'We brought to English journalism all the freshness and some of the absurdities of the amateur. We rolled the sub-editors in the dust. We made monkeys of the trained professional journalist.' During the 1920s the *Express* challenged the *Mail* and by 1935 its daily circulation had reached two million, the highest in the world. In 1918 Beaverbrook founded the *Sunday Express* which, after huge injections of capital and bloody purges of failed editors, had become a thriving concern. And in 1923 he acquired the London *Evening Standard* for nothing, as a result of a complicated deal in which he first bought and then sold (to Rothermere) the Hulton chain of publications.

Like so many of his peers Beaverbrook was no innovator in journalism. He plagiarised and improvised. As he told Arthur Brisbane in 1926, 'I have tried to imitate your methods ... I always read the best American newspapers for ideas and this applies equally to style and treatment in leaders—as let us say to advertising'. Of course, there were some techniques which Beaverbrook never needed to learn. For instance, thoroughly impatient himself, he had a natural gift for compression; endlessly curious (he likened himself to an old concierge) he had an infallible nose for news. Beaverbrook wished the *Express* to have a broad appeal and he eventually created a newspaper that was unique in attracting an equal number of readers of different classes, ages and sexes. He achieved this by snatching and matching appropriate parts from the bodies of his rivals and galvanising the new carcase with his own abundant energy. Thus in 1919 he rejected Blumenfeld's crude method of raising the *Sunday Express*'s circulation by means of 'freaks—mild forms of pornography'. Beaverbrook banned sensation, scandal and the revelation of official secrets. He led the conspiracy of press silence concerning Edward VIII and Mrs Simpson, and never seriously breached the British tradition that information about public affairs is the private property of the government.

He wanted a family newspaper which was lively, gossipy and entertaining—though never ironical, sophisticated forms of humour being beyond the British. It must concern itself chiefly with politics, money and sex (decorously presented), or any combination of these three. It must be superficially dashing but fundamentally respectful towards the proprieties, infernally brilliant but essentially reverent towards Christianity. Consistency was a vice, Beaverbrook maintained, and in some respects his newspapers reflected that view; in the 1920s, for example, the *Daily Express* contradicted itself horribly on the subject of votes for flappers.[25] But, whatever they said, he insisted that the editorials must be as authoritative as the voice of God speaking from on high. It turned out that this voice was not still and small but loud and rasping, with a pronounced Canadian accent. Its favourite means of communication was the telephone and calls were liable to come at any time of the day or night. Behind the Biblical cadences harassed editors could sometimes catch the tinkle of profane laughter. The master was abusing them for the amusement of a mistress.

Beaverbrook's wayward behaviour inspired a fierce sycophancy among his minions. 'He is Allah' said Beverley Baxter, 'and the rest of us are his prophets.'[26] As such Beaverbrook naturally moved in a mysterious way. He dictated letters wearing nothing but a Panama hat, interviewed employees in his bath, received subordinates while seated on the lavatory, gulping down liquid paraffin and cursing his constipation. Beaverbrook cherished the text which the press barons might have adopted as their motto: 'He whom the Lord loveth he chasteneth'. The staff at the *Express* were systematically hounded and insulted. 'It was like living with an earthquake,' said Blumenfeld.[27] Beaverbrook denounced them for making so many 'wicked' mistakes that, 'like the hairs of the head, it is doubtful if they can be numbered'. One editor of the *Evening Standard*, E. T. Raymond, was driven so hard that he suffered a heart attack and died; Blumenfeld himself was humiliated into retirement by being told that his office was required for other purposes, and Arthur Christiansen received similar treatment; lesser fry were bullied so unmercifully that one of them described Beaverbrook as 'the unacceptable face of human nature'.[28] Beaverbrook even taunted them for prostituting their pens to the highest bidder. It is true that, despite momentary anxieties about extravagant spending on items like matches, he paid generously. Yet he was not served exclusively by grovelling masochists or avaricious Fleet Street-walkers.

For if Beaverbrook was a monster of malignity one minute he was a paragon of loving-kindness the next. He attracted by witchery as much as he repelled by savagery. In the words of Peter Howard (Beaverbrook's protégé who later became leader of Moral Rearmament), 'He possessed the genius of planting his boot in your pants and at the same time playing a tune with his hand on your heart-strings'.[29] Beaverbrook's last editor of the *Evening Standard*, Charles Wintour, made much the same point: 'He was an immense mixture of malice and fun, and sometimes the malice got totally out of hand—though he would undoubtedly regard the malice as fun'.[30] Beaverbrook generated around himself an atmosphere of glamour and exhilaration as well as struggle and competition. It was especially palpable on the platform. One *Express* reporter, having watched his employer addressing an Empire Free Trade rally, noted in his diary:

> Lord Beaverbrook, a dreamer, deep-set eyes that look right through you; bubbles with ideas, slogans, acrobatic phrases. Resourceful under fire [from hecklers]; swaggeringly indiscreet in his criticisms, a great showman, an upsetter of custom and tradition, a foe of stupidity and a born heckler himself. A Puck with both hands full of fire-crackers.[31]

Despite Beaverbrook's reputation of being 'a kind of Dracula, Svengali, Iago and Mephistopheles rolled into one', Michael Foot came to love him as 'a second father'.[32] The many Scotsmen whom Beaverbrook employed (both from native partiality and on

Northcliffe's principle that they were hungry men) respected his natural flair for the craft to which their countrymen have made such an outstanding contribution, in the Old World and the New. Perhaps, too, they were inured to the sort of Knoxian fulminations which Beaverbrook trumpeted down the telephone. These were interspersed with frequent cries of 'Hallelujah!', his favourite mode of greeting anonymous items in the *Evening Standard* which he had written himself.

Beaverbrook's journalists were thus willingly energised by his vitality, even at the price of occasional rude shocks. But none of them truly shared his vision, which was Beaverbrook's other chief attribute as a press baron. His imperial ideas were actually a muddle. They were a nostalgic salute to a Chamberlainite past which had anyway been largely fantasy and certainly could not be revived. Neither the incoherence nor the irrelevance mattered, for Beaverbrook's vision was justified by its very perversity. His Empire Free Trade Crusade, which rumbled on between the wars and reached its climax in about 1930, was a larger version of Bennett's 'Old Philadelphia Lady' or Northcliffe's anti-German slogan, 'They will cheat you yet, those Junkers'. It was not a serious attempt to protect imperial commerce via a customs union (which the dominions and colonies wanted even less than the mother country) so much as a trade-mark. People noticed the *Express* because it was bright, interesting and different. The paper was informed by a quixotic spirit and a dogmatic purpose. It was the pulpit of a hobgoblin-like evangelist whose eloquence compelled attention.

His struggle to convert the Tory leader to the gospel of imperial economic unity was especially piquant:

> Mr Baldwin is the champion of all backsliders. We believe we have brought him to grace; we lift up our voices in a hymn of rejoicing; and we have hardly got through the first line of it before we see him crawling down the aisle again.[33]

Baldwin deeply resented being preached at by someone whom he regarded as at once a diabolical corrupter of youth and a 'black Calvinist' who would 'probably end up a religious maniac'.[34] He was profoundly affronted by Beaverbrook's automatic, and often bizarre, recourse to the Scriptures. To give one example out of many: when Beaverbrook was going to make a political speech in mid-Bedfordshire he asked his secretary what the constituency's main crop was, receiving the answer, 'Brussels sprouts'. 'Brussels sprouts, eh,' he mused, 'Find me something in the Bible about Brussels sprouts'.[35] Whenever Beaverbrook was ill, Baldwin said, he (Baldwin) heard the flames of hell roaring for him. Even when Beaverbrook escaped from a motor-car accident and gave him a thank-offering of £25,000 to distribute to charity, Baldwin described it as 'Sucking up to Satan'.[36] Consequently the Conservative leader was only too pleased to use his cousin Kipling's famous phrase in a withering indictment of the alliance which Beaverbrook and Rothermere had deployed against him. By means of 'direct falsehood, misrepresentation, half-truths, . . . suppression', the press barons aimed at 'power without responsibility—the prerogative of the harlot throughout the ages'.[37]

Baldwin's barb is invariably cited as the ultimate denigration of the press barons. Really it was a tribute to their tumultuous independence—instead of bedding down exclusively with a political party they were whoring after strange gods of their own. However, the effect was explosive not just because of the unparliamentary language but because, before Baldwin flung his dart, the two frogs had indeed puffed themselves up to look like bulls. Between them Beaverbrook and Rothermere completely dominated the popular press. But their alliance seemed all the more formidable for each having bought large share-holdings in the other's newspapers. In practice, however, this was a weakness, for the partnership was uneven and uneasy. Beaverbrook benefited from diversifying into a larger press group which disgorged lavish dividends. Rothermere suffered because most of the *Express*'s profits were ploughed back into the business. Thus, in effect, the *Mail* was subsidising its chief competitor. For a time Beaverbrook paid Rothermere in flattery: 'You are incomparably the biggest figure in current journalism', and 'Your bigness of heart and head give me the right to rejoice in the friendship of a very great man'. But after 1929 Rothermere sought payment in a harder currency. Indeed, according to Camrose, he thought about nothing but money, had gone crazy and was following in his brother's footsteps. In reality Rothermere had been hurt by the slump, to such an extent that he went on a rigorous diet at Dr Dengler's sanatorium in Baden-Baden. He told Beaverbrook, 'Physically I desire to conform more to the diminished figure of my fortune'.

Consequently, in 1933 the two press barons severed their financial links. But the friction between them had not only been caused by commercial differences. Despite their superficial agreement on the issue of Greater Britain, Rothermere's priority was political control of the colonies, especially India, whereas Beaverbrook's was economic union with the dominions, especially Canada. Also Beaverbrook wanted the Conservative party to adopt Empire Free Trade whereas Rothermere aspired to create an Imperialist party which would adopt the Conservatives. He suggested that Beaverbrook should build up a caucus of MPs and candidates by giving out 'directorships in your papers'.

For ten or fifteen thousand a year in directorships you can certainly get twenty 'trustys'. If you, with my assistance, can overthrow the Central Conservative organisation, the Conservative Party is ours.

Rothermere did not attempt to conceal his dictatorial assumptions and privately Beaverbrook complained that he trampled all over the Empire Free Trade campaign 'like a bloody elephant'.[38] Beaverbrook disliked the alien forms of extremism to which Rothermere was drawn. Nothing good could come from abroad, he opined, for while Britishers entered the Kingdom of Heaven foreigners went down to Hell. Beaverbrook did not even dissent from the opinion of H. A. Gwynne (editor of the moribund *Morning Post*, whose circulation was said to be declining each day by the number of persons appearing in its death columns): 'Rothermere will kill you not unwittingly by his appalling personality'. Gwynne was a true prophet and Beaverbrook became increasingly inclined to criticise and even to mock his ally, though invariably behind his back. At the time of the abdication crisis he suggested that Mrs Simpson should marry Rothermere and then she could become Queen of Hungary.

Thus Baldwin was able to exploit the differences between the press barons and to chastise Beaverbrook with Rothermere. The breakdown of their alliance demonstrates once more that the press barons were too individualistic to submerge themselves in any kind of a cabal. The effect of Baldwin's final paean of devastation was to show that their power was anyway illusory. Indeed, the failure of the Empire Free Trade crusade provides a classic example of the impotence of the press in the face of hostile public opinion. Of course the press barons did not need Mass-Observation's research to tell them that readers avoided editorials. But even they must have been surprised to discover that only half the 'top people' who, as the advertisements later said, took the *Times*, bothered to glance at its leading articles. The figure for the *News of the World*, which broke all records with a post-war sale of eight and a half million, was one per cent.[39] Most readers paid little attention to their own newspapers' political campaigns and the *Express*'s antics were dismissed by those who did as Beaverbrookian mischief-making, a verbal version of David Low's cartoons. So wayward did its proprietor become that eventually cynics said of the *Daily Express*, as of the Chicago *Tribune*, that no cause was truly lost until that newspaper supported it. But Beaverbrook showed that in an engine of propaganda the engine matters more than the propaganda. His steamed ahead despite its cumbersome freight. Even his personal unpopularity could not slow it down—Beaverbrook scandalised many by announcing that as spending was the way out of the Depression he intended to set an example of extravagance in his own life.

Even the *Daily Herald*, whose mode of progress was to buy readers by means of free gifts, could not for long overtake the *Express*. But for a time, as Rothermere told Beaverbrook, it threatened to force them both 'into a back seat in the newspaper world'. The *Herald*'s colourless controller, Julius Elias (later Lord Southwood), knew nothing about newspapers except how to print them. As far as he was concerned they were a commodity to be manufactured and marketed. He hardly even read them, just brooded over their appearance. Elias employed thousands of door-to-door canvassers to obtain new subscribers by offering free overcoats, underwear, books, boots, tea sets, cutlery, mangles and mincing machines. He thus provoked the most bitter sales war Fleet Street had ever witnessed. Its effect was to extend the habit of taking newspapers down the social scale: the circulation of the national press increased from 4.7 million in 1926 to 10.6 million in 1939. But its cost was breath-taking, £3 million a year at its peak. Elias was compelled to strive for a huge circulation because, with its socialist policies and its working-class readership, his paper could not otherwise appeal to advertisers. As Beverley Baxter observed, the *Herald*'s main attraction was free mangles for it was 'a machine-made product almost completely without personality'. Consequently Elias resisted his competitors' pleas for peace. At the end of one abortive conference at the Savoy Hotel Beaverbrook confronted him furiously. 'Elias! This is war—war to the death.' Then, drawing an imaginary sword, he added, 'I shall fight you to the bitter end', and stabbed his adversary in the heart.[40]

It was an appropriately theatrical gesture, for Beaverbrook preferred play wars to real ones. Rather than risk getting hurt he always sought victory by other means. So he was soon writing friendly letters to Elias, congratulating him on the 'purely personal' success he had achieved with the *Herald*.

> The man makes the business. Momentum may carry the business on. Founding it depends on a single individual in every case. Ecce hommo! [*sic*] Do you know what that means? I do. Somebody told me.

But Beaverbrook's hostility burned more brightly in secret. He bestowed disparaging nicknames on his ennobled rival, among them 'Lord South Pole'. And he attempted to crush the *Herald* by the covert process of raising wages and increasing the *Express*'s work-force. Beaverbrook was sowing the wind and not only his own papers but the whole of Fleet Street would reap the whirlwind. In the short term, however, the policy had two desirable effects from Beaverbrook's point of view. First, it subjected the *Herald*, which was forced to keep pace, to intolerable financial strain. Secondly, it improved the *Express* in technical efficiency and editorial quality. Much to the distress of his tight-fisted general manager, E. J. Robertson, Beaverbrook built up the best journalistic staff that money could buy. He sought talent indefatigably and asserted that 'You cannot run good newspapers without extravagance'.[41] The baby-faced new editor of the *Express*, Arthur Christiansen, even encouraged the stylists among his foreign correspondents to cable their stories with punctuation, including commas at fourpence halfpenny each. But when it was suggested that the paper owed its triumphant advance to Christiansen, Beaverbrook literally beat his breast like an Old Testament prophet.

His indignation was understandable for Christiansen acknowledged himself to be in many respects Beaverbrook's own creation. In the very act of creation Beaverbrook demonstrated his power with a familiar baronial tactic. He promoted Baxter to the managing editorship of the *Express* while appointing Christiansen editor. Neither knew who was in charge. Beaverbrook told the former, 'You'll have to be careful not to let this fellow Christiansen have his head too much at first'. He advised the latter, 'You'll have to watch that fellow Baxter—don't let him sit on you'.[42] In 1933 Christiansen won when Baxter resigned. But (until his heart attack in 1956) there was never any doubt that Christiansen was merely chief technician at the *Express*. And this despite the fact that Beaverbrook made as many curtain calls as a prima donna—journalists greeted the regular announcement that he was relinquishing control of his newspapers with ribald laughter. Nevertheless Christiansen, who worked, at Beaverbrook's insistence, more days than God, deserves credit for transforming the *Express* into the glossiest journalistic package on Fleet Street.

His layout, which focused attention on the main news, was startling and effective. It was imitated even in America and Christiansen in turn imported a number of transatlantic techniques to brighten up the paper. Timestyle, words telescoped, sentences inverted, adjectives jazzed up, he copied from Henry Luce. Luce, incidentally, was fascinated by Beaverbrook: 'My God, what a man, in his huge London Palace-Prison, in his terrifying and fantastically expensive discomfort—Power, Power, Power'.[43] And, like Luce, Christiansen sometimes let style determine content. He preferred trivial stories about people to serious ones about things, and even they were transformed by lavish presentation and injections of human interest. Hearst had aimed to provoke the 'Gee Whiz' emotion in his readers and Christiansen echoed:

My approach to newspapers was based on the idea that when you looked at the front page you said: 'Good heavens,' when you looked at the middle page you said: 'Holy Smoke,' and by the time you got to the back page—well, I'd have to utter a profanity to show how exciting it was.[44]

Of course, profanity was not permitted in the pages of the *Express*. And Beaverbrook ensured that the paper's style, whatever else it did, subserved his policies—in the *Evening Standard*, by contrast, he permitted all sorts of titillating heresies. To sum up, then, Arthur Christiansen was Lord Beaverbrook's poodle. A picture of the two men was once taken which the editor asked the proprietor to autograph for him. Beaverbrook refused on the grounds that it spoke for itself about their relationship. The photograph shows Christiansen smiling obsequiously at his master and receiving in return a glance of sardonic amusement.

Beaverbrook's control over the *Express* was no less effective for being exercised at a distance. For, in spite of living in or near London, he was an absentee proprietor. He claimed never to have set eyes on the opaque glass building, known to its inhabitants as the 'Black Lubyanka', erected to house the *Express*. He became, indeed, something of a metropolitan hermit, seldom accepting invitations and preferring to eat at his own table. This was partly because he was a hypochondriac of fundamentalist convictions. Indeed, he outdid Pulitzer in this respect and rivalled Lord Riddell, controller of the *News of the World*, who was so convinced that a print union leader carried germs that he refused the man admittance to his house and would only speak to him through the letter-box. Beaverbrook was forever taking his temperature and monitoring his bowel movements. He loved to fill the *Express* with tales of new plagues and new cures. The presence of a pimple on his leg caused him such acute anxiety that he persuaded an attractive dinnner guest to rub it better, caressing, in return, a spot on her breast. When the actress Ruby Miller met him for lunch in Monte Carlo Beaverbrook ate only a few nasty-looking gooseberries, talked theosophy for two hours and 'definitely decided that he had only a few more days to live'.[45] His poor health was not quite imaginary. During the war Beaverbrook was so tormented by asthma that he seriously considered flying in a Wellington bomber all night long at ten thousand feet in order to get some sleep.

Another reason for his reclusive behaviour was shyness, strange in a public figure famous for his ebullience. Actually the cartoons which represented him as the little man with the big grin were misleading. True, he was a sparkling host, quick, clever, funny, able to bring out the best in the frequenters (often mutually hostile) of his richly mixed gatherings. And he loved to surround himself with fascinating (and fascinated) women, whom he rewarded well and treated badly—he gave them lavish presents and £100 Christmas bonuses but he was never faithful and when one mistress became pregnant, and wanted to bear his child, he forced her to have an abortion. The fact was that Beaverbrook was only at ease with people he could dominate. At Stornoway House or Cherkely Court (near Leatherhead, which rivalled Sandringham as the ugliest mansion in the country) his whim was law. Harold Nicolson was struck by the fact that all Beaverbrook's visitors were frightened of him. The novelist William Gerhardie, though mesmerised by his host's 'eyes like Ivan the Terrible's', found that his unique charm ('a combination of seemingly irresponsible gaiety and an attitude of appealing confidingness, the whole encased in an armour of power and wealth') was spoilt by an 'air of "What I say, goes"'.[46] At home Beaverbrook could ignore his wife (who died in 1927), bully his children, persecute his servants and master his friends.

He could also escape the bitch boredom which continually dogged his heels—when Winston Churchill addressed Beaverbrook like a public meeting he retaliated by switching on the wireless. At his private cinema he watched all the new films, preferring them to plays because he could talk throughout. His favourite was *Destry Rides Again*, a western starring Marlene Dietrich, which he saw sixteen times and regarded as a greater work of art than the Mona Lisa. Beaverbrook even bought a residence at Newmarket which, as if to propitiate the God of his fathers, he called Calvin House. But he did not enjoy the spectacle of his racehorses finishing last and soon abandoned the sport and the house. Even in his own domestic fortress Beaverbrook could not really relax: visiting the bombed ruin of Stornoway House during the war he urinated in the dining-room, explaining to Percy Cudlipp that for years he had wanted to relieve himself during dinner parties but had always been too nervous to leave the table. Nothing could for long satisfy what Beaverbrook once called his 'restless and meddlesome mind' save the constantly shifting kaleidoscope of journalism. The *Sunday Express* owed its very existence to the fact that 'he was bored on Saturday afternoons'.[47]

War itself, which broke out in defiance of the *Daily Express*'s repeated prognostications, Beaverbrook treated like a newspaper campaign. He had done everything possible to avert the conflict, even treating Nazi persecution of the Jews as though it were a debate, with rights and wrongs on both sides.[48] The *Express* stood for 'Peace, Prosperity and Empire', and by the end of the 1930s the greatest of these was peace. As late as August 1939 it prophesied, 'There will be no war',[49] though some months earlier its owner had ordered the construction of a private air-raid shelter in the garden of Stornoway House. In appeasing the dictators Beaverbrook almost ended his ancient friendship with Winston Churchill, whom he now regarded as politically unreliable and irrelevant. But the two men agreed on the necessity for rearmament. And although Beaverbrook opposed both the blackout and rationing, and still hankered for a negotiated settlement, Churchill revived their intimacy by offering him the vital post of Minister of Aircraft Production in May 1940.

Thus opened what the Canadian called 'the most glittering, glorious, glamorous era of my whole life'.[50] Churchill was not securing Beaverbrook's support as a press baron, in the manner of Lloyd George during the First World War. He was obtaining a vigorous minister and a seductive crony, whose conversation he found almost as stimulating as one of his own monologues. It was a relationship which many found sinister and deplorable. Clementine Churchill begged her husband in vain to 'try ridding yourself of this microbe which some people fear is in your blood—Exorcise this bottle Imp & see if the air is not clearer & purer'.[51] Ernest Bevin summed up their association by comparing Churchill to 'a man who's married a whore; he knows she's a whore but he loves her just the same'.[52] What Bevin especially loathed about Beaverbrook was his inconstancy. Yet journalism is essentially an unstable medium and the new minister achieved more by fits and starts than duller politicians could have done by sustained concentration.

Beaverbrook regarded the Ministry of Aircraft Production as a gigantic stunt designed to increase the circulation of Hurricanes and Spitfires. His function was to quicken the industry with his own pulsating vitality and to ensure that the whole campaign received the fullest publicity. Thus he abandoned the sedate methods of the civil service in favour of the spontaneous energy of businessmen appointed by, and loyal to, himself. According to his slogans, 'Committees take the punch out of war' and 'Organisation is the enemy of impro-visation'.[53] Beaverbrook avoided written memoranda in favour of barked instructions, followed, a few minutes later, by brusque enquiries about whether they had been carried out. A summons from 'the Lord' was a fearful event. One air marshal, urgently sent for to answer the telephone, was told that German planes would be over his aerodrome at any moment. 'Oh my God is that all?' he replied, 'I thought it was a telephone call from Lord Beaverbrook.'[54]

Beaverbrook even discarded programmes because they limited initiative. He merely tightened deadlines and raised targets. The sky was the limit and anything less than total effort was hailed with catarrhal abuse. Beaverbrook not only eliminated bottlenecks, pirated spare parts, cannibalised damaged aeroplanes, dispersed new ones and accelerated production, he ensured that all this was seen to be done. He realised that in a people's war the first rule was display. He roared around the country in a beflagged, armour-plated limousine which disregarded all traffic lights. And by means of the Spitfire Fund and the appeal for aluminium, which produced mountains of saucepans, he turned the weary work of supply into a crusade. The *Daily Mirror*'s star columnist Cassandra commented approvingly that the 'cowardly bureaucracy' strangling the air force was being dismantled by a 'ten-stone parcel of angry brilliance', by 'a tough, stocky little egotist who for fifteen years has been chasing moonbeams, arguing ridiculously about ten ton railway trucks, shouting about isolation, bickering noisily with farmers, surrounding himself with yes men, infuriating his enemies, coining money and generally carrying on like an infuriated blue-bottle in a deserted cathedral'.[55] If Beaverbrook was the most flamboyant minister in the government he was also (just as important in rousing enthusiasm for the war effort) the most accessible. His door was always open and when an unauthorised person gained entry Beaverbrook growled, 'A cat may look at a cannibal'.[56]

Inevitably Beaverbrook's methods caused conflict. Whitehall mandarins were not used to being treated like Fleet Street hacks. 'Brass hats' were rarely subjected to such express contempt for the military mind. Anyway Beaverbrook was soon bored by the stunt. The month after his appointment he submitted his first resignation and at least fourteen more followed in quick succession. Often they were disguised appeals for sympathy or empty dramatic gestures, like the periodic pseudo-abdications from his newspapers. So perhaps he was surprised, even hurt, when Churchill, aware that his friend was now generating more friction than energy, permitted him to go in April 1941. Not that he left the government. First he was made Minister of State, an office with such nebulous duties that he offered to be minister of church as well. Then, in June 1941, he became Minister of Supply, a position which demanded, according to Churchill, a combination of the qualities of Napoleon Bonaparte and Jesus Christ. Sceptics doubted whether Beaverbrook measured up to these requirements. In fact, thanks largely to the obstructiveness of Ernest Bevin, he enjoyed much responsibility and little power—an irony which no one appreciated better than Beaverbrook himself.

However, he was given scope for yet another campaign by the German invasion of Russia, which coincided with his new appointment. Churchill had always regarded the Bolsheviks as a gang of international criminals—their sinister designs in Britain could be gauged from the fact that they had sold Tsarist jewels in order to subsidise the *Daily Herald*. The Prime Minister therefore found it difficult to enthuse over the necessary alliance between Albion's Lion and 'Red Bruin'. Beaverbrook had no such reservations. He quickly became the Kremlin's champion and the early advocate of a Second Front. In September 1941 he and Averell Harriman led an Anglo-American mission to Moscow. There, as a frankly pleasure-loving capitalist, Beaverbrook established a genuine rapport with Stalin. It was a rapport denied to the puritanical British Ambassador, Sir Stafford Cripps, who was so humourless that he saw jokes by appointment only. The dictator and the press magnate amused each other over champagne, which Stalin drank only from his personal bottle, by talking about mistresses. Beaverbrook became a fascinated devotee of the Russian leader. Like the good reporter he was, he noticed every detail, including Stalin's red-pencilled doodles which seemed to consist of the heads of wolves. Beaverbrook promised the Soviet Union generous aid. And he even rescued Stalin from a long harangue by Harriman on the merits of Christianity, interrupting brusquely, 'Promise me that if you become a Christian you'll become a Presbyterian'.[57]

Giving 'these Russians their daily bread' became Beaverbrook's next crusade. Needless to say, it was a sensational one. Like actors who only feel alive when performing, the press barons were inclined to doubt the validity of any cause that did not make headlines. The Soviet Union appealed magically to a Britain bereft of allies and already on the road to the socialism of 1945. Beaverbrook's own course was strangely convoluted, explicable in journalistic rather than political terms. It led him to quit the government in March 1942 and to make a dramatic plea, in America (where he was welcomed ecstatically), for the invasion of Europe. It involved him in justifying 'Stalin the Great's' treason trials and denying the existence of racial or religious persecution in Russia. It resulted in his vendetta against Lord Mountbatten, whom he blamed for 'the loss of Canadian life' during the disastrous raid on Dieppe. It concluded with his trying to ignore the Cold War.

More perverse still, his adulation for the Russian leader prompted him to intrigue against his British hero, even to dream of supplanting him. Beaverbrook privately remarked that the Prime Minister's dislike of Stalin was a symptom of insanity and he toyed with a plot to form an 'anti-Churchill party'.[58] This was not really surprising. No one was more actuated by a spirit of mischief than Beaverbrook. No one more enjoyed pricking pomposity—it was said that he went to America to become another thorn in the crown of Lord Halifax, the pious British ambassador. Conflict was the stuff of publicity and Beaverbrook could not even resist undermining the government in which he was a cabinet minister. Several times Churchill rebuked him for hostile items in the *Express* which could only have emanated from its proprietor. The Prime Minister received the usual bland response that Beaverbrook exercised no control over his newspapers. Anyway, if Beaverbrook's political loyalty to Churchill was always an uncertain quantity, his personal devotion seldom wavered.

He spent the last twenty-one months of the war as Lord Privy Seal, a ceremonial post which gave him ample time to haunt 10 Downing Street after midnight. Francis Williams (sometime editor of the *Herald*) described Beaverbrook as 'the imp with the poltergeist touch, his feet in Vanity Fair, his heart—or so he constantly tells us—with the pilgrims, his head wherever there are secrets to be heard'.[59] As one of Churchill's principal confidants Beaverbrook advised him to attack the Labour party ferociously during the election campaign of 1945. The *Express*, with its vicious headline 'The National Socialists', set the prevailing tone. Attlee said that although the famous speech warning that Labour would rule with a Gestapo was spoken by Churchill the words were those of Beaverbrook, whom he identified as the public figure 'most widely distrusted by decent men of all parties'.[60] Beaverbrook forecast a huge Conservative victory 'in the full knowledge of what happened to the prophets who prophesied falsely before Elijah'.[61]

For once Beaverbrook's estimate of the public mood was wrong and once again his propaganda machine was ineffective, but he was not put to the sword like the prophets of Baal. He simply spent the rest of his days in the political wilderness. This was no real hardship, for newspapers were the pleasure and business of his life. Certainly he experienced what Tom Driberg called 'moods of demonic blackness',[62] some of them doubtless induced by the post-war dislike of his old-fashioned buccaneering ways. Beaverbrook always made a bold show of welcoming criticism, even from his own newspapers. But underneath he was surprisingly sensitive, as Driberg himself discovered when he wrote a hostile biography of his former employer. Beaverbrook responded to the book with fury: 'Man has been falling since the Fall of Adam, but never has any man fallen so low as that fellow Driberg'.[63] Driberg himself told Hannen Swaffer:

> It is saddening to me that like Hearst and Rothermere and Northcliffe and the rest of them he can't really take it at all. Of course, he can enjoy the amiably bantering 'impertinence' that you indulged in at that dinner. But a serious assessment, even though criticism is balanced with praise, is too much for him.

On the whole, though, Beaverbrook enjoyed himself. He campaigned against the United Nations and Britain's involvement with Europe, for imperial consolidation (which he privately admitted to be a lost cause by the 1950s) and the Suez adventure (about which he preferred to print official lies from Whitehall rather than the true reports of his own correspondent on the spot). It amused him to outrage a Royal Commission on the Press by saying that he published his newspapers solely for the purpose of propaganda. He obtained the old thrill of reducing his myrmidons to frenzied activity merely by speaking a few words into the dictaphone. As one of them remarked, it was like working for a benzedrine factory. Only four months before his death Beaverbrook was complaining to Charles Wintour from the Riviera, 'We have not got a telephone. Next to having no bath water, this is the worst experience of my life.'[64] But perhaps Beaverbrook's most characteristic utterance to his editors was, 'Sow the seeds of discontent, Sow the seeds of discontent', sung down the telephone to the tune of 'Polly put the Kettle on'.[65] It was his nearest approach to the Northcliffean megalomania to which, in gloomy moods, Beaverbrook feared he would eventually succumb.

'Newspapers are born to die', Beaverbrook often said, an aphorism that might have sounded more impressive had he applied it less indiscriminately—political parties are born to die, and so on. Be that as it may, press barons were certainly born to die and Beaverbrook's demise, in 1964, left his publications in a more than usually exposed position. Beaverbrook had been the old-style newspaper magnate *par excellence*, bold, independent, quirky, creating newspapers in his own image and sustaining them by his personal vitality. The one little old reader who mattered to journalists on the *Express* had been no mere meddler. He was financial guarantor, protector against external pressure (whether from politicians or advertisers), pre-server of standards. He liked to think of himself as a pillar of cloud by day and a pillar of fire by night. But if 'the Lord' gave, he also took away.

In an effort to improve his newspapers at the expense of their rivals he had encouraged over-manning and over-paying both on the editorial and, much more seriously, on the production side. As early as 1927, Beaverbrook had told Rothermere, 'I have ceased to value my assets in purely money terms. I regard them as a means of carrying out what I think right in the interests of the Empire, and as something which gives me a task in life.' Of course he made his papers pay, but he consistently refused to broaden the *Express*'s financial base. 'We are newspapermen,' he said. 'If we divert our activities, we will undoubtedly damage our newspapers.'[66] Unlike, say, the *Mail*, which diversified into oil, commercial television, pizza restaurants, road haulage, taxicabs, mirror manufacturing, not to mention provincial newspapers, the *Express* had little in the way of subsidiaries and no reserves except Beaverbrook's Canadian fortune. Included in this were large holdings in the great paper and pulp company, Price Brothers, which armoured him against rising costs:

> I do not care what price newsprint reaches . . . If the price goes up, perhaps my Price Brothers shares will go up too . . . So if I can save at the bung-hole while wasting at the spigot, I don't mind.

But in what seemed like 'a final act of mischief from beyond the grave',[67] he bequeathed his Canadian assets to a trust largely devoted to the propagation of Presbyterianism.

Worst of all, Beaverbrook left no heir worthy of the name, as his son Sir Max Aitken modestly acknowledged when refusing to adopt his father's title. Beaverbrook had treated him abominably, giving him duties without authority, and Sir Max, notwithstanding his fine record as a fighter pilot, was a pleasure-lover rather than a fire-eater. The truth was perhaps, as some journalists surmised, that Beaverbrook unconsciously hoped that the *Express* would expire with him—in a sheet of flame and a cloud of smoke, like the ship at a Viking funeral. It sounds improbable but at least one other press baron had shared the feeling, Wilbur F. Storey of Chicago, who remarked in 1876, 'I don't wish to perpetuate my newspaper. *I am the paper!* I wish it to die with me so that the world may know I was the *Times!*'[68]

By the 1960s Beaverbrook's readers and his presses were growing old. In the two decades after 1950 the annual operating expenses of his newspapers rose from under £8 million to almost £50 million. During the inflationary hurricane of the early 1970s costs soared still higher and circulation plummeted. Aitken experimented desperately with new measures and new men. He tried to compete first with the ponderous *Telegraph*, then with the popular *Mirror*. He appointed Jocelyn Stevens to run his newspapers though, in the opinion of a print union leader, the former editor of *Queen* 'couldn't run a bath'.[69] The task was hopeless. By 1977 bankruptcy was imminent and Beaverbrook newspapers had only one real asset left, its buildings. After lengthy negotiations with potential buyers (among them Sir James Goldsmith of Cavenham Foods, who admired Beaverbrook and wanted to see the *Express* crusading again) Aitken sold his newspapers to a vast property conglomerate, Trafalgar House. The new boss, Victor Matthews, now Lord Matthews, also professed esteem for his famous predecessor. He apparently even tried to model himself on Beaverbrook, announcing that 'By and large the editors will have complete freedom, as long as they agree with the policy I have laid down'.[70]

In reality, however, the unsophisticated Matthews bore no relation to the subtle Beaverbrook. He was at first so innocent about the press that he did not know that the initials NPA stood for Newspaper Proprietors' Association. He is not a freebooter, sailing under his own flag, but a mercenary answerable to Trafalgar House's board of directors. And they are not concerned with the publications which earned less than half a million pounds in 1980, but with the hotels, ships and aircraft which contributed chiefly to their profit of £49 million. Matthews's subordinates are not so much editors as divisional managers, not so much reporters as low-echelon executives. His task is less to produce great, or even distinctive, newspapers, than to determine the appropriate marketing strategy for the subsidiary company in a large organisation. Matthews cannot stamp his own character on the *Express* and its sisters because he seldom has time to read them. He is interested in the profits not the contents of his newspapers. Many journalists, threatened with having to conform to the standards of a faceless commercial consortium, feel a strange nostalgia for the hazards and idiosyncrasies of the past. As Neal Ascherson has written, 'The old tycoon, the sometimes crazy plutocrat who ran newspapers and only newspapers was a more reliable master'.[71] Better to serve the devil you know than belong to the management team of a nebulous corporate overlord. In the bleak words of Sir Larry Lamb, former editor of the *Sun*, 'Ever since the *Express* was taken over by the grey-flannel-suit merchants it has been a disaster'.[72]

During his early days on the *Express* Beaverbrook was visited by a pistol-carrying religious maniac who threatened to shoot him unless the Holy Ghost manifested itself over the press baron's head in the shape of a dove. Beaverbrook vainly tried to reason with the man, then knelt down on the floor to pray with him and finally persuaded him that the sacred bird would not appear in the profane atmosphere of a newspaper office. They went downstairs together and in the hubbub of Fleet Street Beaverbrook bolted, reporting the incident to the police who arrested the lunatic. It was a strange and, journalists found, a somewhat droll adventure. It was also a revealing one. Beaverbrook himself was fond of retelling Old Testament stories in the form of what Michael Foot calls 'a blood-soaked Calvinistic horror comic',[73] and the episode might stand as a parable of his life. Beaverbrook's deepest conviction was that his original sin would be visited with ultimate retribution. This did not prevent his exploring all escape routes. They led him into so many contradictions and convolutions that his original aim was all but obscured. The spiritual impulse, aided, of course, by consummate abilities, produced gigantic secular success. And English journalism found itself transformed, for better and for worse, for richer and for poorer, by a psyche which was as complex and 'engaging as a cross-word puzzle'.[74]

However, Beaverbrook was the last of the great British press barons in the sense that no one since has set the stamp of so distinctive a personality on his newspapers. There have been aspirants to Beaverbrook's mantle. Lord Thomson idolised him as the first of the colonial press barons: 'All my life, Max, I have regarded your wonderful life-time accomplishment with awe and admiration'. But Thomson was a single-minded businessman who believed in letting his editors have their heads; what they wrote was merely, in his famous phrase, 'the stuff you separate the ads with'.[75] By discreet silence Beaverbrook assisted Thomson's secret bid to acquire the *Sunday Times* from Lord Kemsley in 1959. But he refused to take Thomson seriously, having years before expressed his contempt for those who claimed that in journalism money could do the work of rare minds and strong sinews:

> You must be ready to put your whole heart and soul, your stomach, your liver, your whole anatomy into a task which will appear most of the time to be dangerously stimulating and on occasion positively revolting. 'Millionaires and their Newspapers'—Humbug and Ignorance.[76]

Mr Rupert Murdoch would agree, but even he is no successor to Beaverbrook. Having created a communications empire on three continents, he constitutes a unique new category, the international press baron, to be discussed later. A few able proprietor-controllers remain, Lord Hartwell, for instance. He is the founder of the only new national Sunday paper to emerge between 1918 and 1981, the *Sunday Telegraph*. Following American precedents, Hartwell modelled it faithfully on his successful *Daily Telegraph*, only to discover that British readers like something different on Sunday. However, he was 'brash enough', as he put it,[77] to request an exclusive story from the Prime Minister, a somewhat surprised Harold Macmillan, for the first issue. And he was dogged enough to devise a novel formula which now gives the *Sunday Telegraph* a circulation of about a million. Nevertheless, his two papers, unsupported by outside interests, facing huge increases in costs and a serious loss of advertising revenue, are now barely profitable. Their future is uncertain. Moreover, Hartwell, a self-effacing, good-humoured man, is anything but a press baron in the old style. He seldom intervenes directly in editorial matters, though he

William Randolph Hearst with Marion Davies

Lord Beaverbrook travels in style

Lord Beaverbrook's eighty-fifth birthday [inset diagram with names]

1. Mr Michael Berry, editor-in-chief,
   Daily Telegraph.
2. Lord Iliffe, vice-chairman,
   Birmingham Post and Mail.
3. Mr Vere Harmsworth, heir to Lord Rothermere.
4. Mr Alick Jeans, managing director,
   Liverpool Daily Post.
5. Sir Geoffrey Harmsworth, chairman,
   Harmsworth Press.
6. Mr Cecil King, chairman, *Daily Mirror.*
7. Mr George Drew, High Commissioner for Canada.
8. Mr Max Aitken, chairman of the board,
   Beaverbrook Newspapers.
9. Lord Camrose, chairman, *Daily Telegraph.*
10. Mr Roy Thomson, chairman,
    Thomson Organisation.
11. Lord Rosebery.
12. Lord Drogheda.
13. Lord Rothermere.
14. Sir Winston Churchill.
15. Lord Beaverbrook.
16. Mr Harold Macmillan.

E. W. Scripps in working clothes

Colonel McCormick

Captain Patterson

Cecil King

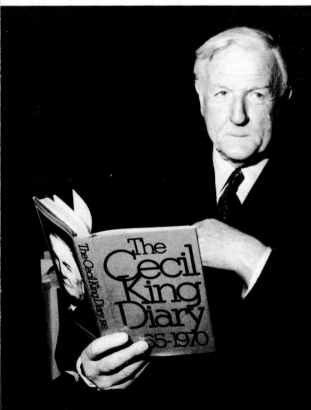

likes to question and criticise. And he is so shy that he has been known to faint at the prospect of making a farewell speech at a journalist's retirement party. Like his peers, Hartwell lacks 'the Lord's' monstrous élan. With Beaverbrook's death Fleet Street lost much of its spirit of ribald nonconformity and the press moved decisively into the era of the conglomerates.

CHAPTER TEN

Chain Gangs

NEWSPAPERS, LIKE OTHER commercial enterprises, have always sought strength through size and found safety in numbers. The press barons, like captains of industry everywhere, tried to cut costs by expansion and consolidation, to eradicate or assimilate competitors, and to establish local monopolies. Thus in the history of newspapers, chains were quite an early development. But diversification outside the field of newspapers altogether has occurred only recently. This new trend is much more pronounced in Britain, where it reflects newspapers' weakness, than in the United States, where it reflects their strength—Fleet Street is so inefficient that it needs external support, whereas American publishing corporations require additional outlets for their capital. Before the Second World War, press magnates on both sides of the Atlantic took Lord Beaverbrook's line that investment in irrelevant concerns would damage their newspapers. They assumed that other businesses would follow suit.

When, in 1929, the International Paper and Power Company proposed to purchase some small newspapers Ralph Pulitzer and other leaders of the American press felt threatened and bewildered. One remarked, as the *Daily Express*'s New York correspondent told Beaverbrook:

> I can understand a newspaper having an interest in a newsprint plant, but, I cannot understand why a newsprint company wants to buy a newspaper. It seems to me like a haberdasher buying a dude in order to dress him.[1]

Beaverbrook rightly foresaw that a conflict of interest would occur if newspapers became the appendages of larger corporations. At best managing editors would be reluctant to hurt, through news reports or editorial comment, other subsidiaries in the company; at worst they would conduct house journals or propaganda sheets. By contrast the press baron, whose private fief, however extensive, consisted entirely or largely of newspapers, could retain his independence. True, he might abuse it grossly. He might make his publications slaves to his passions or projections of his fantasies, but he need never prostitute them for corporate gain. Two of the most striking instances of newspaper-chain proprietors who exercised their freedom to the utmost, though in radically different ways, are provided by the Scripps and the McCormick/Patterson families.

Consciously modelling himself on Gibbon, Edward Willis Scripps laid his journalistic plans during a night spent at the Colosseum in 1878. Climbing onto a broken pillar, he lay under the Italian sky smoking endless cigars and 'strengthened my resolve to be one of the great men of the world'. Power, not glory, would be his aim.

> I decided that I would establish a little kingdom such as Rome was in its prehistoric beginning. I decided that I would extend this kingdom of mine, which would consist of my first newspaper, to another and then another newspaper, and I determined so long as I lived to go on extending my kingdom into perhaps an empire of journalism.[2]

This was the obvious manifestation of Scripps's ambition. Its darker motives were revealed by an earlier experience in London. Wearing a plaid suit, yellow dogskin gloves, diamond studs and carrying an ivory-topped cane, the young American was conscious, as he sauntered through Mayfair, that the English regarded him as a perfect bounder. For his own part, Scripps was horrified by the great gulf which he saw fixed between Britain's arrogant aristocracy and its servile flunkey-dom. The human race was evidently divided into slave-drivers and slaves: Scripps sympathised with the latter but vowed to join the former.

He would die for the poor, as he later said, but he would not live with them. He would even dress like the common people, but he would think for himself. His choice was confirmed by the sight of a dense crowd of city workers crossing London Bridge in the evening rush hour.

> The close contact with so much ugliness, misery, helplessness, and dull blankness of vision had oppressed me. I began to feel something like hysteria ... here I was, a mere drop in the great river of seething humanity. I was myself an intricate part of the waves and eddies of the stream itself. I felt a loathing for the whole

species, including myself. . . . I resolved more than ever before to disassociate myself from the crowd, to climb up and out and over it, no matter by what means, even though crime itself and the worst of crime should form the rungs of the ladder. . . . If not, I would commit suicide.[3]

In his journalistic ventures Scripps was thus inspired by a compassionate wish to protest against the lot of the huddled masses and a misanthropic will to dominate them.

Scripps's aberrant personality had been forged in hardship. He was born in 1854, the thirteenth child of James Mogg Scripps, a failed London bookbinder who had emigrated to farm in America. Edward always reckoned that his birth was 'an accident, the last expiring flame of passion burned to ashes in the aged bodies of my parents'.[4] He probably also attributed the frequent whippings which he received from his mother, James's third wife, to his being unwanted. Julia Scripps was a puritanical school-teacher and she must actually have regarded her awkward youngest son as a particularly rebellious pupil. He was a moody, humourless boy with a plume of red hair, which earned him the nickname 'Turkey Egg', and a sinister cast in his right eye. That eye soon wandered over the bold country girls of Illinois and Scripps embarked on a carnival of lust broken by intervals of tortured celibacy. These brief attempts at self-control filled his mind with such desires that he felt 'unclean clear through to the core'.[5] He later suggested a radical answer to the demands of adolescent sexuality: eugenically ill-adapted females should be sterilised and prostituted to the needs of males between puberty and marriage.

This proposal typified the unorthodox bent of Scripps's mind. At school he was too original to succeed and too contrary to be popular. On the farm he disliked the sordid business of working the land but enjoyed playing in the dirt (and was afterwards to shock editors of his papers by visiting them in muddy boots and filthy clothes). He only felt comfortable in the harsh atmosphere of his parents' house, but in 1872 he left and was soon office boy on his half-brother James's Detroit *Evening News*. The Scripps family, which had included an editor of the London *True Briton* and a founder of the Chicago *Tribune*, was said to be 'a tribe of Ishmaelites, whose hands were against everybody, and against whom everybody's hands were raised'.[6] Of no one was the remark more true than the tribe's newest journalistic recruit.

James Scripps was a pioneer of the low-priced, four-page, big-typed, simple-worded, small-town newspapers which were to be the standard links in his half-brother's chain. The Detroit *Evening News* was run on effort and economy. Copy was penned on flattened-out old envelopes

and every evening James counted the pennies brought in by the newsboys. He also exploited the runt of the Scripps litter, for whom he had
much contempt and little affection. Edward possessed none of the
obvious journalistic skills. He brooded, suffered from poor health and
was barely literate. Yet he was capable of fierce bouts of energy which
he generally employed in devising systems to make others do the work.
He was detailed to deliver papers. In addition he canvassed more
subscribers, developed new suburban routes and hired his own
carriers. Not content with making a healthy profit on the job and
increasing the paper's circulation, he taught himself to write.

At the age of twenty-one he became city editor, a promotion he
celebrated by beginning a spectacular career of drunkenness. From his
editorial desk Scripps urged his reporters 'to raise as much hell as
possible'.[7] He believed that personal journalism in peptonised form
sold newspapers and he was fearless in exposing local malefactors. He
was even candid enough to include himself among their number when
the occasion warranted it. Bob Paine, editor of Scripps's second paper,
the Cleveland *Penny Press* published a report that its owner had been
fined ten dollars for reckless driving (of horses) while intoxicated. Paine
was confronted by Scripps:

> For a full minute his eye was on mine, with all the benevolence of a
> gar-pike glaring at a nice fat minnow. Then the stern features
> relaxed, and into his eyes came that smile which those who knew
> him will never forget.[8]

Paine's salary was increased.

The *Penny Press* was begun on Scripps's return from a European
grand tour in 1878 and it marked the first stage in the realisation of
his imperial dreams. To start with it was a family concern in which
Edward held only a fifth of the stock. But he directed the paper from
the outset and eventually, having exercised what he called 'my own
devilish instinct to scheme',[9] he gained control of it. His policy
remained the same, to print the news as cheaply, briefly and brightly as
possible. The *Press*, helped by Cleveland's spectacular growth, was
instantly successful. Scripps himself published optimistic stories to
encourage the boom, which amazed him. Murdering Tennyson, he
wrote: 'If "ten years of Europe equalled cycles of Cathay", ten months
in America equals ten centuries of Europe'.[10] But Scripps was driven
into furies of resentment by the unequal distribution of Cleveland's
newly created wealth. Moreover he reckoned that a paper which rested
on labour and sold mostly to workers should be the people's champion.

He aimed to put down the mighty from their seat and raise up the humble and meek. *Penny Puke*, as the local plutocrats called it, was scurrilous in its attacks on political corruption and staunch in the promotion of social justice. Nor, until the very end of his life when he became an avowed reactionary, did Scripps's own galloping affluence interfere with his radical beliefs. If anything they grew more violent. Scripps, who supported both Populists and Single Taxers, was inconsistent in politics as in everything else, but for most of his career he was a revolutionary. Socialism was an absurdity but capitalism was a tragedy. So protest was a necessity. As he told Lincoln Steffens, 'I don't think like a rich man. I think more like a left labour galoot, like those dynamiters.'[11] Scripps was referring to the McNamara brothers, whose bombing of the right-wing Los Angeles *Times* in 1910 he defended.

Scripps was proud of his dissident philosophy which he expressed in a number of crackerbarrel 'disquisitions'. These he would read to guests and an 'expression of delighted surprise' would steal over his rugged features at the wisdom he found in them.[12] But if Scripps thought like a renegade he behaved like a businessman. He overcame protracted family opposition and used the existing newspapers as a base on which to build his journalistic confederation. His technique was simple. He chose small, expanding towns in which to found new papers. He invested little in plant or machinery, often renting derelict buildings and buying ancient presses. Young, ambitious men were hired as editors, allowed a minority stake in their paper and given two instructions. They must obey 'all Ten Commandments and make a profit'. As an afterthought, Scripps added that they must also 'serve the interest of the poor and the working classes'.[13]

They sent daily reports to their chief and he exercised detailed management from 'Miramar', the desert retreat which he built outside San Diego to accommodate his growing family. Scripps had married in 1885 and settled down in so far as this was possible for someone who each day smoked forty cigars and drank a gallon of whisky. Doubt has been cast on the latter claim but it was certainly not impossible—Dana had calculated that in the Union army 'a friendly man' would consume this amount in the time.[14] And Scripps paid for his indulgence with numbed flesh, near blindness and attacks of what he called 'the horrors'.

Editors found their rare visits to 'Miramar' an ordeal. Scripps, a hulking, bearded figure clad in a skull-cap (he was terrified of catching colds), rough clothes and rawhide boots, was a fearsome host. Socially ill-at-ease, he was given to bitter tirades against art and education or to the crude horse-play which was his sole idea of fun. He was also a domestic martinet who bawled at his Japanese servants and thrashed his infant children if he was not accorded instant obedience.

Paradoxically, he also insisted that his offspring should express themselves freely and flout every convention. The editors themselves received little mercy, as Edward's strange confession to James Scripps reveals:

> That I am harsh and dictatorial and even cruel in my treatment of men, I have learned by finding so many men crying in my presence, but that I am not so at heart I know, because at such times I feel like crying myself.[15]

Still, a few tears were little to pay for the advantage of an association with Scripps. In the case of his ablest subordinates this could be measured in millions of dollars. No other barracuda of the journalistic deep made such lavish provision for his pilot fish.

Scripps was not infallible. He assumed that one in four of his papers would collapse and he preferred to close down, rather than sell, the failures. An early misjudgement was to challenge Pulitzer's *Post-Dispatch* in St Louis. And such was his detestation for the commercial pressures imposed by advertisements that he several times started newspapers without them. These experiments proved abortive but they showed that Scripps would let nothing erode his independence. Hearst himself was amazed at the degree of control which he exerted within his own domain. In all Scripps founded thirty-two newspapers (some of them short-lived) and held shares in fifteen others. He also created a news service, the United Press, to combat the Conservative Associated Press, and an organisation which disseminated radical editorials to his papers.

Inevitably, no doubt, with increasing prosperity they drifted rightwards. The tendency was strengthened by successive junior partners, first Milton McRae and then Roy Howard (hence the names of his chain, the Scripps-McRae League and the Scripps-Howard League). These lieutenants were Scripps's Babbitts, immensely dedicated men of business who tried to substitute commercial values for his original ideals of public service. Scripps was adamant that his papers should not become organ-grinders for the great and eventually he broke with McRae. 'It is easier for a rich man to enter the Kingdom of Heaven,' Scripps remarked, 'than it is for a successful newspaper publisher to give democracy a square deal.'[16] He disproved his own maxim, sometimes at the expense of his own prejudices: for example, he despised women as the inferior sex but encouraged his papers to campaign for female suffrage. Scripps's publications, which earned him forty million dollars, were the most effective defenders of the underdog in America.

This began to change when Scripps himself changed, during the First World War. He was an ardent Anglophile who urged that the United States should first enter the conflict and afterwards, with the help of her English-speaking allies, police the globe. In 1917 Scripps moved to Washington in order to collate editorial support for the war-effort—there he encountered 'a belligerent old tiger', Lord Northcliffe.[17] Scripps came to the gradual and reluctant conclusion that unbridled free enterprise was America's chief weapon. There was no more powerful incentive than individual selfishness, and the profit motive would be the instrument of victory. Scripps's belated conversion to this theory, the practice of which had dominated his life, was accompanied by a final and well-nigh disastrous family crisis. One of his daughters eloped with Scripps's secretary, his wife took her part, and his son Jim detached his five West-coast papers from the League. Scripps cast them into limbo. He resumed the heavy drinking which he had given up on medical grounds nearly twenty years before, and suffered a paralytic stroke. He recovered but, like Pulitzer, Scripps was now a wreck whose only refuge from nerve storms was to live at sea. Aboard his yacht he began every day with a phonograph performance of 'Onward Christian Soldiers' and spent much of his time playing dominoes.

Yet Scripps's vitality was hardly impaired as guests subjected to his rasping monologues, mostly bullying or boasting, could testify. And with the aid of his loyal son Robert and Roy Howard, he initiated an extraordinary burst of expansion in his chain. Between 1921 and 1925 the Scripps-Howard League founded twelve new papers, a feature syndicate and a picture agency. By the 1920s Scripps could not exercise personal suzerainty over his publications as he had done in the past. Nevertheless, they bore his unmistakable stamp and in this respect differed from the products of today's communications conglomerates, which are all tentacles and no face. They bowed to no will but their owner's, promoted no incidental business interests, resisted advertisers and politicians, maintained their independence against all comers. Unsophisticated but not unenlightened, Scripps's papers, like those of the other great press barons, gave their readers the human contact which many of them, as new immigrants, had lost. For these, as well as for more obvious reasons, H. L. Mencken claimed in 1925 that Scripps was 'probably the most successful newspaper owner America has ever known'.[18] A year later the newspaper magnate was sailing off Liberia when he was seized by a fatal apoplexy. His last words were, 'Too many cigars this evening, I guess'.[19]

The Scripps-Howard League became the second largest newspaper chain in the country (after Hearst's) and still ranks in the top ten. So does the group headed by the Chicago *Tribune*, a paper whose strength awed even Hearst. He wrote to Neylan in 1924,

> The Chicago Tribune, notwithstanding its great age, notwithstanding its firm foundation, the immense business it has, puts an enormous amount of energy back of its editorial and business departments and improves every year in circulation and advertising.

Hearst contrasted its eight million dollar profit with that of his San Francisco *Examiner* which annually made 'a little measly million and a half dollars and thinks it is doing great work'.[20] The *Tribune* owed its massive growth not so much to deep roots as to expert cultivation by the most remarkable newspaper dynasty in American history. Its progenitor, the grandfather of Robert R. McCormick, Joseph M. Patterson and Eleanor M. Patterson, was Joseph Medill. A tough, frontier journalist, he was famous for the virulence of his Republicanism and for telling Lincoln, 'Dammit, Abe, git yore feet off my desk'.[21] Medill, who hailed from New Brunswick, was of Scots-Irish extraction. He had early been attracted towards journalism and was inspired to go West by Horace Greeley. In 1874 he gained financial control of the *Tribune*, itself founded in 1847, which he had dominated for nearly twenty years.

Medill worked to create a newspaper that was a combination of brute virility and god-like authority. He announced that 'the Almighty has ordained' the triumph of both the *Tribune* and of its principles,[22] which were those of aggressively unreconstructed conservatism. They can be gauged from Medill's insistence that the socialist leader should be referred to in the *Tribune* as 'Dictator' Debs and by the tenor of his political diatribes: 'If the chief end of man is to become a lazy lout, a shiftless vagabond, a brawling long-haired idiot, a public nuisance, and an enemy of the human race, let him turn Communist'.[23] Medill also liked to denounce Eastern culture as a form of decadence: Oscar Wilde, an obvious target, would not reproach his 'wicked and imaginative' detractor because, he said, 'the conscience of an editor is purely decorative'.[24] Medill's reactionary beliefs were softened only by a certain innate crankiness, exemplified in his attributing all the world's ills to sunspots, until he discovered that the true villains were microbes. Medill died in 1899 but under his heirs the paper remained an eccentric anachronism. In the twentieth century the *Tribune* was said to be the best nineteenth-century newspaper and its overlord was described as having the finest mind of the thirteenth century.

This medieval personage was Medill's grandson, Robert Rutherford McCormick (1880–1955), known to his intimates as Bertie—though, as an addict of P. G. Wodehouse, he became aware of the effete overtones of that name and later gave instructions that he should be addressed as Bert. Actually, as a small child he had been called Roberta and (until his tantrums put a stop to it) dressed in girl's clothes, an expression of his mother's grief over the death of her baby daughter. Bertie's mother, Katherine Medill, had married Robert S. McCormick in 1876, thus uniting two of Chicago's most prominent clans—the McCormick grain harvester was the first really successful machine of its kind and, by releasing men from the land, it had contributed to the North's victory in the Civil War. But Bertie's genetic inheritance was more problematic than his financial one. Both his paternal grandfather and, after a modest diplomatic career, his father died in lunatic asylums, while his elder brother, who became a Senator, suffered from severe psychological disorders. Bertie used to say that, apart from himself, all the McCormicks were crazy.

Whatever his mental state, Bertie early developed the manias which would obsess him for the rest of his life. His first vivid memory was of being kept indoors while the alien 'brood of vipers'[25] responsible for the Haymarket Riot in 1887 were being executed. Bertie so loathed them that he afterwards shouted at the widow of one of the 'anarchists' and ran over her pug dog on his bicycle. His patriotism was further stimulated by attending a preparatory school in caste-ridden England while his father worked at the American legation in London. Bertie saw Queen Victoria in her old age and was struck by the servile antics of the crowds, who threw their hats in the air like comic-opera villagers. While on holiday in Germany he encountered more royalty. The Prince of Wales (another Bertie) lifted his sailor hat, looked at the name inside and said, 'Ah, a nice little English boy'. 'I am not,' he replied, in an accent of outrage which produced guffaws from the Kaiser, 'I am an American.' Back at Groton, where he was placed in the class above Franklin D. Roosevelt, Bertie was exposed to Eastern snobbery. He responded with a vigorous mid-Western chauvinism. Whereas Stead regarded Chicago as the capital of the English-speaking world, McCormick saw it as the centre of the universe.

It was in every way appropriate that Joseph Medill's last words should have been addressed to Bertie, then a sophomore at Yale: 'What is the news this morning?'[26] Medill exercised a powerful influence over his grandson. He stimulated a permanent interest in military history by confiscating one of Conan Doyle's novels and replacing it with Grant's memoirs. He communicated his fad for revising English spelling along more logical lines, so that under McCormick the *Tribune*'s news and editorial columns were littered with words like 'frate', 'thoro', 'thruout' and 'philosofy'—advertisers successfully resisted pressure to follow suit, on the grounds that unconventional orthography was bad for business. McCormick enjoyed flouting maxims like that. His chief legacy from his grandfather was a combination of stubborn perversity and die-hard ultra-conservatism. What McCormick did not inherit was the Chicago *Tribune* itself. This Medill tied up in a complicated trust, the main beneficiaries of which were his two quarrelsome daughters, Katherine McCormick and Elinor Patterson. Moreover, until his death in 1910, Elinor's husband, R. W. Patterson, would direct the fortunes of the paper. He was a first-rate journalist who both modernised and liberalised the paper, or at any rate palliated its more atavistic ferocity.

This moderate policy was continued by James Keeley whom the trustees appointed to control the paper in 1910. Known as the 'twenty-minute egg' of newspaperdom, he was an uneducated, but extremely able Englishman who treated his journalists like galley-slaves. He not only supported the Progressive party but actually tried to secure his position by engaging Theodore Roosevelt as the *Tribune*'s editor. This plan was thwarted; McCormick and his cousin Joseph Patterson preferred to spend what would have been the ex-President's salary of $15,000 on buying the comic 'Katzenjammer Kids'. Instead Keeley scored innumerable 'pippins' (local scoops) and 'bell-ringers' (national beats), raked muck vigorously and pioneered 'personal service' journalism.[27] He introduced a large number of popular features—advice to the lovelorn, a 'swap' column, beauty hints, a cookery corner and so on—which helped the paper to enter into the every-day life of its readers. But in 1914 Keeley deserted the *Tribune* to edit a rival. Until then McCormick had occupied himself in swimming the Hellespont, qualifying for the bar, engaging in local politics, playing polo and shooting polar bears. However, he had also helped to conduct the business side of the *Tribune*, just as the radical 'Joe' Patterson had served on the paper as a working journalist. Together they took charge. It was the most incongruous and the most successful partnership in the history of the American press.

Joseph Medill Patterson (1879–1946) had experienced the same kind of gilded upbringing as McCormick: private schools, European travel, Groton, Yale. But while his cousin had meant it when he sang 'For God, for Country and for Yale', young Patterson was already in revolt against the beliefs held dear by his family, once 'Scottish cattle rustlers',[28] now Chicago's most determined social climbers. Whereas McCormick had swallowed the Social Darwinist gospel at a gulp, Patterson, though capable of strangling a canary when annoyed by its song, believed in the survival of the unfittest. What is more he regarded life as a challenge which he ought to accept without the advantages conferred on him by position and wealth. Thus on vacation from Yale he went off to run dispatches for the *Tribune*'s correspondent in China during the Boxer Rebellion. Patterson saw himself as a drone and determined to turn himself into a worker. After university he started as a city reporter on the *Tribune*, but though his salary was fifteen dollars a week he could not bring himself to give up his annual allowance of ten thousand.

He compromised by dressing like a proletarian (in stark contrast to McCormick, whose suits were tailored in Savile Row) and by entering local politics as a radical reformer. To everyone's amazement he was elected to the state legislature. Then his masterful father revealed that the victory had resulted from a secret deal between the *Tribune* and a corrupt Republican boss. Disgusted and humiliated, Patterson resigned from the paper. After a brief spell as Commissioner of Public Works in Mayor Dunne's Democratic administration, he announced his conversion to socialism. He quickly established himself as a propagandist against contemporary evils, among which he apparently included Roman Catholicism, writing several novels and plays. His message was that socialism would provide a cure for everything from sweated labour to drug addiction. One critic described him as 'an unpolished Galsworthy',[29] scarcely the most effusive of compliments. Still, his work was successful and he had experienced the power of money as an incentive. Besides, the squabbling of the socialists was incessant. So in 1910 he returned to the *Tribune*, his idealism tarnished but not vanished.

Working with (and against) Keeley, Patterson strengthened the journalistic side of the paper, while McCormick secured its business position by leasing Canadian forests and building paper mills. No one was more adept than Patterson at the crucial task of recruiting readers. Not that he had much time for writers. He preferred to rely on comic strips, photographs, competitions, free gift schemes, self-promotion stunts, crusades, features by the famous (such as the Marquess of Queensberry on sport and Kipling on war) and the smashing impact of a sensational front page. In his office outfit of corduroy trousers, roll-neck sweater and grease-stained cap, Patterson identified with the common man and reckoned to know what appealed to him. The press baron reinforced that understanding by studying newspaper readers on trains, haunting the slums and drinking in low dives, where he sometimes got involved in fights just to prove himself. (In due course his cousin was infected by the desire to play Haroun al Raschid and he walked the streets of Chicago disguised as a blind man—but McCormick's bristling moustache and six feet four inches gave him away.) What gave Patterson away were his sudden fits of aloofness. He would slide down the marble banisters at the *Tribune* building, be the soul of mateyness with reporters, and accompany them on exciting assignments. Then, quite unpredictably, he would withdraw, rebuff those he had befriended, even hound them into leaving the paper. Consequently he was much more loathed by the staff than was McCormick, a lonely paternalist who did not know how to unbend at all. McCormick measured his own and the *Tribune*'s virility by the hostility he provoked. And Patterson never courted popularity. He sought fulfilment by pitting himself against the world. Arthur Brisbane told Lord Beaverbrook that Patterson was the only man he knew, except Hearst, 'who does exactly as he pleases ALL the time'.[30]

The cousins did not work together well but it was surprising that they worked together at all. Not that they disliked each other personally. In fact, Joe was sardonically good-humoured about Bertie's aristocratic airs: watching him greet the *Tribune* staff at a formal reception he remarked, 'Bertie certainly likes to crack the whip and watch the serfs march by'.[31] As for Bertie, he admired the more brilliant and demonstrative Joe. Bertie even supported the Progressives in deference to him and honoured their 'ironbound agreement' not to quarrel.[32] However, their political views were really poles apart. And as each supervised the editorial page for alternate months 'The World's Greatest Newspaper', as the *Tribune* began modestly to call itself, went through some curious convolutions. Odder still, this did not seem to matter. Whatever line it took the *Tribune* was not dull. Keeley's leading articles had been moderate and even-tempered; those of McCormick and Patterson were strident and hard-hitting. Between 1914 and 1921 circulation doubled, to half a million. Inevitably, though, there were clashes and both men must have found it a relief as well as an adventure to go off to war.

McCormick toured both Western and Eastern fronts, sending back atrocity stories to the *Tribune* and making himself an expert on what he called the 'great debauch' of combat. 'I have tasted of the wine of death and its flavour will be forever in my throat.'[33] Patterson visited Mexico and Europe. He returned on a slow British cargo boat, an easy prey for submarines, in order to test his courage, just as he was to do again on the battlefield; when Arthur Brisbane asked him if he had been frightened by the shooting he replied, 'Yes, as frightened as —'.[34] In 1916 the cousins fought in Mexico. Typically, McCormick tried to enter the army at the top, was commissioned as a major and even briefly sported a monocle, while Patterson enlisted as a private. They then both served with distinction in France, McCormick once rallying his troops with a speech which concluded, 'The nearer you are to the enemy, the nearer you are to God'.[35] Afterwards the cousins retained their military titles—Colonel McCormick and Captain Patterson. It was on a dung-heap behind the lines that they agreed, so the story goes, that the *Tribune* was not big enough for both of them. Actually they had long shared this opinion. Just before the Great War McCormick had been negotiating to purchase the New York *Herald* from James Gordon Bennett, whom he regarded as 'perhaps the most enterprising journalist of all time'.[36] Anyway in 1919, prompted by Northcliffe, Patterson launched the New York *Daily News* as a tabloid.

With the Captain preoccupied, the Colonel tightened his grip on the *Tribune*. The paper increasingly became an expression of tumultuous prejudices and the extension of a tigerish personality. But just as McCormick was no mere journalistic Joseph McCarthy, so the *Tribune* was far from being the voice of right-wing orthodoxy. No newspaper in the United States was more rabid in its advocacy of isolationism, in its attacks on the New Deal, and in its cold warriorship. On the *Tribune*'s masthead flew Decatur's toast, 'My Country Right or Wrong' and in its pages chauvinist denunciations of foreigners abroad jostled with racialist diatribes against 'aliens' at home. Chicago was an embattled city—to the North and East were those outposts of the British Empire, Canada and New York, the West was full of 'nuts' and the South was a Democratic wilderness. In the 1930s the paper proclaimed that 'a New Deal vote is an invitation to murder'[37] and represented Roosevelt as one of the four horsemen of the Apocalypse, along with Mussolini, Stalin and Hitler. McCormick personally explained that 'the blowing up of the battleship Maine . . . furnished President F. D. Roosevelt the idea of provoking the Japanese attack on Pearl Harbour 43 years later'.[38] After the war even Eisenhower and Nixon (not to mention Henry Luce) were too 'pink' for a *Tribune* paranoid about the conspiratorial activities of the 'Communists, traitors and homosexuals of the state department'.[39]

Yet, though uttered in more vicious tones, this was a standard rendering of what Oswald Garrison Villard called modern American 'Know-Nothingism'.[40] Where McCormick differed from other bigots was in an intensely idiosyncratic disregard for consistency. Thus the *Tribune* was the great champion of capitalism but it favoured stiff inheritance taxes to break up the large fortunes which threatened the integrity of the Republic. It was the sworn foe of organised labour but it mounted violent campaigns against the excesses of big business— Chicago's traction baron Yerkes was its particular *bête noire*. The *Tribune* intermittently supported the Ku Klux Klan but its philippics against the South were so vitriolic that it became the preferred reading of black intellectuals.̈ The paper approved of J. Edgar Hoover but when, during the war, he threatened to investigate the *Tribune* itself, McCormick was not afraid to vilify the 'FBI "Gestapo"'.[41] The

Tribune's overlord evinced a totalitarian contempt for all restraints, even those of logic.

The Colonel's contradictions were starkly revealed in his treatment of three obsessions, the British Empire, Communism and Chicago. He regarded Britain, with her colonial loot, her pre-eminent navy and her cunning diplomatists, as a major threat to the United States. At the same time he maintained that this transatlantic menace was really ruined by war debts, too decadent to fight and dominated by an incompetent snobocracy. Similarly, Red subversion was everywhere on the rampage (particularly among Waukegan school children, who were influenced by the likes of Clarence Darrow)[42] yet international communism was suffering a series of catastrophic defeats. As for Chicago, it was the Celestial City and Sodom and Gomorrah rolled into one. No doubt all these irreconcilables were the result of stereotyped thinking. They also stemmed from the Colonel's boundless capacity to hate. Like Dana, McCormick bore strange grudges and nursed his malice like a sacred flame. But even the *Sun* did not exhibit the *Tribune*'s reckless disdain for the truth.

Not content with issuing editorials in which Senate investigations became 'government witch-hunts' and crop control 'farm dictatorship',[43] McCormick created the facts in his own image. This was not an occasional lapse, like the New York *Times*'s false reports of anti-Bolshevik uprisings in Russia after 1917. It was a matter of policy. One of the *Tribune*'s most notorious fakes was its picture of the Social Security 'dog-tag' which the New Deal government planned to fasten round the necks of all American workers. In the same year, 1936, the paper's chief notice of a presidential visit to Chicago was a picture of discarded Roosevelt buttons, thoughtfully scattered along his route by the *Tribune*'s own photographer. McCormick's propaganda extended to deeds: when Rhode Island became tainted with Democratic heresy he tried to remove a star from the *Tribune*'s American flag, only desisting when told that defacing the national banner was a criminal offence. It was no wonder that, though other papers made the same mistake, Harry Truman held up the *Tribune*'s proclamation of his defeat on the morning of his Presidential victory in 1948.

Paradoxically, the more the *Tribune* was disparaged the more its circulation grew. If Hearst was the journalistic skunk of America, McCormick was the polecat. A survey conducted in 1937 revealed that, Hearst's publications excepted, the *Tribune* was regarded by Washington correspondents as being the 'least fair and reliable' newspaper in the United States.[44] Yet by 1939 the *Tribune* had beaten all its morning rivals from the field and was the largest standard-sized paper on the continent. More curious still, many of its million purchasers (seventy per cent of whom were Democrats) appeared to detest the *Tribune*. This is well illustrated by the story, apocryphal or not, of the Chicagoan who wanted to contract syphilis because he was 'in favor of anything the *Tribune* was against'.[45] Certainly McCormick, isolated even among the isolationists, was under no illusions about his popularity. He surrounded himself with guard-dogs and body-guards, drove to work every day in a bullet-proof limousine and, so rumour had it, equipped his office with secret doors, concealed machine-guns and other security devices.

He also commissioned an inquiry to find out why people bought the *Tribune*. Its report was rather inconclusive, yet the reason was surely not far to seek. In spite of, and to some extent because of, its glaring faults the *Tribune* was excellent value for money. It gave readers what they wanted in terms of colour, comic strips, features, stunts, campaigns (against Prohibition, for example) and sport. Its news coverage, if not reliable, was exceedingly comprehensive. Its style was zestful, articulate and (compared to that of Hearst's newspapers) sophisticated. Finally, there was something magnificent about McCormick's obscurantism. It was a monumental, adamantine quality, like the 36-storey Gothic Tribune Tower itself, impervious to rust or corruption. Even Harold Ickes, who regarded the *Tribune* (which compared him to Goebbels) as the rottenest paper in America, admitted that, though the Colonel's organ might surrender itself voluntarily, it was no white slave.

It was, indeed, a commercial institution. But this was a matter of pride to McCormick, for a paper with such vast resources would not stoop to prostitution. Even Adolph Ochs, who revived the New York *Times* at the beginning of the century, had been guilty of shameless soliciting—Arthur Brisbane recalled having 'seen him many times, sitting with his stove-pipe hat in his hands, outside the office of some advertiser'.[46] 'The *Tribune* is so prosperous,' McCormick boasted, 'that no bribe is of even passing interest.'[47] Any advertiser who attempted to blackmail the *Tribune* took his life in his hands and his custom elsewhere. Politicians found McCormick equally uncompromising. Chicago's Mayor, 'Big Bill' Thompson, was so incensed by the paper's intransigence that he sued McCormick for damaging the city's credit by defaming its character. The trial confirmed the principle that government cannot be libelled.

Having established a morning monopoly, McCormick abated not a jot of his antagonism towards Roosevelt. Consequently he provoked Marshall Field III to raise up a rival against him, the liberal and interventionist Chicago *Sun*, which first appeared in 1941. Throughout the war McCormick remained a stubborn and fanatical isolationist.

He was widely condemned for giving aid and comfort to the enemy. Few appreciated the fact that he was also preserving the liberty of the press. He was doing so in the most effective way, by exercising it in the face of massive popular hostility. No cause was dearer to McCormick's heart. For example, he made out an irrefutable case against British restrictions on newspaper freedom, imposed through libel laws, contempt of court proceedings, and the Official Secrets Act, and implemented by 'clowns or tyrants' on the bench,[48] only to ruin it by branding Britain as Nazi because of her journalistic silence over Mrs Simpson. Still, there was hardly a murmur of protest from the British when, in 1941, Churchill suppressed the *Daily Worker*. In America during the Great War the Creel Committee on Public Information (to give its full Orwellian title) had imposed similar restrictions on freedom of expression—Max Eastman complained, 'You can't even collect your thoughts without getting arrested for unlawful assemblage'.[49] This censorship was afterwards justified by the Supreme Court which asserted that the First Amendment could be overridden when the state was in 'clear and present danger'. But during the Second World War, although some controls were re-imposed, the *Tribune* and its satellites were too powerful to gag. McCormick's motives may have been selfish and his brand of patriotism pernicious. Nevertheless he sustained the historic right of American newspapers to dissent, even at a time of national crisis.

His cousin performed the same service when the unlikely 'McCormick–Patterson axis' was formed to oppose Roosevelt during the war. But for the two decades of peace Patterson remained a staunch liberal and the New York *Daily News* favoured progressive policies such as the municipal ownership of public utilities. Not that it paid overmuch attention to politics for, as Patterson frankly admitted, his paper was 'built on legs'.[50] At first this well-tried formula seemed in danger of failing, though both Hearst and Arthur Brisbane were worried enough to offer to buy the *News*. But soon circulation began to increase rapidly, rising to 100,000 at the end of 1919, a million in 1925 and reaching a peak of two and a half million by the time of Patterson's death in 1945. Patterson was himself at a loss to explain how the *News* became the best-selling paper in America.

It was by no means more crudely sensational than the yellow journals of the nineties, though many contemporaries asserted that the tabloid revolution marked a new low in the history of the press, 'an unholy blot on the fourth estate'.[51] In fact, Patterson's two tabloid rivals, Hearst's *Mirror* and Macfadden's *Graphic*, both launched in 1924, outdid the *News* in the lurid presentation of sex and crime. Moreover, in their search for thrills they confused fact and fantasy. The difference between their approach and Patterson's was typified by two famous pictures, the *News*'s illicit photograph of Ruth Snyder's execution in the electric chair at Sing-Sing, and the *Graphic*'s 'composograph' showing Caruso welcoming Rudolph Valentino into the spirit world. The first, however repulsive, was news; the second, a fraudulent cross between a camera-work and art-work, was imagination. Similarly, although the *News*'s headlines were often racy to the point of coarseness, they bore some relation to reality: thus 'Singer Croaks on High C' referred to the death of a soprano who was performing at the Metropolitan Opera House.[52] By contrast *Graphic* headlines such as 'I Did Not Marry My Brother' and 'For 36 Hours I Lived Another Woman's Love Life' were obviously spurious.

Hard news was Patterson's grail: he even subsidised experiments to control the sex of unborn rats in the hope that its successful application to man would bring him 'the scientific scoop of the decade'.[53] As the hectic 'twenties turned into the gloomy 'thirties his policy of reporting, however briefly, the serious matters of the day paid dividends. The *Graphic*, having alienated readers by its frenetic pursuit of melodrama (a lesson that is being learnt by today's New York *Evening Post*) closed in 1932 with a loss of some eight million dollars. In 1934 Brisbane thought that only Hearst's presence in New York could save the *Mirror*: 'it would give me great pleasure to teach my young, brown-eyed friend, Joe Patterson, that age cannot wither nor custom stale you'.[54] Hearst was too old. But after Brisbane's death he correctly assessed the reasons for the *News*'s pre-eminence. Writing to the editor of the *Mirror* Hearst accused it of being 'tawdry' and of failing to take account of the improving tastes of a more sophisticated and better educated public. 'I think, in a word, that the Mirror should be a grade above the Daily News instead of a grade below it ... in the long run the meritorious paper wins.'[55]

Hearst saw that public taste was changing: Patterson discovered how it was changing. More even than Northcliffe, Patterson studied to please his readers. He rode on subways, wandered round Coney Island or the Bowery, stood in cinema queues, everywhere gauged popular interests and surveyed public opinion about the *News*. 'You can't publish a successful newspaper by ear,' he told his editors,[56] who were often made to accompany him on these tours. From his surveys Patterson drew various conclusions: that news pictures were 'our life blood', that comic strips and competitions might be low-brow but readers wanted to be treated as high-class, that editorials should be irreverent but respectable and above all short, that the best kind of letters to the paper were those which attacked it most viciously. Patterson contributed some of these 'knocks' himself: 'I hear people say the trouble with the News is the bad paper it's printed on. I tell them it isn't the paper, it is what you put in it.'[57]

It was this tone which Patterson increasingly took towards his underlings. As the success of the *News* became more assured Patterson became more dictatorial. Symbolising this transformation was a new gesture which he adopted to silence employees in mid-sentence—he pushed his hands towards them, palms outwards, as though shoving the words back into their mouths. It was as if he wanted to emphasise that the *News* was no longer the cooperative venture it had been at the outset, but the achievement of one man. 'It won't last five years after I die,' he said.[58] Patterson's self-confidence grew so overweening that he indulged in the kind of caprices that seem inseparable from press baronage. He instructed his architect to build him the ugliest house possible and equip it with steel doors which, in the event of a fire, would not swell and trap its claustrophobic owner inside. Such whims were merely the incidental expression of a fierce independence which Patterson manifested, for instance, when pressed to play down the banking crisis of 1933—he splashed it all over the front page. By the early 1940s Patterson apparently decided either that he knew what was going on in the public mind better than the public did, or that he would ignore it altogether. For, just as the nation was rallying behind Roosevelt as a war leader, Patterson buried his head as firmly as McCormick in the sand of isolationism.

Patterson was not moved by a secret fondness for fascism. Indeed, he saw its leaders as doomed despots: 'Mussolini seems to think he's a pre-1812 Napoleon, not remembering there was also a post-1812 Napoleon'.[59] But, like so many of his generation, he was haunted by the spectre of Armageddon. With unaccustomed fervour he told Beaverbrook in 1939, 'I am not too much given to prayer but I hope God will let the cup of war pass for a while longer from us'.[60] As late as August of that year he was reporting to the *News* from Europe that Germany could not go to war because her road system was incomplete. In 1940 he condemned the Lease-Lend Bill as an act of dictatorship. When the Japanese bombed Pearl Harbour there was a brief reconciliation between Patterson and Roosevelt at the White House. At the meeting the President made the press baron read out some of his more virulent editorials, reducing him to tears in the process.

But soon Patterson returned to opposition, more bitter than ever and driven on by a pathological hatred for Roosevelt. Patterson had always possessed an unscrupulous streak: Harold Ickes had been surprised when he, one of America's most liberal publishers, belied his rhetoric about freedom of the press by openly scheming to keep Marshall Field's new journal *PM* out of the news-stands. Now Patterson employed indefensible tactics, vilifying the administration's Jewish war-mongers and even sneering at the President's physical handicaps. Always inclined to exaggerate the (admittedly considerable) hostility of the press towards himself, Roosevelt responded in kind. He went so far as publicly to present the *News*'s 'sixth columnist', John O'Donnell, with an Iron Cross. The McCormick–Patterson Axis deserved 'neither hate nor praise,' Roosevelt remarked, 'only pity for their unbalanced mentalities'.[61]

The third member of the triumvirate was Eleanor Medill Patterson (1881–1948), always known as 'Cissy'. Less formidable than her brother Joe and her cousin Bert, she was nevertheless important as the first woman editor of a metropolitan newspaper and the voice of the McCormick–Patterson Axis in Washington.

Cissy came late to journalism having spent her early years trying to recover from the trauma of a childhood in which she was alternately spoilt, bullied and neglected. Surrounded by luxury, Cissy was brought up to be a lady. Her domineering mother drilled her in the acquisition of poise and gentility, then sent her away to the correct schools to be 'finished'. Eventually she placed her daughter on the marriage market, having first (if Cissy's autobiographical novel is to be believed) examined her breasts, as though the two women were 'business partners, checking up together on the inventory of their joint account'. Inevitably the red-haired, snub-nosed Cissy rebelled against this treatment. In 1904, despite frantic opposition from her family, she married a Polish fortune-hunter, Count Josef Gizycki. From the first he treated her with feudal callousness, typified in her thinly fictionalised account of the wedding night:

> he had taken her as he preferred to take the young peasant girls on his estate ... silently, without a word or one caress; like a panther rutting in the dark, and she had cried out in her fright and pain.[62]

She endured five years of exile and marriage, loathing his 'Oriental' brutality yet receiving an obscure satisfaction from being dominated. Eventually she ran away and, after an international drama in which the Count kidnapped their daughter Felicia in London and released her only when President Taft personally interceded with the Tsar, they were divorced in 1911.

Cissy spent the next two decades oscillating between the poles of satiety and revulsion. She engaged in a series of love affairs begun with passion and ending in disillusionment. She became a brilliant rider but once shot a horse which threw her. She hunted big game until disgust with blood sports gave rise to a Hearstian sentimentality about animals. Another impulsive and unsatisfactory marriage would have ended in the divorce courts but for the death of her second husband. As a society hostess Cissy possessed every attribute—a thirty-roomed house in Du Pont circle filled with Aubusson carpets and Beauvais tapestries, platoons of green-liveried servants and a feline presence set off by a pack of yapping poodles. Yet, bored by her own parties, she sometimes retired to her silk-sheeted bed with a book. Then, at the age of forty-nine, imbued at once with an extravagant respect for power and the temperament of a mutineer, Cissy persuaded William Randolph Hearst to gamble that she also possessed her family's journalistic flair.

With a circulation of only sixty thousand and mounting losses, Hearst's Washington *Herald* needed to be taken in hand. Hearst obviously relished Cissy's open hero-worship, but recognising a steely determination behind the saccharine manner, the scarlet toe-nails and the extended cigarette-holder, he appointed her to the editorship in 1930. Cissy at once revealed herself as a rank amateur. She confused 'captions' with 'headlines' and refused to print the result of the Kentucky Derby on the front page because horse-racing was vulgar. But she was anxious to learn, remarking that she would rather be a reporter than a lady. To prove her point she disguised herself as an unemployed maid and wrote a first-hand series about the position of women without work in the nation's capital. But she was a better editor than reporter. And she quickly showed that no lady-like modesty would prevent her from exercising her power to the utmost. She dismissed one employee for wearing a red tie, another for sporting a waxed moustache, another for being too handsome. With an expressive mixture of similes a journalist noted that:

> her sub-editors walk in dread of a summons to one of her nightmare interviews on their particular departments. Curled in a corner of a deep leather couch in her private office with her feet tucked under her childishly, she dissects each section of the paper ... With languid tones and words dropped sparingly as vitriol drips from an eye-dropper her criticisms, like a black snake whip, start lazily and end with a crack in the listener's innermost soul.[63]

Like Queen Elizabeth, Cissy surrounded herself with good-looking courtiers whom she reviled or indulged as the spirit moved her. But her caprices were similarly productive. Spurred on by jealousies and resentments, her employees vied with one another to conjure up effective stunts and crusades. Soon it was being said that the clocks ran faster when Cissy Patterson was around, that the paper vibrated with an almost sensual excitement. It needed to because in 1933 Eugene

Meyer bought the Washington *Post* and competition became acute. Cissy tried to steal his four best comic strips and when thwarted by the Supreme Court, she sent her rival a beautifully wrapped box containing a chunk of raw steak. Meyer was puzzled by the gift but his wife had no difficulty in explaining its significance: 'Of course, a dirty Jewish Shylock'.[64] Cissy had to content herself with superiority in reporting. It was rumoured that if a corpse was discovered on the steps of the Washington *Post*'s building the fact would be reported first in the *Herald*. In fact Cissy was so avid for exclusive news that her paper once appeared on the streets with a circumstantial account of the execution of two gangsters several hours before it happened. Apologising to Hearst for her early mistakes, Cissy described herself as 'Scotch Irish conscientious very dumb'. He merely congratulated her on an 'amazing' increase in circulation and a 'very gratifying' rise in advertising revenue.[65]

However, as the 'thirties progressed tensions grew up between owner and editor. Cissy's politics were largely a matter of personalities and she admired her brother Joe even more than she did Hearst. Consequently in 1937 she reprinted some editorials for the *Daily News* favouring the New Deal, instead of Hearst's syndicated attacks on Roosevelt. Hearst remonstrated with her revealingly. He was 'a fish out of water' in the Republican camp:

> I had always been a progressive—a radical. I had nothing in common with reactionaries ... I am in heart and soul a democrat. I believe that the people's will should be obeyed. Moreover I believe that the majority decision is essentially right. Those who differ with it should study the situation themselves and find out wherein THEY are wrong.

However, he disagreed with the President on certain fundamental principles and he could respect Joe only 'as an opponent'. Hearst concluded whimsically, 'I am definitely not a New Dealer or a news dealer'. Cissy protested too much. She had only published the alien editorials in a 'panicky effort to recover from the sock on the jaw we got' at the election. 'I have never sought' to go 'contrary to your policy.... You know, Mr Hearst dear, that I don't lie to you.'[66] Cissy cajoled and flirted (in 1938 she told Hearst that she was coming to see him 'for no reason in the world except I love you')[67] but the constraint remained. She removed it in 1939 by purchasing both Hearst's *Herald* and his Washington *Times*, which she merged. Ironically at just that time she was beginning to follow her brother into Hearstian isolationism.

Loathing subservience yet longing to be mastered, Cissy accepted direction from Joe with a good grace. Indeed, it was his aversion to

Roosevelt's foreign policy which created the McCormick–Patterson Axis, for Cissy had no great respect for her cousin Bertie. Her attitude was doubtless coloured by the fact that, when he visited her in Washington, Cissy had to remove all the breakable objects from his bedroom. For in the dark hours 'terror' overtook him and 'McCormick's shouts and battles with his demon would echo through the whole house'. He never explained, and they did not discuss, what Cissy called 'Bertie's affliction',[68] but it scarcely inspired confidence in his judgement. Nor did the bizarre letter protesting his patriotism which was made public shortly after it was written in 1942:

> You do not know it but the fact is that I introduced the R.O.T.C. into schools; that I introduced machine guns into the army; that I introduced mechanisation; I introduced automatic rifles; I was the first officer to go up in the air and observe artillery fire. Now I have made that a regular practice.

There was a grain of truth in these claims but Carl Sandburg's comment was nevertheless apt: 'And on the seventh day he rested'.[69] McCormick was soon being lampooned as 'Colonel McCosmic'.

Thus it was actually a measure of Cissy's independence that she did not distance herself from such a compromising ally. Instead the Washington *Times-Herald*, like the New York *Daily News*, seemed to vie with the Chicago *Tribune* in its opposition to Roosevelt's government. Representative Elmer Holland named Joe and Cissy Patterson as 'America's No. 1 and No. 2 exponents of the Nazi propaganda line'.[70] His judgement was most strikingly vindicated when Cissy greeted the Yalta agreement with an eight-column banner headline which read 'Crimea Pact a Crime—Berlin'.[71] The approval of Congress was only noted lower down the page and Goebbels made capital out of the *Times-Herald*'s priorities. Unwilling to recognise that the freedom of the press cannot be maintained by a refusal to exercise it and that use often involves abuse, some liberals called for more codes and controls. Why, they asked, should the McCormick–Patterson Axis continue to enjoy legal sanction for behaviour which ranged, in Leo Rosten's phrase, 'from the incendiary to the psychopathic'?[72] Harold Ickes, for instance, who thought Cissy temperamental and unstable, believed that the press magnates should be subject to some kind of regulation. But the First Amendment remained virtually sacrosanct and, as Milton had prophesied, in its free and open encounter with Falsehood, Truth prevailed. Cissy pressed on regardless, asking no favours of the government and giving none. She gained more advertisements, but not at the cost of modifying her editorials. She increased profits and circulation (outstripping all Washington rivals) without compromising her views. Her readers bought the *Times-Herald* not for its views but its news, because it was a bright, interesting sheet full of life and character, Cissy's character.

In 1946, having achieved his ambition to out-live Roosevelt, Joseph Patterson died. Shortly before his death he had become a Roman Catholic but to the end he was preoccupied by the mundane business of journalism—in his oxygen tent there was a telephone directly linked to the *Daily News*. When his cousin vacated the throne, McCormick succeeded him, though not without the usual family feuds. For example, Cissy wanted Joe's liberal daughter Alicia, founder and publisher of the successful Long Island paper *Newsday*, to replace her on the board of directors. At the stock-holders' meeting McCormick resisted furiously and Cissy protested to him:

> There you stood, putting on the six-foot-four business, waving your arms about, glaring like a maniac [,] shouting your denunciations of Alicia. Why?[73]

In 1948 Cissy herself died. McCormick was in Paris when he received the news and from an adjoining room his second wife heard a strange, rumbling kind of song: 'Now I am the last leaf on the tree, the la-a-a-a-ast leaf on the tree-e-e-e!'[74] Having quarrelled with her daughter, Cissy bequeathed the *Times-Herald* to seven of its senior executives, who promptly sold it to McCormick for 4½ million dollars.

From the Tribune Tower he now directed what was, in terms of circulation, the largest American newspaper chain. It proved too big even for McCormick. In particular the *Times-Herald*, lacking Cissy's personal touch, began to lose money. The Colonel's attempts to conduct it by remote control were unsuccessful and a sophisticated metropolitan readership did not appreciate the crude embrace of the Mid-West. In 1954 McCormick sold the *Times-Herald* to Eugene Meyer for 8½ million dollars. The paper was swallowed by its old rival, the *Post*, which McCormick had described as the Washington edition of *Pravda*. McCormick himself died the following year.

He was, if Henry Luce is discounted as a mere magazine magnate and William Loeb (the diehard owner of New Hampshire's *Union-Leader*) is dismissed as a local anachronism, the last of the great press barons in the tradition of the Bennetts, Pulitzer and Hearst. But if he was himself in many respects a throwback to the competitive savagery of the Gilded Age, McCormick was also a living protest against the current shrinkage in 'the market-place of thought'.[75] For though he controlled a chain of journalistic supermarkets, he preserved the attitudes of the proprietor of a corner shop. In the epoch of the mass media he and his Patterson cousins remained, like Scripps, personal journalists. McCormick was not inhibited by any of the worries that constrain the managers of today's public newspaper corporations. He was responsible only to the light as he saw it. And if that light was so dim as often to be indistinguishable from darkness, it at least provided a background against which other newspaper beacons could shine more brightly.

CHAPTER ELEVEN

Uncrowned
King

COMPARED TO THE New York *Daily News*, Britain's leading tabloid, the *Daily Mirror*, was an organ of patriotic propaganda during the war. Yet its harassment by Churchill's government, which resented criticism even from its friends, contrasts starkly with the free conditions enjoyed by the press in America. The contrast is heightened by the fact that the *Mirror* bowed to official pressure and censored itself. This capitulation was all the more poignant because the *Mirror* gloried in its own boldness. Loudly scorning convention, concealment and innuendo, it claimed to reveal the truth, however shocking, without fear or favour. The *Mirror*'s editorial director, Harry Guy Bartholomew (known as 'Bart') took the Duke of Wellington's famous remark as his motto: 'Publish and be Damned!' The slogan was in turn adopted by a successor, Hugh Cudlipp, as the title of a book that purported to be the paper's history. Actually the book was an extended advertisement, belying its much-vaunted brashness with a series of euphemisms. For example, Cudlipp noted that when Northcliffe founded the *Mirror* as a newspaper written by gentlewomen for gentlewomen a number of unfortunate *doubles entendres* crept into the copy. But he coyly omitted the headline for which 'Yesterday in Paris' was substituted—'Our French Letter'.

Even so, there was some justification for the *Mirror*'s boast that it was the most outspoken newspaper in Fleet Street. Bart was the first to break what Edward VIII called 'the "gentleman's agreement" among editors' to suppress news of his desire to marry Mrs Simpson.[1] By American standards, of course, this agreement was a declaration of journalistic bankruptcy in the first place. But British press barons were loath to flout the national convention of reticence, strengthened as it

204

was by inhibiting laws. They professed to live by disclosure, but for the most part they were content to thrive by discretion. Lord Kemsley, for example, thought that there was something vulgar, if not downright improper, in revealing secrets, especially those of the eminent. There was no English McCormick and if there had been the government would have banned his newspaper. Someone like Beaverbrook did have the nerve to speak freely during the war but he was wedded to Churchill. The *Mirror* itself, as the Prime Minister discovered when he enquired into its ownership, had no single, rich proprietor but a multitude of small shareholders (not including, despite MPs' malicious claims, William Randolph Hearst). What resolution it possessed the paper owed to its directors, in particular to Bart and to Northcliffe's nephew, Cecil King. But though the latter was imbued with the courage of his uncle's convictions, he lacked Northcliffe's independence. King aspired to be a press baron in the grand old manner, but he proved to be a new kind of publisher.

Did King see himself during the Second World War as re-living Northcliffe's career during the First? Certainly, he had studied his uncle's history with fascinated attention. The favourite nephew was also given to flourishes of Northcliffean rhetoric. When Chamberlain resigned in 1940, for example, King congratulated himself, 'So at last my campaign to get rid of the old menace had come off'.[2] In the same year, mindful of Northcliffe's achievements as a war propagandist, King placed his experience and abilities at the disposal of the Ministry of Information: to his amazement, they were spurned. Subsequently he strove to make the *Daily Mirror* a political power in the land and to establish himself as a journalistic grey eminence behind the government. But as one of five directors responsible to stockholders he could by no means determine the paper's policy.

Nor did he cherish any true ideal of the press as the fourth estate of the realm. King did not even object to censorship, though he realised that it was being used 'cynically to keep from the British public news that was quite well known to the enemy, but which might have reflected discredit on ministers, generals or admirals'.[3] When the *Daily Worker* was suppressed he merely remarked that this was not in the interest of other newspapers and that it would provide good publicity for the communists. Despite certain more liberal pronouncements he was finally to conclude that a modern state must exert a degree of control over its newspapers. He 'did not see how Government can be conducted with a censorship',[4] which is merely 'negative propaganda'.[5] In other words, King believed that the press was just another weapon, though a potent one, in the political arsenal. His own role, he envisaged, would be to teach Churchill's administration how to use it.

In 1942 he exhorted Brendan Bracken, the Minister of Information:

> if the Government and the newspapers would work more closely
> together a very much more favourable press would result ... the
> newspapers could help the Government in the formulation of
> policy by their knowledge of, and their influence on, public
> opinion.[6]

In advocating collusion between Fleet Street and Downing Street
King was surrendering the pass that Northcliffe had done much to
hold.

For King's pains Churchill tried to have him conscripted (despite
the fact that he was exempted from military service on grounds of
health) and the *Mirror* suppressed. The fact was that the Prime
Minister completely misunderstood the nature of the paper's support
for the war effort. He took the *Mirror*'s raucous attacks on Munich
Muddlers sticking to public office, and bone-headed brass-hats talking
minced drivel, at their face value. In fact King and his fellow directors
were simply coming to terms with popular cynicism over the nation's
traditional rulers in order to mobilise the common people in a total
war. Candour would promote courage, they rightly believed.[7]
Churchill's increasingly old-fashioned view of Britain as a hierarchical
society was summed up in the 'eve of invasion' message which he
addressed to 'all His Majesty's servants in high places'. The Prime
Minister urged them to 'set an example of steadiness' and to 'check and
rebuke the expression of loose and ill-digested opinions in their circles
or by their subordinates'.[8] Churchill's idea of a newspaper was his own
British Gazette, the right-wing propaganda sheet he had run during the
General Strike and which he relished as 'the combination of a first-class
battleship and a first-class general election'.[9] He thus regarded the
Mirror, and its sister the *Sunday Pictorial*, as malignant and subversive.
He ignored the fact that their preoccupation with high society and
correct etiquette proved these papers to be, for all their populist
irreverence, anything but engines of revolution. Disregarding their
chauvinistic witch-hunts against traitors and pacifists, he accused
Cecil King of leading a fifth column.

After various arguments, conducted by letter and in person, the
government threatened to close down the *Mirror* summarily if it did not
become more 'responsible'. Ministers were badly bruised during the
parliamentary debate on the subject, especially when their own former
utterances about the inviolability of press freedom were quoted back at
them. Brendan Bracken, for example, was reminded that he had just
said in America, 'A blindfolded democracy is more likely to fall than to
fight'. The Home Secretary, Herbert Morrison, was in an even more

vulnerable position. As a conscientious objector during the Great War, he had published incitements to British soldiers not to fight their German brothers. And as recently as 23 November 1939 he had written in the *Mirror* itself, 'Public criticism is one of the essentials of good government. Under dictatorship public criticism—even private criticism—is a crime.... Beware of the foes of democracy using the excuse of war for its suppression.' These body blows did not shake the government's resolve. Hammering the table, Churchill vociferated to Brendan Bracken about the *Mirror* men, 'we will flatten them out'.[10] A journalist who knew the Prime Minister wrote that his anger at the press was 'almost uncontrollable, his quest for vengeance endless'.[11] In pursuit of it the Ministry of Information actually considered a scheme by which all newspapers should be compelled to publish the same headline, which it would supply. And it was not until later in the war, when American journalists protested to the State Department about attempts by the British Foreign Office to interfere with their dispatches, that political censorship eased.[12]

Yet throughout the entire dispute King had been conciliatory to the point of subservience. He informed Churchill that if he had only told his secretary to telephone the *Mirror* with orders to 'pipe down', they would have obeyed. In 1941 he assured the Prime Minister 'we now have your point of view clearly before us. The staff have their instructions and you may have already noticed a marked change of tone.'[13] The *Mirror* apologised for caricaturing Colonel Blimp encouraged its radical columnist Cassandra to join the army, and gagged itself for the rest of the war. Thus Churchill squared the *Mirror* by threatening to squash it and Cecil King abdicated his responsibilities. For, as he acknowledged in a liberal moment, 'the press is invariably right to resist' dictation—'It is suppression which distorts news and may cause a malaise in our affairs, not publication.'[14] King's self-imposed censorship was particularly surprising in view of his private conviction that Churchill was the country's 'old man of the sea'.[15] By clinging to power he would, King wrote in his diary for 1942, certainly lead Britain to further disasters if not to final defeat.

Cecil King had cultivated this alarming capacity for silence, hardly the most obvious qualification for the future Chairman of the world's largest publishing company, almost from the year of his birth in 1901. Brought up in the shadow of his uncles Northcliffe and Rothermere, he employed his taciturnity as a defence mechanism against their formidable sister, his mother, Geraldine. She had married Lucas White King, an Indian Civil Servant who later became Professor of Oriental Languages at Trinity College, Dublin. Lucas King was a colourless but irascible figure who once kicked Cecil downstairs for no reason that his offspring could determine. But Cecil felt more menaced by his mother's psychological brutality. Geraldine completely dominated the household and subjected her son to such callous treatment that he was afterwards unable to decide 'whether at bottom she was an evil woman determined to destroy me, or a violent and selfish woman quite indifferent to the threat she presented to a very sensitive emotional child'. Geraldine seems to have alternately scorched and frozen her son. Tall, fair and good-looking, he was an extension of herself and she claimed that he was her favourite child. But she noticed him only to shred his self-confidence and she was 'loveless, capricious and occasionally cruel'.

Cecil responded by repressing his feelings. He withdrew behind a mask of impassivity and developed an icy self-control. Hating himself, he longed, then and afterwards, to commit suicide. But he concluded that life was a struggle in which even an honorary orphan like himself might survive. The trick was to become invisible. He did not literally disappear, of course, though later, when bored or frustrated at parties, he sometimes turned his back on the person talking to him. He practised a calculated muteness, broken only by chilling little blasts of sarcasm; he cut and dried his emotions, snuffed out every spark of animation, vanished in spirit. By a stern effort of will he also governed the rages which boiled up inside him. This was a necessity. For once, during his miserable schooldays at Winchester, Cecil so lost his temper that he felt himself in danger of killing another boy. In youth he learnt to curb his tongue, clench his fists and wait. Later he wrote of his mother, 'I have no wish to do anything with my hands and it has seemed to me over the years that this was because in early childhood I had wanted to strangle her with them.'[16]

After the agonising intimacy of Winchester, where the lavatories had no doors and he was known as the 'Chaste Minerva', King led a solitary existence at Oxford. Shy, awkward, at six foot four physically as well as temperamentally aloof, he presented a frigid exterior to the world. Following an apprenticeship on Rothermere's *Glasgow Herald*, he came to the *Mirror* where he gave the impression 'of having received a crash course in small-talk at a Trappist monastery'.[17] Yet beneath his glacial hauteur there blazed a consuming ambition. All his life King was obsessed by having inherited or acquired the capacity for power without a proper field in which to exercise it. King's autobiography harped on his abilities so dispassionately that the book almost appeared to be an impersonal assessment instead of a monument to frustrated vanity.

I have always had a wider general knowledge than anyone I have ever met.... I have a greater gift of foresight than anyone I have met ... some have thought me the best talker in London.... I have an intuitive comprehension of the thoughts of millions.... [My being] a good judge of people ... explains why I am such a good administrator.[18]

Unfortunately for himself King came into Northcliffe's arrogance but not into his wealth. And his uncle Rothermere gave him nothing more than tokens of affection. In 1940, for example, when the press baron thought he was dying and his entourage believed that he was going mad, he presented his nephew with an Elizabethan silver jug for which Hearst had paid £800 and which Rothermere had bought for ninety. More important, King had earlier persuaded Rothermere to make him a director of the *Mirror*.

There he encouraged Bart to transform the paper from a sagging, orthodox journal read mainly by middle-class women, into a flourishing, nonconformist publication with the largest daily sale in the world. Ironically, having been the initial inspiration of the New York *Daily News*, the *Mirror* owed its revival after 1934 to the deliberate imitation of Patterson's techniques. But, as Hugh Cudlipp rightly remarked, the American tabloid was 'a *newspaper* with pictures' whereas the British one became 'a *picture* paper with news'.[19] The *Mirror* adopted not only the *News*'s dramatic way with photographs but also the sledge-hammer headlines, the condensed style, the strip cartoons and the vehemently demotic tone. The last was typified in Cassandra's column. Its writer, W. N. Connor, prided himself on being crude to the point of brutality, in contrast to the mealy-mouthed hypocrisy which he took to form the basis of most conversation among upper-crust riff-raff. His approach was epitomised in an interview he once conducted at Joseph McCarthy's dentist: he instructed the tooth-puller to hurt his recumbent patient as much as possible and informed the open-mouthed Senator that he resembled no one so much as Mussolini hanging upside down from a lamp-post. Less worthily, he also savaged P. G. Wodehouse for his innocent Berlin broadcasts, harping on the humourist's toffish names: Pelham Grenville mildly enquired whether Connor's own initials stood for Walpurgis Nacht.

Bart was uneducated and inarticulate. He could not write and would not read—an unusual but by no means a unique distinction among newspaper publishers. But having begun on the *Mirror* in 1904 and worked his way up from the bottom, he knew enough to appreciate Cassandra's power as a journalistic demagogue. By nature and nurture Bart was a proletarian. His idea of a good time was to shoot rats in a cellar and he 'dearly loved a dead Tory'.[20] He had an instinctive understanding of the common mind which the aspiring King, with his patrician tastes and intellectual interests, could never match—as King told American newsmen, 'I am a highbrow, a very high highbrow'. Bart had the knack of taking words out of the people's mouth, a form of ventriloquism assisted by devoting a large part of the paper to readers' letters. Consequently, for all its pride in cocking a snook at convention, flouting social taboos and poking fun at the Establishment, the *Mirror* was quite a deferential newspaper. Before the war, especially, it was respectable and respectful. It featured miners' wives ecstatically kissing dukes' buttonholes. It encouraged an abject form of female emancipation—'Men do not want to be commended by women: they want to be admired and adored'.[21] It approved of dressing for dinner. The *Mirror* was not even internally consistent. During the 1930s its opposition to Hitler and to appeasement was much more equivocal than it afterwards liked to pretend. In 1945 the *Mirror* condemned the *Express* for smearing the socialists as fascists but, without positively committing itself to Labour, it hailed Churchill as a potential Führer. As a contemporary remarked, the paper nailed 'its colours to the weathercock'.[22] In short, under Bart the *Mirror* lived up to its name, reflecting rather than directing the opinion of the people.

What for Bart was a visceral identification with his readers Cecil King interpreted as a cynical technique for appealing to a huge new audience of semi-illiterates. Both men possessed a genuine concern for the underdog, but Bart's was founded on sympathy and King's on calculation. King equated poverty and ignorance with present injustice and future disorder. As will appear, the one rogue factor in his cold-blooded political arithmetic was the prospect of imminent apocalypse, with himself somehow emerging as the national saviour. King did wish to improve the condition of the masses. But he also feared and despised them as a dangerous and irrational force.

> It is only the people who conduct newspapers and similar organisations who have any idea quite how indifferent, quite how stupid, quite how uninterested in education of any kind the great bulk of the British public are ... surely the amount of uplift you can fit into any popular medium has got to be kept pretty low ... if you are dealing with masses of people you are dealing in emotional terms most of the time.[23]

Bart naturally loathed King's patronising attitudes. King found it incredible that anyone as intellectually negligible as Bart should be the editorial director of a great newspaper.

Their antipathy was sharpened by a difference in approach towards

Eleanor M. Patterson

General Otis

Harry Chandler

Norman Chandler

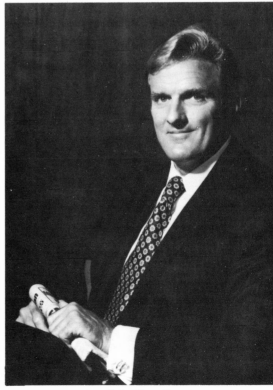

Otis Chandler

Rupert Murdoch—old-fashioned press tycoon

Rupert Murdoch—new-fangled international entrepreneur (flanked by two ex-editors of *The Times*, William Rees-Mogg and, on the left, Harold Evans)

the art of leadership. King issued lucid memoranda from an immaculate desk whereas Bart, in his own argot, ran the *Mirror* by the seat of his pants. Regarding himself as a natural ruler, King seemed bent on emulating General de Gaulle, while Bart behaved like a Tammany boss who had clawed his way to the top. Bart spied on his underlings, tapped their telephones, opened their letters, pursued obscure vendettas against them. He chained their typewriters to the desks and would have liked to shackle his journalists as well. To a senior employee he remarked,

> Let's walk through the news room. Watch them squirm. They need their hate symbol, these boys, and I'm here to fulfil a bloody need. When they hate my guts I know I'm getting across. So's the paper.[24]

Hugh Cudlipp described Bart as a 'thickset, sawn-off shotgun of a man'[25] and he was liable to blast hirelings out of the door at the drop of a whisky—of which he was inordinately fond. Cudlipp himself was fired, despite a talent for writing headlines like 'Maniac Killer Slain in his Floating South Seas Harem', which had helped to give the *Sunday Pictorial* a massive circulation. Bart also had his favourites whom he indulged shamelessly. One of them, Cassandra, summed up his erratic chief as a mixture of horseradish sauce and honey, barbed wire and blue ribbon.

However, Bart's megalomaniac quirks were becoming unendurable. For example, he destroyed the *Mirror*'s priceless picture library because he thought film would supersede it, and he refused to cater for his readers' love of sport. Bart sometimes even claimed to be one of Northcliffe's illegitimate children. Such *lèse-majesté* was intolerable. In 1951 Cecil King organised a revolt. Early one morning, before Bart had drunk himself into his daily state of violent incoherence, King announced that the directors had lost confidence in him and that he would have to go. King's own abilities secured him the succession. But he was to forget that the crown was his by election, not by right. Seventeen years later, overtaken in turn by the hubris of the press barons, King lacked the power to resist a coup staged by his own mayor of the palace Hugh Cudlipp.

Actually Cudlipp, recalled from his exile on Lord Beaverbrook's 'sunny side' of Fleet Street, encouraged King to show more independence. The ebullient Welshman sought to play Montgomery to King's Alexander, though King thought of him as playing Christiansen to his own Beaverbrook. Against his better judgement, King allowed himself to be persuaded that the *Mirror* should oppose both capital punishment and the Suez adventure. These were the most daring policies advanced by the paper until just before the end of King's reign. Perhaps the *Mirror*'s new chief had received a hint of the Labour government's plan, dropped in 1951 after secret Cabinet discussions, to impose a measure of press censorship. (The obsessively secretive Foreign Secretary, Ernest Bevin, reckoned that Britain had something to learn from Russia in this matter, and the security services apparently made it their practice—perhaps still do—to tap the telephones of political journalists who showed unwelcome signs of independence.) Certainly King knew that the Board of Trade had threatened to withhold from his paper licences to buy new machinery unless critical articles were toned down. The paper duly obliged. According to one witness, reports of social deprivation were suppressed because they might have provoked official disapproval.[26] The *Mirror*'s weakness was highlighted in the famous libel suit brought against it by Winston Churchill in 1951. Before the election the paper had accused him of advocating a preventive war against Russia. Instead of fighting the case, the *Mirror* tamely settled out of court, paying Churchill the sum of £1,500.

For all his Olympian arrogance, King knew his place. He was a commentator on the political scene, not a participant, and he condemned the antics of men like Hearst, 'the most odious character of all time'.[27] King was also a newspaper publisher, not an owner. True, by 1963 he controlled, as chairman of the International Publishing Corporation, a total of two hundred periodicals and twenty-one newspapers (twelve of them overseas). But the sheer vastness of that organisation made it susceptible to damage if its director embarked on the kind of crusades traditionally favoured by the press barons. With the bleak logic of which he was a master, King correctly assessed his position: 'The very commercialisation of the Press has made it unrewarding for the publisher to exercise the idiosyncratic power which in their day Northcliffe, Rothermere and Beaverbrook tried to exercise'.[28]

So Cudlipp was encouraged to produce a newspaper whose essential timidity was disguised by a superficial audacity. The *Mirror* never ceased to congratulate itself on being intrepid, enterprising, impertinent, the pricker of pomposity, the flail of snobbery, the torch-bearer of the common man. 'The "Mirror" makes up its mind, and has a mind to make up: this emphatically appeals to a wide British public in an age when politicians are minuetting to-and-fro delivering vacillating speeches about nothing in particular.... Its gaiety is not irresponsible: it smiles with a purpose.'[29] Actually it did little more than perform a series of pseudo-radical charades. For example, the traditional journalistic adulation of the monarchy was given a democratic veneer by the *Mirror*, which invited its readers to vote on whether Princess Margaret should be allowed to marry Group Captain Townsend. A similar stunt was its Debutantes' Ball for Working Girls, which amounted to the back-handed endorsement of a social anachronism.

The *Mirror* distilled its 'vigour and flair' most emphatically, according to Cudlipp, in a rebuke to Nikita Khruschev which took up the entire front page: 'Mr K! (If you will pardon an olde English phrase) Don't Be So Bloody Rude!'[30] Yet, as Raymond Williams noted,[31] the most striking feature of this headline was not its Shavian oath but its apologetic parenthesis. The ingratiating little archaism was a kind of apology within an apology. The *Mirror*'s comments on domestic politics also pretended to be more forceful than they really were. During the election campaign in 1955, for instance, it loudly banged the drum for youth. This was hardly a summons to the barricades. Indeed, it was largely meaningless except as an appeal to the *Mirror*'s predominantly young readership. And it had the disadvantage of clashing with the *Mirror*'s anti-Tory policy. Labour MPs were, on average, five years older than their opponents. Had he been elected, Attlee (aged 72) would have found it difficult to form, as the *Mirror* urged, 'the youngest Cabinet since Adam ruled in Eden'.[32] During the 1950s the *Mirror* pretended to be champagne but was really lemonade—all fizz and no kick. Cecil King's predominant mood was apparently summed up in his categorical declaration that 'popular newspapers are entertainment'.

Yet he also believed that 'a newspaper can have great power if the editor sets about it in the right way'.[33] Having diversified into commercial television at just the right moment, forged a chain of West African newspapers, taken over the Amalgamated Press in 1959 and Odhams in 1961 to establish a publishing group worth about a hundred million pounds (the next largest was Time Inc., valued at £77 million), King was now puffed up by earned success as well as native self-esteem. Not to speak of periodicals, where he exercised a near-monopoly, King controlled national newspapers (*Daily Mirror, Daily Herald, Sunday Pictorial* and *Sunday People*) with a combined circulation of over sixteen million. The New York *Times* described him as a publishing 'czar' who dominated the field 'in a manner unmatched since the death of his uncle'.[34] Such a tribute may have gone to his head, for during a trip he made to the United States shortly afterwards his vainglory was unblushingly on display. King ostentatiously left in the middle of a Chicago dinner given in his honour because half-past nine was his bed-time. And he told a group of newsmen at the National Press Club in Washington that their papers were a 'lot of little parish magazines scattered across the country' full of 'acres of verbiage, cubic miles of repetitious reports, incredibly bad headlines, non-existent layout and ludicrous handling of pictures'.[35]

At home King talked about 'my newspapers', 'my editors', 'my photographers', and his conduct of affairs became, if possible, even more autocratic. According to George Brown, King came to bear an increasing resemblance to his uncle. Brown was well able to judge for he was one of several politicians paid a stipend to advise the *Mirror*—which enabled him to press his views on the paper at all sorts of awkward moments. Brown was a frequent visitor to what journalists called the Glass Menagerie at Holborn Circus and its lavish ninth floor office, full of eighteenth-century furniture and dominated by a portrait of Lord Northcliffe, where King sat in state.[36] He also lived in state, cramming his beautiful Cheyne Walk house with old books and Mycenean art, with antique glass, china and silver. His potted plant stood in an oriental dish two thousand years old, his bedside mat was a silk rug on which a Persian emperor's throne had once rested. Despite such trappings of opulence, King's opposition to the Conservatives hardened, and during the election of 1964 he threw the whole weight of the *Mirror* against them. But whereas under Bart the paper had spoken for the people, now it talked at them. King treated his audience as subjects to be swayed by emotional appeals rather than voters who would be convinced by the articulation of their own views. His *de haut en bas* attitude was well illustrated by the electoral gesture of attaching a red flag to his extra-large Rolls Royce. In the knife-edged contest it is possible that the *Mirror*, with its fifteen million readers, just gave Labour the victory. Harold Wilson apparently thought so: King was invited to Downing Street as his first luncheon guest and offered a peerage. He declined the honour.

He later claimed that his refusal was prompted by a wish to maintain the independence of the press. This is implausible. King had actually thought that his administrative experience and ability made his inclusion in the Cabinet inevitable. But the only government position Wilson offered him was 'the job of understrapper to Douglas Jay' at the Board of Trade. This King considered a 'bitter insult'[37] and there is little doubt that he kept his distance in order to inflate his value in the Prime Minister's eyes. In short, he played hard to get. After the *Mirror* had given its support to a second, and overwhelming, Labour triumph in 1966, King once again turned down a reward out of wounded pride. Having denounced hereditary peerages, Wilson could only make him a life baron. King, who 'saw no reason why I should join their lordships at a lower rank than any of my lesser competitors',[38] would settle for nothing less than an earldom. As a result of this impasse King rapidly moved into outright opposition to the government. Like so many of the press barons, he allowed the political policies of his newspapers to be determined by personal pique. But, in reversing the *Mirror*'s traditional stance, King ignored his own admonition that the controller of a huge modern publishing concern could not, like his individualistic predecessors, 'behave with conspicuous irresponsibility'. He was vulnerable to public obloquy, government intervention and (though King failed to mention this) a boardroom insurrection.

Yet, almost as though he had some premonition of that event, King issued a further warning in his book on the future of the press, in 1967: 'The publisher must smoke out the bees in his own bonnet'.[39] In fact, during that year King's bees buzzed more busily than ever. He increasingly gave way to the obsession that some kind of catastrophe was imminent. All his life King had been haunted by the threat of revolution and the prospect of a totalitarian future. Partly this was a response to Britain's precipitate decline as a world power. Partly it reflected his belief that 'all existing political personalities and parties are utterly discredited'.[40] Partly it was a projection of his own deep pessimism, well illustrated in his diaries for the years 1970 to 1974 which are full of intimations of national and cosmic disaster, each one catalogued with gloomy relish.

> We are entering a new Dark Age with power in the hands of the stupid, the lazy and the ignorant ... a world slump next year ... the balloon is now beginning to go up.... [The United States is] sliding inexorably into chaos ... we may be witnessing the end of Western society.... Democratic government had clearly broken down and a dictatorial regime is all we can look forward to ... appalling calamity of world-wide dimensions ... a revolutionary situation is developing ... so the balloon has begun to go up.[41]

This jeremiad is punctuated by remarks on the grotesque incompetence of elected members of parliament—with two exceptions, both normally regarded as political pariahs, Ian Paisley and Enoch Powell. King concludes that only a form of national government will answer and implies that it should consist of industrial tycoons led by a man of destiny.

Of course, King has rejected the charge that he planned to replace Harold Wilson with a 'business administration': 'I consider the idea neither sensible nor practical'. But King himself was fond of quoting the old journalist's adage, 'Never believe anything until it is officially denied'.[42] And the evidence suggests that the prolonged financial crisis, the extraordinary deviousness of Wilson's government and King's personal frustration combined to provoke him in the spring of 1968.

As a Director of the Bank of England he foresaw an inflationary cataclysm which would destroy the value of money. Men would live by barter, the armed forces would intervene, blood would flow in the streets and, surely, he would be called from the wings of history to play a part in saving the nation. It was in this frame of mind that King paid his celebrated visit to Lord Mountbatten, apparently to explain why Wilson must go and to solicit his support. According to Hugh Cudlipp, Lord Zuckerman, who also attended, broke up the meeting with these words: 'This is rank treachery. All this talk of machine guns at street corners is appalling. I am a public servant and will have nothing to do with it. Neither should you, Dickie.'[43] Two days later, on 10 May 1968, Cecil King launched an 'all-out attack'[44] on the Prime Minister. It took the form of a signed article on the front page of the *Mirror* entitled 'Enough is Enough'. King denounced the government for its lack of foresight, ability, sensitivity and integrity. He accused it of lying about Britain's currency reserves. He described Wilson as 'a brilliant Parliamentary tactician and nothing more', condemned his failure 'to mobilise the talent that is available in this once great country of ours', and called for 'a fresh start under a fresh leader'.

This was the last serious attempt by a newspaper magnate to topple a British Prime Minister, though King naturally disclaimed any such ambition. Like similar assaults in the past, Northcliffe's attempt to unseat Kitchener, for example, it produced the opposite effect to what was intended. Labour MPs forgot their disenchantment with the government and rallied to the defence of their leader. Noting that the *Mirror*'s outburst had considerably strengthened Wilson's position, Richard Crossman exclaimed. 'What a stroke of luck Cecil King has been to Harold'.[45] But King's onslaught backfired in another way. The board of IPC secretly united against him. Cudlipp's role in what King, forgetting his overthrow of Bart, was to denounce as this squalid conspiracy, was equivocal. Believing that King possessed 'sound and proved judgement over an immensely wide range',[46] he had agreed to 'Enough is Enough'. Now he changed his mind and, perhaps with his eye on the succession, stiffened the directors' resistance to King. At the beginning of June 1968 they delivered an ultimatum to their astonished Chairman. His preoccupation with politics and his personal intervention in national affairs was having a bad effect on business: he must therefore resign at once or be dismissed. Characteristically, King preferred deposition to abdication.

Cecil King was ousted because he was an anachronism, an aspiring press baron in the age of media conglomerates. His despotic behaviour was inappropriate to the circumstances of the 1960s. It reflected his conviction that he was in some sense the reincarnation of Northcliffe, sitting crowned upon his throne—when King struck a bronze medal to celebrate the *Mirror*'s fiftieth anniversary he was only with difficulty persuaded that it should not feature his own head on one side and his uncle's on the other. Yet though King's departure was a cause of much rejoicing in Fleet Street, especially among his own employees, it by no means led to an unqualified improvement in the conduct of the press. What it signified, in fact, was the triumph of corporate management over personal control. King himself had stated that a 'publisher has the right, indeed the duty, openly to exert influence through his paper'. And he had contrasted his view with that of Lord Thomson, who imposed no 'centralised and unified philosophy'[47] on his newspapers but gave them complete editorial independence—provided that they did not come out against God or the monarchy. With King's passing, Thomson's method prevailed. But it was not quite so straightforward as it sounded. Editorial liberty was qualified by managerial supervision, which was dominated in turn by the profit motive.

Thomson's favourite colour was gold, his favourite music was 'the sound of radio commercials at ten bucks a whack', his favourite occupation was counting the column inches of advertisements in his papers, his favourite recreation was finding ingenious ways of pinching pennies—like staying at the Savoy hotel for appearances' sake but taking his meals in a Covent Garden porters' café. With his 'deep affection for banks'[48] Thomson was, as he frankly stated, 'a money-making man'.[49] His entire life was a vicious financial circle: 'I buy newspapers to make money to buy more newspapers to make more money'.[50] While King expressed a lordly disdain for lucre, it was Thomson's sole criterion for judging the worth of a newspaper (which accounts for his progressive disillusionment with the London *Times*). His editors knew that eccentric, capricious, outspoken opinions might alienate readers and damage dividends. Consequently there was no room in Thomson's newspapers for the licensed irresponsibility which had been the glory of the press barons, no room for the diversity of view which is the essence of press freedom. Characterised, as a Canadian Senate report said, by their numbing conformity, Thomson's newspapers remain too inoffensive, too balanced. They are the journalistic equivalent of airline food.

After King's dismissal the *Mirror*, now presided over by Cudlipp, vainly tried to prevent its circulation slipping below five million by becoming more respectable. The trend was strengthened in 1970 when the International Publishing Company was taken over by Reed International. Originally a paper company, this huge conglomerate has interests in more than forty countries. In 1977 less than a quarter of its billion pound turnover derived from printing and publishing. The contrast between its mode of wielding authority and King's was well illustrated in the evidence which the *Mirror* submitted to the last two Royal Commissions on the Press. In 1962, declaring the idea that he went round 'steamrolling our poor oppressed editors' to be quite fanciful, Cecil King acknowledged that they had to follow the general strategy laid down by himself, in consultation with Cudlipp. In 1977 the *Mirror* group's editors were said to enjoy 'virtually complete independence', but they were 'surrounded by senior advisers of great experience ... which makes their job more of a consensus position than an arbitrary dictatorship'. Stripped of its corporate verbiage, this simply meant that a committee, and not an individual, made policy. It was no accident that under such remote, amorphous direction the *Mirror*'s own character became less distinctive. It tried to broaden its appeal and to occupy the journalistic middle ground, which meant in practice that it swung uneasily between dispensing information and entertainment. Inevitably, during the 1970s, the *Mirror* lost ground to the *Sun* (which IPC had sold, ironically, as a chronic loss-maker) under the virile personal control of Rupert Murdoch.

With his usual devastating frankness, Cecil King had commented on the 1962 Royal Commission's disquiet over the growing concentration of newspaper ownership:

> The powers that be have not been very interested in the freedom of the press for some years past. They have been stepping up the Official Secrets Act and the operation of the libel law until a very effective press censorship is stifling us all, and the authorities regard such developments with equanimity, so why should they bother if a few newspapers amalgamate?[51]

The post-war Royal Commissions which have three times deliberated on the press were, as the chairman of the latest one incautiously admitted, punitive 'inquisitions'.[52] They were imposed by politicians eager to bring newspapers to heel. So under the circumstances King's jibe was a pertinent one. But he is not quite so inclined to discount the effects of the galloping press consolidation which had occurred since his reign.

Today just three conglomerates, Reed International, Trafalgar House and News International (Rupert Murdoch's corporation), own ten out of Britain's seventeen national newspapers, representing almost 75 per cent of the daily, and some 90 per cent of the Sunday, circulation. A similar concentration has taken place in the provinces where five chains control newspapers (now complete 'commercial operations',[53] according to a recent study) with nearly two-thirds of the total circulation. In most cases the parent companies earn the bulk of their income from other activities, oil, paper, property, shipping, hotels, television, banking, books, and so on. Even the few remaining independent national newspapers have diversified into other enterprises. Of course, all this reflects a general tendency towards the amalgamation of small companies into big business battalions. When it acquired the *Observer* in 1981, Lonrho behaved as though it were simply adding to its growth by a single economic unit. But intellectual goods are more than mere commodities and the political and social implications of conglomerate control of the press are alarming. The watchdog of the people is in danger of becoming the lapdog of international commerce.

This is not to say that major newspapers will be converted into overt instruments of business propaganda. It is to suggest that a subtle erosion of journalistic independence will occur. Evidence that it has already done so in Britain is sparse. But it does exist. In 1974 the *Daily Mail*'s plan to expose atrocious conditions on board a North Sea oil rig was hastily abandoned when journalists discovered that the company to which it belonged, Blackfriars Oil, was one of the paper's own subsidiaries.[54] In its testimony to the Royal Commission in 1977 the *Times* acknowledged that 'Coverage of Thomson Organisation activities in Thomson newspapers tends, certainly, to the drily factual'. More recently, and more revealingly, Conor Cruise O'Brien explained his dilemma as editor-in-chief of an *Observer* which had suddenly been bought and sold (subject to approval by the Monopolies Commission) 'with no more consultation afforded to it than is afforded to a bunch of bananas'. He himself had not, he assured readers, become the personal property of Lonrho's managing director, Mr Roland 'Tiny' Rowland. 'Yet what I write for you is affected by his ownership of the means through which I am able to communicate with you.'

O'Brien recollected his recent harsh words about Rupert Murdoch and continued:

> Am I going to write about Mr Rowland in similar vein? No, reader I am not. And why not? Because Mr Rowland may be the owner of THE OBSERVER. That may not be an admirable reason, but it is true and sufficient: Tis enough, 'twill serve. I am not going to ask that Mr Rowland's ink should print on Mr Rowland's newsprint such words as might induce fits in Mr Rowland. I do not know whether, if I did write such words, they would actually reach you, but they are not going to be written.... There is a rather odd corollary to that, I am never again going to write an unkind word about Mr Rupert Murdoch, so help me

God. Living in a glasshouse now, I shall toss no more rocks in the direction of the other glasshouse.

O'Brien concluded that, though he would not write falsehood there was 'a certain range of topics'—a vast one if he was referring to Lonrho's international interests—towards which he would employ what Edmund Burke called 'an economy of truth'.[55] The *Observer*, a serious liberal paper with a distinguished history, did just that. Nowhere did it mention, in discussing its new owner, the fact that Edward Heath, when Prime Minister, had pilloried Lonrho as 'the unpleasant and unacceptable face of capitalism'.[56]

In general, however, the tightening embrace of the conglomerates receives little attention in the British press. There was no serious outcry when Atlantic Richfield bought the *Observer*, or when they sold it. Radicals have protested that the voice of democracy is being stifled, but there is no agreement about how to prevent it. Stricter legislation to stop undesirable mergers and monopolies is no real solution. Indeed, it might well impede the rescue of weak newspapers by strong chains and thus reduce the existing variety. Several schemes have been proposed by which the state would intervene in the free market economy and stem the corporate tide. Usually these involve giving public money to new or failing publications, with the overall purpose of redistributing power in society. The trouble is that the socialist cure seems likely to be worse than the capitalist disease. For subsidies would make Fleet Street, or a section of it, perilously beholden to Downing Street. Successive Royal Commissions have reluctantly concluded that newspapers are better off being raped by conglomerates than gelded by governments. The BBC and ITV provide a terrible warning. Both depend on parliament in different ways, with the result that their comments on current affairs have all the flair and daring of Musak. Nothing better illustrates the BBC's submissiveness than its withdrawal of the invitation to the radical historian and anti-nuclear campaigner, E. P. Thompson, for fear that a Conservative government would refuse to authorise the imminent increase in its licence fee. But perhaps such caution is understandable. Section 34 of the BBC's new Royal Charter permits the Home Secretary to ban the broadcasting of any programme; section 19 empowers him to send troops to take possession of its studios. If the British press is a torpid Argus, British television is a blinded Cyclops.[57]

As Cecil King himself remarked, 'Radio and television have been castrated by the politicians'.[58] (In America broadcasting suffers from similar handicaps and is not given full protection by the First Amendment on the grounds that the aether, which contains a limited number of transmission frequencies, is public property. Newspapers which own, and in some cases rely on, radio and television stations, are thus subject to official pressure, an additional cause for concern about the growth of communications conglomerates on both sides of the Atlantic.) King recognised impotence when he saw it. But his tragedy was not that he failed to grasp political power (itself a national blessing) but that he never exercised legitimate journalistic influence. With his ability, intelligence and eccentricity, with his personal vanity, his contempt for the established order and his capacity for indiscretion, King was well equipped to extend, willy-nilly, the boundaries of press freedom in Britain. But Cecil King was a press baron in everything but security of tenure. His courage was sapped and his career was dogged by a fatal lack of independence.

CHAPTER TWELVE

From Fief to Empire

IN AMERICA THE passing of the press barons and the transformation of their private fiefs into corporate empires is best illustrated by the remarkable development of the Los Angeles *Times*. Founded in 1881, this struggling frontier sheet was bought soon afterwards by its editor, Harrison Gray Otis. The paper served what was little more than a sprawling village and its water-powered press often had to stop because the pipes became clogged with fish. Otis employed methods of almost unprecedented ruthlessness to give the *Times*, by 1900, a circulation of 30,000 and to make it the most profitable newspaper in the West. When Otis died in 1917 his son-in-law, Harry Chandler, turned the paper into a prospectus for the proliferating business enterprises which earned him several hundred million dollars. As Hearst primly informed Fremont Older:

> The Times is not a public institution run in the service of the people. It is a private institution run for the personal business advantage of Mr Chandler. . . . It is even worse than this; it is an instrument for the promotion of Mr Chandler's unpatriotic enterprises and crooked deals. In other words, the newspaper is being prostituted for the private unworthy ends [of] its proprietor.[1]

During the 1940s, under Harry's son Norman, the *Times* stuck its fingers into other commercial pies, beginning a chain, buying television stations and investing in timber land and paper mills. In 1960, the fourth member of the dynasty, appropriately named Otis Chandler, turned the *Times* into a public company, the first American newspaperman to take that course.

Today, a century after its foundation, the *Times* heads the largest newspaper-based conglomerate in the country. The Times-Mirror Company owns several other newspapers, including Long Island's *Newsday*, the Dallas *Times-Herald*, and the Hartford *Courant*. Its most recent acquisition is the Denver *Post*, once the yellow journal of Harry Tammen and Fred Bonfils, two of the most notorious press barons in American history, who ran it from a red-painted office known as the 'Bucket of Blood'.[2] Controlling massive interests in publishing, broadcasting and wood products, the Times-Mirror Company is the most widely diversified of the newspaper groups and it has an annual turnover of more than a billion dollars. At the turn of the century the *Times* was one of the worst newspapers in the United States; now it is one of the best. Yet, as will appear, the change is not entirely for good. An individual sink of iniquity has become a corporate well of knowledge, but the pollution which remains is all the more insidious for being less perceptible.

Harrison Gray Otis was a journalistic primitive. He was not so much a press baron as a robber baron and he brought to the *Times* such a combination of innate personal savagery and acquired military skill as to make it invincible. He also managed to provoke some of the most vicious invective ever bestowed upon a newspaperman; witness the famous diatribe of Hiram Johnson, Governor of California.

> He sits there in senile dementia with gangrene heart and rotting brain, grimacing at every reform, chattering impotently at all things that are decent, frothing, fuming, violently gibbering, going down to his grave in snarling infamy ... disgraceful, depraved, corrupt, crooked, putrescent—that is Harrison Gray Otis.[3]

Otis was born on an Ohio farm in 1837, the youngest of sixteen children and the grandson of a noted revolutionary soldier. He served a printing apprenticeship and received a commercial education before himself fighting with distinction in the Union Army. The tall, blond, blue-eyed Lieutenant-Colonel was discharged after being wounded. He then used his political connections to obtain work as a government printer, a Patent Officer and finally a Special Agent for the Treasury Department in the Alaska seal islands. There he prevented poaching and prohibited the sale of whisky to the natives. As a stern Methodist and a rigid teetotaller he relished this job. But, driven by ambition and feeling the pull of California, 'the fattest land I was ever in', he did not remain for long. As one journalist wrote, 'He envisioned himself to be an empire builder, a big man destined to do big things'.[4] The things

Otis did, once he had gained complete control of the Los Angeles *Times* in 1886, made Colonel McCormick seem like a mild-mannered liberal.

Journalism, for Otis, was the prosecution of war by other means. His new *Times* building, aptly situated on Fort Street, was constructed like a block-house. Completed in 1887 at a cost of $25,000, it was the first granite edifice in Los Angeles. Otis provided the staff, known as 'the Phalanx', with an arsenal of rifles and shot-guns. And, dressed, as usual, in full military uniform, he conducted regular drills in their use. A contemporary journalist, commenting on the way in which Otis's 'powerful personality' and 'overwhelming individuality' 'permeated and dominated his whole establishment', naturally reached for a military metaphor. 'He marched his martial way through every department—editorial, news, mechanical and business'.[5] During the worst of the labour troubles which he did so much to provoke, Otis charged to the office from his homes, called The Outpost and The Bivouac, in a car with a cannon mounted on the roof. The *Times* itself was a daily barrage of high explosive, directed at the countless enemies who gave point and purpose to Otis's life. There were vicious personal feuds, for example. Otis attacked Hearst as 'yellow Yawp' and nicknamed his former partner, who had established the rival *Tribune*, 'Smoothy' Boyce. When Boyce threatened to sue him for libel Otis replied characteristically, 'The Times is always ready to back up what it says, and, in fact, to force the fighting'.[6]

Otis conducted vitriolic campaigns against businesses which refused to advertise, against institutions like the Democratic party and the closed shop, against customs such as unlicensed drinking and undisciplined garbage disposal, even against places. For instance, the *Times* did not as a rule report earthquakes because it was bad for property prices; but Otis sometimes wrongly reported them as having occurred in Santa Barbara, where he had received a social snub. However, his especial loathing was reserved for San Francisco, for he was investing everything in the supremacy of Los Angeles. Such was his local chauvinism that a reader of the *Times* might have been pardoned for assuming that the two cities were at war. Otis constantly boomed Southern California's climate, its real estate values, its fertility, its growth. His General Order No 1 read simply 'Push things'.[7] By contrast, he described San Francisco as 'the buckle on the Northern Murder Belt'.[8] Its safest bank was a sand bank. Its inhabitants were degenerates and aliens. It was ruled by criminals and 'Wobblies' (a word which Otis coined for the Industrial Workers of the World).

It was as a haven of militant labour that Otis especially reviled San Francisco. For since 1883, when his own printers mutinied out of sympathy for strikers in the Bay City, he had regarded trade unionism as an insufferable form of dictatorship. For the last thirty years of his life (interrupted only by the war of extermination which Otis waged against the Filipinos in 1898–1899, becoming a general as a result) he dedicated himself to resisting its incursions southward. He would not even compromise in order to obtain the Assistant Secretaryship of War. His nomination was defeated by the unions and he told President McKinley, 'I would not change the attitude I have deliberately and successfully held for years past for the sake of securing any office on earth'.[9] All was fair in his prolonged and bloody conflict with organised labour. Otis created a blackleg Printers' Protective Fraternity, stiffened the resistance of other press barons, mobilised the police and the commercial community, employed spies, *agents provocateurs* and vigilantes, resorted to bribery, fraud, blackmail and coercion. The *Times* itself was his principal weapon and it sniped ceaselessly at 'the "labor leader", who leads in the wrong direction, and who fights shy of labor as a means of subsistence'.[10] As for the rank and file, they were 'butchers', 'wolves', 'industrial vampires', 'socialistic freaks', 'thugs and ruffians', 'dynamitards and bludgeon-wielders', 'corpse defacers'.[11] The *Times* even printed a fake picture of Samuel Gompers, leader of the American Federation of Labour, trampling on the Stars and Stripes. The trade unions retaliated with nation-wide financial levies, strikes, pickets, boycotts, intimidation and sporadic violence.

In 1903 they induced Hearst to found the Los Angeles *Examiner* in order to combat the *Times*. It promised to 'support with its whole power the proposition that labor is justified in demanding a fair share of the wealth it produces'. Otis denounced the *Examiner* as 'an emissary of chaos', receiving in return some choice vilification from W. C. Brann of the *Iconoclast*:

> I can wonder what will become of the *Times* editor when the breath leaves his feculent body and death stops the rattling of his abortive brain, for he is unfit for heaven and too foul for hell. He cannot be buried in the earth lest he provoke a pestilence, nor in the sea lest he poison the fish, nor swing in space like Mahomet's coffin lest the circling worlds, in trying to avoid contamination, crash together.[12]

Words could not hurt Otis. Nor could the *Examiner*. For in 1904 he secretly bought the progressive Los Angeles *Herald* and employed it as a fifth column, a 'skeleton regiment' he called it, to subvert the liberal cause while seeming to sustain it. By the turn of the century General Otis congratulated himself on having made Los Angeles 'the Mecca of the independent worker'.[13] Others knew it as Scab City, or simply Otistown.

At a few minutes past one o'clock in the morning of 1 October 1910 the hostilities reached a climax. Los Angeles was rocked by a huge explosion as the new *Times* building was dynamited. Complete with turrets and battlements, this half-million-dollar structure was even more of a castle than its predecessor. Yet it was almost completely destroyed by the blast. A score of Otis's employees perished, many of them in the resulting fire, for Otis's stronghold resembled a prison as well as a fortress and they could not escape. Only the *Times*'s emblem was undamaged. It was a circumstance on which the General harped in the mighty curse he pronounced over the bombers:

> O you anarchic scum, you cowardly murderers, you leeches upon honest labor, you midnight assassins, you whose hands are dripping with the innocent blood of your victims . . . look up—if you dare raise your eyes in that direction—and behold the stone image of the eagle that you could not reach.[14]

Otis was further provoked by the discovery that 'infernal machines' had been placed outside his own and an associate's house. He clamoured for an arrest, earning himself the nickname Harrison Bray Otis.

Eventually two brothers named McNamara, both union men, were charged with what Otis called 'the Crime of the Century'.[15] They pleaded innocent. The case divided the nation; capital and labour drew up their battle-lines. But some radicals, convinced of the McNamaras' guilt, justified their action. E. W. Scripps, for example, argued that employers possessed and used every weapon—the power to give and withhold jobs, the financial whip-hand, control over the bar and the bench, government and police. Workers had only brute force and could not be blamed for resorting to it. Scripps advocated negotiations with the prosecution before the trial commenced. His friend Lincoln Steffens, the muck-raking journalist, arranged for the McNamaras to confess in return for long sentences of imprisonment instead of the death penalty. Otis was initially outraged by the bargain. 'I want those sons-of-bitches to hang', he thundered.[16] But his subtle son-in-law, Harry Chandler, convinced him that victory was preferable to vengeance. By their admission the McNamaras thoroughly discredited and demoralised the labour movement. At the impending mayoral election the socialist candidate was decisively defeated and the rule of big business, unhampered by trade unionism, was secured. The *Times*'s triumph was to shape the history of Los Angeles for a generation or more.

With his massive bulk, his shaggy walrus moustache and goatee beard, with his combative spirit and refractory nature, Otis resembled nothing so much as a grizzly bear of the Sierras. Unreconstructed Republican though he was in theory, his political rampages were governed in practice by private whims. Otis was afraid of no one, not even the mighty Southern Pacific railroad. After an epic fight the *Times* thwarted the Southern Pacific's attempt to build Los Angeles's principal harbour in Santa Monica (where it had bought land) instead of at San Pedro. Otis regarded his paper as a commercial institution but profits were not his sole concern. He was quite prepared to ban an advertiser who spent $50,000 a year for trying to dictate the content of the news columns. And he threw a leader of society out of his office when he accused a *Times* reporter of lying. Arguably, too, Otis's prolonged struggle with the unions was a financial dead loss, for, apart from the incidental costs, he had to pay high wages in order to demonstrate the advantages of paternalism.

Even before 1886, when he was trying to gain complete financial control of the paper, Otis refused an offer from some bankers who wanted him to support their political candidate in return for an indefinite loan: 'The Times belongs to the public and I cannot sell it out.'[17] In valuing his own independence above lucre, Otis was a true press baron. Upton Sinclair had a different view. He claimed that the Los Angeles *Times*, which he regarded as the Madam in the brothel of journalism, was undeviatingly mercenary. It was inevitable:

> Someone has said that to talk of regulating capital is to talk of moralizing a tiger; I would say that to expect justice and truth-telling of a capitalist newspaper is to expect asceticism at a cannibal feast.[18]

In likening the press barons to wild beasts and savages Sinclair undermined his own central contention. This was that newspaper owners were engaged in a plot to maintain industrial autocracy's control over political democracy. In fact, press barons were too uninhibited to endure the discipline of a conspiracy. Certainly General Otis took orders from no one, fought no battles but his own and numbered capitalists as well as socialists among the legion of his foes.

However, Harry Chandler (1864–1944) seemed bent on making the *Times* imitate Upton Sinclair's account of it. Chandler became a Californian Midas and the paper helped him to turn everything he touched into gold. Born in New Hampshire, he had come to the West Coast as a young man seeking a cure for pneumonia. He obtained work in the circulation department of the *Times*. Like Scripps, he made his first real money by gaining control of the newsboys' delivery routes but, unlike him, Chandler was only interested in the newspaper as a commodity. In 1894 he married Otis's daughter, Marian, and was soon appointed business manager of the *Times*. Now he began to buy property and before the general's death he had acquired the largest real estate network in California, not to mention hundreds of thousands of acres in Mexico. With these acres in mind Chandler, like Hearst, urged the American government to intervene during the Mexican Revolution and he may actually have supplied arms to the conservative forces of General Huerta.

Chandler's most spectacular coup was to divert the Owens River, via an aqueduct, through the San Fernando Valley—huge tracts of which he had purchased—to Los Angeles. The inhabitants of the Owens Valley saw their farms reduced to desert while Chandler's syndicate profited to the tune of some $100 million. The *Times* boomed the scheme and played a crucial part in accomplishing what has recently been called 'one of the greatest water "steals" in history'.[19] It also became an advertising brochure for Harry Chandler's other investments—in cattle, cotton, oil, ship-building, book publishing, insurance, catering, clothing manufacture and so on. Chandler was involved in almost every development of the expanding economy of Southern California. He did much to attract the automobile and aircraft industries to Los Angeles: the *Times* became their champion. He bought property in Hollywood and backed Warner Brothers: the *Times* puffed motion pictures. Republicanism was good for business and the *Times* enabled Chandler to become the *éminence grise* of the party in California. But where money was concerned he was no ideologue. While his syndicate was engaged in what proved to be abortive negotiations to develop oil and coal fields in Siberia, the *Times* (much to Hearst's delight) muted its vociferous hostility towards Bolshevism.

It was a brief aberration. For the next forty years the *Times* specialised in horror stories about Reds subverting Californian churches and communising American girls. Norman Chandler (1899–1977), who became publisher of the *Times* after his father's death in 1944, was a hard-line Republican. Indeed, he was mainly responsible for discovering Richard M. Nixon as a politician and giving him the kind of press support that made him feel he could do no wrong. But even more than Harry, Norman was a pragmatist. He had served a long apprenticeship on the *Times*, starting as a floor-sweeper and serving a turn in every department, and the only doctrine in which he really believed was that of commercial success. (The creed was softened by his adoption of a familiar American practice: he gave back to the public in the form of well-advertised charity a small portion of what his forebears had taken by means of concealed rapacity.) Thus between 1945 and 1955 the *Times* rose from thirty-fourth to first among

American daily newspapers in the amount of linage it carried. However, it was clear that there was a large section of the growing population of Los Angeles which resisted this dropsical production, though it might buy a cheaper, racier, less reactionary newspaper. So in 1948 Norman Chandler launched the afternoon tabloid *Mirror*. He gave the editor two instructions. 'One: not to favour Communism in any way. Two: not to print anything that couldn't go into the American home.'[20]

The *Mirror* thus resembled its London namesake in seeming to be more daring than it really was. It conducted campaigns against saloons, organised crime, the black market in babies, and ugly female legs. It even raised gasps by running a series of articles on the menopause. And it favoured Eisenhower for President instead of Taft, the *Times*'s candidate. Norman was eventually reconciled to this by his forceful wife Dorothy, who threatened to go on sexual strike unless he supported Eisenhower—one occasion when the *Times* did succumb to the closed shop. The *Mirror* was a failure and, after internal convulsions, it expired—at the same time as the Hearst *Examiner*, a coincidence which probably involved a breach of the anti-trust laws and certainly gave the *Times* a morning monopoly. Like the *Times*'s immensely profitable television station KTTV (begun in 1949), the *Mirror* afforded another indication that the Chandlers' expanding family enterprise had become an integral part of the economy of Southern California. Of course, businesses had controlled newspapers before. But, in the spirit of the First Amendment, the press barons had largely remained outside the established order. General Otis was a maverick: the Chandlers were part of the herd.

Between 1958 and 1962 the Los Angeles *Times* was transformed. It became a somewhat lumbering version of other *Times* newspapers, those in New York and London. There were several reasons for this startling change. The *Times*'s last old-fashioned, Red-baiting, Labour-hating campaign had backfired disastrously in 1958, when the Democratic candidate for the Governorship of California, Pat Brown, was elected with an overwhelming majority. Los Angeles, now the third largest city in the United States, had become too sophisticated for the *Times*'s crude methods to produce anything but revulsion. A new editor, Nick Williams, was appointed in that year and he moved to occupy the ideological middle ground, which still put the paper, when judged by standards other than those of Norman Chandler, distinctly to the right of centre. But though the *Times* endorsed Nixon in 1960, it reported Kennedy fairly. Such balance was unprecedented, and so was the *Times*'s new-found enthusiasm for some of the social causes that appealed to the young such as gun control and civil liberties.

This all reflected the fact that Norman's son Otis became publisher in 1960 and he was significantly more liberal-minded than his father. True, Otis Chandler believed that the prime responsibility of the *Times* was to make money. But he recognised that respectability could confer even greater profitability. By adopting a tone of magisterial impartiality the *Times* could claim to speak for, and aspire to be bought by, the entire community. This was especially necessary if it was to beat off the challenge of its New York namesake which, in 1962, began to print a West Coast edition. In the event, the Los Angeles *Times* did much to ensure the failure of this attempt to produce America's first national newspaper. However, Otis Chandler had an even more pressing reason for trying to make the *Times* moderate and objective. In 1960 the Times-Mirror Company 'went public', issuing 6 million shares, 4·1 million of which were sold, 1·9 million being held back for trading purposes. From now on the *Times* was bound to be responsible, if only to its stockholders.

Otis Chandler was responding to the economic logic which dictated that a business could only succeed through expansion and diversification. The individual press baron could not survive, burdened as he was by the rising cost of newsprint and new technology, by competition for advertisements from television and by a threefold fiscal burden, corporation tax, income tax and inheritance tax. Advised by business consultants, Chandler turned the Times-Mirror Company into a huge conglomeration of commercial interests. The corporation, which he likes to call 'an information company, or a communications company',[21] avoided tax by ploughing back its earnings. Using unissued stock certificates or borrowing on assets, it bought other newspapers and enterprises unrelated to journalism, obtaining generous new allowances for plant depreciation. The plan was to invest mainly outside the field of newspapers, whose potential for growth seemed limited.

Soon the company owned subsidiaries which produced timber and associated goods, published Bibles, paperbacks, telephone directories, road maps, medical and legal books. It also had a considerable stake in cable television. Only about 40 per cent of its income came from newspapers. Chandler himself, the blond, six-foot-three athlete who had apparently possessed few enthusiasms outside surfing and big-game hunting, now followed in his father's footsteps. He became involved in countless other business ventures. He sat on the boards of many large companies, such as the Union Bank and Pan-American Airways. And he increased his personal interests in property, agriculture and oil, the last of which led to his being charged in 1973 with violations of the federal securities law. The case against him was eventually dropped and the *Times* reported the story with marvellous circumspection.

As the parent company's non-journalistic concerns proliferated this was but one occasion among many when the paper had to tread warily. Although some of Paul Conrad's cartoons were banned (for example, his representation, entitled 'Leaks', of Spiro Agnew urinating over selected American newspapers), there was not much in the way of overt censorship on Otis Chandler's *Times*. Indeed, his great-grandfather would have been astonished by the degree of editorial latitude. But the corporate consensus was imposed on journalists by means of subtle pressures. Optimistic articles about the delights of sunny California were preferred to hard-hitting investigations into the seamy side of its life. The *Times*, which employed no black reporters, played down the prospect of racial disharmony in Los Angeles. In 1965, when the riots occurred in the black suburb of Watts, the paper found itself in the embarrassing position of relying for its news on reports from the local police and the national wire services. To give Chandler his due, however, he publicly admitted that the *Times* had been at fault. And the paper's inquest on the violence won a Pulitzer Prize.

In general, though, the *Times* was the cheer-leader of commerce, especially commerce in which Otis Chandler had a hand. It shamelessly supported civic developments that would increase the value of its own property. And it still fails to give adequate coverage to the interests of poor minority groups in Los Angeles for the simple reason, as Otis Chandler explains, that to do so 'would not make sense financially . . . that audience does not have the purchasing power and is not responsive to the kind of advertising we carry'.[22] The paper's assistant metropolitan editor, Noel Greenwood, concluded:

> The real conflict of interest at the *Times*, and at other papers—in fact, of the newspaper business—is that the publisher has a stake in the larger business and industrial establishment. The staff is constantly pulled back and forth: trying to act as a watchdog for the public; but, at the same time, developing that more 'realistic' sentiment that it's a job and they're practicing a trade as best they can under some very real constraints.[23]

Otis Chandler himself acknowledges that, despite the advantages of group ownership, there is an equally strong 'argument on the other side for independence, that the loss of independent newspapers and voices around the country is a bad thing, and so I guess I'm kind of on the fence.'[24]

Thinking corporately, managing through a team, writing by committee, the *Times* today identifies itself with the great industrial and financial institutions of America. The paper resembles other commercial monoliths in everything but its responsibilities as a member of the fourth estate and its accompanying constitutional privileges. But, as an integral part of the country's power structure, the *Times* tends to neglect its public responsibilities. Its elaborate neutrality masks a positive determination to maintain the company's place in that structure. Consequently, its privileges could be threatened. Already there is much talk in the United States of treating communications conglomerates like any other monopolistic enterprise and 'Busting the Media Trusts'.[25] In 1978 the distinguished journalist John Hohenberg wrote:

> The growth of conglomerates which make news part of their general business, does not tend to increase public confidence in the integrity of the public intelligence that is offered ... if there is a continued flaunting of power by the news media in the years to come, the First Amendment is not likely to prove a great barrier to antitrust action.[26]

The First Amendment was drafted on the understanding that newspapers would be voices crying in the wilderness. It did not matter how raucous or even how deceitful they were, for reason would triumph in the open lists and verity would prevail amidst diversity. The flagrant lies of a press baron like General Otis were easy enough to detect, even had there not been competitors enough to expose them. The subtle ways in which Otis Chandler's *Times* distorts the truth are more difficult to spot and there are fewer independent newspapers to do the spotting.

Indeed, the complete disappearance of the independent newspaper has been widely forecast. In 1960 the chains controlled well under half of all daily circulation, whereas today they control almost three-quarters. In an authoritative survey of present trends, the Washington *Post* reckoned that within the next twenty years nearly all America's 1750 newspapers will be owned by fewer than two dozen great communications conglomerates.[27] The chairman of the National News Council recently estimated that eight or nine groups would own 85 per cent of the nation's dailies by 1990.[28] Already only eight chains control 50 per cent of the daily circulation and more than a score have followed the Los Angeles *Times* in becoming public companies. Chains are swallowing other chains—the eager bidding of rival publishers for the recently-sold Speidel chain made its vice-president feel 'like a virgin at a stag party.'[29] In addition to the tax advantages, there are further incentives towards consolidation. The chains save money by central management, bulk buying of newsprint and easier selling of advertising space. Possible economies of scale will soon be dramatically increased. Electronic typesetting and satellite communication could serve newspapers scattered all over the continent from a single media complex. The *Wall Street Journal* already has a nation-wide string of 'zoned editions',[30] full of local news and advertising, and many city papers are taking similar steps to follow their readers into the suburbs. Newspaper offices, at present cottage industries, may well be transformed into mere assembly plants and distribution centres for the products of one large factory. That this poses a threat to good journalism has been proved by the New York *Times*'s abortive West Coast edition. One journalist, Gay Talese, likened it to *Pravda* because the '"reporters" were technicians processing what officials elsewhere decided should go into the paper'.[31]

The factories are growing all the time. Adolph Ochs, who rescued the New York *Times* when it fell on evil days after George Jones's death, abjured conflicts of interest by pledging himself 'never to dabble in Wall Street'.[32] Now the paper has twenty-seven subsidiaries, including thirteen other newspapers, shares in large Canadian newsprint companies, radio and television stations, assorted magazines, and three publishing firms. Eugene Meyer, who helped to make the Washington *Post* America's second most influential paper, regarded the preservation of its independence almost as a sacred trust. But today the *Post* stands 'at the head of a burgeoning conglomerate'.[33] Newspapers account for less than a quarter of its revenue, most of which comes from magazine and broadcasting interests. Once Henry Luce refused to add a publishing house to his magazine empire because he would not have time to read all the books it issued in his name. Now *Time* is junior partner in a huge timber and paper conglomerate with a net income (in 1977) of $90 million. Multinational corporations are significantly represented among the proprietors of the American press. The Thomson Organisation owns fifty-seven newspapers. And Rupert Murdoch has expatiated on the attractions of acquiring newspapers in the United States: 'You pay three times the revenue because it's a monopoly and a licence to steal money forever.'[34] There is nothing to prevent other industrial giants such as oil companies or car manufacturers from investing in the profitable field of newspapers and a few have already done so. America stands poised to follow the British example. Paradoxically, there is more concern in the United States about what might happen than in the United Kingdom about what has happened.

Of course, there is a bright side to the picture and American newspaper publishers are quick to point it out. They argue that only large press consortia have the resources to oppose an increasingly powerful government and stress their good record over the twin crises of Vietnam and Watergate. Actually, that record was by no means as impeccable as the newspapers afterwards liked to pretend. And, as President Nixon showed when he threatened the New York *Times*'s Florida radio stations, the conglomerates are vulnerable precisely because of their non-journalistic interests. However, as Katherine Graham remarks, in a revealing mixture of ethical and commercial phraseology, the Washington *Post* is a

> living demonstration that a publicly owned firm can do what a news company should do, which is to take risks for news stories, to stand behind its new product even if it hurts you occasionally, and to do what your First Amendment obligations require you to do. And I think that, in the long run, that pays.

Other defenders of the corporate press claim that only papers like the New York and Los Angeles *Times* and the Washington *Post* can resist the threats to journalistic freedom posed by recent decisions about rights of privacy, libel, the protection of news sources and official secrets.

They also say that, although there are vicious asset-strippers and flagrant propagandists, most chains improve the newspapers they buy. As Alvah H. Chapman of the Knight-Ridder group contends, 'Many, many newspapers across this country were pervasively mediocre, unprofessional and timid. They often lacked the economic strength— or will—to resist the special interests which called the shots in their communities.'[34] He is correct, and he could have elaborated his case by showing how many of the stronger newspapers were money-minded prostitutes, citing perhaps the bitter indictment of a turn-of-the-century journalist, William Salisbury:

> The majority of these owners and managers have no more poetry in their souls than have wholesale grocers, or dealers in other merchandise. They are concerned about such things as art and learning, about public morals, about the fate of the American public itself, as much as are other business men—no more. The biggest newspapers much resemble department stores, their chief patrons, and their twin product of American commercialism.[35]

But when Alvah Chapman, whose chain has been described by one of its editors as computerised and dehumanised, accuses his critics of remembering 'the good old days that never were',[36] he himself is guilty of selective amnesia. He forgets the positive achievements of the press barons.

Certainly a large body of informed opinion in America deplores the organisations which have succeeded them. It asserts that the ideas and information men live by are too important to be left in the care of 'diversified corporations with far-ranging interests'.[37] And it quotes the Supreme Court's verdict (Associated Press v. United States, 1945) that the First Amendment 'rests on the assumption that the widest possible dissemination of information from diverse and antagonistic sources is essential to the welfare of the public'. In Senator Edward Kennedy's words, 'The possibility that newspapers and other media will be swallowed into stifling conglomerates that will shut down rivals and shut off differing viewpoints is, naturally, intensely worrying in our democracy.'[38] Another leading opponent of 'the titans of the chains', Representative Morris K. Udall of Arizona, reinforced the point with his much-quoted pronouncement in 1977: 'I fear that the quest for profits and higher dividends for their growing list of stockholders will transcend their responsibility to maintain an independent and dedicated influence in the community.'[39] Inevitably, in the ninety-eight per cent of American cities where there are daily newspaper monopolies, editors lack the incentive to improve their products. For the most part they are content to rely on the news services, accept shoddy work from their underlings and cut costs at the behest of superiors who regard the press as simply a business operation. The widespread belief is soundly based: never in the history of American journalism have editorial values been so systematically sacrificed to commercial ones.

Criticism has come from within the press as well. Ben Bagdikian, sometime internal ombudsman of the Washington *Post*, has commented on the 'severe ideological ossification' of the press corporations. And he has exposed the sinister ways in which papers like the Wilmington (Del) *Journal* and *News* and the Houston *Chronicle* became a means to their 'parent company's non-journalistic ends'.[40] Bagdikian and others have proposed solutions to the problems of corporate ownership. They range from imposing further anti-trust measures to publicising who owns what, from achieving true journalistic autonomy to giving statutory freedom of access to the press. Unfortunately it seems that what might be enforceable would not be effective and what might be effective would not be enforceable—and this is not to consider the inherent dangers of press legislation. There is nothing to stop the growth of the conglomerate empires; the despotism of an Otis seems petty by comparison.

CHAPTER THIRTEEN

International Baronage

CERTAINLY NOTHING HAS been able to halt the spectacular expansion of Rupert Murdoch's international press corporation. Starting thirty years ago with a bare majority of shares in the feeble Adelaide *News*, Murdoch has built up a conglomerate worth well over £100 million. His antipodean holdings include the only national newspaper, the *Australian*, the Sydney *Mirror* and *Telegraph*, a large number of provincial and suburban papers, magazines, the sole independent airline (which he bought because it controlled a television station), not to mention interests in books, records, films, printing, farming, mining, natural gas and the New South Wales Lottery. In the United States Murdoch owns the largest evening newspaper, the New York *Post*, several other metropolitan journals, the national weekly *Star*, magazines, the San Antonio *Express* and *News*, and a dozen suburban news-sheets in the Houston area. His national papers in Britain are the *Sun* and the *News of the World* (which have the biggest daily and Sunday circulations respectively, 3·8 million and 4·5 million), the *Times* and the *Sunday Times*. Murdoch also owns twenty-seven provincial papers and has a stake in London Weekend Television, in printing, papermaking, recording and publishing.

His newspapers always seem to be the best or the worst. Inevitably the latter attract most attention—which, of course, is precisely what they try to do with stories like this (from the San Antonio *News*):

> A divorced epileptic, who told police she was buried alive in a bathtub full of wet cement and later hanged upside down in the nude, left San Antonio for good this week-end. The tiny, half-blind woman, suffering from diabetes, recounted for the *News* a bizarre horror story filled with rape, torture and starvation.[1]

Despite such sensationalism, and because of it, Murdoch is the biggest figure to walk down Fleet Street since Lord Northcliffe. On a global scale he has perhaps achieved the greatest spread of newspaper power in history. Personally he is a remarkable cross between the new-fangled multi-national tycoon and the old-fashioned press baron. Yet thanks to Murdoch's dramatic commercial forays over three continents, the fact that he is a direct beneficiary of 'the Chief of All Journalists (of all ages)', as his father called Northcliffe,[2] has gone largely unrecognised.

Sir Keith Murdoch, Rupert's father, was the son of a Presbyterian minister who emigrated to Australia from that cradle of journalists, Aberdeenshire, in the late nineteenth century. After a frugal childhood Keith obtained his first job in 1903, as district correspondent for the Melbourne *Argus*. He was a forceful, ambitious man, 'physically and mentally massive'.[3] But he was hampered by a severe stammer which he only overcame in middle age, and even then his conversation was punctuated by long silences. By 1914 Murdoch had improved himself and his position in Australian journalism, having saved up to take a course at the London School of Economics and afterwards become Melbourne correspondent of the Sydney *Sun*. He had also gained the friendship of the Labour Prime Minister, Andrew Fisher, who commissioned him to investigate the postal arrangements for Australian troops in Gallipoli. This he did, finding the Postal Department an 'inert mass of congealed incompetency'. But, appalled by what he saw in the Dardanelles and scenting a sensation, Murdoch went further.

He wrote a report which exposed the 'gross bungling' of the general staff, the 'terrible atrophy' in the trenches and the disastrous failure of the expedition as a whole.[4] It was an inflammatory document, largely (but not wholly) accurate, crackling with memorable phrases: 'Sedition is talked around every tin of bully beef on the peninsula'.[5] Though addressed to Fisher, this 'Guy Fawkes epistle' as its chief victim General Sir Ian Hamilton called it, was read by Lloyd George, who characterised Murdoch as 'exceptionally intelligent and sane'.[6] Northcliffe was also sent a copy and, like Lloyd George, he urged Murdoch to circulate it to other ministers. The Australian complied and his report helped the government to make up its mind to recall Hamilton and to evacuate Gallipoli. More important, from Murdoch's personal point of view, it established him in the good graces of Northcliffe. The Colossus of Fleet Street became 'the biggest influence and the biggest force' in his life.[7] Modelling himself on his hero Murdoch earned, in his own hemisphere, the title of 'Lord Southcliffe'.[8]

Until 1920 Murdoch spent most of his time managing the United Cable Service which sent news to Australian newspapers from London. Northcliffe assisted by giving advice, letting him see early proofs of the *Daily Mail* and introducing him to important people. He also invited Murdoch to Sutton Place for what the Australian gleefully called 'lovely girls, golf and one week more of yourself'. Even on questions relating to 'the sex' (Northcliffe's term) Murdoch treated him as a confidant: 'I recentlly met an Adorable Person in the shape of a Slade School art student and have only just recovered my stance.'[9] He also tickled Northcliffe's palate with just the right kind of tit-bits, about 'Australians getting narrow eyes owing to the sunshine',[10] for example. But mostly they talked newspapers. Murdoch flattered Northcliffe's vanity—'You have reduced your control of your vast organisation to a set of coherent principles which these fellows follow and understand'— and received in return valuable hints about their common craft.[11] In 1920 Murdoch was even employed to cover the Prince of Wales's tour of Australia and New Zealand for the *Times*. At the end of that year Murdoch accepted, on Northcliffe's advice, the editorship of the Melbourne *Herald*.

Northcliffe further helped him by sending detailed criticisms of the paper. They amount to a distillation of Northcliffean wisdom on the subject of popular journalism.

> The first editorial should be the second thing read every day, the first being the main news.... Smiling pictures make people smile.... I, personally, prefer short leading articles.... People like to read about profiteering. Most of them would like to be profiteers themselves, and *would* if they had the chance.... The church notes are good. People who drink, smoke and swear, have no idea of the interest in church matters.... [Sport] can be overdone I believe, even in Australia.... The desk habit is, of course, one of the curses of journalism.... Every woman in the world would read about artificial pearls.... The late Gordon Bennett, when his staff could not print pictures, introduced the engineer of his yacht and told him to print pictures. The man did it.... The 'Herald' has a very bad name in Australia ... just as a man is always the last to hear about his wife's sideslips, so is an editor the last to hear about his paper. You have got to live down a past.... I still notice in the 'Herald' an absence of 'items'. Columns of items a day give the reader a great feeling of satisfaction with his three-halfpenny worth.... My young men say you don't have enough stockings in the paper. I am afraid that I am no longer a judge of that.[12]

Murdoch hailed Northcliffe as 'Chief' and told him, 'Your notes are my bible. I go to them daily.'

This was not obsequiousness. Murdoch's missives to Northcliffe, which catalogue the progress of the *Herald* under his direction, show that he followed his mentor's precepts in letter and in spirit. Murdoch promoted the first beauty contest in Australia. He published serials, started a woman's page, mounted stunts, conducted campaigns over hospitals, police, tramways, and hatched other 'schemes for forcing ourselves forward'. He kept his editorials crisp and human, illustrated them, concentrated on local issues. Within a year the *Herald*'s circulation had risen from 95,000 to 140,000. Rivals attacked Murdoch as a 'yellow' newspaperman who had 'brought *Daily Mail* journalism to Australia'.[13]

They also imitated his methods, as well as employing more standard techniques—such as assaulting the *Herald*'s newsagents and setting fire to its building. Journalism in Australia has always been a vicious business and its leaders yielded nothing to press barons elsewhere in the violence of their behaviour. Witness Cyril Pearl's remarkable account of the career of John Norton, owner of *Truth*, who was denounced by one competitor as a 'human plague-rat'.[14] His son carried on the family tradition—Peter Packer, proprietor of the Sydney *Morning Telegraph*, went to the grave bearing on his ear the marks of Ezra Norton's teeth. Lord Thomson, who made a study of the Australian press, concluded that it was too dangerous to invest there: the inhabitants carried guns and their main occupation seemed to be rape.

When Keith Murdoch entered this arena in 1920 he provoked new bloodshed and inaugurated the most ruthless era in the history of Australian newspapers. With his news sellers menaced by gangs wielding bicycle chains, Murdoch distributed his paper through fruiterers, barber-shops and tobacconists.[15] His staff became a private army and he employed a revolver-carrying bodyguard. Remorselessly the *Herald* advanced. Murdoch used it as a base from which he expanded into other enterprises. He began a number of specialist magazines and became the first Australian newspaperman to exploit the new possibilities of radio. By acquiring huge timber concessions in Tasmania and building a paper mill he virtually created the antipodean newsprint industry. Imbued with Northcliffe's dynamism, Murdoch also shared some of his hero's lesser quirks. He was a hypochondriac. He was suspicious of men who wore beards. He selected smart youngsters of good social background as reporters, promised them advancement in glowing terms and promptly forgot all about them. He was a fervent patriot and a preacher of 'constructive Australianism'. Yet his Tory views were tempered by a form of radical populism. Indeed, Murdoch called himself, as Northcliffe might have done, a 'revolutionary conservative'.[16]

The term might equally be applied to his son Rupert, who was brought up in the paternal shadow. Admittedly, at boarding school in Geelong he was known as 'Red Rupert' and at Oxford University he kept a bust of Lenin in his rooms. But he soon reverted to type and now disparages the long-haired, suede-booted Left as much as he does the snobbish élitism of the Right. Today he is partial to jokes which offend liberal susceptibilities. He has even been quoted as saying that there is nothing wrong with the blacks of Brixton that being hit over the head with a bottle won't put right. More important even than his political opinions, however, are his journalistic ones. Under the forceful guidance of his father, Rupert was steeped in Northcliffean ideas. Almost from birth, in 1931, he lived and breathed newspapers. Together father and son would pore over the *Herald*, analysing its defects, discussing improvements. Nurture played its vital part, but Rupert Murdoch is also a natural press magnate.

He is temperamentally restless, driven by bursts of nervous energy, and even now has such a low threshold of boredom that he sometimes simply walks away from people who do not interest him. One who knew him at both school and university declared, 'the key to Murdoch . . . is that he is a fidget.'[17] He is also charming, brash, ambitious and independent. At Geelong he was a nonconformist who turned cartwheels on the cricket field. As a contemporary remarked, Rupert was 'a perfect pest' at school: 'whatever authority was for he was against.'[18] At Oxford he tried to take a short cut to office in the University Labour Club by illegally canvassing for election. He lacked the concentration to read at length but managed to gain a poor degree (in Politics, Philosophy and Economics) as a result of six weeks cramming before the examination. After Oxford Murdoch exploited his father's friendship with Lord Beaverbrook to obtain a job as sub-editor on the *Daily Express*. He earned £10 a week, stayed at the Savoy Hotel and quickly learnt the butcher's art of chopping up copy. Aged only twenty-one he also tried to buy the Melbourne *Argus* from Cecil King, who looked askance at such presumption. Then, in 1952, Keith Murdoch died and (to his son's lasting fury) much of the family property was realised to pay inheritance tax. Rupert flew home to build his fortune on the ruins of his father's estate.

He did so by adapting the Northcliffean methods learnt on his father's knee to modern circumstances. Of course, the old reliance on stunts, self-promotion, crusades, competitions and insurance schemes remained, as did *Answers* articles like 'My Crazy Cat thinks Mice are Nice'. Moreover Murdoch employed, and employs, many familiar business techniques. He has always been fond of appointing two men to the same post and watching them fight for survival. In London he travelled to work by tube and studied the reading habits of other commuters. Like Northcliffe, too, he uses office spies. He is known as 'a great sacker'; he specialises in abrupt dismissals and paid £79,000 to buy out the contract of Stafford Somerfield, editor of the *News of the World*. But Murdoch's journalism was, and remains, especially in Australia and Britain, much more sensational than anything Northcliffe would have countenanced and it has added a new dimension to the term 'muck-raker'.

Huge headlines scream 'Wives Sell Sex for Food', 'Uncle Tortures Tots with Hot Fork', 'Colour it Blood Red and Call it Kill City USA', 'Leper Rapes Virgin, Gives Birth to Monster Baby'. The stories and serials in Murdoch's papers—for example, the memoirs of the prostitute Christine Keeler and the train-robber Ronald Biggs—exploit sex and crime with such unadulterated relish that in Britain they frequently earn him the censure of the Press Council. Pictures of bare-breasted girls decorate so many of his pages that he has been dubbed the 'Dirty Digger' and Rupert 'Thanks-for-the-Mammary' Murdoch: it cannot be long before he trumps his rivals in this respect by playing the pubic card. Also Murdoch's political campaigns are far cruder than anything hitherto practised in the Old World. He gives every appearance of relishing the exercise of his power and influence in the newspaper world, and he feels that it is his right as a controller of newspapers in a free society to criticise politicians.[19] Finally, Murdoch's drive for commercial expansion is more ruthless than Northcliffe's and he is much more daring as an entrepreneur.

Still, newspapers are his first love and remain the largest part of his business. He is never happier than when taking off his coat and acting the part of editor-in-chief, as he did when the New York *Post* covered the 'Son of Sam' murders in such lurid detail in 1977. But from the start modern economic logic dictated that in order to grow he must diversify. With only one newspaper he could not achieve economies of scale, let alone security. Having made the Adelaide *News* a rip-roaring radical news-sheet, Murdoch bought the moribund Perth *Sunday Times* and, employing his familiar tactic of lowering its tone in order to raise its circulation, soon whipped it back to life. With a chain of newspapers Murdoch could buy better information, more eye-catching articles, serials like *The Sensuous Woman* and *The Love Machine*. But without more revenue he could not afford a chain. So he acquired Channel Nine television in Adelaide, which soon began to make large profits. He was thus able to raise bigger loans. In 1960 he moved to Sydney, purchasing another television station, some suburban newspapers and eventually Ezra Norton's ramshackle empire which included the *Daily* and *Sunday Mirror*.

These two papers had been deliberately run down before being sold and their resuscitation at Murdoch's hands was one of the hardest fights of his career. His first move was to redecorate the *Mirror* building and give everyone a by-line, thus restoring morale at a stroke. On Pulitzer's principle he increased staff holidays in order to find out what was happening in his own office. Following Northcliffe's dictum— 'telephones multiply the man'—he rang up his employees (as he still does) at all hours of the day and night, praising, suggesting, gossiping, badgering, cursing. Murdoch worked incessantly and invested the business of trouncing the opposition with all the excitement of a crusade. This brought him into conflict with Sydney's leading press baron Frank Packer. Their bitter struggle involved at least one affray between minions, in which Frank's son Clyde was lucky to escape with mere broken bones, and endless financial wheeling and dealing. It ended in 1972 when Murdoch bought Packer's *Daily* and *Sunday Telegraph*. Long before that, in 1964, Murdoch had founded the *Australian*, widely regarded as a fig-leaf of respectability designed to hide the sins being committed in what the *Sunday Times* (before Murdoch became its proprietor) described as his 'bordello of papers'.[20] But while Murdoch is by no means averse to the prestige which accrues to him as owner of the sole national newspaper, he has also created a monument to his genuine patriotism. One former journalist has a vivid memory of the *Australian*'s birth pangs: at the 'magic moment' when Murdoch reached up into the entrails of an ancient press, housed in a converted jam factory in Canberra, and pulled out the first copy, everyone was acutely conscious of his 'fierce pride in what he had produced'.

In 1968 Murdoch made the first of his major overseas purchases, buying the *News of the World* and the *Sun* in a couple of lightning raids which took Fleet Street completely by surprise. The take-over of the *News of the World* was an astonishing coup. Murdoch himself described it as 'the biggest steal since the Great Train Robbery'. He traded on the proprietors' detestation of a rival bidder, the socialist millionaire Robert Maxwell, saying that he would travel half-way round the world to throw Maxwell a concrete lifebelt. Murdoch managed to disguise the poverty of his own offer for the paper by padding it out with meaningless concessions, such as the 'right to distribute magazines in Tasmania'.[21] Murdoch's acquisition of the *Sun* was the product of competing versions of arrogance. Hugh Cudlipp was convinced that since he had failed with the paper no one could succeed. Murdoch, who had studied the files of Bart's *Mirror* and talked to Cecil King, believed that he was the exception to this rule. With the help of his outstanding editor, Larry Lamb, he proved to be correct.

Why did Murdoch invade Britain? He himself is apt to explain his acquisitive urge in personal terms, as a matter of responding to a challenge, an instinct to compete and to gamble. In a rare interview he explained to the *Guardian*, 'Coming here you begin to think, is Cudlipp all that damned good? You know, they all think he's God. Or is Cecil King God or something? Maybe one could mix it over here. . . . It was almost bravado.'[22] Doubtless this is part of the truth. Behind his tough, noisy exterior Murdoch is surprisingly sensitive—he is terrified of women and hates being branded as a pedlar of pornography. So he loathed being patronised by Cudlipp, who had never even edited a daily newspaper, and was determined to teach him a lesson. Moreover, gambling has always been the breath of life to Murdoch. The greater the risk the greater the thrill—as an impoverished student hitch-hiking through France he spent his last pound at a casino and paid for the rest of his holiday with his winnings. He is not interested in amassing capital but in acquiring a stake. Money burns a hole in Murdoch's bank account and investment for him is little more than an elevated form of pitch-and-toss.

The most hazardous gamble of his life was the assault on America. This took place in 1973 when Murdoch purchased the San Antonio *Express* and *News* for almost twenty million dollars. By then he was disenchanted with Britain. There were the 'daily bloody arguments' with recalcitrant trade unions. There was the snobbish Establishment to which Murdoch would not sacrifice his independence: the day on which the Queen paid a ceremonial visit to Fleet Street happened to coincide with the news of Princess Margaret's impending divorce and only the *Sun* was vulgar enough to splash the story. Despite the nipples, Murdoch was several times offered a knighthood but he would not sell out: 'The last thing I wanted was to be a bloody press lord.'[23] Finally there was the planned kidnapping of Murdoch's wife Anna by the Hosein brothers—in the event they took, and later murdered, the wrong woman. A more positive reason for Murdoch's stepping westwards was his itch to try his luck in the greatest journalistic lottery on earth.

For the odds were not, he calculated, as long as they looked. First, the conglomerates had induced a degree of blandness and boredom into their newspapers which made them vulnerable to a bright, aggressive competitor. As one of Murdoch's managers elegantly remarked, 'American newspapers . . . are yuk.'[24] Murdoch himself was more specific: American publishers are out to impress their advertisers and colleagues instead of their readers; American editors print too many tedious columns; American sub-editors are 'bloody lazy'; and American reporters 'can't even bloody write'.[25] Secondly Murdoch reckoned that San Antonio resembled Sydney in being a violent kind of frontier city where his brand of 'blood and guts' journalism would be effective. Of course, there were constraints. 'I want a tear-away paper with a lot of tit,' he had told the editors of the London *Sun*.[26] But even in Texas this crude formula had to be toned down. Nevertheless, as Murdoch discovered after having initially pitched the San Antonio *News* and the national *Star* (founded in 1974) too low, American readers were more sophisticated than Australian ones and less self-consciously working-class than British ones.

So when he rode in triumph to New York in 1977, having bought Dorothy Schiff's liberal evening *Post*, Murdoch moderated his sensationalism to suit a somewhat more refined taste. As he explained,

> This is a middle-class city. Everybody in this country wants to get ahead, get a piece of the action. That's the fundamental difference between the New World and the Old World. There's not the self-improvement ethic in England that there is in this country. If you drop below that level, you're talking about the ghettos. And there's a question as to whether those people can even read, let alone afford a newspaper.

Of course, Murdoch's *Post* was still appealing to the lower end of the market. It was and is a frankly sensational newspaper, full of headlines like 'Mass Baby Killer Stalks Hospital' and 'Warped Genius Tortures His Mom'. It revels in scandal, gossip, crime, sport, titillating features, spicy serials, million-dollar contests (Wingo, the *Post*'s variation on Bingo) and occasional fits of hysteria (such as the 'Son of Sam' murders or the nuclear accident at Three Mile Island). Yet if the *Post* is superficial it also contains a large amount of serious news, much of it accurate. Like the Powder River, its coverage is a mile wide and an inch deep. Thus the *Post* hardly attempted to emulate the New York *Times* but it did set out to compete with the *Daily News*.

Even this seemed an incredible piece of effrontery in 1977. The *Post* was a metropolitan evening paper with a circulation of 450,000, squeezed between television and suburban competitors, unable to attract much advertising because of the low purchasing power of its readers. However, Murdoch had detected two fatal weaknesses in the opposition. Without Joe Patterson the *Daily News* lacked the clear impression of a personality, the *sine qua non* of successful journalism. And its highly-paid staff of (effectively) 5,000 was four times larger than the *Post*'s. In short, it was over-tired and over-manned. Murdoch thus embarked on a bitterly-fought circulation war. He tried to lure away the *New*'s readers by exciting competitions, its writers by inflated salaries, its advertisers by special offers. In 1978 he broke ranks with the other New York publishers during a protracted strike, signed a separate agreement with the unions and put the *Post*, bulging with advertisements, on the streets while his competitors were still locked in negotiations. This desertion was greeted with cries of outrage by the *News* and the *Times* which described Murdoch, respectively, as 'a dirty street fighter' and 'a bad element, practicing mean, ugly, violent journalism'.[27]

The *News* hit back. In 1980 it launched a Tonight edition, pricing it cheaply, promoting it hugely and filling it with fashionable 'life-style' features otherwise known as 'boutique journalism'. Murdoch at once retaliated by lowering his own price and producing a morning edition of the *Post*. The conflict was now being waged all day on all fronts. Some choice tactics were, and are, employed. The *News* crows over a scoop and the *Post* accuses it of interfering with the course of justice by making improper revelations. The *News* responds to Wingo with its own Zingo, which the *Post* disparages as Sleep-O. The *News* brands Murdoch's managers as aliens and the *Post* counters by characterising its rival as the 'Chicago-owned News'. By the end of 1981 it was clear that Murdoch was winning. The *Post* had doubled its advertising and its circlation, which was approaching the magic million mark. The *News* abandoned its Tonight edition which had only achieved a sale of 75,000. In December, with losses running at about twelve million dollars for the year, America's largest general newspaper became what the *Post* had long been calling it—an 'ailing tabloid'. It was put up for sale.

Murdoch played a cunning but inconspicuous part in the complex negotiations which followed. For he was determined that the *News* should be closed rather than sold. 'Rupert thinks the *News* is doomed,' said one of his henchmen, 'He wants to wipe it out.'[28] So, as various bidders tried to extract advantageous terms from the *News*'s unions and management, Murdoch schemed to thwart them. When it seemed as though the Texas banking millionaire Joe Allbritton had secured the *News* Murdoch sabotaged his offer by making one of his own which was much more favourable to the trade unions. The *News*'s management rejected it as 'patently illusory' and denounced it as 'an anti-competitive and predatory act'.[29] But the act was successful. At the time of writing (May 1982) the *News* has been withdrawn from the market. It intends to soldier on, sustained by cash from its parent Chicago Tribune Company and (with luck) concessions from the unions. Meanwhile Murdoch proposes to fight to the finish. To quote his own melodramatic words: the *News* and the *Post* 'are engaged in a dance of death which must end in the disappearance of one or both newspapers.'[30]

Which will survive? Murdoch suggests that the *News* will give up the ghost when its contracts with the unions (guaranteeing heavy redundancy payments) expire in 1984. The *News*'s publisher, Robert M. Hunt, replies angrily:

> Absolute rubbish. The News is here to stay. The fact that Rupert Murdoch, the Australian publisher, continually uses his New York Post to rush into print with ugly, unfounded rumors shows just how panicky he is getting. The Post is losing $20 million per year and is in far worse financial shape than the Daily News. Murdoch and his executive crew of aliens are putting out a paper that has far less circulation, little advertising and virtually no credibility.[31]

Perhaps so, but only a rash punter would bet on the *Post*'s demise at the hands of the *News*. For Murdoch abides by the rule which Patterson discovered long ago (as did Northcliffe in Britain) and which the conglomerates sedulously follow today—that there is a level in American journalism below which it is not profitable to fall. Murdoch is not making the mistake of Macfadden's pornographic or even of Hearst's yellow journal. Yet he still practises vigorous personal journalism of a distinctly jaundiced hue and it is easy to see why contemporary commentators regard him as 'a throwback, a late nineteenth century Hearstian figure who has seemingly materialized in the New York City of the late 1970s through some curious time warp.'[32]

For, like a press baron of old, he controls all his newspapers in a dynamic and dictatorial fashion. As he informed Stafford Somerfield, the editor he inherited on the *News of the World*, 'I did not come all this way not to interfere.' The paper was going to speak with only one voice and 'That voice is mine.'[33] Murdoch glories in being 'a working boss'[34] and he likes to pump adrenalin into his employees by directing operations for sixteen hours a day. He functions in obsessional bursts of enthusiasm which sometimes produce a slick, professional treatment of the news and sometimes provoke crude effusions such as the *Sun*'s notoriously jingoistic headline gloating over the loss of the Argentine battle-cruiser *General Belgrano*—'Gotcha'. Unlike, say, Beaverbrook, Murdoch is not possessed by malice, but some of his habits in the news-room are distinctly autocratic. He is quite capable of sweeping accumulated paper off desks and then complaining that the office is untidy. He once chastised an editor thus for wearing suede shoes: 'What do you think you're running, a newspaper or a bloody jazz band?'[35] He conducts rows with his employees in which the swear-words fly like fists—at the end of one of them Ernest Bridges, managing director of News Ltd in Australia collapsed and died, to Murdoch's intense distress. And he is merciless in the hunt for news. He defines 'real news' as 'someone inventing a pill to make mad people sane'. After being goaded to produce more and more lurid sensations one reporter of the New York *Post* said in 1977, 'I'm supposed to come up with something new on [Son of] Sam tonight. I don't know where I'll start. I'm sick of the whole story. I feel pretty slimy.'[36]

Inevitably Murdoch's tactics have brought him into conflict with his own employees, especially with those wedded to the high professional standards taught in schools of journalism. In a business dominated by corporations and managed by teams, journalists are now unaccustomed to such baronial behaviour. In 1975 some staff members of the *Australian* went on strike claiming that the news coverage as well as the editorial content was being manipulated in an effort to destroy Gough Whitlam, the Labour Prime Minister. A similar complaint was made during Mayor Koch's election campaign by journalists on the New York *Post*. Fifty of them signed a petition complaining about the paper's biased reporting, to which Murdoch gave his standard answer: 'It's not your paper, it's *my* paper.'[37] The interior walls of the *Post*'s office were daubed with xenophobic graffiti such as 'Send This Wallaby Back, Jack'.[38] And Murdoch learnt that if he tried to vulgarise the Greenwich *Village Voice* its entire staff would resign. Consequently it remains a perpetual thorn in his flesh, scarcely more reverent about Murdoch than about the Chicago Tribune Company which, the *Voice* remarks sweetly, is so unsmart that it 'could fuck up a two-car funeral'. Apparently Murdoch wants to sell the *Voice* which sounds the one discordant note in his international nest of singing birds.

Testifying before the Royal Commission on the Press in 1977 William Rees-Mogg, editor of the *Times*, said:

> Mr Murdoch's writ does run in his own building and, much as I respect his energy and vigour, because of his views on the proprietorial function I would never myself be willing to work for him.

When Murdoch bought the *Times* four years later Rees-Mogg duly resigned, but not without assuring his readers that the guarantees of editorial freedom given by the new proprietor 'are very far reaching and there is no reason to doubt that he will abide by them'.[39] American observers were less sanguine. Chris Welles of the Columbia School of Journalism remarked, 'He has a history of promising not to meddle with editorial policy—and then meddling with it anyway. He couldn't just sit on a piece of property like the *Times* and let it be.'[40]

Oddly enough, the *Times* itself was quite sceptical about the worth of the safeguards which 'Tiny' Rowland offered, with equal fervour, when he purchased the *Observer* later on in 1981. Like every other serious newspaper, the *Times* echoed the view of the minority report of the Monopolies Commission (the majority report was taken seriously only by Lonrho and the Conservative government). This said that the relationship between Mr Rowland and any editor of the *Observer* would be 'too close, subtle and continuous to be subject to control' by the 'independent directors' whom Lonrho proposed to appoint. A leading article in the *Times* concluded that Rowland's undertakings to preserve editorial independence were 'too nebulous to be of any value. They would be hard to enforce effectively against a proprietor who was determined to infringe them'.[41] The *Times* is, of course, in the very same case vis-à-vis Rupert Murdoch. When Murdoch maintains that he has a right to insist on excellence, that only a successful editor enjoys complete freedom in his organisation, that 'if the *Times* was in danger of folding up . . . I would have to step in', he is obviously leaving himself every latitude to intervene. It is scarcely surprising that when asked to sum up his advice to journalists on the *Times* under the new dispensation Robert Spitzler, formerly Managing Editor of the New York *Post*, said simply, 'Run!'[42] Recent developments, notably interference with both staff and stories and the dismissal of the editor, Harold Evans, tend to confirm the wisdom of this advice.

As has been said, the similarities between Northcliffe's acquisition of the *Times* in 1908 and Murdoch's in 1981 are uncanny. Northcliffe too swore that the Old Lady of Printing House Square should remain inviolate. He would preserve her as a great independent institution, like, he said ironically, the British Museum. Murdoch is caught in exactly Northcliffe's trap over the *Times*. It cannot go on as it is. Yet if Murdoch follows his familiar policy of making the paper more popular, of turning it into a de luxe edition of the *Sun* perhaps, he will destroy the very distinction which makes it worth having in the first place. Worse still, if he increases its circulation he may also increase its already gigantic losses. Such are the weird economics of Fleet Street that this actually happened in the late 1960s when costs rose with readers but advertising revenue did not.[43] At the moment this pattern, with slight variations, seems to be repeating itself. It is likely that the main problem for the *Times*, if it survives, will be too little income from advertisements rather than too much expenditure on over-manning.

Murdoch's style is scarcely cramped at all by the *Times*'s independent national directors and his relationship with Harold Evans closely resembled Northcliffe's with his editors. Not, of course, that Evans ever prostrated himself before his proprietor in the terms that Wickham Steed used to Northcliffe:

> As to the Paper, you know that your wishes are my wishes, your views are my views. . . . I am determined that no one shall succeed in making bad blood between us as many people would like to do. I have been loyal to you in deed, in thought and in word.[44]

Evans's record, exemplified in his struggle against the legal gags imposed on the press during the Thalidomide case, is generally good. He deplores that pervasive feature of the journalistic scene, politicians' attempts to exert backstairs pressure on editors. It was almost with horror that Evans recently quoted the astounding confession made by a much-respected ex-editor of the *Guardian*, Alstair Hetherington. On the subject of President Johnson's request for more British involvement in Vietnam Hetherington told Harold Wilson: 'I thought we should keep out, but if he [Wilson] felt we ought to go in I was willing to turn the paper's line round over the next week or two.'[45] A former editor of the *Northern Echo*, Evans was imbued with something of the baronial independence which distinguished his predecessor on that paper, W. T. Stead, whom he much admires. Yet Evans found it impossible to resist when Murdoch followed the Northcliffean course of cajolery, interference, bullying, threats and dismissal. It is doubtful if his successor, Charles Douglas-Home, will fare any better under a proprietor who is said to want Genghis Khan in charge of the editorial pages. Nevertheless the prime lesson which the history of the press barons teaches is that modern editors must cultivate a ruthless independence if they are to prevent press freedom from being eroded by the great communications conglomerates.

For the crucial difference between Murdoch's *Times* and Northcliffe's is that the former is part of an international business much of which is not concerned with newspapers. In the United Kingdom, for instance, some 35 per cent of Murdoch's turnover came from non-publishing sources in 1980 (by far the lowest figure among the great newspaper-owning corporations). Much of Murdoch's strength, and weakness, stems from his international diversification. The complex structure of companies based on three continents gives him more financial independence from the banks than he would otherwise have. This means that he can be as tight-fisted over dividends as he is over expenditure and can plough back profits at will, reaping the appropriate tax advantage. Furthermore Murdoch's varied business interests help each other. They do so in obvious ways such as shared printing facilities for different journals, bulk buying of newsprint and the syndication of articles. But there are more subtle and more damaging varieties of mutual support.

For example, in Australia Murdoch's radio and television stations promote his newspapers and vice-versa. And on a number of occasions his news interests have supported his non-journalistic concerns. His campaign against the Australian Prime Minister Robert Menzies can be traced back to that politician's refusal to grant him a television license. At a recent broadcasting tribunal set up to scrutinize Murdoch's control of Melbourne's Channel Ten Television evidence was produced to show that his newspapers had printed a number of stories hostile to Trans Australia Airlines, the rival to his own Ansett Airlines. Similarly the political policies of Murdoch's newspapers often appear to have been determined by his desire to wring concessions (loans, franchises and so on) from governments for the benefit of his other commercial concerns. He is uneasily aware that he is betraying his trust as a controller of the fourth estate and in 1977 he pronounced, 'that's why I'm getting out of minerals. It leaves me wide open. It's a mistake for me to own anything but newspapers.'[46] However Murdoch still directs a multinational communications conglomerate whose diversified interests his publications are often made to serve.

The extent to which Murdoch's non-journalistic interests will further shape the organisation and content of his publications remains to be seen. It largely depends on whether he becomes, as seems probable, an entrepreneur fully engaged in directing companies, raising loans and organising takeovers, or whether he remains primarily what his upbringing made him, a newspaperman. Certainly he thinks of himself as a journalist and his professionalism in that sphere is never in doubt. Larry Lamb found him easy to work with for that very reason. 'You can't bullshit him,' as another employee remarked, 'he knows the game from start to finish'. But, like Otis Chandler, Murdoch talks of 'the communications industry'.[47] He likes to represent himself as a mere run-of-the-mill chief executive and invariably refers to 'our' operations, employing the corporate rather than the royal 'we'. Moreover he is heavily preoccupied with defending and expanding an empire which is always stretched to its financial limits. Murdoch owes his strength to being a potent hybrid, at once an international business man who draws his strength from a conglomeration of enterprises and a press baron who drives his publications forward with the traditional ferocity of the breed. Whether he can sustain this dual role and where it will lead him are matters of conjecture. Rupert Murdoch has risen like a comet but his present course is ambivalent and his destination is uncertain.

CHAPTER FOURTEEN

Conclusion:
The Death of the Barons

IT IS IMPOSSIBLE to say whether the volatile medium of journalism made citizens like Kane or whether it attracted them because they resembled him in the first place—doubtless a bit of both. But there is no escaping the uncanny similarities between the press barons or the associated paradox that few, in an era of unbridled individualism, were more individualistic. Other entrepreneurs, such as Andrew Carnegie, were as creative in their own spheres. Some, Rothschilds and Rockefellers, were richer. A few had personalities which were as flamboyant and as powerful—J. P. Morgan, for example. Nevertheless, being the gaudiest beasts in the jungle of nascent capitalism as well as directors of the fourth estate, the press barons placed their mark more flagrantly than other commercial magnates on the history of their times. This should not obscure the fact that, like captains of industry everywhere, they were far from being complete masters of their fate. Their public organs were also private enterprises, large ones to be sure, but dependent ultimately on a favourable economic climate.

At the beginning of the Victorian age the sun shone on journalism and the press barons sprang up like weeds, though more rapidly in America than in Britain where their growth was stunted by hostile governments. The French Revolution and the Industrial Revolution had produced a substantial newspaper readership, at once stimulated by the atmosphere of democratic change and prosperous enough to buy not only the public prints but also the goods they advertised. Revenue from advertising really made the press barons, who defined themselves by the independence which they could now afford to display. Emerging from their political and commercial tutelage and interpreting the gospel of *laissez-faire* with fanatical latitude, the lords

251

of journalism exercised their new freedom in a profusion of differing ways.

Some became victims of Kane's syndrome—megalomania, elephantiasis of the ego, confusion of pen with sceptre—the occupational hazard of the press barons. The younger Bennett, the older Hearst and Northcliffe, for instance, employed their power in an arbitrary, eccentric and sometimes crazy manner. In youth, by contrast, Hearst and Northcliffe, like Beaverbrook, had adopted what was perhaps an even more characteristic attitude. This was a form of conservative populism which uneasily accommodated both their own and their readers' predilections. But though the press barons often imitated each other dissent abounded. There were radical subversives like Scripps and the early Patterson, liberal faddists like Greeley and Stead, reactionary bigots like McCormick and Otis. There were misanthropists like Barnes, iconoclasts like Dana, altruists like the later Pulitzer. There were originals like the elder Bennett, plagiarists like Burnham, T. P. O'Connor and Cissy Patterson, oafs like the first Viscount Rothermere. As Delane and Raymond proved, there was even room for orthodoxy.

Enjoying not only press liberty but capitalist licence, the owners of newspapers felt free to tyrannise over their work-force and to exploit the public. At worst, newspaper offices became outposts of pandemonium ruled by capricious and evil spirits. More often journalists were regarded as subsidiary cogs in the engine of the rotary press and their productions were in every sense machine-made. At best the press lords treated their minions as accomplices and, by exercising titanic energy and skill amounting at times to genius, they created newspapers which were worthy members of the fourth estate. However, as far as the health of the British and American bodies politic was concerned, it was not the quality of these publications which chiefly mattered but the variety. Amid the babel which swelled from Fleet Street and Park Row something like the truth, safeguard of all civil liberty, was to be heard. It was by no means always first enunciated by the most respectable publications or for the best motives. As a rule in journalism irresponsibility is the highest form of responsibility. And often it was the most popular newspapers which were prepared, for reasons of sensationalism, to flout taboos, to rake muck and to divulge inconvenient information.

Such revelations were, of course, easier to publish in the United States than in Britain, where official secrecy is a disease, ritual promises of open government are ritually broken and what interests the public is not in the public interest. Instances are legion. Witness the covert way in which the decision was taken to build Concorde. Or the attempt to suppress publication of the Crossman diaries. Or the Ministry of Defence's nonchalant refusal, in 1981, even to discuss American reports that East Anglia might have been reduced to a desert as the result of a nuclear accident at Lakenheath air base in 1956. Or the Contempt of Court Act (1981) which, belying its stated aim to increase freedom, has empowered the Attorney-General to embark on a series of prosecutions against outspoken journalists—this amounts to a legal purge against the press and it has already led to some silent self-censorship by newspapers. (As Bennett Snr. said, 'it is an old, worm-eaten, Gothic dogma of the Courts' that publicity is destructive to the operations of justice. It is based on the patronising premiss that a juror cannot discriminate between what he hears in court and what he reads in the press; whereas if he really were incapable of such an elementary intellectual exercise he would be unfitted to sit in judgement at all'.) The British equivalent of the Watergate conspiracy was collusion over the attack on Suez, details of which were only vouchsafed to a grateful nation as a result of French and Israeli disclosures. At the same time, however, freedom of information in America has its limitations and newsmen have been arrogant enough not to trust a democratic people with facts which they know to be important—to their country's cost. For example, it seems likely that neither the U2 incident nor the Bay of Pigs fiasco would have occurred if journalists had not censored themselves in what they were persuaded to be the national interest. Nor did American newspapers (with notable exceptions) distinguish themselves during the McCarthy era—Bill Hearst actually provided the Senator with reporters to help him fill in the 205 blanks on his famous list of subversives.

Still, on both sides of the Atlantic the very diversity of the press did act, incidentally, as some sort of check on the executive power. This served the public interest particularly well as governments became more monolithic. Disciplined political parties, bureaucracy and other instruments of state control developed. And eventually that apparatus of dissimulation known as public relations was set up—today there are twice as many publicity agents in Washington as journalists. Moreover Westminster and Washington based their legitimacy firmly on more or less democratic elections. Only the tribunes of the people could plausibly resist the dictatorship of the majority.

The likes of Delane, Greeley, Pulitzer and Beaverbrook might extol the political and social mission of the press but there was no denying the fact that it was essentially a business. Whatever personal axe they had to grind most newspaper owners regarded it as such and tried to adapt to changing economic conditions. These began to favour the survival of larger enterprises as the nineteenth century waned. An early spur to the concentration of ownership was the advent of limited liability companies in the 1850s. Soon after the American Civil War Charles Francis Adams Jnr. wrote prophetically (in *Chapters of Erie*) 'The system of corporate life and corporate power, as applied to industrial development, is yet in its infancy. It tends always to development,—always to consolidation. . . . We shall see these great corporations spanning the continent.'

This transformation did not happen at a constant pace in every concern. The age of individualism lasted longer in newspapers than in other commercial operations because, being born again each day, they were so dependent on the personal vitality of their controllers. But with the growth of the consumer society, whose city-dwellers bought the goods displayed in newspaper advertisements and sold in new department stores, the press itself had to become a modern mass-production industry. Technological advances, especially the high-speed Hoe presses and linotype machines, enabled it to meet the demand but vastly increased costs. This manufacturing revolution made it inevitable that the private fiefs of the press barons would develop into public companies and that the rule of the proprietors would give way to corporate management. Joint-stock capital was superseding personal inspiration as the main driving force in newspaperdom.

Press barons whose income came largely or exclusively from their publications were especially vulnerable to the economic tempests of the twentieth century. Of all major industries newspapers are most easily disrupted and two world wars, as well as the intervening depression and the subsequent inflation, brought many weaker ones to their knees. The growing power (and expectations) of organised labour, the rising price of newsprint, the intensifying competition (including that from radio and television, chiefly in the field of advertisements), the cost of new plant—all this helped to squeeze the life-blood out of the press barons. They responded in different ways. Some, like Ralph Pulitzer, meekly succumbed to strangulation. Others—Northcliffe, Scripps, Rothermere, Hearst, McCormick, the Chandlers—sought to defend themselves by establishing a pattern of mergers, local monopolies and chains, by standardising products, eliminating rivals and consolidating holdings. Still others, like Beaverbrook, fought the good fight, increased their circulation and sustained themselves into a new era.

By the 1960s, however, winter had set in with a vengeance. As the career of Cecil King amply demonstrates, the press barons were an anachronism. History was on the side of the big boardrooms, the more diversified their interests the better. The lonely press baron was doomed. He was unable to save through bulk buying, central management or other economies of scale. He was hit by spiralling inflation and rocketing costs, and threatened by annihilating personal as well as company taxation. If he did not transmute his business into a giant corporation he would be devoured by one. In Britain, where the national press was enfeebled by atrocious industrial relations (caused as much by the blind ambition of the press barons as by the entrenched intransigence of the trade unions) newspapers were either taken over by conglomerates or developed into conglomerates. In the United States, where virtually all newspapers are local and most enjoy a monopoly, those with the largest profits were best able to expand, which they usually did in the field of communications media. In both countries, however, the economic logic of conglomeration was, and is, irrefutable.

A large public company with subsidiaries in variegated enterprises can spread its risks, make the best use of professional managers and benefit from a number of important fiscal advantages (especially through debenture financing and 'paper exchanges'). Above all it can pay for the expensive new electronic printing technology and for yet further growth from a new Eldorado. Over the last two decades vast pension funds, unit trusts and other such institutions have come to dominate the British and American stock markets. They prefer to invest substantial sums in quoted companies, which can expand and take over rivals accordingly. Such infusions of capital are to the conglomerates what advertising revenue was to the press barons who, as they lived by lucre, died of financial anaemia—relative in America, absolute in Britain. Apart from that virile hybrid Rupert Murdoch, and odd survivors like Lord Hartwell and William Loeb, the press barons have passed away. The controllers of today's newspapers are simply corporate men, the personifications of anonymity.

The implications of this change are both profound and paradoxical. For the new controllers of the press are at once too captive and too free. Unlike the old press barons they are answerable to their stockholders. So their paramount commitment is to profits, and they are disposed to apply only commercial criteria to what is a trust as well as a business. This can warp and dehumanise the organisation of a newspaper and reduce its contents to universally acceptable blandness. At worst the subsidiary units of huge conglomerates are soulless bureaucracies and their publications are anodyne pap whose serious purpose is to promote the capitalist order in general and the interests of its parent company in particular. These interests are so many and various that conglomerates always need the good-will of governments, which can, and do, exert pressure on their newspapers.

On the other hand, a conglomerate, by virtue of its gigantic resources, may enjoy a degree of freedom which was seldom exercised by the press barons themselves. For they were, in one sense, responsible to their readers. True, the more uncompromising of them—the younger Bennett, Dana, Stead, McCormick and to some extent Beaverbrook—refused to accept the restraints imposed on them by public opinion. Others, such as Hearst and Pulitzer, sometimes mirrored it and sometimes tried to mould it. All of them—one thinks especially of the elder Bennett, Barnes, Delane, Raymond, Northcliffe—knew that they opposed popular views at their peril. After all, a newspaper without readers was like a fief without villeins: it could not survive. Sir Denis Hamilton, sometime editor-in-chief of Times Newspapers, was referring to this degree of dependence when he wrote that wherever the ownership of a newspaper lies ultimate 'control is with its readers'. But today this is no longer the case. Diversified corporations can sustain newspapers which have circulations in thousands and losses in millions—can even, to the gall of their critics, improve them. Conglomerates may well consider that unprofitable newspapers which bang their drum or enhance their prestige are a sound investment, just like expenditure on advertising. Take Lonrho, for example: in 1980 printing and publishing contributed only £86 million to its turnover of £2.1 billion. The *Observer*, on which 'Tiny' Rowland apparently expressed a willingness to lose £2 million a year, might be the ideal mask to conceal the unacceptable face of capitalism. If Rupert Murdoch turns out to be more of an entrepreneur than a press baron the *Times* may become merely his British fig-leaf.

Clearly under these circumstances editors and working journalists have new and awesome responsibilities. Without benefit of wealth they must maintain press freedom against politicians and others (trade unionists, civil servants, pressure groups) bent on distorting or suppressing the news in the name of some supposedly higher duty. With little or no security of tenure they must aspire to preserve variety and individuality in a contracting market-place of thought and information. Possessing responsibility without power, they must fight to purify the wells of knowledge threatened by subtle and unprecedented pollution. In this well-nigh impossible task they might seek inspiration from that exotic episode in the history of capitalism whose villainous heroes were the founders of their profession. If their spirit of tigerish independence were to live on among the leading practitioners of modern journalism few would mourn the death of the press barons.

Bibliography

Principal Unpublished Sources
  The following were consulted.
  Bancroft Library, Berkeley: Hearst Papers, Oral History Records.
  British Library: Northcliffe Papers, Gladstone Papers (Stead letters).
  Butler Library, Columbia University: Pulitzer Papers, Oral History Records.
  House of Lords Record Office: Beaverbrook Papers, Blumenfeld Papers.
  New York Public Library: James Gordon Bennett Papers, Don C. Seitz Papers.
  Newberry Library, Chicago: Hearst Letters, Hecht Papers, Lawson Papers.
  Times Archives, New Printing House Square: Delane Papers, Northcliffe Papers.

  Note: Certain chapters in this book rely very heavily on primary materials. The general reader would find the citing of each reference wearisome and repetitive; the interested scholar will want to visit the archives. So I have left a considerable number of manuscript quotations unidentified. All those in Chapter III are taken from the Delane Papers at the Times Archives, those in Chapter VII from the Pulitzer Papers in the Butler Library, Columbia University, those in Chapter VIII from the Hearst Papers at Berkeley, and those in Chapter IX from the Beaverbrook Papers at the House of Lords Record Office.

Principal Published Sources
A. Particular
The following is a short selection of the basic works (mostly biographies) about the press barons discussed in this book. The place of publication is London unless otherwise stated—as is the case in the subsequent, more comprehensive, list of references.

F. Brown, *Raymond of the Times* (New York, 1951)

A. I. Dasent, *John Thadeus Delane* (2 vols., 1908)

G. G. Van Deusen, *Horace Greeley: Nineteenth Century Crusader* (Philadelphia, 1953)

P. Ferris, *The House of Northcliffe* (1971) [Rothermere]

R. Gottlieb and I. Wolt, *Thinking Big* (New York, 1977) [Otis and the Chandlers]

D. Hudson, *Thomas Barnes of* The Times (Cambridge, 1943)

C. King, *Strictly Personal* (1969)

O. Knight (ed.), *I Protest* by E. W. Scripps (Madison, Wis., 1966)

R. Pound and G. Harmsworth, *Northcliffe* (1959)

S. Regan, *Rupert Murdoch** (1976)

D. C. Seitz, *The James Gordon Bennetts* (Indianapolis, 1928)

W. A. Swanberg, *Citizen Hearst* (1961)

W. A. Swanberg, *Pulitzer* (New York, 1967)

A. J. P. Taylor, *Beaverbrook* (1972)

J. Tebbel, *An American Dynasty* (New York, 1968) [McCormick and the Pattersons]

F. Whyte, *The Life of W. T. Stead* (2 vols., 1925)

J. H. Wilson, *The Life of Charles A. Dana* (New York, 1907)

B. General

The following is a brief selection of general books on the history of the modern British and American press. Unfortunately there is no book which covers the British press in a way that is both scholarly and readable: Francis Williams's *Dangerous Estate* is jejune beside Edwin Emery's (admittedly somewhat text-bookish) *The Press and America*. By way of compensation Stephen Koss has provided a masterly survey, which has no equivalent in America, of a major aspect of British journalism.

A. Aspinall, *Politics and the Press 1780–1850* (1973)

W. G. Bleyer, *Main Currents in the History of American Journalism* (Boston, 1927)

G. Boyce, J. Curran and P. Wingate (eds.), *Newspaper History* (1978)

E. Emery, *The Press and America* (Englewood Cliffs, N.J., 1978)

S. Koss, *The Rise and Fall of the Political Press in Britain* I (1981)

The History of 'The Times' (5 vols., 1935–)

E. C. Hynds, *American Newspapers in the 1980s* (New York, 1980)

A. J. Lee, *The Origins of the Popular Press in England, 1855–1914* (1976)

S. Morison, *The English Newspaper* (Cambridge, 1932)

F. L. Mott, *American Journalism* (New York, 1947)

A. Nevins, *The Evening Post* (New York, 1968)

M. Schudson, *Discovering the News* (New York, 1978)

A. Smith, *The Newspaper* (1979)

F. Williams, *Dangerous Estate* (1959)

---

* This is perhaps the worst book ever written about a press magnate, but until Michael Leapman's book is published it remains the only extended treatment of its subject.

Notes

CHAPTER 1 (pages 7–8)

1. C. H. Levermore, 'The Rise of Metropolitan Journalism, 1800–1840' in *American Historical Review* VI (1900–01), 463.
2. New York *Herald*, 29 April 1837.
3. *Foreign Quarterly Review* XXXI (1843), 272.
4. I. Pray, *Memoirs of James Gordon Bennett and His Times* (New York, 1855), 162.
5. New York Public Library: J. G. Bennett Collection, Diary, 12 June–18 Aug. 1831.
6. J. Parton, *Famous Americans of Recent Times* (New York, 1867), 269.
7. D. C. Seitz, *The James Gordon Bennetts* (Indianapolis, 1928), 32.
8. *Foreign Quarterly Review* XXX (1842), 198.
9. R. O'Connor, *The Scandalous Mr Bennett* (New York, 1962), 17.
10. W. G. Bleyer, *Main Currents in the History of American Journalism* (Boston, 1927), 190.
11. J. W. Robertson Scott, *The Life and Death of a Newspaper* (1952), i.
12. *The Idler*, 11 Nov. 1758.
13. F. L. Mott, *American Journalism* (New York, 1947 edn.), 146.
14. S. K. Padover (ed.), *Democracy by Thomas Jefferson* (1942), 149.
15. C. Mackay, *Through the Long Day* I (1887), 50.
16. H. Herd, *The March of Journalism* (1952), 137.
17. H. R. Fox Bourne, *English Newspapers* II (1887), 89.
18. W. Cobbett, *Political Register* (1 Nov. 1823), Col. 87.
19. G. A. Cranfield, *The Press and Society* (1978), 74.
20. L. R. Ingpen (ed.), *The Autobiography of Leigh Hunt* I (1903), 172.
21. S. Morison, *John Bell, (1745–1831)* (Cambridge, 1930), 10.
22. Ingpen, *Autobiography of Hunt* I, 169.
23. A. Aspinall, *Politics and the Press 1780–1850* (1973 edn.), 204.

24. C. Pebody, *English Journalism and the Men Who Have Made It* (1882), 75.
25. Aspinall, *Politics and Press*, 296.
26. A. Andrews, *The History of British Journalism* I (1859), 232.
27. P. L. Gordon, *Personal Memoirs* I (1830), 252–3.
28. F. Knight Hunt, *The Fourth Estate* I (1850), 257.
29. Andrews, *British Journalism* II, 108.
30. D[ictionary of] N[ational] B[iography]. See also I. R. Christie, *Myth and Reality in Late Eighteenth-Century British Politics* (1970), 352.
31. Aspinall, *Politics and Press*, 365 and 198.
32. F. E. Mineka (ed.), *The Earlier Letters of John Stuart Mill 1812–1848* (Toronto, 1963), 39.
33. New York Public Library: Bennett Diary.
34. Pray, *Memoirs of Bennett*, 84 and 255.
35. S. Bent, *Ballyhoo* (New York, 1927), 317.
36. Mott, *American Journalism*, 146.
37. A. de Tocqueville, *Journey to America* ed. by A. J. Mayer (1959), 239.
38. E. Emery, *The Press and America* (Englewood Cliffs, N.J., 1972 edn.), 118.
39. F. Hudson, *Journalism in the United States* (New York, 1872), 353.
40. J. L. Crouthamel, *James Watson Webb* (Middletown, Conn., 1969), 72. See also pp. 44–5 for Crouthamel's verdict that the bribery charge against Webb must be regarded as 'Not Proved'.
41. *Foreign Quarterly Review* XXX (1842), 204.
42. Hudson, *Journalism in United States*, 244.
43. Padover (ed.), *Democracy by Jefferson*, 150.
44. H. C. Allen, *The United States of America* (1964), 71.
45. Padover (ed.), *Democracy by Jefferson*, 143.
46. Andrews, *History of British Journalism* I, 62.
47. Aspinall, *Politics and Press*, 33.
48. C. D. Yonge, *The Life and Administration of Robert Banks, Second Earl of Liverpool* II (1868), 411 and 434.
49. A. J. Lee, *The Origins of the Popular Press in England 1855–1914* (1976), 42.
50. E. P. Thompson, *The Making of the English Working Class* (1963), 721.
51. W. H. Wickwar, *The Struggle for the Freedom of the Press 1819–1832* (1928), 215.
52. J. W. Osborne, *William Cobbett: his thought and his times* (New Brunswick, 1966), 72.
53. R. K. Webb, *The British Working Class Reader 1780–1848* (1955), 80.
54. Cranfield, *Press and Society*, 153.
55. I. Collins, *The Government and the Newspaper Press in France 1814–1881* (Oxford, 1959), 42.
56. Cranfield, *Press and Society*, 138.
57. J. Bentham, *Collected Works* VIII, edited by J. Bowring (1843), 487.
58. 'Half-a-Crown's Worth of Cheap Knowledge' in *Fraser's Magazine* XVII (Mar. 1838), 280.
59. L. Shepherd, *The History of Street Literature* (Newton Abbot, 1973), *passim*.
60. R. D. Altick, *The English Common Reader* (Chicago, 1957), 321.

61. R. Straus, *Sala* (1942), 57.
62. R. Williams, *The Long Revolution* (Harmondsworth, 1965), 212.
63. P. Hollis, *The Pauper Press* (Oxford, 1970), 122.
64. H. J. Perkin, 'The Origins of the Popular Press' in *History Today* VII (1957), 430.
65. T. Carlyle, *Sartor Resartus* (1910 edn.), 48.
66. L. Filler, *Appointment at Armageddon* (Westport, Conn., 1977), 35.

CHAPTER 2 (pages 19–36)

1. Pray, *Memoirs of Bennett*, 228.
2. W. J. Abbott, *Watching the World Go By* (Boston, 1933), 149.
3. Pray, *Memoirs of Bennett*, 267, 466, 221 and 30.
4. O. Carlson, *The Man who made the News: James Gordon Bennett* (New York, 1942), 175.
5. *Herald*, 10 Oct. 1835.
6. Carlson, *Man who made the News*, 175 and 174.
7. A. Nevins, *The Evening Post* (New York, 1968 edn.), 159.
8. Carlson, *Man who made the News*, 209.
9. *Foreign Quarterly Review* XXI (1843), 270.
10. Carlson, *Man who made the News*, 185 and 211.
11. *Herald*, 17 Oct. 1835.
12. Pray, *Memoirs of Bennett*, 39.
13. Carlson, *Man who made the News*, 164.
14. New York Public Library: Bennett Diary.
15. Pray, *Memoirs of Bennett*, 172.
16. Carlson, *Man who made the News*, 233.
17. Pray, *Memoirs of Bennett*, 466.
18. Carlson, *Man who made the News*, 177.
19. *Herald*, 14 Sept. 1835.
20. Mott, *American Journalism*, 232.
21. Seitz, *James Gordon Bennetts*, 29.
22. M. Schudson, *Discovering the News* (New York, 1978), 21.
23. Pray, *Memoirs of Bennett*, 465.
24. Bleyer, *History of American Journalism*, 191.
25. Mott, *American Journalism*, 229 and 232.
26. Pray, *Memoirs of Bennett*, 194.
27. J. H. Wilson, *The Life of Charles A. Dana* (New York, 1907), 485 and 487.
28. Carlson, *Man who made the News*, 176.
29. J. Parton, *Famous Americans*, 291.
30. E. H. Ford and E. Emery, *Highlights in the History of the American Press* (Minneapolis, 1954), 157.
31. Seitz, *James Gordon Bennetts*, 74.
32. Carlson, *Man who made the News*, 179, 149, 150 and 166.
33. A. M. Hughes, *News and the Human Interest Story* (Chicago, 1940), 8.

34. Pray, *Memoirs of Bennett*, 299.
35. *Herald*, 30 Oct. 1835.
36. F. M. O'Brien, *The Story of the Sun* (New York, 1928), 62.
37. Carlson, *Man who made the News*, 185.
38. *American Historical Review* VI, 463.
39. *Times*, 29 Oct. 1842.
40. D. Ayerst, *Guardian, Biography of a Newspaper* (1971), 104.
41. *Temple Bar* VII (Mar. 1863), 196.
42. K. Tillotson (ed.), *The Letters of Charles Dickens* IV (Oxford, 1977), 11. See also 13, for the suggestion that Webb was 'perhaps recalled in Col. Diver', and III, 84 and 431 for Dickens's view of the *Herald*.
43. *Foreign Quarterly Review* XXX, 199.
44. Ibid., XXXI, 268.
45. Pray, *Memoirs of Bennett*, 221.
46. *Herald*, 18 Jan. 1837 and 28 Sept. 1835.
47. Pray, *Memoirs of Bennett*, 266.
48. Seitz, *James Gordon Bennetts*, 206.
49. Wilson, *Dana*, 486.
50. Carlson, *Man who made the News*, 242.
51. *Foreign Quarterly Review* XXX, 211.
52. Bleyer, *American Journalism*, 209.
53. Seitz, *James Gordon Bennetts*, 179.
54. *American Historical Review* VI, 461.
55. O'Connor, *Scandalous Mr Bennett*, 162.
56. Carlson, *Man who made the News*, 207–11.
57. *Smithsonian* (Nov. 1978), 132.
58. O'Connor, *Scandalous Mr Bennett*, 148.
59. Seitz, *James Gordon Bennetts*, 221.
60. O. Knight (ed.), *I Protest* by E. W. Scripps (Madison, Wis., 1966), 334. The remark is not attributed to Bennett but no one else, surely, could have made it.
61. A. S. Crockett, *When James Gordon Bennett was Caliph of Bagdad* (New York, 1926), 400.
62. A. Laney, *Paris Herald* (New York, 1968), 19.
63. R. D. Blumenfeld, *The Press in My Time* (1937), 158.
64. Seitz, *James Gordon Bennetts*, 352.
65. T. Dreiser, *A Book about Myself* (1929), 469.
66. Columbia [University Library], P[ulitzer] P[apers], 14 January 1897.
67. R. D. Blumenfeld, *R. D. B.'s Diary, 1887–1914* (1930), 53.
68. F. Lundberg, *Imperial Hearst: A Social Biography* (New York, 1937), 115.
69. O'Connor, *Scandalous Mr Bennett*, 291 and 226.
70. Crockett, *When Bennett was Caliph*, 91.
71. O'Connor, *Scandalous Mr Bennett*, 296.
72. *Smithsonian* (Nov. 1978), 140.
73. J. Luskin, *Lippmann, Liberty and the Press* (Alabama, 1972), 79.
74. G. Britt, *Forty Years—Forty Millions* (New York, 1935), 185.

CHAPTER 3 (pages 37–49)

1. Pray, *Memoirs of Bennett*, 412.
2. W. Hazlitt, *Selected Writings* edited by R. Blythe (Harmondsworth, 1970), 259.
3. Fox Bourne, *English Newspapers* I, 366.
4. Knight Hunt, *Fourth Estate* II, 154.
5. *The History of 'The Times'* I (1935), 80.
6. Fox Bourne, *English Newspapers* I, 359.
7. Pebody, *English Journalism*, 101.
8. Pray, *Memoirs of Bennett*, 395.
9. P. Fitzgerald (ed.), *The Life, Letters and Writings of Charles Lamb* I (1895), 259–60.
10. D. Hudson, *Thomas Barnes of* The Times (Cambridge, 1943), 16, 29 and 64.
11. *History of 'The Times'* I, 198.
12. A. Aspinall (ed.), *Three Early Nineteenth Century Diaries* (1952), 364.
13. H. Hobson, P. Knightley and L. Russell, *The Pearl of Days* (1972), 48.
14. Hudson, *Barnes*, 110.
15. W. Dowden (ed.), *The Letters of Thomas Moore* II (Oxford, 1964), 613.
16. Lord J. Russell (ed.), *Memoirs, Journal and Correspondence of Thomas Moore* V (1856), 293.
17. *Times*, 26 Nov. 1835.
18. *History of 'The Times'* I, 368.
19. Cranfield, *Press and Society*, 158.
20. T. Carlyle, *Life of John Sterling* (1851), 303.
21. Hudson, *Barnes*, 93 and 91.
22. Fox Bourne *English Newspapers* I, 72.
23. *Times*, 10 Jan. 1835.
24. Aspinall (ed.), *Three Diaries*, 117.
25. L. Strachey and R. Fulford (eds.), *The Greville Memoirs* III (1938), 104.
26. *Times*, 1 Jan. 1835.
27. Aspinall, *Politics and Press*, 198.
28. A. I. Dasent, *John Thadeus Delane* I (1908), 26.
29. *History of 'The Times'* II, 481.
30. Dasent, *Delane* I, 18.
31. A. C. Benson and Viscount Esher (eds.), *The Letters of Queen Victoria* II (1911 edn.), 57.
32. A. Trollope, *The Warden* (1855), Ch. 14.
33. Dasent, *Delane* II, 34.
34. *Times*, 14 Oct. 1862.
35. G. Meredith, *Diana of the Crossways* (1885), Ch. 33.
36. Dasent, *Delane* II, 129.
37. *History of 'The Times'* II, 264.
38. R. Blake, *Disraeli* (1969 edn.), 381.
39. A. W. Kinglake, *The Invasion of the Crimea* VII (6th edn., 1883), 234–5 and 240–41.

40. *Manchester Guardian*, 7 May 1860.
41. *History of 'The Times'* II, 205 and 162.
42. *Times*, 14 Mar. 1854.
43. *Edinburgh Review* CII (Oct. 1855), 492.
44. G. Boyce, J. Curran and P. Wingate (eds.), *Newspaper History* (1978), 22.
45. H. Maxwell, *Life and Letters of the Fourth Earl of Clarendon* II (1913), 313.
46. E. T. Cook, *Delane of 'The Times'* (1916), 165.
47. *History of 'The Times'* II, 264.
48. D. N. B. (John Walter II).
49. Cook, *Delane*, 259.
50. B[ritish] M[useum], Northcliffe Papers, Add. MSS. 4890. CVI.
51. Pebody, *English Journalism*, 129.
52. J. Tunstall, '"Editorial Sovereignty" in the British Press, its past and present' in *Royal Commission on the Press* (1977), 260.
53. *Edinburgh Review* CII (Oct. 1855), 471.

CHAPTER 4 (pages 50–68)

1. 'The Political Press of America' in *Fraser's Magazine* LI (June, 1855), 683.
2. J. Parton, *Life of Horace Greeley* (New York, 1855), 35.
3. J. A. Isely, *Horace Greeley and the Republican Party* (Princeton, 1947), 12.
4. Parton, *Greeley*, 421.
5. Ibid., 239.
6. G. Fowler, *Timber Line* (New York, 1933), 97.
7. *Putnam's Magazine* VI (July 1855), 82.
8. *Courier & Enquirer*, 27 Jan. 1844.
9. G. T. McJimsey, *Genteel Partisan: Manton Marble 1834–1917* (Ames, Iowa, 1973), 86.
10. Parton, *Greeley*, 239.
11. R. Ogden, *Life and Letters of Edwin Lawrence Godkin* I (New York, 1907), 254.
12. G. G. Van Deusen, *Horace Greeley: Nineteenth Century Crusader* (Philadelphia, 1953), 148.
13. W. H. Hale, *Horace Greeley* (New York, 1950), 124.
14. Van Deusen, *Greeley*, 51.
15. F. W. Zabriskie, *Horace Greeley* (1890), 377.
16. Hale, *Greeley*, 320.
17. H. Greeley, *Recollections of a Busy Life* I (New York, 1971 edn.), 137.
18. Mott, *American Journalism*, 271.
19. C. Sandburg, *Abraham Lincoln: The War Years* I (New York, 1939), 401.
20. Zabriskie, *Greeley*, 159.
21. Van Deusen, *Greeley*, 69.
22. A. H. Sotheran, *Horace Greeley and Other Pioneers of American Socialism* (New York, 1915), 233.
23. Isely, *Greeley*, 16.
24. H. L. Stoddard, *Horace Greeley* (New York, 1946), 64.

25. J. H. Browne, 'Horace Greeley' in *Harper's Monthly Magazine* XLVI (1873), 736.
26. Nevins, *Evening Post*, 332.
27. R. Ogden, *Life of Godkin* I, 168.
28. Van Deusen, *Greeley*, 21.
29. Zabriskie, *Greeley*, 152.
30. Hale, *Greeley*, 190.
31. D. C. Seitz, *Horace Greeley* (Indianapolis, 1926), 405.
32. Greeley, *Recollections* I, 146.
33. D. McLellan, *Karl Marx: His Life and Thought* (1973), 285.
34. Zabriskie, *Greeley*, 12.
35. Stoddard, *Greeley*, 88 and 81.
36. Hale, *Greeley*, 351.
37. Van Deusen, *Greeley*, 420.
38. Ibid., 320
39. E. L. Godkin, *Reflections and Comments* (New York, 1895), 54.
40. F. Brown, *Raymond of the Times* (New York, 1951), 22.
41. Van Deusen, *Greeley*, 320.
42. J. Benton (ed.), *Greeley on Lincoln* (New York, 1873), 127–8.
43. A. Maverick, *Henry J. Raymond and the New York Press* (Hartford, Conn., 1870), 26.
44. Brown, *Raymond*, 8.
45. Maverick, *Raymond*, 31.
46. *Tribune*, 19 June 1869.
47. Brown, *Raymond*, 24.
48. *Courier and Enquirer*, 27 Jan. 1844.
49. E. Davis, *History of the New York Times 1851–1921* (New York, 1921), 11.
50. Brown, *Raymond*, 104.
51. Ibid., 126.
52. Hale, *Greeley*, 155.
53. *Times*, 18 Sept. 1851.
54. Times MSS. 27 Sept. 1866.
55. J. E. Pollard, *The Presidents and the Press* (New York, 1947), 436.
56. Brown, *Raymond*, 287.
57. Ibid., 318.
58. C. J. Rosebault, *When Dana Was the Sun* (New York, 1931), 17.
59. C. A. Dana, *The Art of Newspaper Making* (1895), 42.
60. Rosebault, *Dana*, 56.
61. Wilson, *Dana*, 277.
62. O'Brien, *Story of the Sun*, 174.
63. Hudson, *Journalism in the United States*, 679.
64. B[ancroft] L[ibrary, Berkeley, California, Hearst Papers], October 1927.
65. Mott, *American Journalism*, 376.
66. C. Stone, *Dana and the Sun* (New York, 1938), 129.
67. Nevins, *Evening Post*, 546.
68. Stone, *Dana and the Sun*, 117.
69. R. Cortissoz, *The Life of Whitelaw Reid* I (1921), 239.

70. Dana, *Newspaper Making*, 22 and 43–4.
71. Stone, *Dana and the Sun*, 41.
72. P. Kinsley, *The Chicago Tribune* I (New York, 1943), 304.
73. Bleyer, *American Journalism*, 257.

CHAPTER 5 (pages 69–85)

1. Hudson, *Journalism in the United States*, 545.
2. *British Quarterly Review* LIII (Jan. 1871), 4.
3. F. B. Wilkie, *Personal Reminiscences of Thirty-five Years in Journalism* (Chicago, 1891), 114.
4. K. Marx and F. Engels, *Collected Works* XIV (1980), 122.
5. G. M. Trevelyan, 'The White Peril' in *Nineteenth Century* I (1901), 1047.
6. Lord Burnham, *Peterborough Court* (1955), 76, 9 and 88.
7. Straus, *Sala*, 203.
8. Hobson *et al*, *Pearl of Days*, 186.
9. Straus, *Sala*, 138.
10. Burnham, *Peterborough Court*, 30.
11. H. Fyfe, *Sixty Years of Fleet Street* (1949), 201.
12. Burnham, *Peterborough Court*, 22.
13. F. Whyte, *The Life of W. T. Stead* I (1925), 114.
14. E. W. Stead, *My Father* (1913), 4, 21 and 50.
15. R. L. Schults, *Crusader in Babylon* (Lincoln, Nebraska, 1972), 9.
16. B. M. Gladstone Papers, Add MSS. 44, 303, 18 Mar. 1880.
17. Schults, *Crusader in Babylon*, 12–13.
18. Robertson Scott, *Life and Death of a Newspaper*, 241 ff.
19. H. Kingsmill, *After Puritanism* (1929), 208.
20. Robertson Scott, *Life and Death of a Newspaper*, 42.
21. R. H. Super (ed.), *The Last Word* [*The Complete Prose Works of Matthew Arnold* XI] (Ann Arbor, Michigan, 1977), 202.
22. K. Bird, 'Who Conducted the First Interview?' in *Journalism Studies Review* No. 4 (July, 1979), 9.
23. J. O. Baylen, 'The "New Journalism" in Late Victorian Britain' in *Australian Journal of Politics and History* XVII (Dec. 1972), 370.
24. S. Morison, *The English Newspaper* (Cambridge, 1932), 281.
25. W. T. Stead, 'Government by Journalism' in *The Contemporary Review* XLIX (May, 1886), 655.
26. Robertson Scott, *Life and Death of a Newspaper*, 226.
27. Schults, *Crusader in Babylon*, 66.
28. *Pall Mall Gazette*, 6 July 1885.
29. Schults, *Crusader in Babylon*, 140.
30. J. Gross, *The Rise and Fall of the Man of Letters* (1969), 26.
31. J. Saxon Mills, *Sir Edward Cook* (1921), 66.
32. J. Morley, *Recollections* I (1917), 209–10.
33. *Contemporary Review* XLIX, 665 ff and L, 667 ff.
34. Whyte, *Stead* I, 202.

35. *Contemporary Review* L, 678.
36. Whyte, *Stead* I, 311.
37. J. W. Robertson Scott, *'We' and Me* (1956), 123.
38. K. Jones, *Fleet Street and Downing Street* (1920), 116.
39. Robertson Scott, *Life and Death of a Newspaper*, 137.
40. R. Jenkins, *Sir Charles Dilke* (Fontana, 1968), 218.
41. J. L. Garvin, *The Life of Joseph Chamberlain* II (1932–), 291.
42. H. Friederichs, *The Life of Sir George Newnes* (1911), 116–17.
43. Schults, *Crusader in Babylon*, 248 and 251.
44. W. T. Stead, *If Christ Came to Chicago* (1894), 103.
45. Whyte, *Stead* I, 332.
46. W. T. Stead, *After Death* (1915), 151.
47. Whyte, *Stead* II, 314.
48. E. K. Harper, *Stead the Man* (1914), 14.
49. H. Fyfe, *T. P. O'Connor* (1934), 141.
50. Fyfe, *Fleet Street*, 98.
51. Morison, *English Newspaper*, 289.
52. T. P. O'Connor, 'The New Journalism' in *The New Review* I (Oct., 1889), 423.
53. A. L. Thorold, *The Life of Henry Labouchere* (1913), 455.
54. F. Moy Thomas (ed.), *Fifty Years of Fleet Street* by Sir John Robinson (1904), 207.
55. J. Hatton, *Journalistic London* (1882), 43 and 182.
56. S. Koss, *The Rise and Fall of the Political Press in Britain* (1981), 410 and *passim*.
57. F. Greenwood, 'The Press and Government' in *Nineteenth Century* XXVIII (July, 1890), 110.

CHAPTER 6 (pages 86–107)

1. G. Juergens, *Joseph Pulitzer and the* New York World (Princeton, 1966), 16.
2. W. R. Reynolds, 'Joseph Pulitzer' (Columbia University Ph.D. thesis, 1950), 370 and 469.
3. J. W. Barrett, *Joseph Pulitzer and His New World* (New York, 1941), xiii.
4. A. Churchill, *Park Row* (New York, 1958), 39.
5. Reynolds, 'Pulitzer', 377 and 454.
6. D. C. Seitz, *Joseph Pulitzer: His Life and Letters* (New York, 1926), 50.
7. H. Saalberg, 'The *Westliche Post* of St. Louis ...' (Missouri Ph.D. thesis, 1967), 197.
8. I. Cobb, *Exit Laughing* (New York, 1941), 119.
9. Reynolds, 'Pulitzer', 156.
10. W. A. Swanberger, *Pulitzer* (New York, 1967), 29.
11. Seitz, *Pulitzer*, 91.
12. Swanberg, *Pulitzer*, 29.
13. J. S. Rammelkamp, *Pulitzer's* Post-Dispatch *1878–1883* (Princeton, 1967), 62.

14. Ibid., *passim*.
15. Swanberg, *Pulitzer*, 220.
16. Rammelkamp, Post-Dispatch, 94.
17. Columbia University Oral History Office, 'Reminiscences of Joseph Pulitzer Jr.', 12 Dec. 1906.
18. Juergens, *Pulitzer*, 4.
19. Barrett, *Pulitzer*, 57.
20. Swanberg, *Pulitzer*, 70.
21. *World*, 11 May 1883.
22. H. W. King, *Pulitzer's Prize Editor* (Durham, N.C., 1965), 210.
23. Reynolds 'Pulitzer', 212.
24. Ibid., 469.
25. *World*, 3 Oct. 1886.
26. Ibid., 22 Nov. 1885.
27. Reynolds, 'Pulitzer', 155.
28. Juergens, *Pulitzer*, 112.
29. Reynolds, 'Pulitzer', 280.
30. Swanberg, *Pulitzer*, 219.
31. Juergens, *Pulitzer*, 36.
32. J. L. Heaton, *The Story of A Page* (1913), 123.
33. Reynolds, 'Pulitzer', 538 and 642.
34. Ibid., 448.
35. Swanberg, *Pulitzer*, 132.
36. Ibid., 163.
37. Cobb, *Exit Laughing*, 131.
38. Swanberg, *Pulitzer*, 288.
39. Reynolds, 'Pulitzer', 260.
40. Dreiser, *Book About Myself*, 469.
41. Reynolds, 'Pulitzer', 266.
42. Ibid., 272 and 311.
43. Cobb, *Exit Laughing*, 143.
44. J. M. Lee, *History of American Journalism* (New York, 1923), 373.
45. M. and D. Berg, 'The Rhetoric of War Preparation: The New York Press in 1898' in *Journalism Quarterly* XLV (1968), 657.
46. S. Brooks, 'The American Yellow Press' in *Fortnightly Review* 96 (1911), 137.
47. Reynolds, 'Pulitzer', 451.
48. Heaton, *Story of A Page*, 153 and 171.
49. L. M. Starr, 'Joseph Pulitzer and his most "indegoddampendent" editor' in *American Heritage* XIX (June, 1968), 83 and 84.
50. J. Pulitzer, 'The College of Journalism' in *North American Review* DLXX (May, 1904), 667.
51. A. Ireland, *An Adventure with a Genius* (1938), 50.
52. Ibid., 75.
53. Ibid., 115.
54. *North American Review* (1904), 680.

55. S. Walker, 'Symphony in Brass' in *Post Biographies of Famous Journalists*, edited by J. E. Drewry (New York, 1942), 420.
56. R. Steel, *Walter Lippmann and the American Century* (1980), 269.
57. E. P. Hoyt, *Alexander Woollcott: The Man Who Came to Dinner* (1968), 312.

CHAPTER 7 (pages 108–125)

1. Columbia P. P., Seitz to Pulitzer, 4 Jan. 1901.
2. R. N. Pierce, 'How the tabloid was born' in *Journalism Studies Review* I, No. 2, (June, 1977), 29.
3. H. Fyfe, *Northcliffe: An Intimate Biography* (1930), 335.
4. Columbia P. P., Seitz to Pulitzer, 4 Jan. 1901.
5. *Editor and Publisher*, 17 Aug. 1929.
6. Blumenfeld, *Press in My Time*, 191.
7. *Daily Mail*, 1 Nov. 1911.
8. R. Pound and G. Harmsworth, *Northcliffe* (1959), 15 and 5.
9. H. G. Wells, *Experiment in Autobiography* I (1934), 325.
10. *Daily Mail*, 5 May 1896.
11. Pound and Harmsworth, *Northcliffe*, 42.
12. Times MSS.
13. N. Angell, *The Press and the Organisation of Society* (1933), 14.
14. *Answers to Correspondents*, 2 June 1888 and *passim*.
15. Pound and Harmsworth, *Northcliffe*, 201.
16. *Daily Mail*, 7 May and 7, 17, 31 Oct. 1896.
17. Ibid., 13 May, 1896.
18. T. Clarke, *Northcliffe in History* (1950), 153.
19. Robertson Scott, *'We' and Me*, 74.
20. *Daily Mail*, 1896, *passim*.
21. *Answers*, 3 Nov. 1888.
22. Columbia P. P., Seitz to Pulitzer, 4 Jan. 1901.
23. T. Clarke, *My Northcliffe Diary* (1931), 37.
24. T. Driberg, *'Swaff'* (1974), 27–8.
25. *History of 'The Times'* III, 577.
26. B. Falk, *Bouquets for Fleet Street* (1951), 120.
27. Fyfe, *Fleet Street*, 115.
28. A. G. Gardiner, *Portraits and Portents* (1926), 290.
29. B. M. Add. MSS. 4890. I, J. S. Sandars to Northcliffe, 13 Dec. 1909.
30. H[ouse] of L[ords Record Office. Beaverbrook Papers.] Northcliffe to Aitken, 11 Nov. 1911.
31. Robertson Scott, *"We" and Me*, 45.
32. J. A. Hammerton, *With Northcliffe in Fleet Street* (n.d.), 211.
33. E. D. Coblentz, *Newsmen Speak* (Berkeley, 1954), 98.
34. R. M. Wilson, *Doctor's Progress* (1938), 118.
35. Clarke, *Northcliffe Diary*, 80.
36. F. Dilnot, *The Adventures of a Newspaper Man* (1913), 224.
37. Pound and Harmsworth, *Northcliffe*, 341.

38. S. Huddleston, *In My Times* (1938), 205.
39. C. Beaumont, *A Rebel in Fleet Street* (1944), 70.
40. Pound and Harmsworth, *Northcliffe*, 850.
41. E. Wallace, *People* (1926), 164.
42. Cobb, *Exit Laughing*, 117.
43. Times MSS, May 1913.
44. *History of 'The Times'* III, 769.
45. B. Falk, *Five Years Dead* (1937), 137.
46. Times MSS, 1908.
47. *History of 'The Times'* IV, 131 and III, 769.
48. C. Stuart, *Opportunity Knocks Once* (1952), 91.
49. F. H. Kitchin, *Moberly Bell and His Times* (1925), 262.
50. Wells, *Autobiography* II, 696.
51. A. M. Gollin, *The Observer and J. L. Garvin* (1960), 165.
52. P. Ferris, *The House of Northcliffe* (1971), 126.
53. E. Wrench, *Geoffrey Dawson and Our Times* (1955), 95.
54. Pound and Harmsworth, *Northcliffe*, 289.
55. Blumenfeld, *Press in My Time*, 49.
56. Lord Northcliffe, *At the War* (1916), 183.
57. J. M. McEwen, 'The Press and the Fall of Asquith' in *Historical Journal* XXI (1978), 863.
58. Ferris, *House of Northcliffe*, 202.
59. Pound and Harmsworth, *Northcliffe*, 782.
60. Falk, *Five Years Dead*, 169.
61. A. Harmsworth, 'The Making of a Newspaper' in A. Lawrence, *Journalism as a Profession* (1903), 186.
62. Pound and Harmsworth, *Northcliffe*, 741.
63. *Atlantic Monthly*, CXIX (Jan. 1917), 116.
64. W. Smith, *Spilt Ink* (1932), 206.
65. Wilson, *Doctor's Progress*, 120.
66. Lord Northcliffe, *My Journey Round the World* 1921–22 (1923), *passim*.
67. Times MSS.
68. Pound and Harmsworth, *Northcliffe*, 879.
69. H. of L., Northcliffe to Beaverbrook, 19 Dec. 1920.

CHAPTER 8 (pages 126–153)

1. *Britannia*, 5 Oct. 1928.
2. T. Lippmann Jnr. (ed.), *A Gang of Pecksniffs* by H. L. Mencken (New York, 1975), 59.
3. G. Seldes, *Lords of the Press* (New York, 1938), 234.
4. M. Davies, *The Times We Had: Life with William Randolph Hearst* (1976), Introduction by Orson Welles.
5. P. Kael, *The Citizen Kane Book* (1971), 82 and 65.
6. F. C. Howe, *Confessions of a Reformer* (New York, 1925), 245.
7. *Newsweek*, 25 Aug. 1934.

8. S. Brooks, 'The Significance of Mr Hearst' in *Fortnightly Review* LXXXII (Dec. 1907), 924.
9. L. Steffens, 'Hearst, The Man of Mystery' in *American Magazine* LXIII (Nov. 1906), 6.
10. L. Chaney and M. Cieply have also made some use of this collection in *The Hearsts* (New York, 1981). But, as its subtitle indicates, their book is mainly concerned with the family's later years and the development of what is perhaps the largest private corporate empire in America.
11. B.L., E. H. Clark, 'Reminiscences of the Hearst Family'.
12. Mrs F. Older, *William Randolph Hearst: American* (1936), 51.
13. W. A. Swanberg, *Citizen Hearst* (1961), 30.
14. C. Chaplin, *My Autobiography* (1964), 334.
15. W. Neale, *The Life of Ambrose Bierce* (New York, 1929), 89.
16. J. Creelman, 'The Real Mr. Hearst' in *Pearson's Magazine* (May, 1906), 257.
17. See, for example, the modern-sounding strictures on them for shaping the policies of their newspapers by 'non-journalistic considerations' in E. A. Ross, *Changing America: Studies in Contemporary Society* (New York, 1912), 116 ff. For a list of the chief magnate-owners see F. Lundberg, *America's 60 Families* (New York, 1962), 244 ff.
18. W. J. Abbott, *Watching the World*, 138.
19. J. Tebbel, *The Life and Good Times of William Randolph Hearst* (1953), 125.
20. L. Pratt, 'A Park Row Interlude: Memoir of Albert Pulitzer' in *Journalism Quarterly* XL (1963), 539.
21. B.L., Brisbane to Hearst, 7 July 1927.
22. Bleyer, *American Journalism*, 358.
23. Columbia, P.P., n.d.
24. J. K. Winkler, *W. R. Hearst, An American Phenomenon* (1928), 109.
25. Tebbel, *Hearst*, 126.
26. *American*, 26 Feb. 1918.
27. Columbia P.P., n.d.
28. O. Carlson, *Brisbane* (1937), 108.
29. M. Koenigsberg, *King News* (New York, 1941), 337.
30. E. D. Coblentz (ed.), *William Randolph Hearst—A Portrait in His Own Words* (New York, 1952), 59.
31. Abbott, *Watching the World*, 216.
32. J. E. Wisan, *The Cuban Crisis as Reflected in the New York Press (1895–1898)* (New York, 1934), 153.
33. *Journal*, 17 Feb. 1898.
34. C. H. Brown, *The Correspondents' War* (New York, 1967), 266.
35. J. Creelman, *On the Great Highway* (Boston, 1901), 212 and *Pearson's Magazine* (1906), 259.
36. *Journal*, 25 Sept. 1898.
37. Columbia P.P., Seitz to Pulitzer, 1902.
38. Creelman, *Pearson's Magazine* (1906), 263.
39. Coblentz, *Newsmen Speak*, 113.
40. B. Hecht, *Charlie* (New York, 1957), 50.

41. Newberry Library, Chicago, J. Whittaker to G. Fowler, 6 Aug. 1956.
42. B. Hecht, *A Child of the Century* (New York, 1955), 120.
43. Older, *Hearst*, 369.
44. Times MSS, 13 Jan. 1909 and 1 Dec. 1919.
45. J. Thurber, *The Years With Ross* (1959), 134.
46. 'In the News' (Hearst's syndicated editorial), 20 Mar. 1940.
47. *Anti-Hearst Examiner*, 23 Oct. 1935.
48. Chicago Historical Society, Hearst to Mrs W. J. Chalmers, 1933.
49. Drewry (ed.), *Biographies of Famous Journalists*, 18.
50. E. Gauvreau, *My Last Million Readers* (New York, 1941), 219.
51. O. G. Villard, *Prophets, true and false* (1928), 302.
52. Hughes, *Human Interest Story*, 224 and 234.
53. H. of L., 18 Jan. 1932.
54. *New Yorker*, 19 Nov. 1938.
55. B.L., Walter Steilberg's reminiscences.
56. Ibid., E. H. Clark, 'Reminiscences of the Hearst Family'.
57. Davies, *Hearst*, 122.
58. R. Lasch, 'Chicago Patriot' in *Atlantic Monthly* (June 1942), 694.
59. B.L., E. H. Clark, 'Reminiscences of the Hearst Family'.
60. Tebbel, *Hearst*, 283.
61. Coblentz (ed.), *Hearst*, 213.
62. Grover Smith (ed.), *Letters to Aldous Huxley* (1969), 593.
63. F. L. Guiles, *Marion Davies* (1973), 8.
64. *Life*, 19 Aug. 1951.
65. Cobb, *Exit Laughing*, 123.

CHAPTER 9 (pages 154–179)

1. Quoted by H. Ickes, *America's House of Lords* (Westport, Conn., 1967 edn.), 52.
2. B.L., 21 Nov. 1924.
3. U. Sinclair, *The Brass Check* (Pasadena, 1919), 412.
4. J. Curran and J. Seaton, *Power Without Responsibility* (Fontana, 1981), 77 and *passim*.
5. Scripps, *I Protest*, 34.
6. C. M. Vines, *A Little Nut-Brown Man* (1968), 195.
7. A. J. P. Taylor, *Beaverbrook* (1972), 497.
8. Wood, *Beaverbrook*, 329.
9. K. Young, (ed.), *The Diaries of Sir Robert Bruce Lockhart* II (1981), 40 and 219.
10. Lord Beaverbrook, *Friends* (1959), 6.
11. Wood, *Beaverbrook*, 181.
12. A. B. Baxter, *Strange Street* (1935), 196.
13. *Times*, 28 Mar. 1980.
14. Taylor, *Beaverbrook*, 164.

15. Lord Beaverbrook, *My Early Life* (Fredericton, New Brunswick, 1965), 50.
16. T. Wilson (ed.), *The Political Diaries of C. P. Scott, 1911–1928* (1970), 336.
17. Wood, *Beaverbrook*, 68.
18. Lord Beaverbrook, *Men and Power* (1956), 184.
19. R. Rhodes James, *Memoirs of a Conservative* (1966), 28.
20. Wells, *Autobiography* II, 697.
21. Taylor, *Beaverbrook*, 241.
22. F. A. Mackenzie, *Beaverbrook* (1931), 162.
23. Lord Beaverbrook, *The Decline and Fall of Lloyd George* (1963), 126.
24. Lord Beaverbrook, *Politicians and the Press* (1925), 16.
25. Cf. *Express* 1 Mar. 1924 and 30 Mar. 1927.
26. Mackenzie, *Beaverbrook*, 179.
27. Fyfe, *Fleet Street*, 139.
28. D. Edgar, *Express '56* (1981), 124.
29. P. Howard, *Beaverbrook* (1964), 21.
30. Charles Wintour to the author, 15 Dec. 1981.
31. H. Rose, *Before I Forget* (1942), 103.
32. M. Foot, *Debts of Honour* (1980), 79.
33. T. Driberg, *Beaverbrook* (1956), 211.
34. Howard, *Beaverbrook*, 115.
35. Lord Boyd of Merton to the author, 21 Nov. 1981.
36. Lord Vansittart, *The Mist Procession* (1958), 368.
37. Driberg, *Beaverbrook*, 213.
38. Taylor, *Beaverbrook*, 272.
39. C. Madge and T. Harrisson, *Mass Observation: The Press and its Readers* (1949), 49.
40. R. J. Minney, *Viscount Southwood* (1954), 268–9.
41. Charles Wintour to the author, 15 Dec. 1981.
42. Driberg, *Beaverbrook*, 145.
43. W. A. Swanberg, *Luce and His Empire* (1972), 112.
44. A. Christiansen, *Headlines All my Life* (1961), 147.
45. Wood, *Beaverbrook*, 160.
46. W. Gerhardie, *Memoirs of A Polyglot* (1973 edn.), 271, 273 and 276.
47. George Malcolm Thomson to the author, 23 Nov. 1981.
48. A. Sharf, *The British Press and Jews Under Nazi Rule* (Oxford, 1964), 15.
49. *Express*, 7 Aug. 1939.
50. K. Young, *Churchill and Beaverbrook* (1966), 141.
51. M. Soames, *Clementine Churchill* (1979), 314.
52. A. Bullock, *Life and Times of Ernest Bevin* II (1967), 178.
53. D. Farrer, *The Sky's the Limit* (1943), 35.
54. Howard, *Beaverbrook*, 128.
55. A. C. H. Smith, *Paper Voices* (1975), 96–7.
56. Farrer, *Sky's the Limit*, 24.
57. G. M. Thomson, *Vote of Censure,* (1968), 54.
58. D. Farrer, *G- for God Almighty* (1969), 83.
59. F. Williams, *Dangerous Estate* (1959), 217.

60. Driberg, *Beaverbrook*, 303.
61. Young, *Churchill and Beaverbrook*, 264.
62. Driberg, *Beaverbrook*, 305.
63. David Farrer to the author, 11 Nov. 1981.
64. Letter in possession of Charles Wintour, 17 Feb. 1964.
65. Vines, *Nut-Brown Man*, 272.
66. S. Jenkins, *Newspapers: The Power and the Money* (1979), 29.
67. L. Chester and J. Fenby, *The Fall of the House of Beaverbrook* (1979), 218.
68. J. E. Walsh, *To Print the News Raise Hell* (Chapel Hill, N. Carolina, 1969), 270.
69. Chester and Fenby, *House of Beaverbrook*, 183.
70. Curran and Seaton, *Power without Responsibility*, 112.
71. J. Curran (ed.), *The British Press: A Manifesto* (1978), 131.
72. Sir Larry Lamb to the author, 22 Oct. 1981.
73. Foot, *Debts of Honour*, 91.
74. Gardiner, *Portraits and Portents*, 47.
75. R. Braddon, *Roy Thomson of Fleet Street* (1965), 127.
76. Mackenzie, *Beaverbrook*, 177–8.
77. *Sunday Telegraph*, 1 Feb. 1981.

CHAPTER 10 (pages 180–203)

1. H. of L., H.17. J. W. T. Mason to Beaverbrook, 29 Apr. 1929.
2. Scripps, *I Protest*, 36.
3. C. McCabe, *Damned Old Crank* (New York, 1931), 21.
4. Scripps, *I Protest*, 19.
5. McCabe, *Damned Old Crank*, 75.
6. Ibid., 64.
7. Scripps, *I Protest*, 32.
8. Bent, *Ballyhoo*, 271.
9. Scripps, *I Protest*, 66.
10. A. Britt, *Ellen Browning Scripps* (Oxford, 1960), 46.
11. L. Steffens, *Autobiography* (1932), 667.
12. M. Eastman, *Great Companions* (1959), 10.
13. N. D. Cochran, *E. W. Scripps* (New York, 1972 edn.), 289.
14. Wilson, *Dana*, 214.
15. Scripps, *I Protest*, 67.
16. Cochran, *Scripps*, 296.
17. Ibid., 168.
18. Mencken, *A Gang of Pecksniffs*, 94.
19. G. Gardner, *Lusty Scripps* (New York, 1932), 246.
20. B. L., 4 May 1924.
21. Emery, *Press and America*, 225.
22. Kinsley, *Chicago Tribune* I, 41.
23. J. Gies, *The Colonel of Chicago* (New York, 1979), 9.

24. Kinsley, *Chicago Tribune* III, 35.
25. Ibid., 95.
26. Chicago *Tribune*, 6 Jan. and 13 Apr. 1952.
27. J. W. Linn, *James Keeley* (New York, 1937), 40 and 183.
28. Chicago *Tribune*, 28 Dec. 1952.
29. *New Yorker*, 13 Aug. 1938.
30. H. of L., 11 May 1935.
31. Drewry, *Post Biographies*, 221.
32. L. Wendt, *Chicago Tribune* (Chicago, 1979), 397.
33. R. R. McCormick, *With the Russian Army* (New York, 1915), 252.
34. H. of L., Brisbane to Beaverbrook, 11 May 1935.
35. Chicago *Tribune*, 28 June 1953.
36. Ibid., 16 Mar. 1952.
37. Ibid., 28 Dec. 1952.
38. Ibid., 13 Apr. 1952.
39. Ibid., 30 Mar. 1952.
40. O. G. Villard, 'The World's Greatest Newspaper' in *Nation* (1 Feb. 1922), 118.
41. Chicago *Tribune*, 28 Dec. 1952.
42. J. E. Edwards, *The Foreign Policy of Colonel McCormick's Tribune, 1929–41* (Reno, Nevada, 1971), 59.
43. S. S. Sargent, 'Emotional Stereotypes in the Chicago Tribune' in *Sociometry* II (1939) 69–75.
44. L. C. Rosten, *The Washington Correspondents* (New York, 1937), 356–7.
45. Drewry, *Post Biographies*, 224.
46. B.L., Brisbane to Hearst, 29 Dec. 1934.
47. Villard, *Nation*, 1 Feb. 1922.
48. R. R. McCormick, *The Freedom of the Press* (New York, 1936), 89.
49. D. Aaron, *Writers on the Left* (New York, 1967), 53.
50. New York *Times*, 27 May 1946.
51. S. M. Bessie, *Jazz Journalism* (New York, 1938), 19.
52. J. Chapman, *Tell it to Sweeney* (New York, 1961), 168.
53. Hughes, *News and Human Interest Story*, 273.
54. B.L., 23 Nov. 1934.
55. B.L., Hearst to McCabe, 21 Dec. 1937.
56. *New Yorker*, 13 Aug. 1938.
57. Chapman, *Tell it to Sweeney*, 70–71.
58. Ibid., 9.
59. H. of L., Patterson to Beaverbrook, 31 July 1936.
60. H. of L., 6 Feb. 1939.
61. G. J. White, *FDR and the Press* (Chicago, 1979), 44 and 50.
62. E. Gizycka, *Autumn Flight* (1930), 76 and 157.
63. Quoted by P. Healy, *Cissy* (New York, 1966), 296–7.
64. D. Halberstam, *The Powers That Be* (1979), 182.
65. B.L., 15 and 7 Apr. 1932.
66. B.L., letters between Hearst and Cissy Patterson, 2 Mar., 25 Mar. and 14 June 1937.

67. Ibid., 9 Sept. 1938.
68. F. Waldrop, *McCormick of Chicago* (Westport, Conn., 1966), 163.
69. *Time*, June 1947, quoted in Ford and Emery, *Highlights in History of American Press*, 379.
70. *Time*, 24 Aug. 1942.
71. J. Tebbel, *An American Dynasty* (New York, 1968), 314.
72. Rosten, *Washington Correspondents*, 302.
73. Healy, *Cissy*, 377–8.
74. Waldrop, *McCormick*, 265.
75. Tebbel, *American Dynasty*, 338.

CHAPTER 11 (pages 204–221)

1. H. Cudlipp, *Publish and be Damned!* (1953), 97.
2. C. King, *With Malice Towards None* (1970), 39.
3. C. King, *Strictly Personal* (1969), 115.
4. *The Cecil King Diary 1970–1974* (1977), 102.
5. Cecil King to the author, 3 Nov. 1981.
6. King, *Malice*, 115.
7. See I. McLaine, *Ministry of Morale* (1979), 281.
8. Winston S. Churchill, *The Second World War* II (1949), 211.
9. R. Rhodes James, *Churchill: A Study in Failure* (1970), 173.
10. W. P. Crozier, *Off the Record* edited by A. J. P. Taylor, (1973), 311.
11. T. Margach, *The Abuse of Power* (1978), 70.
12. F. Williams, *Nothing so Strange* (1970), 166 and 173.
13. Cudlipp, *Publish and be Damned!*, 157 and 167.
14. *Twentieth Century* (Spring, 1965), 100.
15. King, *Malice*, 194
16. King, *Strictly Personal*, 36, 71 and 72.
17. R. Connor, *Cassandra* (1969), 30–1.
18. King, *Personally Speaking*, 37 and 40.
19. H. Cudlipp, *At Your Peril* (1962), 18.
20. M. Edelman, *The Mirror: A Political History* (1966), 38–9.
21. Smith, *Paper Voices*, 89.
22. T. S. Matthews, *The Sugar Pill* (1957), 87.
23. Smith, *Paper Voices*, 101.
24. C. Morris, *I Bought a Newspaper* (1963), 13.
25. Cudlipp, *Published and be Damned!*, 50.
26. Morris, *I Bought a Newspaper*, 17.
27. *Observer*, 29 Apr. 1962.
28. C. King, *The Future of the Press* (1967), 87.
29. *Royal Commission on the Press* P.P. XII (1962), 114.
30. Cudlipp, *At Your Peril*, opp. 160.
31. *Observer*, 29 Apr. 1962.
32. Smith, *Paper Voices*, 154.
33. *Books and Bookmen*, May and July 1980.

34. New York *Times*, 2 Mar. 1961.
35. Cudlipp, *At Your Peril*, 18.
36. G. Brown, *In My Way* (1971), 62.
37. *King Diary, 1965–1970*, 144.
38. King to the author, 14 Oct. 1981.
39. King, *Future of the Press*, 94 and 92.
40. King, *Malice*, 209.
41. *King Diary 1965–1970* and *1970–1974, passim*.
42. *Books and Bookmen*, Jan. and June 1979.
43. Cudlipp, *Walking on the Water*, 326. See also *Encounter* (Sept. 1981), 15.
44. *King Diary 1965–1970*, 192.
45. A. Howard (ed.), *The Crossman Diaries* (1979), 440.
46. Cudlipp, *At Your Peril*, 14.
47. King, *Future of the Press*, 89 and 92.
48. R. Thomson, *After I Was Sixty* (1973), 87.
49. Braddon, *Thomson*, 138 and 276.
50. *Columbia Journalism Review* (Mar.–Apr. 1977), 19.
51. *Royal Commission on the Press* (1962), 472.
52. O. R. McGregor, 'Communication in a Changing World—The Role of the Press' in *Gazette* XXIV (1978), 244.
53. D. H. Simpson, *Commercialisation of the Regional Press* (1981), 3 and *passim*.
54. *New Statesman*, 4 Oct. 1974.
55. *Observer*, 8 Mar. 1981.
56. *Times*, 26 June 1981.
57. For a polemic against the 'doctored pap' broadcast by the BBC see D. Hare, *Ah Mischief: The Role of Public Broadcasting* (1982).
58. *Books and Bookmen*, July 1980.

CHAPTER 12 (pages 222–235)

1. B.L., 30 Apr. 1919.
2. Fowler, *Timber Line*, 101.
3. Halberstam, *Powers That Be*, 103. There are a number of versions of this speech. See, e.g., G. E. Mowry, *The California Progressives* (Berkeley, 1951), 47.
4. R. Gottlieb and I. Wolt, *Thinking Big* (New York, 1977), 19 and 20.
5. *Dictionary of American Biography*.
6. L[os] A[ngeles] *Times*, 29 Apr. 1887.
7. *Newsweek*, 30 Apr. 1956.
8. L.A. *Times*, 9 Jan. 1887.
9. Gottlieb and Wolt, *Thinking Big*, 41.
10. L.A. *Times*, 20 Dec. 1903.
11. Ibid., *passim*.
12. Gottlieb and Wolt, *Thinking Big*, 48–9 and 24.
13. L.A. *Times*, 13 Dec. 1903.
14. Ibid., 3 Oct. 1910.

15. J. and L. Caughey, *Los Angeles* (Berkeley, 1976), 260.
16. Gottlieb and Wolt, *Thinking Big*, 96.
17. L.A. *Times*, 31 July 1917.
18. Sinclair, *Brass Check*, 224.
19. R. D. Delmatier *et al.*, *The Rumble of Californian Politics 1848–1970* (New York, 1970), 201.
20. *Newsweek*, 30 Apr. 1956.
21. Washington *Post*, 27 July 1977.
22. *Columbia Journalism Review* (Jan./Feb., 1979), 53.
23. Gottlieb and Wolt, *Thinking Big*, 485.
24. Washington *Post*, 24 July 1977.
25. *Harper's*, July 1977.
26. J. Hohenberg, *A Crisis for the American Press* (New York, 1978), 279.
27. Washington *Post*, 24 July 1977.
28. E. C. Hynds, 'Trends in Daily Newspapers in the United States' in *Gazette* XXV (1979), 136.
29. Quoted by B. M. Compaine (ed.), *Who Owns the Media?* (White Plains, N.Y., 1979), 34.
30. A. Smith, *Goodbye Gutenberg* (New York, 1980), 153.
31. G. Talese, *The Kingdom and the Power* (1971), 334.
32. D. Faber, *Printer's Devil to Publisher* (New York, 1963), 131.
33. *Columbia Journalism Review* (Mar./Apr., 1978), 52 and 19.
34. Washington *Post*, 31 July and 24 July 1977.
35. W. Salisbury, *The Career of a Journalist* (New York, 1908), 520–21.
36. Washington *Post*, 24 July 1977.
37. *Gazette* (1979), 137.
38. Washington *Post*, 24 July 1977.
39. Hohenberg, *American Press*, 183.
40. B. H. Bagdikian, *The Effete Conspiracy* (New York, 1972), 11, 88 and *passim*.

CHAPTER 13 (pages 236–250)

1. *Time*, 17 Jan. 1977.
2. B.M. Add. MSS. 4890, XXVII, Murdoch to Northcliffe, 9 Apr. 1921.
3. J. Hetherington, *Australians* (Melbourne, 1961), 83.
4. B.M. Add. MSS. 4890, XXVII, Murdoch to Northcliffe, 23 Sept. 1915.
5. A. Moorehead, *Gallipoli* (Four Square edn., 1963), 287.
6. I. Colvin, *The Life of Lord Carson* III (1936), 87.
7. B.M. Add. MSS. 4890, XXVII, Murdoch to Northcliffe, 4 Mar. 1920.
8. T. Clarke, *Marriage at 6 A.M.* (1934), 251.
9. B.M. Add. MSS. 4890, XXVII, 17 Feb. 1921.
10. Ibid., Northcliffe to Murdoch, 12 Nov. 1921.
11. Ibid., Murdoch to Northcliffe, 9 Apr. 1921.
12. Ibid., Dec. 1921.
13. Ibid., 30 Dec. 1921, 1 Jan. and 24 Mar. 1922.
14. C. Pearl, *Wild Men of Sydney* (1966), 169.

15. H. Mayer, *The Press in Australia* (Melbourne, 1966), 29–30.
16. *Keith Murdoch, Journalist* (Melbourne, 1952), 27 and 22.
17. S. Regan, *Rupert Murdoch* (1976), 40.
18. *Observer*, 16 Nov. 1969.
19. Ibid., 25 Jan. 1981.
20. *Sunday Times* (colour magazine), 21 April 1974.
21. Peter Grose to the author, Dec. 1981.
22. *Guardian*, 28 Aug. 1974.
23. *Village Voice*, 29 Nov. 1976.
24. P. Edgar, *The Politics of the Press* (Melbourne, 1979), 22.
25. *Village Voice*, 29 Nov. 1976.
26. *More*, Feb. 1977.
27. *Esquire*, 22 May 1979.
28. *Financial Times*, 18 Aug. 1981.
29. New York *Post*, 1 May 1982.
30. *Village Voice*, 11 May 1982.
31. *Daily News*, 4 May 1982.
32. *Esquire*, 22 May 1979.
33. S. Somerfield, *Banner Headlines* (1979), 187 and 142.
34. *Observer*, 16 Nov. 1969.
35. C. Wintour, *Pressures on the Press* (1972), 193.
36. Hohenberg, *American Press*, 253.
37. M. Block, 'News Wars' in *Journalism Studies Review* No. 6 (July, 1981), 28.
38. *Newsweek*, 17 Jan. 1977.
39. *Times*, 13 Feb. 1981.
40. *Observer*, 25 Jan. 1981.
41. *Times*, 30 June 1981.
42. BBC *Panorama* programme, 16 Feb. 1981.
43. H. Henry (ed.), *Behind the Headlines* (1978), 75–6.
44. B.M. Add. MSS. 4890, XCVI, 5 Dec. 1920.
45. *Times*, 29 Oct. 1981.
46. *More*, Feb. 1977.
47. *New Statesman*, 11 Oct. 1974.

INDEX

PIERS BRENDON lives in Cambridge, England, with his wife and two sons. He has written and edited a number of books, including *Eminent Edwardians* and *Hurrell Froude and the Oxford Movement*, and he is a regular contributor to *The Times* (London), *The Observer*, and other journals.